Network Security
Know It All

Network Security
Know It All

James Joshi

Saurabh Bagchi

Bruce S. Davie

Adrian Farrel

Bingrui Foo

Vijay K. Garg

Matthew W. Glause

Gaspar Modelo-Howard

Prashant Krishnamurthy

Pete Loshin

James D. McCabe

Lionel M. Ni

Larry L. Peterson

Rajiv Ramaswami

Kumar N. Sivarajan

Eugene H. Spafford

George Varghese

Yu-Sung Wu

Pei Zheng

ELSEVIER

AMSTERDAM • BOSTON • HEIDELBERG • LONDON
NEW YORK • OXFORD • PARIS • SAN DIEGO
SAN FRANCISCO • SINGAPORE • SYDNEY • TOKYO

Morgan Kaufmann is an imprint of Elsevier

MORGAN KAUFMANN PUBLISHERS

Publishing Director: Chris Williams
Publisher: Denise E. M. Penrose
Senior Acquisitions Editor: Rick Adams
Publishing Services Manager: George Morrison
Production Editor: Lianne Hong
Assistant Editor: Gregory Chalson
Cover Design: Joanne Blank
Cover Image: Jupiter Images
Composition: Charon Tec Ltd (A Macmillan Company)
Proofreader: Phyllis Coyne et al.
Indexer: Distributech
Interior printer: RR Donnelley Harrisonburg, North Plant
Cover printer: Phoenix Color Corporation

Morgan Kaufmann Publishers is an imprint of Elsevier.
30 Corporate Drive, Suite 400, Burlington, MA 01803, USA

Library of Congress Cataloging-in-Publication Data
Network security : know it all / by James Joshi ... [et al.].
    p. cm.
    Includes bibliographical references and index.
    ISBN 978-0-12-374463-0 (hardcover : alk. paper)   1. Computer networks—Security measures.
I. Joshi, James B. D.
    TK5105.59.N338 2008
    005.8—dc22

                                                                                        2008012262

ISBN: 978-0-12-374463-0

For information on all Morgan Kaufmann publications, visit our
Web site at *www.mkp.com* or *www.books.elsevier.com*

Printed and bound in the United Kingdom
Transferred to Digital Printing, 2011

Working together to grow
libraries in developing countries
www.elsevier.com | www.bookaid.org | www.sabre.org

ELSEVIER   BOOK AID
            International   Sabre Foundation

Contents

About the Authors

Saurabh Bagchi (Chapter 10) is an assistant professor in the School of Electrical and Computer Engineering at Purdue University, West Lafayette, Indiana. He is a faculty fellow of the Cyber Center and has a courtesy appointment in the Department of Computer Science at Purdue University. He received his M.S. and Ph.D. from the University of Illinois at Urbana–Champaign in 1998 and 2001, respectively. At Purdue, he leads the Dependable Computing Systems Lab (DCSL), where he and a group of wildly enthusiastic students try to make and break distributed systems for the good of the world. His work is supported by NSF, Indiana 21st Century Research and Technology Fund, Avaya, and Purdue Research Foundation, with equipment grants from Intel and Motorola. His papers have been runner-ups for best paper in HPDC (2006), DSN (2005), and MTTS (2005). He has been an Organizing Committee member and Program Committee member for the Dependable Systems and Networks Conference (DSN) and the Symposium on Reliable Distributed Systems (SRDS). He also contributed to *Information Assurance: Dependability and Security in Networked Systems*, published by Elsevier, 2007.

Bruce S. Davie (Chapter 1) joined Cisco Systems in 1995, where he is a Cisco Fellow. For many years, he led the team of architects responsible for Multiprotocol Label Switching and IP Quality of Service. He recently joined the Video and Content Networking Business Unit in the Service Provider group. He has 20 years of networking and communications industry experience and has written numerous books, RFCs, journal articles, and conference papers on IP networking. He is also an active participant in both the Internet Engineering Task Force and the Internet Research Task Force. Prior to joining Cisco, he was director of internetworking research and chief scientist at Bell Communications Research. Bruce holds a Ph.D. in computer science from Edinburgh University and is a visiting lecturer at M.I.T. His research interests include routing, measurement, quality of service, transport protocols, and overlay networks. He is also a co-author of *Computer Networks: A Systems Approach*, published by Elsevier, 2007.

Adrian Farrel (Chapter 5) has over two decades of experience designing and developing communications protocol software. As Old Dog Consulting, he is an industry-leading freelance consultant on MPLS, GMPLS, and Internet routing, formerly working as MPLS Architect for Data Connection Ltd., and as director of Protocol Development for Movaz Networks, Inc. He is active within the Internet Engineering Task Force, where he is co-chair of the CCAMP working group responsible for GMPLS, the Path Computation Element (PCE) working group, and the Layer One VPN (L1VPN) working group. Adrian has co-authored and contributed to numerous Internet drafts and RFCs on MPLS, GMPLS, and related technologies. He is also the author of *The Internet and Its Protocols: A Comparative Approach*, published by Elsevier, 2004.

Bingrui Foo (Chapter 10) is a Ph.D. student in the School of Electrical and Computer Engineering at Purdue University in West Lafayette, Indiana. Presently, he is involved in two research projects: one in the field of network security, specifically the design of intrusion-tolerant systems and automated response mechanisms, and one in the field of statistical modeling, which consists of extending mixture models by adding hierarchal structure to images and videos. His papers have appeared in DSN and ACSAC. He also contributed to *Information Assurance: Dependability and Security in Networked Systems*, published by Elsevier, 2007.

Vijay K. Garg (Chapter 7) has been a professor in the Electrical and Computer Engineering Department at the University of Illinois at Chicago since 1999, where he teaches graduate courses in Wireless Communications and Networking. Dr. Garg was a Distinguished Member of Technical Staff at the Lucent Technologies Bell Labs in Naperville, Illinois, from 1985 to 2001. He received his Ph.D. from the Illinois Institute of Technologies, Chicago, Illinois, in 1973, and he received an M.S. from the University of California at Berkeley, California, in 1966. Dr. Garg has co-authored several technical books, including five in wireless communications. He is a fellow of ASCE and ASME, and a senior member of IEEE. Dr. Garg is a registered professional engineer in the states of Maine and Illinois. He is an academic member of the Russian Academy of Transport. Dr. Garg was a feature editor of Wireless/PCS Series in *IEEE Communication Magazine* from 1996 to 2001. He is also the author of *Wireless Communications & Networking*, published by Elsevier, 2007.

Matthew W. Glause (Chapter 10) Center for Education and Research in Information Assurance and Security (CERIAS), Dependable Computing Systems Laboratory, School of Electrical and Computer Engineering, Purdue University. He also contributed to *Information Assurance: Dependability and Security in Networked Systems*, published by Elsevier, 2007.

Gaspar Modelo-Howard (Chapter 10) is a Ph.D. student in the Department of Electrical and Computer Engineering and a member of the Center for Education and Research in Information Assurance and Security (CERIAS) at Purdue University, West Lafayette, Indiana. He came to Purdue after spending seven years as an information security officer for the Panama Canal Authority and five years as a college professor for network security courses. His current research interests include machine-learning techniques for intrusion response and the convergence between security and dependability. He has an M.S. in information security from Royal Holloway, University of London, and a B.S. in electrical engineering from Universidad Tecnologica de Panama. He also contributed to *Information Assurance: Dependability and Security in Networked Systems*, published by Elsevier, 2007.

James Joshi (Chapter 2) is an assistant professor in the School of Information Sciences at the University of Pittsburgh, Pennsylvania. He is a cofounder and the director of the Laboratory of Education and Research on Security Assured

Information Systems (LERSAIS). At Pitt, he teaches several information assurance (IA) courses and coordinates the IA program. His research interests include access control models, security and privacy of distributed multimedia systems, trust management, and information survivability. His research has been supported by the National Science Foundation, and he is a recipient of the NSF-CAREER award in 2006. He received his M.S. in computer science and a Ph.D. in electrical and computer engineering from Purdue University, West Lafayette, Indiana, in 1998 and 2003, respectively. He is also a co-author of *Information Assurance: Dependability and Security in Networked Systems*, published by Elsevier, 2007.

Prashant Krishnamurthy (Chapter 2) is an associate professor with the graduate program in Telecommunications and Networking at the University of Pittsburgh, Pennsylvania. At Pitt, he regularly teaches courses on wireless communication systems and networks, cryptography, and network security. His research interests are wireless network security, wireless data networks, position location in indoor wireless networks, and radio channel modeling for indoor wireless networks. His research has been funded by the National Science Foundation and the National Institute of Standards and Technology. He is the co-author of the books *Principles of Wireless Networks: A Unified Approach* and *Physical Layer of Communication Systems* (Prentice Hall; 1st edition, December 11, 2001). He served as the chair of the IEEE Communications Society, Pittsburgh Chapter, from 2000 to 2005. He obtained his Ph.D. in 1999 from Worcester Polytechnic Institute, Worcester, Massachusetts. He is also a co-author of *Information Assurance: Dependability and Security in Networked Systems*, published by Elsevier, 2007.

Pete Loshin (Chapter 6) writes and consults about Internet protocols and open source network technologies. Formerly on the staff of *BYTE Magazine, Information Security Magazine*, and other publications, his work appears regularly in leading trade publications and websites, including *CPU, Computerworld, PC Magazine*, EarthWeb, Internet.com, and CNN. He is also the author of *IPv6: Theory, Protocol, and Practice*, published by Elsevier, 2003.

James D. McCabe (Chapter 3) was an advisor on networking to NASA and the Department of Commerce OCIOs. He is the recipient of multiple NASA awards and holds patents in supercomputer network research. He has been architecting, designing, and deploying high-performance networks for over 20 years. He also consults, teaches, and writes about network analysis, architecture, and design. McCabe holds degrees in chemical engineering and physics from Georgia Institute of Technology and Georgia State University. He is also the author of *Network Analysis, Architecture, and Design*, published by Elsevier, 2007.

Lionel M. Ni (Chapter 8) is a professor and head of the Computer Science Department at the Hong Kong University of Science and Technology. Dr. Ni earned his Ph.D. in electrical and computer engineering from Purdue University,

West Lafayette, Indiana, in 1981. He was a professor in the Computer Science and Engineering Department at Michigan State University, where he started his academic career in 1981. He has been involved in many projects related to wireless technologies, 2.5G/3G cellular phones, and embedded systems. He is also a co-author of *Smart Phone and Next Generation Mobile Computing*, published by Elsevier, 2005.

Larry L. Peterson (Chapter 1) is a professor and chair of Computer Science at Princeton University. He is the director of the Princeton-hosted PlanetLab Consortium and chair of the planning group for NSF's GENI Initiative. His research focuses on the design and implementation of networked systems. Peterson is a fellow of the ACM. He received his Ph.D. from Purdue University in 1985. He is also a co-author of *Computer Networks: A Systems Approach*, published by Elsevier, 2007.

Rajiv Ramaswami (Chapter 9) leads a group in planning and designing photonic switching products at Nortel Networks. He has worked on optical networks since 1988, from early research to product development, that includes stints at IBM research, Tellabs, and Xros (now part of Nortel). He is an IEEE Fellow and a recipient of the IEEE W.R.G. Baker and W.R. Bennett prize paper awards, as well as an Outstanding Innovation award from IBM. Rajiv received a Ph.D. in electrical engineering and computer science from the University of California at Berkeley. He is also a co-author of *Optical Networks: A Practical Perspective*, published by Elsevier, 2001.

Kumar N. Sivarajan (Chapter 9) is cofounder and chief technology officer at Tejas Networks, an optical networking start-up in Bangalore, India. He has worked on optical, wireless, ATM, and Internet networking technologies for over a decade, first at IBM Research and then at the Indian Institute of Science, Bangalore. He is a recipient of the IEEE W.R.G. Baker and W.R. Bennett prize paper awards. Kumar received his Ph.D. in electrical engineering from the California Institute of Technology. He is also a co-author of *Optical Networks: A Practical Perspective*, published by Elsevier, 2001.

Eugene H. Spafford (Chapter 10) is one of the most senior and recognized leaders in the field of computing. He has an ongoing record of accomplishments as a senior advisor and consultant on issues of security, education, cyber crime, and computing policy to a number of major companies, law enforcement organizations, and academic and government agencies, including Microsoft, Intel, Unisys, the U.S. Air Force, the National Security Agency, the GAO, the Federal Bureau of Investigation, the National Science Foundation, the Department of Energy, and for two presidents of the United States. With nearly three decades of experience as a researcher and instructor, Dr. Spafford has worked in software engineering, reliable distributed computing, host and network security, digital forensics, computing policy, and computing curriculum design. He is responsible for a number of "firsts" in several of these areas. Dr. Spafford is a professor with a joint appointment in computer science and electrical and computer engineering at Purdue University, West Lafayette, Indiana, where he has served on the faculty since 1987. He is also a professor of philosophy (courtesy) and a professor of communication (courtesy). He is the executive director of the Purdue University Center for Education and Research in Information Assurance and Security (CERIAS). As of 2007, Dr. Spafford is also an adjunct professor of computer science at the University of Texas at San Antonio, and is executive director of the Advisory Board of the new Institute for Information Assurance there. Dr. Spafford serves on a number of advisory and editorial boards, and he has been honored several times for his writing, research, and teaching on issues of security and ethics. He also contributed to *Information Assurance: Dependability and Security in Networked Systems*, published by Elsevier, 2007.

George Varghese (Chapter 4) is a widely recognized authority on the art of network protocol implementation. Currently a professor in the Department of Computer Science at UC–San Diego, he has previously worked for Digital Equipment Corporation and taught at Washington University. Elected a fellow of the ACM in 2002, he holds (with colleagues) 14 patents in the general field of network algorithmics. Several algorithms that he helped develop have found their way into commercial systems, including Linux (timing wheels), the Cisco GSR (DRR), and MS Windows (IP lookups). He is also the author of *Network Algorithmics: An Interdisciplinary Approach to Designing Fast Networked Devices*, published by Elsevier, 2004.

Yu-Sung Wu (Chapter 10) is a Ph.D. student in the School of Electrical and Computer Engineering at Purdue University, West Lafayette, Indiana, since 2004. His primary research areas are information security and fault tolerance in computer systems. He is a member of the Dependable Computing Systems Laboratory at Purdue, where he participates in the research projects for ADEPTS (an intrusion response system) and CIDS (a correlation framework for intrusion detection). Yu-Sung also has been working closely with researchers at Avaya Labs on building the IDS/IPS solutions for voiceover IP systems. He also contributed to *Information Assurance: Dependability and Security in Networked Systems*, published by Elsevier, 2007.

Pei Zheng (Chapter 8) was an assistant professor in the Computer Science Department at Arcadia University and a consultant working in the areas of mobile computing and distributed systems during the writing of this book. Dr. Zheng received his Ph.D. in computer science from Michigan State University in 2003. He was a member of the technical staff in Bell Laboratories/Lucent Technologies. He joined Microsoft in 2005. His research interests include distributed systems, network simulation and emulation, and mobile computing. He is also a co-author of *Smart Phone and Next Generation Mobile Computing*, published by Elsevier, 2005.

Network Security Overview

Computer networks are typically a shared resource used by many applications representing different interests. The Internet is particularly widely shared, being used by competing businesses, mutually antagonistic governments, and opportunistic criminals. Unless security measures are taken, a network conversation or a distributed application may be compromised by an adversary.

Consider some threats to secure use of, for example, the World Wide Web. Suppose you are a customer using a credit card to order an item from a website. An obvious threat is that an adversary would eavesdrop on your network communication, reading your messages to obtain your credit card information. How might that eavesdropping be accomplished? It is trivial on a broadcast network such as an Ethernet, where any node can be configured to receive all the message traffic on that network. Wireless communication can be monitored without any physical connection. More elaborate approaches include wiretapping and planting spy software on any of the chain of nodes involved. Only in the most extreme cases, such as national security, are serious measures taken to prevent such monitoring, and the Internet is not one of those cases. It is possible and practical, however, to encrypt messages so as to prevent an adversary from understanding the message contents. A protocol that does so is said to provide *confidentiality*. Taking the concept a step further, concealing the quantity or destination of communication is called *traffic confidentiality*—because merely knowing how much communication is going where can be useful to an adversary in some situations.

Even with confidentiality there still remain threats for the website customer. An adversary who can't read the contents of your encrypted message might still be able to change a few bits in it, resulting in a valid order for, say, a completely different item or perhaps 1,000 units of the item. There are techniques to detect, if not prevent, such tampering. A protocol that detects such message tampering provides *data integrity*. The adversary could alternatively transmit an extra copy of your message in a *replay attack*. To the website, it would appear as though you had simply ordered another of the same item you ordered the first time. A protocol that detects replays provides *originality*. Originality would not, however, preclude the adversary intercepting your order, waiting a while, then transmitting it—in effect, delaying your order. The adversary could thereby arrange for the item to arrive on your doorstep while you are away on vacation, when it can be easily snatched. A protocol that detects such delaying tactics is said to provide *timeliness*. Data integrity, originality, and timeliness are considered aspects of the more general property of *integrity*.

Another threat to the customer is unknowingly being directed to a false website. This can result from a DNS attack, in which false information is entered in a domain name server or the name service cache of the customer's computer. This leads to translating a correct URL into an incorrect IP address—the address of a false website. A protocol that ensures that you really are talking to whom you think you're talking is said to provide *authentication*. Authentication entails integrity since it is meaningless to say that a message came from a certain participant if it is no longer the same message.

The owner of the website can be attacked as well. Some websites have been defaced; the files that make up the website content have been remotely accessed and modified without authorization. That is an issue of *access control*: enforcing the rules regarding who is allowed to do what. Websites have also been subject to denial of service (DoS) attacks, during which would-be customers are unable to access the website because it is being overwhelmed by bogus requests. Ensuring a degree of access is called *availability*.

Finally, the customer and website face threats from each other. Each could unilaterally deny that a transaction occurred, or invent a nonexistent transaction. *Nonrepudiation* means that a bogus denial (repudiation) of a transaction can be disproved, and *nonforgeability* means that claims of a bogus (forged) transaction can be disproved.

Although these examples have been based on Web transactions, there are comparable security threats in almost every network context. Although the Internet was designed with the redundancy to survive physical attacks such as bombing, it was not originally designed to provide the kind of security we have been discussing. Internet security mechanisms have essentially been patches. If a comprehensive redesign of the Internet were to take place, integrating security would likely be the foremost driving factor. That possibility makes this chapter all the more pertinent.

The main tools for securing networked systems are cryptography and firewalls. The bulk of this chapter concerns cryptography-based security.

1.1 CRYPTOGRAPHIC TOOLS

We introduce the concepts of cryptography-based security step by step. The first step is the cryptographic algorithms—ciphers and cryptographic hashes—that are introduced in this section. They are not a solution in themselves, but rather building blocks from which a solution can be built. The next step (Section 1.2) addresses the problem of distributing the keys, the secret parameters that are input to cryptographic algorithms. In the next step (Section 1.3), we describe how to incorporate the cryptographic building blocks into protocols that provide secure communication between participants who possess the correct keys. Finally, Section 1.4 examines several complete security protocols and systems in current use.

1.1.1 Principles of Ciphers

Encryption transforms a message in such a way that it becomes unintelligible to any party that does not have the secret of how to reverse the transformation. The sender applies an *encryption* function to the original *plaintext* message, resulting in a *ciphertext* message that is sent over the network, as in Figure 1.1. The receiver applies a secret *decryption* function—the inverse of the encryption function—to recover the original plaintext. The ciphertext transmitted across the network is unintelligible to any eavesdropper, assuming she doesn't know the decryption function. The transformation represented by an encryption function and its corresponding decryption function is called a *cipher*.

Cryptographers have been led to the principle, first stated in 1883, that encryption and decryption functions should be parameterized by a *key*, and furthermore that the functions should be considered public knowledge—only the key need be secret. Thus, the ciphertext produced for a given plaintext message depends on both the encryption function and the key. One reason for this principle is that if you depend on the cipher being kept secret, then you have to retire the cipher (not just the keys) when you believe it is no longer secret. This means potentially

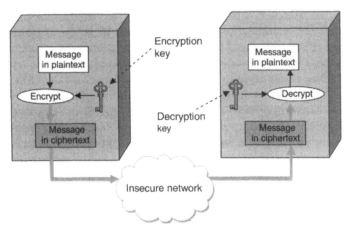

FIGURE 1.1

Symmetric-key encryption and decryption.

frequent changes of cipher, which is problematic since it takes a lot of work to develop a new cipher. Also, one of the best ways to know that a cipher is secure is to use it for a long time—if no one breaks it, it's probably secure. (Fortunately, there are plenty of people who will try to break ciphers and who will let it be widely known when they have succeeded, so no news is generally good news.) Thus, there is considerable cost and risk in deploying a new cipher. Finally, parameterizing a cipher with keys provides us with what is in effect a very large family of ciphers; by switching keys we essentially switch ciphers, thereby limiting the amount of data that a *cryptanalyst* (code-breaker) can use to try to break our key/cipher, and the amount she can read if she succeeds.

The basic requirement for an encryption algorithm is that it turns plaintext into ciphertext in such a way that only the intended recipient—the holder of the decryption key—can recover the plaintext. What this means is that encrypted messages cannot be read by people who do not hold the key.

It is important to realize that when a potential attacker receives a piece of ciphertext, he may have more information at his disposal than just the ciphertext itself. For example, he may know that the plaintext was written in English, which means that the letter *e* occurs more often in the plaintext that any other letter; the frequency of many other letters and common letter combinations can also be predicted. This information can greatly simplify the task of finding the key. Similarly, he may know something about the likely contents of the message; for example, the word "login" is likely to occur at the start of a remote login session. This may enable a *known plaintext* attack, which has a much higher chance of success than a *ciphertext only* attack. Even better is a *chosen plaintext* attack, which may be enabled by feeding some information to the sender that you know the sender is likely to transmit—such things have happened in wartime, for example.

The best cryptographic algorithms, therefore, can prevent the attacker from deducing the key even when the individual knows both the plaintext and the ciphertext. This leaves the attacker with no choice but to try all the possible keys—exhaustive, "brute-force" search. If keys have n bits, then there are 2^n possible values for a key (each of the n bits could be either a zero or a one). An attacker could be so lucky as to try the correct value immediately, or so unlucky as to try every incorrect value before finally trying the correct value of the key, therefore, she would have tried all 2^n possible values; the average number of guesses to discover the correct value is halfway between those extremes, $2^n/2$. This can be made computationally impractical by choosing a sufficiently large key space and by making the operation of checking a key reasonably costly. What makes this difficult is that computing speeds keep increasing, making formerly infeasible computations feasible. Furthermore, although we are concentrating on the security of data as it moves through the network—that is, the data is sometimes vulnerable for only a short period of time—in general, security people have to consider the vulnerability of data that needs to be stored in archives for tens of years. This argues for a generously large key size. On the other hand, larger keys make encryption and decryption slower.

Most ciphers are *block ciphers*: they are defined to take as input a plaintext block of a certain fixed size, typically 64 to 128 bits. Using a block cipher to encrypt each block independently—known as *electronic codebook (ECB) mode* encryption—has the weakness that a given plaintext block value will always result in the same ciphertext block. Hence recurring block values in the plaintext are recognizable as such in the ciphertext, making it much easier for a cryptanalyst to break the cipher.

To prevent this, block ciphers are always augmented to make the ciphertext for a block vary depending on context. Ways in which a block cipher may be augmented are called *modes of operation*. A common mode of operation is *cipher block chaining (CBC)*, in which each plaintext block is XORed with the previous block's ciphertext before being encrypted. The result is that each block's ciphertext depends in part on the preceding blocks (i.e., on its context). Since the first plaintext block has no preceding block, it is XORed with a random number. That random number, called an *initialization vector (IV)*, is included with the series of ciphertext blocks so that the first ciphertext block can be decrypted. This mode is illustrated in Figure 1.2. Another mode of operation is *counter mode*, in which successive values of a counter (e.g., 1, 2, 3, . . .) are incorporated into the encryption of successive blocks of plaintext.

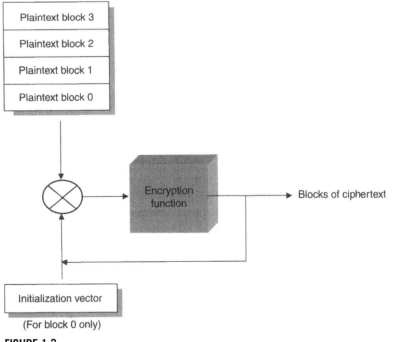

FIGURE 1.2

Cipher block chaining (CBC).

1.1.2 Symmetric-Key Ciphers

In a symmetric-key cipher, both participants[1] in a communication share the same key. In other words, if a message is encrypted using a particular key, the same key is required for decrypting the message. If the cipher illustrated in Figure 1.1 were a symmetric-key cipher, then the encryption and decryption keys would be identical. Symmetric-key ciphers are also known as secret-key ciphers since the shared key must be known only to the participants.

The U.S. National Institute of Standards and Technology (NIST) has issued standards for a series of symmetric-key ciphers. *Data Encryption Standard (DES)* was the first, and it has stood the test of time in that no cryptanalytic attack better than brute-force search has been discovered. Brute-force search, however, has gotten faster. DES's keys (56 independent bits) are now too small given current processor speeds. Consequently, NIST updated the DES standard in 1999 to indicate that DES should only be used for legacy systems. Nonetheless, DES is still widespread.

NIST also standardized the cipher *Triple DES (3DES)*, which leverages the cryptanalysis resistance of DES while in effect increasing the key size. A 3DES key has 168 (= 3 * 56) independent bits, and is used as three DES keys; let's call them DES-key1, DES-key2, and DES-key3. 3DES-encryption of a block is performed by first DES-encrypting the block using DES-key1, then DES-*de*crypting the result using DES-key2, and finally DES-encrypting that result using DES-key3. Decryption involves decrypting using DES-key3, then encrypting using DES-key2, then decrypting using DES-key1.

The reason 3DES encryption uses DES *de*cryption with DES-key2 is to interoperate with legacy DES systems. If a legacy DES system uses a certain key, then 3DES can compute the same encryption function by using that key for each of DES-key1, DES-key2, and DES-key3: In the first two steps we encrypt and then decrypt with the same key, producing the original plaintext, which we then encrypt again.

Although 3DES solves DES's key-length problem, it inherits some other shortcomings. Software implementations of DES/3DES are slow because it was originally designed, by IBM, for implementation in hardware. Also, DES/3DES uses a 64-bit block size; a larger block size is more efficient and more secure.

3DES is being superseded by the *Advanced Encryption Standard (AES)* issued by NIST in 2001. The cipher selected to become that standard (with a few minor modifications) was originally named Rijndael (pronounced roughly like "Rhine dahl") based on the names of its inventors, Daemen and Rijmen. AES supports key lengths of 128, 192, or 256 bits, and the block length is 128 bits. AES permits fast implementations in both software and hardware. It doesn't require much memory, which makes it suitable for small mobile devices. AES has some mathematically

---

[1]We use the term *participant* for the parties involved in a secure communication since that is the term we have been using throughout the chapter to identify the two endpoints of a channel. In the security world, they are typically called *principals.*

proven security properties and, as of 2005, there are not known to have been any successful attacks against it.

1.1.3 Public-Key Ciphers

An alternative to symmetric-key ciphers is asymmetric, or public-key, ciphers. Instead of a single key shared by two participants, a public-key cipher uses a pair of related keys, one for encryption and a different one for decryption. The pair of keys is "owned" by just one participant. The owner keeps the decryption key secret so that only the owner can decrypt messages; that key is called the *private key*. The owner makes the encryption key public, so that anyone can encrypt messages for the owner; that key is called the *public key*. Obviously, for such a scheme to work it must not be possible to deduce the private key from the public key. Consequently, any participant can get the public key and send an encrypted message to the owner of the keys, and only the owner has the private key necessary to decrypt it. This scenario is depicted in Figure 1.3.

Because it is somewhat unintuitive, we emphasize that the public encryption key is useless for decrypting a message—you couldn't even decrypt a message that you yourself had just encrypted unless you had the private, decryption key. If we think of keys as defining a communication channel between participants, then another difference between public-key and symmetric-key ciphers is the topology of the channels. A key for a symmetric-key cipher provides a channel that is two-way between two participants—each participant holds the same (symmetric)

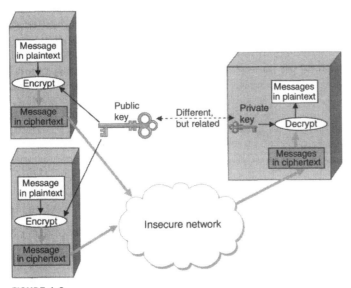

FIGURE 1.3

Public-key encryption.

key that either one can use to encrypt or decrypt messages in either direction. A public/private key pair, in contrast, provides a channel that is one-way, and many-to-one from everyone who has the public key to the (unique) owner of the private key, as illustrated in Figure 1.3.

An important additional property of public-key ciphers is that the private decryption key can be used with the encryption algorithm to encrypt messages so that they can only be decrypted using the public encryption key. This property clearly wouldn't be useful for confidentiality since anyone with the public key could decrypt such a message. (Indeed, for two-way confidentiality between two participants, each participant needs its own pair of keys, and each encrypts messages using the other's public key.) This property is, however, useful for authentication since it tells the receiver of such a message that it could only have been created by the owner of the keys (subject to certain assumptions that we will get into later). This is illustrated in Figure 1.4. It should be clear from the figure that anyone with the public key can decrypt the encrypted message, and assuming that the result of the decryption matches the expected result, it can be concluded that the private key must have been used to perform the encryption. Exactly how this operation is used to provide authentication is the topic of Section 1.3. As we will see, public-key ciphers are used primarily for authentication and to confidentially distribute symmetric keys, leaving the rest of confidentiality to symmetric-key ciphers.

A bit of interesting history: The concept of public-key ciphers was first published in 1976 by Diffie and Hellman. Subsequently, however, documents have come to light proving that Britain's Communications-Electronics Security Group had discovered public-key ciphers by 1970, and the U.S. National Security Agency (NSA) claims to have discovered them in the mid-1960s.

The best-known public-key cipher is RSA, named after its inventors: Rivest, Shamir, and Adleman. RSA relies on the high computational cost of factoring large numbers. The problem of finding an efficient way to factor numbers is one that mathematicians have worked on unsuccessfully since long before RSA appeared in 1978, and RSA's subsequent resistance to cryptanalysis has further bolstered

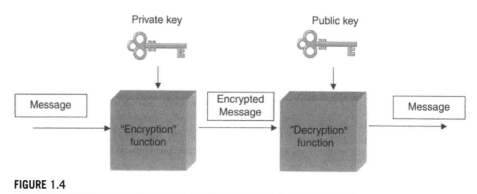

FIGURE 1.4

Authentication using public keys.

confidence in its security. Unfortunately, RSA needs relatively large keys, at least 1,024 bits, to be secure. This is larger than keys for symmetric-key ciphers because it is faster to break an RSA private key by factoring the large number on which the pair of keys is based than by exhaustively searching the key space.

Another public-key cipher is ElGamal. Like RSA, it relies on a mathematical problem, the discrete logarithm problem, for which no efficient solution has been found, and requires keys of at least 1,024 bits. There is a variation of the discrete logarithm problem, arising when the input is an elliptic curve, that is thought to be even more difficult to compute; cryptographic schemes based on this problem are referred to as elliptic curve cryptography.

Public-key ciphers are, unfortunately, several orders of magnitude slower than symmetric-key ciphers. Consequently, symmetric-key ciphers are used for the vast majority of encryption, while public-key ciphers are reserved for use in authentication (Section 1.1.4) and session key establishment (Section 1.2).

1.1.4 Authenticators

Encryption alone does not provide data integrity. For example, just randomly modifying a ciphertext message could result in a value that decrypts into valid-appearing plaintext, in which case the tampering would be undetectable by the receiver. Nor does encryption alone provide authentication. It is meaningless to say that a message came from a certain participant if the contents of the message have been modified. To some extent one may focus on either of authentication or data integrity temporarily, but they are fundamentally inseparable.

An *authenticator* is a value, to be included in a transmitted message, that can be used to verify simultaneously the authenticity and the data integrity of a message. We defer discussion of the use of authenticators in protocols to Section 1.3. Here we focus on the algorithms that produce authenticators.

To support data integrity, an authenticator includes redundant information about the message contents; it is like a checksum or cyclic redundancy check (CRC). To support authentication, an authenticator includes some proof that whoever created the authenticator knows a secret that is known only to the alleged sender of the message; for example, the secret could be a key, and the proof could be some value encrypted using the key. There is a mutual dependency between the form of the redundant information and the form of the proof of secret knowledge. We discuss several workable combinations.

We initially assume that the original message need not be confidential—that a transmitted message will consist of the plaintext of the original message plus an authenticator. Later we will consider the case where confidentiality is desired.

One kind of authenticator combines encryption and a *cryptographic hash function*. A cryptographic hash function (also known as a cryptographic checksum) is a function that outputs sufficient redundant information about a message to expose any tampering. Just as a checksum or CRC exposes bit error introduced by noisy links, a cryptographic checksum is designed to expose deliberate corruption of messages by an adversary. The value it outputs is called a *message digest* and, like an ordinary checksum, is appended to the message. All the message digests produced by a given hash have the same number of bits regardless of the length of the original message. Since the space of possible input messages is larger than the space of possible message digests, there will be different input messages that produce the same message digest, like collisions in a hash table. Cryptographic hash algorithms are treated as public knowledge, as with cipher algorithms.

An authenticator can be created by encrypting the message digest. The receiver computes a digest of the plaintext part of the message, and compares that to the decrypted message digest. If they are equal, then the receiver would conclude that the message is indeed from its alleged sender (since it would have to have been encrypted with the right key) and has not been tampered with. No adversary could get away with sending a bogus message with a matching bogus digest because she would not have the key to encrypt the bogus digest correctly. An adversary could, however, obtain the plaintext original message and its encrypted digest by eavesdropping. The adversary could then (since the hash function is public knowledge) compute the digest of the original message, and generate alternative messages looking for one with the same message digest. If she finds one, she could undetectably send the new message with the old authenticator. Therefore, security requires that the hash function have the *one-way* property: It must be computationally infeasible for an adversary to find any plaintext message that has the same digest as the original.

For a hash function to meet this requirement, its outputs must be fairly randomly distributed. For example, if digests are 128 bits long and randomly distributed, then you would need to try 2^{127} messages, on average, before finding a second message whose digest matches that of a given message. If the outputs are not randomly distributed—that is, if some outputs are much more likely than others—then for some messages you could find another message with the same digest much more easily than this, which would reduce the security of the algorithm. If you were instead just trying to find any *collision*—any two messages that produce the same digest— then you would need to compute the digests of only 2^{64} messages, on average. This surprising fact is the basis of the birthday attack—see the exercises for more details.

The most common cryptographic hash algorithms are Message Digest 5 (MD5) and Secure Hash Algorithm 1 (SHA-1). MD5 outputs a 128-bit digest, and SHA-1 outputs a 160-bit digest. Researchers have recently discovered techniques for finding MD5 collisions much more efficiently than brute force, and well within computational feasibility. This led to recommendations to shift from MD5 to SHA-1. Even more recently researchers have discovered techniques that find SHA-1 collisions somewhat more efficiently than brute force, but are not yet computationally feasible. Although *collision attacks* (attacks based on finding any collision) are not as great a risk as *preimage attacks* (attacks based on finding a second message that collides with a given first message), these are nonetheless serious weaknesses. NIST has proposed to phase out SHA-1 by 2010, in favor of four variants of SHA that are collectively known as SHA-2.

In this approach (encrypted message digest) to generating an authenticator, the digest encryption could use either a symmetric-key cipher or a public-key cipher. If a public-key cipher is used, the digest would be encrypted using the sender's private key (the one we normally think of as being used for decryption), and the receiver—or anyone else—could decrypt the digest using the sender's public key.

A digest encrypted with a public-key algorithm but using the private key is called a *digital signature* because it provides nonrepudiation like a written signature. The receiver of a message with a digital signature can prove to any third party that the sender really sent that message, because the third party can use the sender's public key to check for herself. (Symmetric-key encryption of a digest does not have this property because only the two participants know the key; furthermore, since both participants know the key, the alleged receiver could have created the message herself.) Any public-key cipher can be used for digital signatures. *Digital Signature Standard (DSS)* is a digital signature format that has been standardized by NIST. DSS signatures may use any one of three public-key ciphers, one based on RSA, another on ElGamal, and a third called Elliptic Curve Digital Signature Algorithm.

Another kind of authenticator is similar, but instead of encrypting a hash, it uses a hashlike function that takes a secret value (known to only the sender and the receiver) as a parameter, as illustrated in Figure 1.5. Such a function outputs an authenticator called a *message authentication code (MAC)*. The sender appends the MAC to her plaintext message. The receiver recomputes the MAC using the plaintext and the secret value, and compares that recomputed MAC to the received MAC.

A common variation on MACs is to apply a cryptographic hash (such as MD5 or SHA-1) to the concatenation of the plaintext message and the secret value, as illustrated in Figure 1.5. The resulting digest is called a *hashed message authentication*

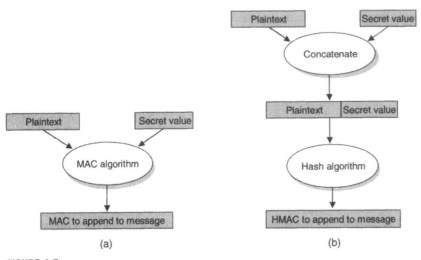

(a)   (b)

FIGURE 1.5

Computing a MAC (a) versus computing an HMAC (b).

code (HMAC) since it is essentially a MAC. The HMAC, but not the secret value, is appended to the plaintext message. Only a receiver who knows the secret value can compute the correct HMAC to compare with the received HMAC. If it weren't for the one-way property of the hash, an adversary might be able to find the input that generated the HMAC and compare it to the plaintext message to determine the secret value.

Up to this point, we have been assuming that the message wasn't confidential, so the original message could be transmitted as plaintext. To add confidentiality to a message with an authenticator, it suffices to encrypt the concatenation of the entire message including its authenticator—the MAC, HMAC, or encrypted digest. Remember that, in practice, confidentiality is implemented using symmetric-key ciphers because they are so much faster than public-key ciphers. Furthermore, it costs little to include the authenticator in the encryption, and it increases security. A common simplification is to encrypt the message with its (raw) digest, such that the digest is only encrypted once; in this case, the entire ciphertext message is considered to be an authenticator.

Although authenticators may seem to solve the authentication problem, we will see in Section 1.3 that they are only the foundation of a solution. First, however, we address the issue of how participants obtain keys in the first place.

1.2 KEY PREDISTRIBUTION

To use ciphers and authenticators, the communicating participants need to know what keys to use. In the case of a symmetric-key cipher, how does a pair of participants obtain the key they share? In the case of a public-key cipher, how do participants know what public key belongs to a certain participant? The answer differs depending on whether the keys are short-lived *session keys* or longer-lived predistributed keys.

A session key is a key used to secure a single, relatively short episode of communication: a session. Each distinct session between a pair of participants uses a new session key, which is always a symmetric-key key for speed. The participants determine what session key to use by means of a protocol—a session-key establishment protocol. A session-key establishment protocol needs its own security (so that, for example, an adversary cannot learn the new session key); that security is based on the longer-lived predistributed keys.

There are several motivations for this division of labor between session keys and predistributed keys:

- Limiting the amount of time a key is used results in less time for computationally intensive attacks, less ciphertext for cryptanalysis, and less information exposed should the key be broken;

- Predistribution of symmetric keys is problematic;

- Public-key ciphers are generally superior for authentication and session-key establishment but too slow to use encrypting entire messages for confidentiality.

This section explains how predistributed keys are distributed, and Section 1.3 will explain how session keys are then established. We henceforth use "Alice" and "Bob" to designate participants, as is common in the cryptography literature. Bear in mind that although we tend to refer to participants in anthropomorphic terms, we are more frequently concerned with the communication between software or hardware entities such as clients and servers that often have no direct relationship with any particular person.

1.2.1 Predistribution of Public Keys

The algorithms to generate a matched pair of public and private keys are publicly known, and software that does it is widely available. So if Alice wanted to use a public-key cipher, she could generate her own pair of public and private keys, keep the private key hidden, and publicize the public key. But how can she publicize her public key—assert that it belongs to her—in such a way that other participants can be sure it really belongs to her? Not via email or Web, because an adversary could forge an equally plausible claim that key x belongs to Alice when x really belongs to the adversary.

A complete scheme for certifying bindings between public keys and identities—what key belongs to whom—is called a *public key infrastructure (PKI)*. A PKI starts with the ability to verify identities and bind them to keys out-of-band. By "out-of-band," we mean something outside the network and the computers that comprise it, such as in the following scenarios. If Alice and Bob are individuals who know each other, then they could get together in the same room and Alice could give her public key to Bob directly, perhaps on a business card. If Bob is an organization, Alice the individual could present conventional identification, perhaps involving a photograph or fingerprints. If Alice and Bob are computers owned by the same company, then a system administrator could configure Bob with Alice's public key.

Establishing keys out-of-band doesn't scale well, but it suffices to bootstrap a PKI. Bob's knowledge that Alice's key is x can be widely, scalably disseminated using a combination of digital signatures and a concept of trust. For example, suppose that you have received Bob's public key out-of-band, and that you know enough about Bob to trust him on matters of keys and identities. Then Bob could send you a message asserting that Alice's key is x and—since you already know Bob's public key—you could authenticate the message as having come from Bob. (Remember that to digitally sign the statement, Bob would append a cryptographic hash of it that has been encrypted using his private key.) Since you trust Bob to tell the truth, you would now know that Alice's key is x, even though you had never met her or exchanged a single message with her. Using digital signatures,

Bob wouldn't even have to send you a message; he could simply create and publish a digitally signed statement that Alice's key is *x*. Such a digitally signed statement of a public-key binding is called a *public-key certificate*, or simply a certificate. Bob could send Alice a copy of the certificate, or post it on a website. If and when you need to verify Alice's public key, you could do so by getting a copy of the certificate, perhaps directly from Alice—as long as you trust Bob and know his public key. You can see that by starting from a very small number of keys (in this case, just Bob's) you could build up a large set of trusted keys over time. More on this topic below.

One of the major standards for certificates is known as X.509. This standard leaves a lot of details open, but specifies a basic structure. A certificate clearly must include

- The identity of the entity being certified;
- The public key of the entity being certified;
- The identity of the signer;
- The digital signature;
- A digital signature algorithm identifier (which cryptographic hash and which cipher).

An optional component is an expiration time for the certificate. We will see a particular use of this feature below.

Since a certificate creates a binding between an identity and a public key, we should look more closely at what we mean by "identity." For example, a certificate that says, "This public key belongs to John Smith" may not be terribly useful if you can't tell which of the thousands of John Smiths is being identified. Thus, certificates must use a well-defined namespace for the identities being certified. For example, certificates are often issued for email addresses and DNS domains.

There are different ways a PKI could formalize the notion of trust. We discuss the two main approaches.

Certification Authorities

In this model of trust, trust is binary; you either trust someone completely, or not at all. Together with certificates, this allows the building of *chains of trust*. If *X* certifies that a certain public key belongs to *Y*, and then *Y* goes on to certify that another public key belongs to *Z*, then there exists a chain of certificates from *X* to *Z*, even though *X* and *Z* may have never met. If you know *X*'s key—and you trust *X* and *Y*—then you can believe the certificate that gives *Z*'s key. In other words, all you need is a chain of certificates, all signed by entities you trust, as long as it leads back to an entity whose key you already know.

A *certification authority* or *certificate authority (CA)* is an entity claimed (by someone) to be trustworthy for verifying identities and issuing public-key certificates. There are commercial CAs, governmental CAs, and even free CAs. To use a CA, you must know its own key. You can learn that CA's key, however, if you can obtain a chain of CA-signed certificates that starts with a CA whose key you already know. Then you can believe any certificate signed by that new CA.

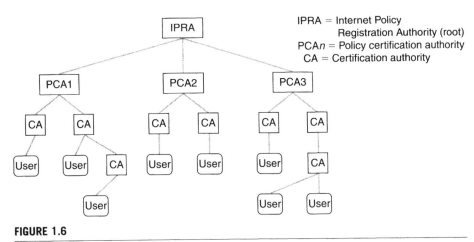

FIGURE 1.6

Tree-structured certification authority hierarchy.

A common way to build such chains is to arrange them in a tree-structured hierarchy, as shown in Figure 1.6. If everyone has the public key of the root CA, then any participant can provide a chain of certificates to another participant and know that it will be sufficient to build a chain of trust for that participant.

Alternatively, there could be multiple CAs whose public keys are considered well known (i.e., obtained out-of-band). As a bookkeeping device, such a CA can generate its own certificate, signing it with the very key defined in the certificate. Such certificates are known as *self-certifying certificates*. Web browsers such as Firefox and Microsoft's Internet Explorer come preequipped with self-certifying certificates for a set of CAs; in effect, the browser's producer has decided these keys can be trusted. These certificates are accepted by SSL/TLS, the protocol most often used to secure Web transactions (Section 1.4.3).

There are still significant issues with building chains of trust. First of all, even if you are certain that you have the public key of the root CA, you need to be sure that every CA from the root on down is doing its job properly. If just one CA is willing to issue certificates to entities without verifying their identities, then what looks like a valid chain of certificates becomes meaningless. X.509 certificates provide the option of restricting the set of entities that the subject of a certificate is, in turn, trusted to certify.

Web of Trust

An alternative model of trust is the *web of trust* exemplified by Pretty Good Privacy (PGP), which is further discussed in Section 1.4.3. PGP is a security system for email, so email addresses are the identities to which keys are bound and by which certificates are signed. In keeping with PGP's roots as protection against government intrusion, there are no CAs. Instead, every individual decides whom he trusts and how much he trusts them—in this model, trust is a matter of degree.

In addition, a public-key certificate can include a confidence level indicating how confident the signer is of the key binding claimed in the certificate. So a given user may have to have several certificates attesting to the same key binding before he is willing to trust it.

For example, suppose you have a certificate for Bob provided by Alice; you can assign a moderate level of trust to that certificate. However, if you have additional certificates for Bob that were provided by C and D, each of whom is also moderately trustworthy, that might considerably increase your level of confidence that the public key you have for Bob is valid. In short, PGP recognizes that the problem of establishing trust is quite a personal matter and gives users the raw material to make their own decisions, rather than assuming that they are all willing to trust in a single hierarchal structure of CAs. To quote Phil Zimmerman, the developer of PGP, "PGP is for people who prefer to pack their own parachutes."

PGP has become quite popular in the networking community, and PGP key-signing parties are a regular feature of IETF meetings. At these gatherings, an individual can

- Collect public keys from others whose identity he knows;
- Provide his public key to others;
- Get his public key signed by others, thus collecting certificates that will be persuasive to an increasingly large set of people;
- Sign the public key of other individuals, thus helping them build up their set of certificates that they can use to distribute their public keys;
- Collect certificates from other individuals whom he trusts enough to sign keys.

Thus, over time a user will collect a set of certificates with varying degrees of trust.

Certificate Revocation

One issue that arises with certificates is how to revoke, or undo, a certificate. Why is this important? Suppose that you suspect that someone has discovered your private key. There may be any number of certificates in the universe that assert that you are the owner of the public key corresponding to that private key. The person who discovered your private key thus has everything he needs to impersonate you: valid certificates and your private key. To solve this problem, it would be nice to be able to revoke the certificates that bind your old, compromised key to your identity, so that the impersonator will no longer be able to persuade other people that he is you.

The basic solution to the problem is simple enough. Each CA can issue a *certificate revocation list (CRL)*, which is a digitally signed list of certificates that have been revoked. The CRL is periodically updated and made publicly available. Because it is digitally signed, it can just be posted on a website. Now, when Alice receives a certificate for Bob that she wants to verify, she will first consult the latest CRL issued by the CA. As long as the certificate has not been revoked, it is valid. Note that if all certificates have unlimited life spans, the CRL would always be getting longer, since you could never take a certificate off the CRL for fear that some copy of the revoked certificate might be used. However, by attaching an expiration date to a certificate when it is issued, we can limit the length of time that a revoked certificate needs to stay on a CRL. As soon as its original expiration date is passed, it can be removed from the CRL.

To overcome certain deficiencies of CRLs, *Online Certificate Status Protocol (OCSP)* was created. OCSP is used to communicate with, and between, OCSP servers called *OCSP responders* to check a certificate's validity.

1.2.2 Predistribution of Symmetric Keys

If Alice wants to use a secret-key cipher to communicate with Bob, she can't just pick a key and send it to him because, without already having a key, they can't encrypt this key to keep it confidential and they can't authenticate each other. As with public keys, some predistribution scheme is needed. Predistribution is harder for symmetric keys than for public keys for two obvious reasons:

- While only one public key per entity is sufficient for authentication and confidentiality, there must be a symmetric key for each pair of entities who wish to communicate. If there are N entities, that means $N(N-1)/2$ keys.

- Unlike public keys, secret keys must be kept secret.

In summary, there are a lot more keys to distribute, and you can't use certificates that everyone can read.

The most common solution is to use a *key distribution center (KDC)*. A KDC is a trusted entity that shares a secret key with each other entity. This brings the number of keys down to a more manageable $N-1$, few enough to establish out-of-band for some applications. When Alice wishes to communicate with Bob, that communication does not travel via the KDC. Rather, the KDC participates in a protocol that authenticates Alice and Bob—using the keys that the KDC already shares with each of them—and generates a new session key for them to use. Then Alice and Bob communicate directly using their session key. Kerberos (Section 1.3.3) is a widely used system based on this approach.

1.3 AUTHENTICATION PROTOCOLS

We described how to encrypt messages and build authenticators in Section 1.1, and how to predistribute the necessary keys in Section 1.2. It might seem as if all we have to do to make a protocol secure is append an authenticator to every message and, if we want confidentiality, encrypt the message.

There are two main reasons why it's not that simple. First, there is the problem of a *replay attack*: an adversary retransmitting a copy of a message that was previously sent. If the message was an order you had placed to a website, for example, then the replayed message would appear to the website as though you had ordered more of the same. Even though it wasn't the original incarnation of the message, its authenticator would still be valid; after all, the message was created by you, and it wasn't modified. In a variation of this attack called a *suppress-replay attack*, an adversary might merely delay your message (by intercepting and later replaying it), so that it is received at a time when it is no longer appropriate. For example, an adversary could delay your order to buy stock from an auspicious time to a time when you would not have wanted to buy. Although this message would in a sense be the original, it wouldn't be timely. Originality and timeliness may be considered aspects of integrity. Ensuring them will in most cases require a nontrivial, back-and-forth protocol.

The other problem we have not yet solved is how to establish a session key. A session key is a symmetric-key cipher key generated on the fly and used for just one session, as described in Section 1.2. This too involves a nontrivial protocol.

What these two issues have in common is authentication. If a message is not original and timely, then from a practical standpoint we want to consider it as not being authentic, not being from whom it claims to be. And when is it more critical to be sure whom a message is from than when you are arranging to share a new session key? Usually, authentication protocols establish a session key at the same time, so that at the end of the protocol Alice and Bob have authenticated each other and they have a new symmetric key to use. Without a new session key, the protocol would just authenticate Alice and Bob at one point in time; a session key allows them to efficiently authenticate subsequent messages. Generally, session-key establishment protocols perform authentication (a notable exception is Diffie-Hellman, Section 1.3.4). So the terms authentication protocol and session-key establishment protocol are almost synonymous.

There is a core set of techniques used to ensure originality and timeliness in authentication protocols. We describe those techniques before moving on to particular protocols.

1.3.1 Originality and Timeliness Techniques

We have seen that authenticators alone do not enable us to detect messages that are not original or timely. One approach is to include a timestamp in the message. Obviously the timestamp itself must be tamperproof, so it must be covered by the authenticator. The primary drawback to timestamps is that they require distributed clock synchronization. Since our system would then depend on synchronization, the clock synchronization itself would need to be defended against security threats; this in addition to the usual challenges of clock synchronization. Another issue is that distributed clocks are synchronized to only a certain degree—a certain margin of error. Thus, the timing integrity provided by timestamps is only as good as the degree of synchronization.

Another approach is to include a *nonce*—a random number used only once—in the message. Participants can then detect replay attacks by checking whether

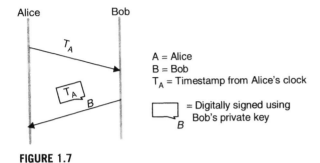

FIGURE 1.7

A challenge-response protocol.

a nonce has been used previously. Unfortunately this requires keeping track of past nonces, of which a great many could accumulate. One solution is to combine the use of timestamps and nonces, so that nonces are required to be unique only within a certain span of time. That makes ensuring uniqueness of nonces manageable while requiring only loose synchronization of clocks.

Another solution to the shortcomings of timestamps and nonces is to use one or both of them in a *challenge-response* protocol. Suppose we use a timestamp. In a challenge-response protocol, Alice sends Bob a timestamp, challenging Bob to encrypt it in a response message (if they share a symmetric key) or digitally sign it in a response message (if Bob has a public key, as in Figure 1.7). The encrypted timestamp is like an authenticator that additionally proves timeliness. Alice can easily check the timeliness of the timestamp in a response from Bob since that timestamp comes from Alice's own clock—no distributed clock synchronization needed. Suppose instead that the protocol uses nonces. Then Alice need only keep track of those nonces for which responses are currently outstanding and haven't been outstanding too long; any purported response with an unrecognized nonce must be bogus.

The beauty of challenge-response, which might otherwise seem excessively complex, is that it combines timeliness and authentication; after all, only Bob (and possibly Alice, if it's a symmetric-key cipher) knows the key necessary to encrypt the never-before-seen timestamp or nonce. Timestamps or nonces are used in most of the authentication protocols that follow.

1.3.2 Public-Key Authentication Protocols

Both of the public-key authentication protocols we present assume that Alice and Bob's public keys have been predistributed to each other via some PKI (Section 1.2.1). We mean this to include the case where Alice includes her certificate in her first message to Bob, and the case where Bob searches for a certificate about Alice when he receives her first message.

This first protocol (Figure 1.8) relies on Alice and Bob's clocks being synchronized. Alice sends Bob a message with a timestamp and her identity in plaintext plus

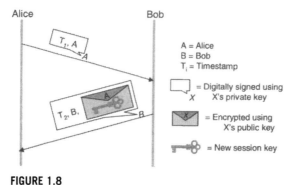

FIGURE 1.8

A public-key authentication protocol that depends on synchronization.

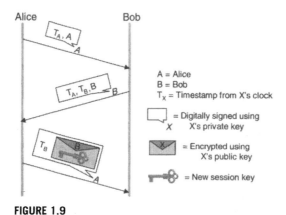

FIGURE 1.9

A public-key authentication protocol that does not depend on synchronization. Alice checks her own timestamp against her own clock, and likewise for Bob.

her digital signature. Bob uses the digital signature to authenticate the message, and the timestamp to verify its freshness. Bob sends back a message with a timestamp and his identity in plaintext, and a new session key encrypted (for confidentiality) using Alice's public key, all digitally signed. Alice can verify the authenticity and freshness of the message, so she knows she can trust the new session key. To deal with imperfect clock synchronization, the timestamps could be augmented with nonces.

The second protocol (Figure 1.9) is similar but does not rely on clock synchronization. In this protocol, Alice again sends Bob a digitally signed message with a timestamp and her identity. Because their clocks aren't synchronized, Bob cannot be sure that the message is fresh. Bob sends back a digitally signed message with Alice's original timestamp, his own new timestamp, and his identity. Alice can verify the freshness of Bob's reply by comparing her current time against the timestamp that originated with her. She then sends Bob a digitally signed message with his original

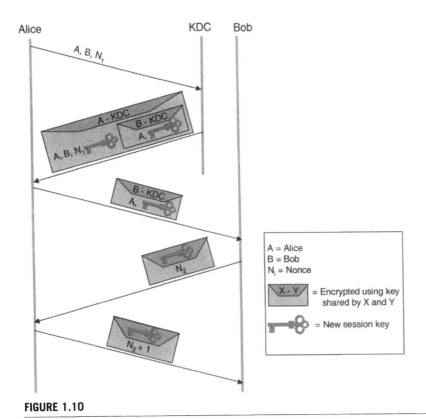

FIGURE 1.10

The Needham-Schroeder authentication protocol.

timestamp and a new session key encrypted using Bob's public key. Bob can verify the freshness of the message because the timestamp came from his clock, so he knows he can trust the new session key. The timestamps essentially serve as convenient nonces, and indeed this protocol could use nonces instead.

1.3.3 Symmetric-Key Authentication Protocols

As explained in Section 1.2.2, only in fairly small systems is it practical to predistribute symmetric keys to every pair of entities. We focus here on larger systems, where each entity would have its own *master key* shared only with a KDC. In this case, symmetric-key-based authentication protocols involve three parties: Alice, Bob, and a KDC. The end product of the authentication protocol is a session key shared between Alice and Bob that they will use to communicate directly, without involving the KDC.

The Needham-Schroeder authentication protocol is illustrated in Figure 1.10. Note that the KDC doesn't actually authenticate Alice's initial message and doesn't communicate with Bob at all. Instead the KDC uses its knowledge of Alice's and

Bob's master keys to construct a reply that would be useless to anyone other than Alice (because only Alice can decrypt it), and contains the necessary ingredients for Alice and Bob to perform the rest of the authentication protocol themselves.

The nonce in the first two messages is to assure Alice that the KDC's reply is fresh. The second and third messages include the new session key and Alice's identifier, encrypted together using Bob's master key. It is a sort of symmetric-key version of a public-key certificate; it is in effect a signed statement by the KDC (because the KDC is the only entity besides Bob who knows Bob's master key) that the enclosed session key is owned by Alice and Bob. Although the nonce in the last two messages is intended to assure Bob that the third message was fresh, there is a flaw in this reasoning.

Kerberos

Kerberos is an authentication system based on the Needham-Schroeder protocol and specialized for client-server environments. Originally developed at MIT, it is an IETF standard and available as both open source and commercial products. We will focus here on some of Kerberos's interesting innovations.

Kerberos clients are human users, and users are authenticated using passwords. Alice's master key, shared with the KDC, is derived from her password—if you know the password, you can compute the key. Kerberos assumes anyone can physically access any client machine; therefore, it is important to minimize the exposure of Alice's password or master key not just in the network, but also on any machine where she logs in. Kerberos takes advantage of Needham-Schroeder to accomplish this. In Needham-Schroeder, the only time Alice needs to use her password is when decrypting the reply from the KDC. Kerberos client-side software waits until the KDC's reply arrives, prompts Alice to enter her password, computes the master key and decrypts the KDC's reply, and erases all information about the password and master key to minimize its exposure. Also note that the only sign a user sees of Kerberos is when the user is prompted for a password.

In Needham-Schroeder, the KDC's reply to Alice plays two roles: It gives her the means to prove her identity (only Alice can decrypt the reply), and it gives her a sort of symmetric-key certificate or "ticket" to present to Bob—the session key and Alice's identifier, encrypted with Bob's master key. In Kerberos, those two functions—and the KDC itself, in effect—are split up (Figure 1.11). A trusted server called an authentication server (AS) plays the first KDC role of providing Alice with something she can use to prove her identity—not to Bob this time, but to a second trusted server called a ticket-granting server (TGS). The TGS plays the second KDC role, replying to Alice with a ticket she can present to Bob. The beauty of this scheme is that if Alice needs to communicate with several servers, not just Bob, then she can get tickets for each of them from the TGS without going back to the AS.

In the client-server application domain for which Kerberos is intended, it is reasonable to assume a degree of clock synchronization. This allows Kerberos to use timestamps and life spans instead of Needham-Shroeder's nonces, and thereby eliminate the Needham-Schroeder security weakness explored in Exercise 4.

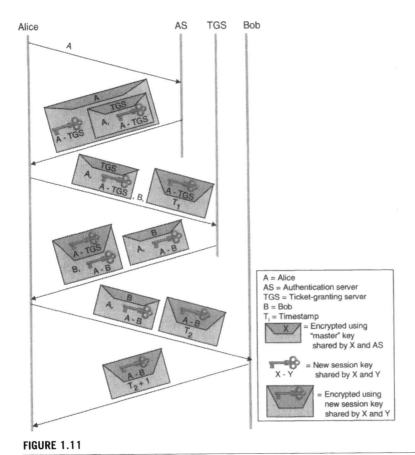

FIGURE 1.11

Kerberos authentication.

Kerberos supports a choice of cryptographic algorithms including the hashes SHA-1 and MD5 and the symmetric-key ciphers AES, 3DES, and DES.

1.3.4 Diffie-Hellman Key Agreement

The Diffie-Hellman key agreement protocol establishes a session key without using any predistributed keys. The messages exchanged between Alice and Bob can be read by anyone able to eavesdrop, and yet the eavesdropper won't know the session key that Alice and Bob end up with. On the other hand, Diffie-Hellman doesn't authenticate the participants. Since it is rarely useful to communicate securely without being sure whom you're communicating with, Diffie-Hellman is usually augmented in some way to provide authentication.

The protocol has two parameters, p and g, both of which are public and may be used by all the users in a particular system. Parameter p must be a prime number.

The integers mod p (short for modulo p) are 0 through $p - 1$, since $x \bmod p$ is the remainder after x is divided by p, and form what mathematicians call a *group* under multiplication. Parameter g (usually called a generator) must be a *primitive root* of p: for every number n from 1 through $p - 1$ there must be some value k such that $n = g^k \bmod p$. For example, if p were the prime number 5 (a real system would use a much larger number), then we might choose 2 to be the generator g since:

$$1 = 2^0 \bmod p$$
$$2 = 2^1 \bmod p$$
$$3 = 2^3 \bmod p$$
$$4 = 2^2 \bmod p$$

Suppose Alice and Bob want to agree on a shared symmetric key. Alice and Bob, and everyone else, already know the values of p and g. Alice generates a random private value a and Bob generates a random private value b. Both a and b are drawn from the set of integers $\{1, \ldots, p - 1\}$. Alice and Bob derive their corresponding public values—the values they will send to each other unencrypted—as follows. Alice's public value is

$$g^a \bmod p$$

and Bob's public value is

$$g^b \bmod p$$

They then exchange their public values. Finally, Alice computes

$$g^{ab} \bmod p = (g^b \bmod p)^a \bmod p$$

and Bob computes

$$g^{ba} \bmod p = (g^a \bmod p)^b \bmod p.$$

Alice and Bob now have $g^{ab} \bmod p$ (which is equal to $g^{ba} \bmod p$) as their shared symmetric key.

Any eavesdropper would know p, g, and the two public values $g^a \bmod p$ and $g^b \bmod p$. If only the eavesdropper could determine a or b, she could easily compute the resulting key. Determining a or b from that information is, however, computationally infeasible for suitably large p, a, and b; it is known as the discrete logarithm problem.

On the other hand, there is the problem of Diffie-Hellman's lack of authentication. One attack that can take advantage of this is the *man-in-the-middle attack*. Suppose Mallory is an adversary with the ability to intercept messages. Mallory already knows p and g since they are public, and she generates random private values c and d to use with Alice and Bob, respectively. When Alice and Bob send their public values to each other, Mallory intercepts them and sends her own public values,

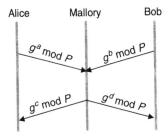

FIGURE 1.12

A man-in-the-middle attack.

as in Figure 1.12. The result is that Alice and Bob each end up unknowingly sharing a key with Mallory instead of each other.

A variant of Diffie-Hellman sometimes called *fixed Diffie-Hellman* supports authentication of one or both participants. It relies on certificates that are similar to public-key certificates but instead certify the Diffie-Hellman public parameters of an entity. For example, such a certificate would state that Alice's Diffie-Hellman parameters are p, g, and $g^a \bmod p$ (note that the value of a would still be known only to Alice). Such a certificate would assure Bob that the other participant in Diffie-Hellman is Alice—or else the other participant won't be able to compute the secret key, because she won't know a. If both participants have certificates for their Diffie-Hellman parameters, they can authenticate each other. If just one has a certificate, then just that one can be authenticated. This is useful in some situations; for example, when one participant is a web server and the other is an arbitrary client—the client can authenticate the web server and establish a session key for confidentiality before sending a credit card number to the web server.

1.4 SECURE SYSTEMS

At this point, we have seen many of the components that are required to build a secure system. These components include cryptographic algorithms, key predistribution mechanisms, and authentication protocols. In this section we examine some complete systems that use these components.

These systems can be roughly categorized by the protocol layer at which they operate. Systems that operate at the application layer include Pretty Good Privacy (PGP), which provides electronic mail security, and Secure Shell (SSH), a secure remote login facility. At the transport layer, there is the IETF's Transport Layer Security (TLS) standard and the older protocol from which it derives, SSL (Secure Socket Layer). The IPsec (IP security) protocols, as their name implies, operate at the IP (network) layer. 802.11i provides security at the link layer of wireless networks. This section describes the salient features of each of these approaches.

These security protocols have the ability to vary which cryptographic algorithms they use. The idea of making a security system algorithm-independent is a very good one, because you never know when your favorite cryptographic algorithm might be proved to be insufficiently strong for your purposes. It would be nice if you could quickly change to a new algorithm without having to change the protocol specification or implementation.

1.4.1 Pretty Good Privacy (PGP)

Pretty Good Privacy (PGP) is a widely used approach to providing security for electronic mail. It provides authentication, confidentiality, data integrity, and nonrepudiation. Originally devised by Phil Zimmerman, it has evolved into an IETF standard known as OpenPGP.

PGP's confidentiality and receiver authentication depend on the receiver having a known public key. PGP's sender authentication and nonrepudiation depend on the sender having a known public key. These public keys are predistributed using certificates and a web-of-trust PKI, as described in Section 1.2.1. PGP supports RSA and DSS for public-key certificates. These certificates may additionally specify which cryptographic algorithms are supported or preferred by the key's owner.

Note that "PGP" refers to both a protocol and an application that uses the protocol. The protocol involves only a single message transmitted in one direction, with the interesting feature being the format of that message.

When Alice has a message to email to Bob, her PGP application goes through the steps illustrated in Figure 1.13. First, the message is digitally signed by Alice; MD5 and SHA-1 are among the hashes that may be used in the digital signature. Then her PGP application generates a new session key for just this one message; AES and 3DES are among the supported symmetric-key ciphers. The digitally signed message is encrypted using the session key. Then the session key itself, encrypted using Bob's public key, is appended to the message. Alice's PGP application reminds her of the level of trust she had previously assigned to Bob's public key, based on the number of certificates she has for Bob and the trustworthiness of the individuals who signed the certificates. Finally—not for security, but to conform to email's SMTP protocol—a base64 encoding is applied to the message to convert it to an ASCII-compatible representation. Upon receiving the PGP message in an email, Bob's PGP application reverses this process step-by-step to obtain the original plaintext message and confirm Alice's digital signature—and reminds Bob of the level of trust he has in Alice's public key.

Email has unusual characteristics that allow PGP to embed an adequate authentication protocol in this one-message data transmission protocol, avoiding the need for any prior message exchange. Alice's digital signature suffices to authenticate her. Although there is no proof that the message is timely, legitimate email isn't timely, and the session key and the data it encrypts arrive simultaneously anyway. Although there is no proof that the message is original, Bob is an email user and probably a fault-tolerant human who can recover from duplicate emails. Alice can be sure that only Bob could read the message because the session key was encrypted with his

Hi...= The plaintext message

1) Digitally sign
using Alice's private key

2) Encrypt using a newly
generated one-time session key

3) Encrypt the session key using
Bob's public key, and append
that

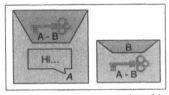

4) Use base64 encoding to
obtain an ASCII-compatible
representation

base64

FIGURE 1.13

PGP's steps to prepare a message for emailing from Alice to Bob.

public key. Although this protocol doesn't prove to Alice that Bob is actually there
and received the email, email doesn't guarantee delivery anyway.

1.4.2 Secure Shell (SSH)

The Secure Shell (SSH) protocol is used to provide a remote login service, and is
intended to replace the less-secure Telnet and rlogin programs used in the early
days of the Internet. (SSH can also be used to remotely execute commands and
transfer files, like the Unix **rsh** and **rcp** commands, respectively, but we will focus
on how SSH supports remote login.) SSH is most often used to provide strong
client/server authentication/message integrity—where the SSH client runs on the
user's desktop machine and the SSH server runs on some remote machine that
the user wants to log into—but it also supports confidentiality. Telnet and rlogin
provide none of these capabilities. Note that "SSH" is used to refer to both the SSH
protocol and applications that use it.

To better appreciate the importance of SSH on today's Internet, consider that a few short years ago telecommuters used dialup modems to connect their home computers to work (or school). This meant that when they logged in, their passwords were sent in the clear over a phone line and the LAN at work. Sending your password in the clear over a LAN isn't a great idea, but at least it's not as risky as sending it across the Internet. Today, however, telecommuters often subscribe to ISPs that offer high-speed cable modem or DSL service, and they go through these ISPs to reach work. This means that when they log in, both their passwords and all the data they send or receive potentially pass through any number of untrusted networks. SSH provides a way to encrypt the data sent over these connections, and to improve the strength of the authentication mechanism they use to log in.

The latest version of SSH, version 2, consists of three protocols:

- SSH-TRANS, a transport layer protocol;
- SSH-AUTH, an authentication protocol;
- SSH-CONN, a connection protocol.

We focus on the first two, which are involved in remote login. We briefly discuss the purpose of SSH-CONN at the end of the section.

SSH-TRANS provides an encrypted channel between the client and server machines. It runs on top of a TCP connection. Any time a user uses an SSH application to log into a remote machine, the first step is to set up an SSH-TRANS channel between those two machines. The two machines establish this secure channel by first having the client authenticate the server using RSA. Once authenticated, the client and server establish a session key that they will use to encrypt any data sent over the channel. This high-level description skims over several details, including the fact that the SSH-TRANS protocol includes a negotiation of the encryption algorithm the two sides are going to use. For example, AES is commonly selected. Also, SSH-TRANS includes a message integrity check of all data exchanged over the channel.

The one issue we can't skim over is how the client came to possess the server's public key that it needs to authenticate the server. Strange as it may sound, the server tells the client its public key at connection time. The first time a client connects to a particular server, the SSH application warns the user that it has never talked to this machine before, and asks if the user wants to continue. Although it is a risky thing to do, because SSH is effectively not able to authenticate the server, users often say "yes" to this question. The SSH application then remembers the server's public key, and the next time the user connects to that same machine, it compares this saved key with the one the server responds with. If they are the same, SSH authenticates the server. If they are different, however, the SSH application again warns the user that something is amiss, and the user is then given an opportunity to abort the connection. Alternatively, the prudent user can learn the server's public key through some out-of-band mechanism, save it on the client machine, and thus never take the "first time" risk.

Once the SSH-TRANS channel exists, the next step is for the user to actually log onto the machine, or more specifically, authenticate himself to the server.

SSH allows three different mechanisms for doing this. First, since the two machines are communicating over a secure channel, it is OK for the user to simply send his password to the server. This is not a safe thing to do when using Telnet since the password would be sent in the clear, but in the case of SSH, the password is encrypted in the SSH-TRANS channel. The second mechanism uses public-key encryption. This requires that the user has already placed his public key on the server. The third mechanism, called host-based authentication, basically says that any user claiming to be so-and-so from a certain set of trusted hosts is automatically believed to be that same user on the server. Host-based authentication requires that the client *host* authenticate itself to the server when they first connect; standard SSH-TRANS only authenticates the server by default.

The main thing you should take away from this discussion is that SSH is a fairly straightforward application of the protocols and algorithms we have seen throughout this chapter. However, what sometimes makes SSH a challenge to understand is all the keys a user has to create and manage, where the exact interface is operating system dependent. For example, the OpenSSH package that runs on most Unix machines supports a **ssh-keygen** command that can be used to create public/private key pairs. These keys are then stored in various files in directory **.ssh** in the user's home directory. For example, file ~/**.ssh/known_hosts** records the keys for all the hosts the user has logged into, file ~/**.ssh/authorized_keys** contains the public keys needed to authenticate the user when he logs into this machine (i.e., they are used on the server side), and file ~/**.ssh/identity** contains the private keys needed to authenticate the user on remote machines (i.e., they are used on the client side).

Finally, SSH has proven so useful as a system for securing remote login, it has been extended to also support other insecure TCP-based applications, such as X Windows and IMAP mail readers. The idea is to run these applications over a secure SSH tunnel. This capability is called *port forwarding* and it uses the SSH-CONN protocol. The idea is illustrated in Figure 1.14, where we see a client on

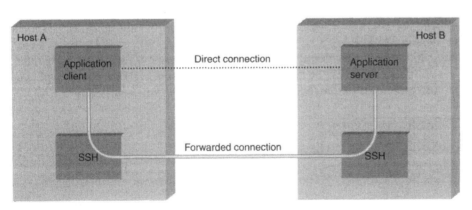

FIGURE 1.14

Using SSH port forwarding to secure other TCP-based applications.

host A indirectly communicating with a server on host B by forwarding its traffic through an SSH connection. The mechanism is called port forwarding because when messages arrive at the well-known SSH port on the server, SSH first decrypts the contents, and then forwards the data to the actual port at which the server is listening.

1.4.3 Transport Layer Security (TLS, SSL, HTTPS)

To understand the design goals and requirements for the Transport Layer Security (TLS) standard and the Secure Socket Layer (SSL) on which TLS is based, it is helpful to consider one of the main problems that they are intended to solve. As the World Wide Web became popular and commercial enterprises began to take an interest in it, it became clear that some level of security would be necessary for transactions on the Web. The canonical example of this is making purchases by credit card. There are several issues of concern when sending your credit card information to a computer on the Web. First, you might worry that the information would be intercepted in transit and subsequently used to make unauthorized purchases. You might also worry about the details of a transaction being modified, for example, to change the purchase amount. And you would certainly like to know that the computer to which you are sending your credit card information is in fact one belonging to the vendor in question and not some other party. Thus, we immediately see a need for confidentiality, integrity, and authentication in Web transactions. The first widely used solution to this problem was SSL, originally developed by Netscape and subsequently the basis for the IETF's TLS standard.

The designers of SSL and TLS recognized that these problems were not specific to Web transactions (i.e., those using HTTP) and instead built a general-purpose protocol that sits between an application protocol such as HTTP and a transport protocol such as TCP. The reason for calling this "transport layer security" is that, from the application's perspective, this protocol layer looks just like a normal transport protocol except for the fact that it is secure. That is, the sender can open connections and deliver bytes for transmission, and the secure transport layer will get them to the receiver with the necessary confidentiality, integrity, and authentication. By running the secure transport layer on top of TCP, all of the normal features of TCP (reliability, flow control, congestion control, etc.) are also provided to the application. This arrangement of protocol layers is depicted in Figure 1.15.

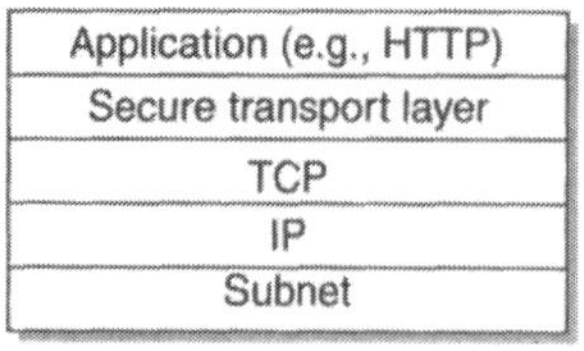

| Application (e.g., HTTP) |
| Secure transport layer |
| TCP |
| IP |
| Subnet |

FIGURE 1.15

Secure transport layer inserted between application and TCP layers.

When HTTP is used in this way, it is known as HTTPS (Secure HTTP). In fact, HTTP itself is unchanged. It simply delivers data to and accepts data from the SSL/TLS layer rather than TCP. For convenience, a default TCP port has been assigned to HTTPS (443). That is, if you try to connect to a server on TCP port 443, you will likely find yourself talking to the SSL/TLS protocol, which will pass your data through to HTTP provided all goes well with authentication and decryption. Although stand-alone implementations of SSL/TLS are available, it is more common for an implementation to be bundled with applications that need it, primarily web browsers.

In the remainder of our discussion of transport layer security, we focus on TLS. Although SSL and TLS are unfortunately not interoperable, they differ in only minor ways, so nearly all of this description of TLS applies to SSL.

Handshake Protocol

A pair of TLS participants negotiate at runtime which cryptography to use. The participants negotiate a choice of:

- Data integrity hash, MD5 or SHA, used to implement HMACs.

- Symmetric-key cipher for confidentiality. Among the possibilities are DES, 3DES, and AES.

- Session-key establishment approach. Among the possibilities are Diffie-Hellman, fixed Diffie-Hellman, and public-key authentication protocols using RSA or DSS.

Interestingly, the participants may also negotiate the use of a compression algorithm, not because this offers any security benefits, but because it's easy to do when you're negotiating all this other stuff and you've already decided to do some expensive per-byte operations on the data.

In TLS, the confidentiality cipher uses two keys, one for each direction, and similarly two initialization vectors. The HMACs are likewise keyed with different keys for the two participants. Thus, regardless of the choice of cipher and hash, a TLS session requires six keys. TLS derives all of them from a single shared *master secret*. The master secret is a 384-bit (48-byte) value that is in turn derived in part from the session key that results from TLS's session-key establishment protocol.

The part of TLS that negotiates the choices and establishes the shared master secret is called the *handshake protocol*. (Actual data transfer is performed by TLS's *record protocol*.) The handshake protocol is at heart a session-key establishment protocol, with a master secret instead of a session key. TLS supports a choice of approach to session-key establishment, ranging from public-key certificates to Diffie-Hellman. These call for correspondingly different protocols. Furthermore, the handshake protocol supports a choice between mutual authentication of both participants, authentication of just one participant (this is the most common case; e.g., authenticate a website but not a user), or no authentication at all (anonymous Diffie-Hellman). Thus, the handshake protocol knits together several session-key establishment protocols into a single protocol.

Rather than trying to explain in detail how the handshake protocol is able to accommodate all these variations, we describe it at a high level (Figure 1.16). The client initially sends a list of the combinations of cryptographic algorithms that it supports, in decreasing order of preference. The server responds giving the single combination of cryptographic algorithms it selected from those listed by the client. These messages also contain a *client-nonce* and a *server-nonce*, respectively, that will be incorporated in generating the master secret later.

At this point the negotiation phase is complete. The server now sends additional messages based on the negotiated session-key establishment protocol (one of the possibilities is anonymous Diffie-Hellman, so it wouldn't be accurate to call it an authentication protocol). That could involve sending a public-key certificate

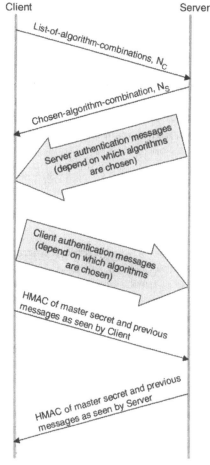

FIGURE 1.16

Handshake protocol to establish TLS session.

or a set of Diffie-Hellman parameters. If the server requires authentication of the client, it sends a separate message indicating that. The client then responds with its part of the negotiated key exchange protocol.

Now the client and server each have the information necessary to generate the master secret. The session key that they exchanged is not in fact a key, but instead what TLS calls a *premaster secret*. The master secret is computed (using a published formula incorporating both MD5 and SHA) from this premaster secret, the client-nonce, and the server-nonce.

Using the keys derived from the master secret, the client then sends a message that includes a hash of all the preceding handshake messages, to which the server responds with a similar message. This enables them to detect any discrepancies between the handshake messages they sent and received, such as would result, for example, if a man-in-the-middle modified the initial unencrypted client message to weaken its choices of cryptographic algorithms.

Record Protocol

Within a session established by the handshake protocol, TLS's record protocol adds confidentiality and integrity to the underlying transport service. Messages handed down from the application layer are:

1. Fragmented or coalesced into blocks of a convenient size for the following steps;
2. Optionally compressed;
3. Integrity-protected using an HMAC;
4. Encrypted using a symmetric-key cipher;
5. Passed to the transport layer (normally TCP) for transmission.

The record protocol uses an HMAC as an authenticator. The HMAC uses MD5 or SHA-1, whichever was negotiated by the participants. The client and server have different keys to use when computing HMACs, making them even harder to break. Furthermore, each record protocol message is assigned a sequence number, which is included when the HMAC is computed—even though the sequence number is never explicit in the message. This implicit sequence number prevents replays or reorderings of messages. This is needed because, although TCP guarantees sequential no-duplicate messages under normal assumptions, those assumptions do not include an adversary that can intercept TCP messages and send bogus ones. On the other hand, it is TCP's delivery guarantees that make it possible for TLS to rely on a legitimate TLS message having the next implicit sequence number in order.

Another interesting feature of the TLS protocol, which is quite a useful feature for Web transactions, is the ability to "resume" a session. To understand the motivation for this, it is helpful to understand how HTTP makes use of TCP connections. Each HTTP operation, such as getting a page of text or an image from a server, requires a new TCP connection to be opened. Retrieving a single page with a number of embedded graphical objects might take many TCP connections. Opening a TCP connection requires a three-way handshake before data transmission can start.

Once the TCP connection is ready to accept data, the client would then need to start the TLS handshake protocol, taking at least another two RTTs (and consuming some amount of processing resources and network bandwidth) before actual application data could be sent. The resumption capability of TLS alleviates this problem.

Session resumption is an optimization of the handshake that can be used in those cases where the client and the server have already established some shared state in the past. The client simply includes the session ID from a previously established session in its initial handshake message. If the server finds that it still has state for that session, and the resumption option was negotiated when that session was originally created, then the server can reply to the client with an indication of success, and data transmission can begin using the algorithms and parameters previously negotiated. If the session ID does not match any session state cached at the server, or if resumption was not allowed for the session, then the server will fall back to the normal handshake process.

1.4.4 **IP Security (IPsec)**

Easily the most ambitious of all the efforts to integrate security into the Internet happens at the IP layer. Support for IPsec, as the architecture is called, is optional in IPv4 but mandatory in IPv6.

IPsec is really a framework (as opposed to a single protocol or system) for providing all the security services discussed throughout this chapter. IPsec provides three degrees of freedom. First, it is highly modular, allowing users (or more likely, system administrators) to select from a variety of cryptographic algorithms and specialized security protocols. Second, IPsec allows users to select from a large menu of security properties, including access control, integrity, authentication, originality, and confidentiality. Third, IPsec can be used to protect narrow streams (e.g., packets belonging to a particular TCP connection being sent between a pair of hosts) or wide streams (e.g., all packets flowing between a pair of gateways).

When viewed from a high level, IPsec consists of two parts. The first part is a pair of protocols that implement the available security services. They are the Authentication Header (AH), which provides access control, connectionless message integrity, authentication, and antireplay protection, and the Encapsulating Security Payload (ESP), which supports these same services, plus confidentiality. AH is rarely used so we do not discuss it further. The second part is support for key management, which fits under an umbrella protocol known as Internet Security Association and Key Management Protocol (ISAKMP).

The abstraction that binds these two pieces together is the *security association (SA)*. An SA is a simplex (one-way) connection with one or more of the available security properties. Securing a bidirectional communication between a pair of hosts—corresponding to a TCP connection, for example—requires two SAs, one in each direction. Although IP is a connectionless protocol, security depends on connection state information such as keys and sequence numbers. When created, an SA is assigned an ID number called a *security parameters index (SPI)* by the receiving machine. A combination of this SPI and the destination IP addresses uniquely identifies an SA. ESP's header includes the SPI so the receiving host can determine which SA an incoming packet belongs to, and hence, what algorithms and keys to apply to the packet.

SAs are established, negotiated, modified, and deleted using ISAKMP. It defines packet formats for exchanging key generation and authentication data. These formats aren't terribly interesting because they provide a framework only—the exact form of the keys and authentication data depend on the key generation technique, the cipher, and the authentication mechanism that is used. Moreover, ISAKMP does not specify a particular key exchange protocol, although it does suggest the Internet Key Exchange (IKE) as one possibility, and IKE is what is used in practice.

ESP is the protocol used to securely transport data over an established SA. In IPv4, the ESP header follows the IP header; in IPv6, it is an extension header. Its format uses both a header and a trailer, as shown in Figure 1.17. The **SPI** field lets the receiving host identify the security association to which the packet belongs. The **SeqNum** field protects against replay attacks. The packet's **PayloadData** contains the data described by the **NextHdr** field. If confidentiality is selected, then the data is encrypted using whatever cipher was associated with the SA. The **PadLength** field records how much padding was added to the data; padding is sometimes necessary because, for example, the cipher requires the plaintext to be a multiple of a certain number of bytes, or to ensure that the resulting ciphertext terminates on a 4-byte boundary. Finally, the **AuthenticationData** carries the authenticator.

IPsec supports a *tunnel mode* as well as the more straightforward *transport mode*. Each SA operates in one or the other mode. In a transport mode SA, ESP's payload data is simply a message for a higher layer such as UDP or TCP. In this mode, IPsec acts as an intermediate protocol layer, much like SSL/TLS does between TCP and a higher layer. When an ESP message is received, its payload is passed to the higher-level protocol.

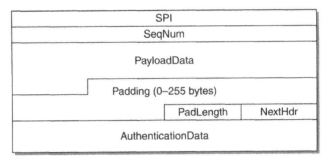

FIGURE 1.17

IPsec's ESP format.

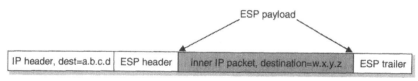

FIGURE 1.18

An IP packet with a nested IP packet encapsulated using ESP in tunnel mode. Note that the inner and outer packets have different addresses.

In a tunnel mode SA, however, ESP's payload data is itself an IP packet, as in Figure 1.18. The source and destination of this inner IP packet may be different from those of the outer IP packet. When an ESP message is received, its payload is forwarded on as a normal IP packet. The most common way to use the ESP is to build an IPsec tunnel between two routers, typically firewalls. For example, a corporation wanting to link two sites using the Internet could open a pair of tunnel-mode SAs between a router at one site and a router at the other site. An IP packet outgoing from one site would, at the outgoing router, become the payload of an ESP message sent to the other site's router. The receiving router would unwrap the payload IP packet and forward it on to its true destination.

These tunnels may also be configured to use ESP with confidentiality and authentication, thus preventing unauthorized access to the data that traverses this virtual link and ensuring that no spurious data is received at the far end of the tunnel. Furthermore, tunnels can provide traffic confidentiality, since multiplexing multiple flows through a single tunnel obscures information about how much traffic is flowing between particular endpoints. A network of such tunnels can be used to implement an entire virtual private network (VPN). Hosts communicating over a VPN need not even be aware that it exists.

1.4.5 Wireless Security (802.11i)

Wireless links are particularly exposed to security threats due to the lack of any physical security. The IEEE 802.11i standard provides authentication, message integrity, and confidentiality to 802.11 (Wi-Fi) at the link layer. *Wi-Fi Protected Access 2 (WPA2)* is often used as a synonym for 802.11i, although it is technically a trademark of The Wi-Fi Alliance that certifies product compliance with 802.11i.

For backward compatibility, 802.11i includes definitions of first-generation security algorithms—Wired Equivalent Privacy (WEP) and 802.11 entity authentication—that are now known to have major security flaws. We will focus here on 802.11i's newer, stronger algorithms.

802.11i authentication supports two modes. In either mode, the end result of successful authentication is a shared pairwise master key. *Personal mode*, also known as *pre-shared key (PSK) mode*, provides weaker security but is

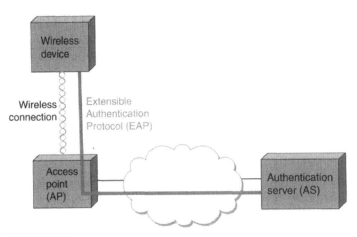

FIGURE 1.19

Use of an authentication server in 802.11i.

more convenient and economical for situations like a home 802.11 network. The wireless device and the access point (AP) are preconfigured with a shared *passphrase*—essentially a very long password—from which the pairwise master key is cryptographically derived.

802.11i's stronger authentication mode is based on the IEEE 802.1X framework for controlling access to a LAN, which uses an authentication server (AS), as in Figure 1.19. The AS and AP must be connected by a secure channel and could even share the same host. The AP forwards authentication messages between the wireless device and the AS. The protocol used for authentication is the Extensible Authentication Protocol (EAP). EAP is designed to support multiple authentication methods—smart cards, Kerberos, one-time passwords, public-key authentication, and so on—as well as both one-sided and mutual authentication. So EAP is better thought of as an authentication framework than a protocol. Specific EAP-compliant protocols, of which there are many, are called *EAP methods*. For example, EAP-TLS is an EAP method based on TLS authentication. 802.11i does not place any restrictions on what the EAP method can use as a basis for authentication. It does, however, require an EAP method that performs *mutual* authentication because not only do we want to prevent an adversary accessing the network via our AP, we also want to prevent an adversary fooling our wireless devices with a bogus, malicious AP. The end result of a successful authentication is a pairwise master key shared between the wireless device and the AS, which the AS then conveys to the AP.

With a pairwise master key in hand, the wireless device and the AP execute a session-key establishment protocol called the 4-way handshake to establish a pairwise transient key. This pairwise transient key is really a collection of keys that includes a session key called a temporal key. This session key is used by the protocol, called *CCMP*, that provides 802.11i's data confidentiality and integrity.

CCMP stands for CTR (counter mode) with CBC-MAC (Cipher-Block Chaining with Message Authentication Code) protocol. CCMP uses AES in counter mode to encrypt for confidentiality. Recall that in counter-mode encryption, successive values of a counter are incorporated into the encryption of successive blocks of plaintext (Section 1.1.1).

CCMP uses a message authentication code (MAC) as an authenticator. The MAC algorithm is based on CBC (Section 1.1.1), even though CCMP doesn't use CBC in the confidentiality encryption. In effect, CBC is performed without transmitting any of the CBC-encrypted blocks, solely so that the last CBC-encrypted block can be used as a MAC (only its first 8 bytes are actually used). The role of initialization vector is played by a specially constructed first block that includes a 48-bit packet number—a sequence number. (The packet number is also incorporated in the confidentiality encryption, and serves to expose replay attacks.) The MAC is subsequently encrypted along with the plaintext in order to prevent birthday attacks, which depend on finding different messages with the same authenticator (Section 1.1.4).

1.5 FIREWALLS

A firewall is a system that is the sole point of connectivity between the site it protects and the rest of the network, as illustrated in Figure 1.20. It is usually implemented as part of a router, although a personal firewall may be implemented on an end-user machine. Firewall-based security depends on the firewall being the only connectivity to the site from outside; there should be no way to bypass the firewall via other gateways, wireless connections, or dial-up connections. The "wall" metaphor is misleading in the context of networks since it is the absence of connectivity—not the presence of a barrier—that prevents communication. In terms of walls, a firewall is like the only door (connection) through a wall (the absence

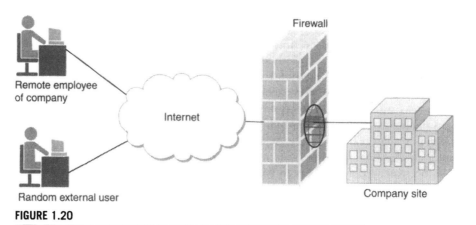

FIGURE 1.20

A firewall filters packets flowing between a site and the rest of the Internet.

of any other connection). A firewall provides access control by restricting which messages it will relay between the site and the rest of the network; it forwards messages that are allowed, and filters out messages that are disallowed. For example, it might filter out all incoming messages addressed to a particular IP address or to a particular TCP port number.

In effect, a firewall divides a network into a more-trusted zone internal to the firewall, and a less-trusted zone external to the firewall. This is useful if you do not want external users to access a particular host or service within your site. Much of the complexity comes from the fact that you want to allow different kinds of access to different external users, ranging from the general public, to business partners, to remotely located members of your organization. A firewall may also impose restrictions on outgoing traffic, to prevent certain attacks and to limit losses if an adversary succeeds in getting access inside the firewall.

Firewalls may be used to create multiple *zones of trust*, such as a hierarchy of increasingly trusted zones. A common arrangement involves three zones of trust: the internal network, the *demilitarized zone (DMZ)*, and the rest of the Internet. The DMZ is used to hold services such as DNS and email servers that need to be accessible to the outside. Both the internal network and the outside world can access the DMZ, but hosts in the DMZ cannot access the internal network. Therefore, if an adversary succeeds in compromising a host in the exposed DMZ, it still cannot access the internal network. The DMZ can be periodically restored to a "clean" state.

Firewalls filter based on IP, TCP, and UDP information, among other things. They are configured with a table of addresses that characterizes the packets they will, and will not, forward. By addresses, we mean more than just the destination's IP address, although that is one possibility. Generally, each entry in the table is a 4-tuple: It gives the IP address and TCP (or UDP) port number for both the source and destination.

For example, a firewall might be configured to filter out (not forward) all packets that match the following description:

$$< 192.12.13.14, 1234, 128.7.6.5, 80 >$$

This pattern says to discard all packets from port 1234 on host 192.12.13.14 addressed to port 80 on host 128.7.6.5. (Port 80 is the well-known TCP port for HTTP.) Of course it's often not practical to name every source host whose packets you want to filter, so the patterns can include wildcards. For example,

$$< *, *, 128.7.6.5, 80 >$$

says to filter out all packets addressed to port 80 on 128.7.6.5, regardless of what source host or port sent the packet. Notice that address patterns like these require the firewall to make forwarding/filtering decisions based on level 4 port numbers, in addition to level 3 host addresses. It is for this reason that network layer firewalls are sometimes called *level 4 switches*.

In the preceding discussion, the firewall forwards everything except where specifically instructed to filter out certain kinds of packets. A firewall could also filter out everything unless explicitly instructed to forward it, or use a mix of the two strategies. For example, instead of blocking access to port 80 on host 128.7.6.5, the firewall might be instructed to only allow access to port 25 (the SMTP mail port) on a particular mail server, for example,

$$< *, *, 128.19.20.21, 25 >$$

but to block all other traffic. Experience has shown that firewalls are very frequently configured incorrectly, allowing unsafe access. Part of the problem is that filtering rules can overlap in complex ways, making it hard for a system administrator to correctly express the filtering she intends. A design principle that maximizes security is to configure a firewall to discard all packets other than those that are explicitly allowed.

Many client-server applications dynamically assign a port to the client. If a client inside a firewall initiates access to an external server, the server's response would be addressed to the dynamically assigned port. This poses a problem: How can a firewall be configured to allow an arbitrary server's response packet but disallow a similar packet for which there was no client request? This is not possible with a *stateless firewall*, which evaluates each packet in isolation. It requires a *stateful firewall*, which keeps track of the state of each connection. An incoming packet addressed to a dynamically assigned port would then be allowed only if it is a valid response in the current state of a connection on that port.

Modern firewalls also understand and filter based on many specific application-level protocols such as HTTP, Telnet, or FTP. They use information specific to that protocol, such as URLs in the case of HTTP, to decide whether to discard a message.

1.5.1 Strengths and Weaknesses of Firewalls

At best, a firewall protects a network from undesired access from the rest of the Internet; it cannot provide security to legitimate communication between the inside and the outside of the firewall. In contrast, the cryptography-based security mechanisms described in this chapter are capable of providing secure communication between any participants anywhere. This being the case, why are firewalls so common? One reason is that firewalls can be deployed unilaterally, using mature commercial products, while cryptography-based security requires support at both endpoints of the communication. A more fundamental reason for the dominance of firewalls is that they encapsulate security in a centralized place, in effect factoring security out of the rest of the network. A system administrator can manage the firewall to provide security, freeing the users and applications inside the firewall from security concerns—at least some kinds of security concerns.

Unfortunately, firewalls have serious limitations. Since a firewall does not restrict communication between hosts that are inside the firewall, the adversary who does manage to run code internal to a site can access all local hosts. How might an adversary get inside the firewall? The adversary could be a disgruntled employee with legitimate access. Or the adversary's software could be hidden in some software installed from a CD or downloaded from the Web. Or an adversary could bypass the firewall by using wireless communication or telephone dial-up connections.

Another problem is that any parties granted access through your firewall, such as business partners or externally located employees, become a security vulnerability. If their security is not as good as yours, then an adversary could penetrate your security by penetrating their security.

Another problem for firewalls is that a service that appears safe to expose may have a bug that makes it unsafe. A classic example is PHF, a phone booklike service that was available on many websites for looking up names and addresses. A buffer-overflow bug in PHF made it possible for anyone to execute an arbitrary command on the web server by using her browser to enter the command in an input field of the PHF form. Such bugs are discovered regularly, so a system administrator has to constantly monitor announcements of them. Administrators frequently fail to do so, since firewall security breaches routinely exploit security flaws that have been known for some time and have straightforward solutions.

In addition to the (unintended) bugs that may be left accessible by a firewall, there are also what could be thought of as intended, deliberate bugs. *Malware* (malicious software) is software that is designed to act on a computer in ways concealed from and unwanted by the computer's user. Viruses, worms, and spyware are common types of malware. ("Virus" is sometimes used synonymously with malware, but we will use it in the narrower sense in which it refers to only a particular kind of malware.) Like buggy software, malware code need not be natively executable object code; it could as well be interpreted code such as a script or an executable macro such as those used by Microsoft Word.

Viruses and *worms* are characterized by the ability to make and spread copies of themselves; the difference between them is that a worm is a complete program, while a virus is a bit of code that is inserted (and inserts copies of itself) into another piece of software, so that it is executed as part of the execution of that piece of software. Viruses and worms typically cause problems such as consuming network bandwidth as mere side effects of attempting to spread copies of themselves. Even worse, they can also deliberately damage a system or undermine its security in various ways. They could, for example, install a *backdoor*, which is software that allows remote access to the system without the normal authentication. This could lead to a firewall exposing a service that should be providing its own authentication procedures but has been undermined by a backdoor.

Spyware is software that, without authorization, collects and transmits private information about a computer system or its users. Usually spyware is secretly embedded in an otherwise useful program, and is spread by users deliberately installing copies. The problem for firewalls is that the transmission of the private information looks like legitimate communication.

A natural question to ask is whether firewalls (or cryptographic security) could keep malware out of a system in the first place. Most malware is indeed transmitted via networks, although it may also be transmitted via portable storage devices such as CDs and memory sticks. One of the two approaches used by antimalware applications is to observe programs for suspicious behavior as they execute—clearly not feasible for a firewall that is not on the end-user machine. The other approach is searching for segments of code from known malware, an approach already limited by the ability of clever malware to tweak its representation in various ways. The main problem with implementing this approach in a firewall is the impact on network performance. Cryptographic security cannot eliminate the problem either, although it does provide a means to authenticate the originator of a piece of software and detect any tampering, such as when a virus inserts a copy of itself.

1.6 CONCLUSION

Networks such as the Internet are shared by parties with conflicting interests. The job of network security is to keep them from spying on or interfering with each other's use of the network. Confidentiality is achieved by encrypting messages. Data integrity can be assured using cryptographic hashing. The two techniques can be combined to guarantee authenticity of messages.

Symmetric-key ciphers such as AES and 3DES use the same secret key for both encryption and decryption, so sender and receiver must share the same key. Public-key ciphers such as RSA use a public key for encryption, and a secret, private key for decryption, so any party can use the public key to encrypt a message so that it is readable only by the holder of the private key. The fastest technique known for breaking established ciphers such as AES and RSA is brute-force search of the space of possible keys, which is made computationally infeasible by the use of large keys. Most encryption for confidentiality uses symmetric-key ciphers due to their vastly superior speed, while public-key ciphers are usually reserved for authentication and session-key establishment.

An authenticator is a value attached to a message to verify the authenticity and data integrity of the message. One way to generate an authenticator is to encrypt a message digest that is output by a cryptographic hash function such as MD5 or SHA-1. If the message digest is encrypted using the private key of a public-key cipher, the resulting authenticator is considered a digital signature, since the public key can be used to verify that only the holder of the private key could have generated it. Another kind of authenticator is a message authentication code, which is output by a hashlike function that takes a shared secret value as a parameter. A hashed MAC is a MAC computed by applying a cryptographic hash to the concatenation of the plaintext message and the secret value.

A session key is used to secure a relatively short episode of communication. The dynamic establishment of a session key depends on longer-lived predistributed keys.

The ownership of a predistributed public key by a certain party can be attested to by a public-key certificate that is digitally signed by a trusted party. A public-key infrastructure is a complete scheme for certifying such bindings, and depends on a chain or web of trust. Predistribution of keys for symmetric-key ciphers is different because public certificates can't be used and because symmetric-key ciphers need a unique key for each pair of participants. A key distribution center is a trusted entity that shares a predistributed secret key with each other participant, so that they can use session keys, not predistributed keys, between themselves.

Authentication and session-key establishment require a protocol to assure the timeliness and originality of messages. Timestamps or nonces are used to guarantee the freshness of the messages. We saw two authentication protocols that use public-key ciphers, one that required synchronized clocks and one that did not. Needham-Schroeder is a protocol for authenticating two participants who each share a master symmetric-key cipher key with a key distribution center. Kerberos is an authentication system based on the Needham-Schroeder protocol and specialized for client-server environments. The Diffie-Hellman key agreement protocol establishes a session key without predistributed keys and authentication.

We discussed several systems that provide security based on these cryptographic algorithms and protocols. At the application level, PGP can be used to protect email messages and SSH can be used to securely connect to a remote machine. At the transport level, TLS can be used to protect commercial transactions on the World Wide Web. At the network level, the IPsec architecture can be used to secure communication among any set of hosts or gateways on the Internet.

A firewall filters the messages that pass between the site it protects and the rest of the network. Firewalls filter based on IP, TCP, and UDP addresses, as well as fields of some application protocols. A stateful firewall keeps track of the state of each connection so that it can allow valid responses to be delivered to dynamically assigned ports. Although firewall security has important limitations, it has the advantage of shifting some responsibility for security from users and applications to system administrators.

Unlike attacks on confidentiality, where an adversary is trying to gain access to information it is not allowed to see, a *denial-of-service (DoS)* attack involves an adversary trying to keep you from accessing information or resources you have every right to access.

One well-known denial-of-service attack is called a SYN attack, named after the TCP's connection setup packet. In a SYN attack, a remote attacker floods your machine with SYN packets, causing it to spend all its cycles setting up bogus TCP connections. The key to this attack is that, unlike simply flooding a machine with bogus data packets, each SYN packet requires nontrivial processing to determine that it's OK to just throw the packet away. Firewalls offer some level of protection, in that they can be programmed to drop all packets from a known attacking host, but it's easy for the attacker to simply put a different source IP address in each SYN packet.

Another well-known DoS attack is to send a stream of "Christmas tree packets" to a router—packets with all the "lights" turned on (e.g., all known IP options enabled). The router spends so much time processing these options that it fails to process BGP updates.

A less well-known example illustrates how subtle a denial-of-service attack can be. An attacker flooded an ISP's router with IP packets carrying a serial sequence of IP addresses. The sequence blew the router's first-level route cache, which ultimately caused the router's processor to spend all its time building new forwarding tables. This happened at the expense of the router responding to its neighbors' routing probes, which caused the neighbors to believe the router was down.

Protecting against denial-of-service attacks involves three steps. The first is to account for all resources consumed by every user (or flow). The second is to detect when the resources consumed by a given user exceed those allowed by some system policy. Once an attack is detected, the final step is to reclaim the consumed resources using as few additional resources as possible; otherwise, removal of an offending user becomes a denial-of-service attack in its own right. Unfortunately, few of today's systems—including both hosts and routers—accurately account for all resources used in the system, let alone define a policy as to what constitutes a denial-of-service attack.

In general, however, it is difficult to detect when a resource-usage policy has been violated because the attacker doesn't necessarily send a large stream of attack packets from the same source. Instead, the attacker may bombard you with innocent-looking packet streams from many sources. This is known as a *distributed denial-of-service (DDoS)* attack, and involves the attacker first compromising a large set of machines (so-called *zombies*) and then turning all of these zombies against you at the same time. For example, highly visible sites like CNN, Yahoo!, eBay, and Amazon were brought down by a DDoS attack in February 2000. In the end, DDoS attacks are problematic because it is almost impossible to distinguish between a legitimate heavy load from many sources (i.e., a flash crowd) and a DDoS attack.

FURTHER READING

The first two security-related papers, taken together, give a good overview of the topic. The article by Lampson et al. contains a formal treatment of security, while the Satyanarayanan paper gives a nice description of how a secure system is designed in practice. The third paper gives an overview of the IPsec security architecture and is the right place to start to fully understand the state of security in the Internet today.

Lampson, B., et al. "Authentication in Distributed Systems: Theory and Practice." *ACM Transactions on Computer Systems*, 10(4): 265–310, November 1992.

Satyanarayanan, M. "Integrating Security in a Large Distributed System." *ACM Transactions on Computer Systems*, 7(3): 247–280, August 1989.

Kent, S., and K. Seo. "Security Architecture for the Internet Protocol." *Request for Comments* 4301, December 2005.

There are several good books covering the full gamut of network security. We recommend Schneier [Sch95], Stallings [Sta03], and Kaufman et al. [KPS02]. The first two give comprehensive treatments of the topic, while the last gives a very readable overview of the subject. The full IPsec architecture is defined in a series of RFCs: [Ken05a], [Eas05], [MG98a], [MG98b], [MD98], [Ken05b], [Kau05]. A book by Barrett and Silverman [BS01] gives a thorough description of SSH. Menezes et al. [MvOV96] is a comprehensive cryptography reference (a copy can be freely downloaded from the URL listed below).

A discussion of the problem of recognizing and defending against denial-of-service attacks can be found in Moore et al. [MVS01], Spatscheck and Peterson [SP99], and Qie et al. [QPP02]. Recent techniques used to identify the source of attacks can be found in papers by Bellovin [Bel00], Savage et al. [SWKA00], and Snoeren et al. [SPS+01]. The increasing threat of DDoS attacks is discussed by Garber [Gar00] and Harrison [Har00], and early approaches to defending against such attacks are reported in a paper by Park and Lee [PL01].

Finally, we recommend the following live references:

ftp://cert.org/pub: A collection of security-related notices posted by the Computer Emergency Response Team (CERT).

http://www.cacr.math.uwaterloo.ca/hac/: Downloadable copy of [MvOV96], a comprehensive cryptography reference.

Network Attacks

2.1 INTRODUCTION

Information assurance (IA) deals with security and dependability of systems and networks. In this chapter, we provide an overview of issues, terminology, and techniques related to the security of the *network*. Network security comprises of ongoing activities that (a) assess the network for its current state of security, (b) have in place protection and prevention mechanisms against security threats, (c) implement detection mechanisms to rapidly identify security attacks that may have been successful, and (d) have policies, procedures, and techniques in place to respond to attacks. We discuss these aspects in a succinct manner in this chapter. In Section 2.2, we describe the network communications and how they are vulnerable to security attacks and provide a brief overview of security services. Section 2.3 is devoted to mechanisms that are used to protect networks from security threats or prevent successful attacks and here we discuss firewalls and cryptographic protocols. Intrusion detection is examined in Section 2.4 and response mechanisms are considered in Section 2.5.

2.2 NETWORK ATTACKS AND SECURITY ISSUES

In this section, we provide a very brief overview of communications across networks and discuss some specific attacks that illustrate how security is impacted in networks.

2.2.1 Network Communications

It is instructive to examine, at a very high level, how two hosts on the Internet usually make connections to one another to understand how attacks occur over the network. However, our goal here is not to explain protocols from a communications perspective (such as performance, reliability, and so on) or explore their details. Please note that what is described below corresponds only to a typical **47** scenario and there are exceptions and many different possible variations for communications across the Internet.

Let us suppose that a client application on host A on network P wishes to connect to a server application on host B on network Q. The client and server applications run as processes on the respective hosts. The client application creates data that is sent down the protocol stack to the transport layer. The transport layer adds information to this data in a structured manner creating a *segment* that is passed down to the network layer. The transmission control protocol (TCP) and the user datagram protocol (UDP) are two common transport layer protocols. The transport layer segment forms the payload of a network layer *packet* or *datagram* usually carried by the Internet protocol (IP). The IP datagram is further carried by a link or medium access control (MAC) layer protocol in a *frame* on each link between host A and host B (examples are Ethernet and WiFi). Each link may have its own physical layer-dependent transmission mechanisms.

At the transport layer, a *port number* will identify the process in host A; let us denote this port number as P_A. Host A will have an IP address that belongs to network P; let us denote this as IP_A. The tuple $<P_A, IP_A>$, which is sometimes called a *socket*, is a globally unique identifier of the client process that intends to communicate with the server process. Similarly, the server process will be associated with a port number P_B and an IP address IP_B. A connection between the client and server can thus be uniquely identified through the tuple $<P_A, IP_A, P_B, IP_B>$. The transport layer segment consists of a header containing the source port P_A and the destination port P_B. The IP datagram has a header that contains the source IP address IP_A and the destination IP address IP_B.

Network interface cards only recognize the MAC address. When the network interface card in host A creates a MAC frame on the physical medium of network P, it typically uses a 48-bit source MAC address and a 48-bit destination MAC address. Obviously, host B is on a different network, possibly using a different link and physical layer. Thus, the destination MAC address does not belong to host B, but instead to a gateway or router that connects network P to other networks or the Internet. The IP address of the gateway is either manually installed in host A or host A finds this information using a *dynamic host configuration protocol* (DHCP). DHCP is also used to dynamically assign IP addresses to hosts in a network. However, knowledge of simply the IP address of the gateway does not suffice since the MAC address is necessary for the frame to be received by the gateway. A mapping of the IP address to the MAC address can be obtained using the *address resolution protocol* (ARP). Similarly, when a frame arrives at the gateway from the Internet to the host on the network Q, the gateway will have to use the ARP to determine the MAC address of the destination host. The gateway is responsible for routing the IP datagram in the received MAC frame to another router in the Internet, which forms a node on one of the available paths to the destination network Q. Such paths are determined using routing information through routing protocols like the routing information protocol (RIP), open shortest path first (OSPF), and border gateway protocol (BGP).

How does the application process on host A know the IP address of host B? Usually, the IP address is not known, instead a domain name such as "www.cnn .com" that is human friendly is used in the application. It is necessary for host A to use the *domain name service* (DNS) to determine the IP address of host B. This has to happen *prior* to the actual data being sent in an IP packet to host B. Each network has a local name server that is known to every host in that network (possibly through DHCP). Host A contacts the local name server when the application process in host A desires to send a packet to host B with information about host B (say "www.cnn.com"). If the local name server has cached information about the IP address of host B, it provides that information to host A immediately. If not, it contacts a root name server (there are only 13 of these worldwide). The root name servers have information about authoritative name servers that in turn have information related to hosts on their networks. In the above example, the root name server may provide the local name server of network P, the IP address of the authoritative name server for network Q. The local name server of network P then contacts the authoritative name server of network Q to obtain the IP address of host B. Then the IP address is forwarded to host A.

Now suppose that host A was successful in finding the IP address of host B using DNS. The application process in host A with port number P_A sends data to a process in host B with port number P_B. How did the process in host A know the port number P_B? Standard applications have standard port numbers. For example, a web server usually employs the port number 80, a telnet server uses 23, a web server running the secure sockets layer (SSL) uses 443, the simple mail transport protocol (SMTP) uses 25, and so on. Port numbers may also be changed after initial contact as in the case of protocols like the file transfer protocol (FTP) or applications like Skype. Although port numbers for standard services are well known, this does not automatically imply that such services are not available at other port numbers. For instance, it is quite possible to run a web server at a port number other than 80.

Services on servers "listen" for initial contact from clients at the standard port numbers. These are what we call "open" ports. When a packet from host A arrives at host B, it is sent up the protocol stack to the transport layer where the server that is listening at port number P_B receives the application data in the transport layer segment. The server processes the data appropriately and responds to the client at port number P_A, which is known because of the initial received packet.

Figure 2.1 shows a very simplified view of some of the many protocols and applications that are common in networked communications today. It is to be noted that this is just a very small fraction of the protocols and applications in use. Each of these protocols could perhaps create security problems because they are capable of being abused by malicious entities in ways in which they were not anticipated to be used.

Security problems occur for a variety of reasons, but one common reason is that servers listening at known ports have bugs in their implementation (e.g., buffer

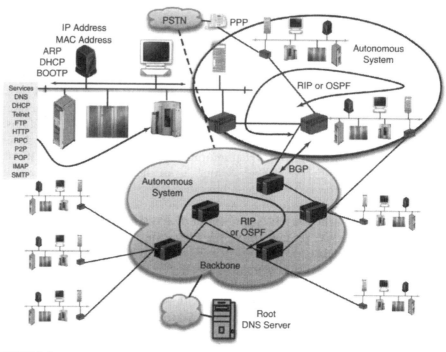

FIGURE 2.1

Simplified view of the many protocols that impact network communications.

overflows). For example, it is possible for a malicious entity (we will refer to a malicious entity—a human, a criminal organization, or software—as Oscar in this chapter) to craft packets that can be sent to buggy services. When a service is compromised, it can enable Oscar to take control over the host. This means Oscar can perhaps install malicious software on the host, use the host to launch other malicious packets, steal files that are stored on the host or on other hosts on the network that trust the compromised host, and so on as described in the following examples.

2.2.2 Some Example Security Attacks

The emergence of very large cyber-crime operations has moved network security attacks from the realm of hobbyists to criminal organizations, making them more dangerous with potential for great economic harm. In this section, we discuss some specific security attacks that will lead us to a general discussion of security attacks and security services in the next section. We do not provide an exhaustive list of attacks but have picked a few for illustration. The web site of US-CERT

(United States Computer Emergency Readiness Team) [1] is a good source for past and recent vulnerabilities and security incidents.

TCP SYN Flood Attack

As mentioned earlier, TCP is the most common transport layer protocol. It is used by many application layer protocols like the HyperText Transfer Protocol (HTTP) and FTP. TCP was designed to provide reliable service on top of the unreliable network layer provided by IP. So among other things, TCP is connection oriented and it carefully maintains buffers, windows, and other resources to count segments and track lost segments. When host A wants to connect to host B, a "three-way" handshake occurs to set up the connection. First, host A sends a TCP segment with a SYN flag set (this is one of six flags used for synchronization—bits—in TCP for indicating information). Host B acknowledges the SYN segment with its own TCP segment with the SYN flag and ACK flag (used to acknowledge the receipt of the SYN packet) set. Host A completes the handshake with a TCP segment with the ACK flag set. Then data transfer begins. Whenever a server receives a SYN segment from a client, it sets aside some resources (e.g., memory) anticipating a completed handshake and subsequent data transfer. As there are limited resources at a server, only a set number of connections can be accepted. Other requests are dropped. Oscar can make use of this "feature" to deny services to legitimate hosts by sending a flood of crafted SYN segments to a server with possibly spoofed source IP addresses. The server responds with SYN-ACK segments and waits for completion of the handshake, which never happens. Meanwhile, legitimate requests for connection are dropped. Such an attack is called a SYN flood attack and has been the cause of denial of service to popular web servers in recent years. Note that Oscar primarily makes use of a feature in a communications protocol to launch denial of service (DoS). The absence of authentication of the source IP address makes it difficult to block such attacks since it is hard to separate legitimate requests from malicious requests. Similarly, Internet Control Message Protocol (ICMP) and other protocols can be used to launch floods that result in DoS. Distributed DoS (DDoS) attacks have recently made headlines by bringing down several popular web sites in recent years as well as launching attacks on root DNS servers. A taxonomy of DDoS attacks is available in Mirkovic and Reiher [2].

Address Spoofing and Sequence Number Guessing Attacks

Several services use the IP address or host name to provide access to the service. As discussed previously, it is very easy for Oscar to craft packets. Spoofing IP addresses is as trivial as spoofing host names. There have been instances of attacks where root access to certain hosts has been obtained by sending crafted packets with spoofed IP addresses. In many of the attacks, it is not sufficient to spoof IP addresses; it is also necessary to guess sequence numbers (of other protocols carried in the IP packet as payload such as TCP or DNS). For example, we previously discussed the TCP three-way handshake. As part of the handshake, both the client and the server use initial sequence numbers that are incremented in the corresponding acknowledgments. If the IP address is spoofed and Oscar wishes to fool the server into believing that a legitimate client has connected with it, Oscar needs to "guess" the sequence number generated by the server. This is because the server's SYN-ACK segment is delivered to an IP address that does not belong to Oscar (and hence Oscar may not receive the response from the server). The server sequence number is supposed to be random and difficult to guess. However, poor implementations of TCP have allowed malicious entities to easily guess the sequence number generated by the server. Similarly, spoofed DNS responses that can poison the DNS cache (see the section below on pharming) can be generated if the sequence numbers associated with DNS requests can be guessed.

Worm Attacks

Worms are self-replicating, malicious software programs that can crash hosts or services, open trapdoors for installing keyboard sniffers, or perform other malicious activity. Once a worm is installed on a host, it probes other networked hosts for bugs or vulnerabilities in services that can be exploited. This essentially means that the worm sends crafted packets to certain port numbers at IP addresses. If the services listening to such port numbers are vulnerable, the worm can exploit such vulnerabilities to install itself on such hosts. For example, in July 2001, web servers running Microsoft's Internet Information Server (IIS) software were discovered to have a buffer overflow bug. Although a patch was issued for this bug, not every host running IIS was patched. The Code Red (two versions) and Code Red II worms exploited this bug and spread it rapidly across the Internet [3]. It is estimated that Code Red infected at least 350,000 hosts.

The speed with which a worm spreads depends on the design of the worm (e.g., the rate at which it scans for other vulnerable hosts), whether patches exist for the vulnerability exploited by the worm, the number of hosts running the vulnerable software, and the clean-up rate [4]. The way worms find other hosts to exploit can also influence their spread. Many early worms would randomly pick IP addresses to probe for vulnerabilities. This, however, meant that many IP addresses would either not belong to hosts that existed or to hosts that did not run the vulnerable service or operating system, thereby limiting the spread of the worm. Others had a hard-coded sequence of IP addresses that would be probed. This meant that infected hosts would likely probe other infected hosts first.

Recent worms are intelligent—they look for "neighboring" IP addresses first. Some worms use Internet search engines to discover vulnerable hosts. However, most search engines present the same set of results for a query, thereby reducing the set of hosts scanned for vulnerabilities. The most rapidly spreading worms use email and entries in the address books of infected hosts to reach a variety of legitimate and potentially vulnerable hosts. In the past, exploits for vulnerabilities would not appear quickly, but it is common to see so-called "zero-day" exploits today. A zero-day exploit, for instance, can result in a worm that can be released on the same day that a vulnerability is discovered in a service. This makes it almost impossible to patch the exploit in time, enabling the worm to spread extremely rapidly.

Phishing, Evil Twins, and Pharming

Phishing is an example of a social engineering security attack where legitimate users are fooled into revealing information such as logins, passwords, credit card numbers, and so on by making them visit web sites that look like legitimate sites, but are actually fake ones run by criminal organizations. Legitimate users can visit such sites, for instance, by clicking on links that appear in emails that look legitimate. Most phishing attacks target financial organizations like banks or e-commerce sites like Paypal or eBay.

Recently, a special form of phishing attacks, called "evil twins," has appeared whereby WiFi access points are placed in areas (e.g., hot spots like coffee shops or hotels) close to where legitimate service is being provided by some service provider. When a legitimate user tries to connect to such access points placed by Oscar, a web page, similar to ones displayed by legitimate service providers, is displayed. It is common for subscribers to enter credit card and other sensitive information on these web pages, enabling Oscar to steal such information.

Pharming is a more dangerous security attack. As described previously, DNS is used to discover IP addresses associated with domain names. In the case of pharming, DNS caches can be poisoned with fake entries so that a user sees a fake web site even if a legitimate URL is typed in the browser. DNS cache poisoning is possible when name servers use vulnerable versions of software that can be exploited with unsolicited DNS responses. Once again, the impact is similar to phishing attacks where a legitimate user will reveal sensitive information to the criminals.

2.2.3 Security Attacks, Services, and Architecture

In the previous section, we have seen some examples of security attacks, such as denial of service, session hijacking, worms, and social engineering. One way of classifying security attacks is to consider their nature—whether they are passive or active. In the case of passive attacks, Oscar does not interfere with the information flow or storage (e.g., eavesdropping), making such attacks hard to discover. It is important to prevent such attacks. Active attacks (such as masquerading) involve interference and participation by Oscar. As they are hard to prevent, they must be detected and stopped as rapidly as possible.

Security attacks can be of many types: eavesdropping (interception) on information and revealing such information; interrupting the flow or availability of information; masquerading as a legitimate entity to access services, information, or resources; and fabricating information with the aim of causing damage are all different security attacks. Security attacks usually do not occur in one shot. Oscar typically first engages in mapping out the victim's network, resources, IP addresses, open services, and so on. This is sometimes called reconnaissance, and Oscar may try to get information that appears to be harmless if revealed, but may impact security later. This is followed up by exploitation of vulnerabilities, theft of information, taking over of hosts, and so on. An excellent treatment of the security attack process is available in Bejtlich [5].

The common security services to protect against security attacks as defined in the literature are *confidentiality, authentication, integrity, nonrepudiation*, and *availability* [6]. *Confidentiality* implies that information or data is kept secret from unauthorized entities, specifically Oscar. In the case of *authentication*, it is necessary for communicating parties to (a) ensure at the start of communications that they are communicating with who they think they are communicating with, that is, Oscar should not fool an honest Alice into thinking that she is communicating with an honest Bob, and (b) ensure that after communications have been established and verified to be between legitimate parties, that Oscar does not hijack the communications session and interpose himself as one of the legitimate parties. The second part of authentication is often called *message authentication* and it is combined with *integrity*. In such a case, once legitimate communications have been established, it is necessary to ensure that any messages exchanged have not been modified, fabricated, reordered, replayed, or deleted. *Nonrepudiation* refers to a security service where once a person has sent a message, he or she cannot deny having created the message. *Availability* refers to a security service that ensures that services are made available to an authorized person in a timely manner.

Note that all security services may not be present all the time, and different protocols and applications support different subsets of security services. Sometimes architectural methods (using firewalls, screened subnets, and demilitarized zones) are necessary for ensuring some of the security services (e.g., *confidentiality* or *availability*).

2.3 PROTECTION AND PREVENTION

In this section, we consider security mechanisms for protection against and prevention of security attacks. We consider firewalls and perimeter security in Section 2.3.1 and cryptographic protocols in Section 2.3.2. The interested reader is referred to Northcutt et al. [7] and Cheswick et al. [8] for more details on firewalls. A good reference that considers cryptography and cryptographic protocols is Stinson [9].

2.3.1 Firewalls and Perimeter Security

To block malicious packets from entering a network, it is common to employ firewalls. Firewalls in olden days referred to thick walls of brick constructed especially for preventing the spread of fires from one building to another. Firewalls today refer to hardware, software, and policies to prevent the spread of security attacks into an organization's (or individual's) network or host. As discussed previously in Section 2.2, attacks of many kinds occur due to maliciously crafted packets that arrive at the target network. If such packets can be identified and discarded, they

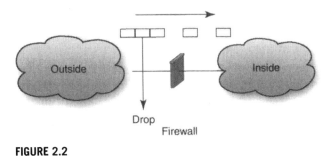

FIGURE 2.2

Schematic of a firewall.

will no longer be a threat to the security of the network. This is in essence the idea behind firewalls. However, it is not trivial to efficiently identify such packets correctly all the time. As shown in Figure 2.2, the firewall sits between the "inside" and the "outside." The inside is usually what needs to be protected. The term *firewall* can mean many things today, from a simple packet filter to a complex intrusion prevention system that is capable of examining a series of packets and reconstructing sessions for comparison with known attack signatures.

A *packet filter* is the simplest type of firewall. It filters incoming or outgoing packets based on *rules* created manually by the administrator of a network. Packet filters usually have a default "drop" policy. This means that if a packet does not satisfy any of the rules that allow it into the inside, it is dropped. Each packet is considered independently without consideration of previous or future packets, making packet filters fast and capable of handling high data rates. The simpler the rules are, the faster the filtering and the smaller the performance hit. Cisco's standard access control lists (ACLs) filter packets based solely on source IP addresses. In this case, it is easy to filter packets with source IP addresses that are obviously spoofed or other packets from sources that are not expected to communicate with the inside. Examples are IP packets that arrive from the outside with non-routable source IP addresses, loopback IP addresses, or IP addresses that belong to hosts on the inside. However, standard ACLs cannot block packets to specific hosts on the inside or packets that correspond to specific protocols. The extended ACL from Cisco allows a packet filter to look at source and destination IP addresses, TCP or UDP port numbers, and TCP flags and make decisions on whether or not a packet should be allowed into the inside. Other firewall software (e.g., IPTables in Linux) and hardware have equivalent access control lists for filtering packets.

The rules in the packet filter are considered in strict order creating potential for configuration errors as the list of rules grows in size. One way of overcoming this problem is to use so-called dynamic packet filters or stateful firewalls. Dynamic packet filters build rules on the fly. The assumption is that hosts on the inside are to be trusted. When they send packets to open connections with hosts on the outside, a stateful firewall builds a rule on the fly that allows packets from the specific external host (and port number at that host) to the specific internal host (and the port number at this host). The rule is deleted when the connection is terminated. This reduces the number of hard-coded rules and makes it difficult for Oscar to guess what packets may make it through a firewall.

Packet filters can still be fooled through a variety of loopholes that exist (e.g., by sending fragmented packets). In order to determine whether or not packets are legitimate, it is often necessary to look at the application payload. Sometimes it is even necessary to reconstruct the application data. This is possible if proxy firewalls are used. Proxy firewalls consist of hardened hosts (usually dual-homed) that run reduced modules of certain applications. When an internal host makes a connection to the outside, it really makes a connection (say, TCP) with the proxy firewall. The proxy then makes a connection to the external host. Thus, there are two connections that exist. External hosts only see the proxy firewall. They are not even aware of the existence of other internal hosts. When packets are returned, they make their way up the protocol stack where the application (with reduced features) reconstructs the data. If the data is legitimate, it is forwarded to the internal host. Moreover, Oscar can gain very little knowledge during reconnaissance because internal hosts are not visible to the outside world. However, proxy firewalls create performance bottlenecks. They also do not support a variety of applications, often frustrating legitimate network communications.

Architectural approaches can approximate the benefits of proxy firewalls, and yet keep performance levels reasonable. One common approach is to screen the inside from the outside by using one or more packet filters. In Figure 2.3, for example, packet filter A allows packets (from most legitimate hosts on the outside) through interface p to reach either the web server or the mail server. As almost anyone can reach these servers, this is called a *demilitarized zone* (DMZ). If it is also a router, it does not advertise the existence of the inside network to the outside world. Similarly, packet filter B allows packets from either the web server or the mail server to the inside through interface r. Thus, the inside network is screened from the outside.

Note that packet filters can also be used to stop packets from the inside from going out (e.g., through interfaces s and q in Figure 2.3). This may be necessary if

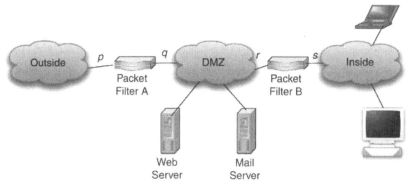

FIGURE 2.3

Schematic of a screened subnet and demilitarized zone.

hosts on the inside have been compromised and are launching attacks, or hosts are trying to access services not allowed by corporate policy.

Nowadays, firewalls are more than simple packet filters. They can maintain state, do load balancing (if multiple firewalls are used), do some inspection of application payloads, detect attacks based on known signatures, maintain logs useful for forensics or analysis, and also act as endpoints for connectivity to mobile users who need to connect to the inside from the outside. For example, firewalls can now be the terminating points for virtual private network (VPN) connections using IPSec or SSL, which make use of cryptography to prevent outsiders from connecting to the inside or monitoring connections made by mobile employees. We discuss cryptographic protocols next.

2.3.2 **Cryptographic Potocols**

Security services such as confidentiality and integrity can be provided to communication protocols using cryptography. In this section, we provide a brief overview of the important topics in cryptography and cryptographic protocols. More details can be found in Stallings [6], Cheswick et al. [8], and Kaufmann [10].

Cryptographic protocols make use of cryptographic *primitives* that are used to provide the required security services. A classification of such primitives is shown in Figure 2.4. Cryptology is the broad discipline that includes the science of designing

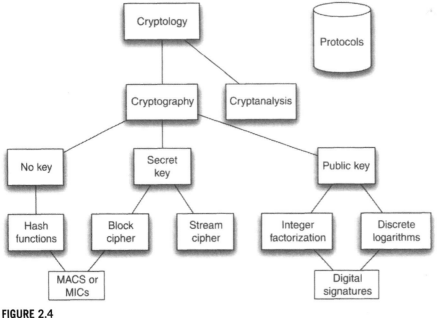

FIGURE 2.4

Classification of cryptographic primitives.

ciphers (cryptography) and that of breaking ciphers (cryptanalysis). Data that is encrypted is called "plaintext" and the result of encryption is called "ciphertext." Ciphers or encryption algorithms can be classified into secret key and public key categories.

In the case of secret key encryption, two honest parties, say Alice and Bob, share a secret key k that is used with an encryption algorithm. Both encryption and decryption make use of the same key k and both parties have knowledge of the key. Secret key algorithms can further be classified into block ciphers and stream ciphers. Block ciphers encrypt "blocks" of data (e.g., 64, 128, or 256 bits) at a time. Each block is encrypted with the same key. Common block ciphers include the Advanced Encryption Standard (AES), Blowfish, and CAST. Stream ciphers use the key k to generate a key stream. The key stream is XORed with the data stream to create the ciphertext. At the receiver, the same key stream is generated and XORed with the ciphertext to obtain the data. Block ciphers can be used to create key streams through standard modes of operation [6, 9]. RC-4 is a common stream cipher that is not derived from a block cipher. It is recommended that the key size for good security with block or stream ciphers should be at least 128 bits today. It is common to assume that everyone, including Oscar, knows the encryption algorithms, but the key is secret and known only to honest communicating parties, in this case, Alice and Bob.

Public key encryption is based on the property that given a pair of related information, one part of the information can be revealed. However, the other part of the information cannot be discovered even with knowledge of the first part. For example, if some large prime numbers are randomly selected and multiplied, revealing the product does not enable others to guess or calculate the prime numbers that are factors of the product. This property is used in RSA. The information that is revealed is called the "public key" and the information kept secret is called the "private key." To encrypt information, the public key is used. To decrypt information, the private key is used. Another mathematical technique used for public key encryption is based on discrete logarithms. Because of the mathematical nature of public key encryption, key sizes are typically longer for good security—around 1,024 bits for RSA.

Public key encryption is also computationally expensive. Consequently, it is common to use public key encryption for key establishment and digital signatures. Confidentiality and integrity of bulk data are achieved using secret key schemes. Although the public key of an honest party like Alice can be made public, its authenticity needs to be verified since Oscar can claim to be Alice and publish his key as hers. It is common to use digital certificates signed by one of a few trusted certification authorities to verify the authenticity of the public key (see below for more on digital signatures). This approach is used in modern web browsers for e-commerce applications.

We also include hash functions in the classification in Figure 2.4. They are not strictly encryption schemes. They map any sized data to a fixed-size digest. Given the digest, it is considered infeasible to obtain any data that maps to the digest if the size of the digest is at least 160 bits. Popular hash functions in use today are MD-5 and SHA.

Block ciphers and hash functions can be used to create *message authentication codes* (MACs) or *message integrity checks* (MICs). These are checksums on data created using block ciphers or hash functions with a shared secret key between the communicating parties. MACs or MICs provide message authentication and integrity. If Oscar were to fabricate a message or modify a legitimate message, the checksum would always fail, alerting the receiver of a problem with the received data. The Cipher Block Chaining MAC (CBC-MAC) that uses block ciphers and keyed-hash MAC (HMAC) that employs hash functions are popular standard implementations of MACs.

Digital signatures are like physical signatures. They attest some information and are bound to that information. Typically this involves encrypting the hash value of some information with the private key of a public key/private key pair. Suppose Alice generated some data and created a digital signature of the data. Anyone can verify the signature because decrypting the signature requires the public key, which is available to everyone. No one except Alice can generate the signature because she is the only one in possession of the private key. Recall that knowledge of the public key does not help Oscar or others deduce the private key.

The cryptographic primitives discussed above are used in cryptographic protocols, which are designed with specific security objectives in mind. Cryptographic protocols are notoriously hard to design since they will likely have pitfalls that are hard to detect [10]. A good example of a cryptographic protocol that fails to meet most of its security objectives is the *Wired Equivalent Privacy* (WEP) protocol used in legacy IEEE 802.11 wireless local area networks [11]. Moreover, cryptographic primitives make use of keys shared between communicating parties. Establishing secret keys between legitimate parties interested in communicating, such that Oscar does not obtain any knowledge of the keys, is not trivial and requires cryptographic protocols. Key establishment is usually based on master keys established with trusted third parties or public key cryptography.

Most well-designed cryptographic protocols have three phases. In the first phase, the communicating entities *identify* or *authenticate* themselves to one another. In some cases the entity authentication is unilateral (i.e., Alice authenticates herself to Bob, but not vice versa). Entity authentication makes use of passwords, PIN, pass phrases, biometrics, security tokens, and the like. Challenge-response protocols that do not require an entity to reveal the password, but only demonstrate knowledge of the password, are commonly used for entity authentication. In the second phase, or as part of the first phase, the communicating entities also establish keys for security services to be provided next. Establishment of keys can be in two ways: key transport or distribution, where one party generates the keys (or a master key) and transports them securely to the other party, or key agreement, where both parties exchange information used in the secure creation of the same key at both ends. It is common for both parties to exchange random numbers, sequence numbers, or time stamps (called nonces, or numbers used once) that are used as input in key generation. In the third phase, the established keys are used to provide confidentiality (through encryption with a block or stream cipher) and integrity (through MACs or MICs). We briefly describe some examples in the following sections.

Kerberos

Kerberos is used for authenticating users when they access services from workstations, typically on a local area network. An authentication server shares a password with all users and a key with a ticket-granting server. When a user logs on to a workstation, the workstation contacts the authentication server. The authentication server issues a ticket to the user and also sends a key that the user will share with the ticket-granting server. This key is encrypted with the user's password. The workstation will not be able to retrieve the key if the user is not legitimate. Thus, recovery of the key to be shared with the ticket-granting server indirectly authenticates the user. Note that in this phase, a key has been transported to the user as well. Of course, this assumes that a password has been manually shared between the user and the authentication server. The ticket itself is encrypted with a key shared between the authentication server and the ticket-granting server. It includes, among other things, the key that has been transported to the user. When the user desires to access a service, the workstation presents the ticket to the ticket-granting server and a message authentication code created using the key that was initially received from the authentication server. This verifies the user's legitimacy to the ticket-granting server, which then issues a key and a ticket to the workstation for use with the requested service. A similar authentication mechanism is used with the server providing the service. Kerberos is more complicated than what has been described here. More details are available in Stallings [6] and Kaufmann et al. [10].

IPSec

IPSec encrypts all IP traffic between two hosts, or two networks, or combinations of hosts with possibly different terminating points for different security services. Keys may be manually established or a very complex protocol called *Internet Key Exchange* (IKE) can be used for authenticating entities to one another and establishing keys. Keys are established as part of a unidirectional "security association" that specifies the destination IP address, keys, encryption algorithms, and "protocol" to be used. "Protocol" here corresponds to one of two specific security services provided by IPSec: *Authentication Header* (AH) and *Encapsulated Security Payload* (ESP). In AH, a MAC is created on the entire IP packet minus the fields in the IP header that change in transit. This enables the receiver to detect spoofed or modified IP packets. However, the payload is in plaintext and visible to anyone who may be capable of capturing the IP packet. ESP provides confidentiality and integrity to the payload of the IP packet but not the header. Use of the two protocols in the above manner is called "transport mode." It is also possible to use a "tunnel mode" where the original IP packet is tunneled in another IP packet. This makes the original IP packet the payload, thereby protecting it completely.

SSL

The secure sockets layer (the latest version is called transport layer security, or TLS) is used in web browsers to secure data transfer, especially for e-commerce applications, banking, and other confidential transactions. At a high level, the browser is not required to be authenticated by the server (although this is possible and optional in SSL). The user employing the web browser is authenticated using passwords or other techniques proprietary to the organization using the server. The server, however, is authenticated by the browser through its digital certificate. This provides the user some assurance that the transaction is taking place with a legitimate bank or e-commerce site. Note that the use of SSL is not the assurance of authenticity of the server since any site or any server could use SSL. It is the information contained in the digital certificate that authenticates the server. The digital certificate contains the public key of the server, signed by a certification authority. The browser creates a random secret, encrypts it with the server's public key, and sends it to the server. This random secret, along with previously exchanged nonces, is used to generate keys (at both the server and the browser) that are used for encryption with block or stream ciphers (RC-4 is commonly used) and integrity with message authentication codes.

2.4 DETECTION

Irrespective of the protection and prevention mechanisms in place, it is possible that security attacks succeed and proceed in an organization's network. It is extremely important to detect such attacks at the earliest onslaught so that action can be taken to stop further damage. More details of detection mechanisms and processes can be found in Bejtlich [5], Northcutt and Novak [12], and Amoroso [13].

Intrusion detection is the broad term used to describe the process for identifying the fact that a security attack has occurred (or is occurring). There is no single method for identifying attacks; typically, three methods are used. In host-based intrusion detection, audit trails, logs, deployment of suspicious code, logins, and so on are monitored to detect the occurrence of a security attack. In network-based intrusion detection, the packets entering the network are examined to see if they correspond to signatures of known security attacks. Anomaly-based intrusion detection looks for abnormal usage of network or system resources and flags potential problems.

Audit trail processing, used with host-based intrusion detection, is usually done offline. Care has to be taken to ensure that logs in hosts have not been tampered with. Logs from many hosts and systems may have to be correlated to detect attacks. Network-based intrusion detection is in real time as packets are captured. This can be problematic if the amount of data flowing into the network is extremely large, as the buffering capacity may be limited and packets may be dropped by an intrusion detection system (IDS). Using signatures of known attacks is a common technique used for intrusion detection. However, this may miss new and unidentified attacks.

If signatures are made too specific, security attacks may be missed resulting in false negatives. If signatures are made too general, it is likely that some normal traffic and activity are flagged as a security attack resulting in false positives. Thus, careful tuning are often necessary to detect intrusions with low false positives or negatives. The algorithms used for intrusion detection can be fairly complex, making use of data mining, pattern matching, decision making, and so on.

Often, IDSs deploy *sensors* to probe or monitor the network or systems in question. It is necessary to deploy sensors on either side of a firewall to get an idea of the attacks that are being blocked. Multiple redundant sensors may be necessary depending on the network topology. Sensors themselves may have to be networked to correlate the collected data. Such a network may or may not be separate from the network that is being monitored. The Internet Engineering Task Force is working on formats for exchange of intrusion detection information.

It is possible that IDSs may themselves be subject to security attacks. There are techniques that Oscar may employ to thwart detection by IDSs (such as fragmentation, flooding, unrelated attacks). Recent trends in intrusion detection include *distributed intrusion detection* where system administrators from all over the world submit their monitored information to a service that then performs correlations to detect and identify attacks.

There are several kinds of intrusion detection systems available today including specialized appliances from vendors. SNORT is an open-source intrusion detection system that is available for free. While evaluating an IDS, it is necessary to consider the types of attacks that an IDS can detect, the operating systems it supports, whether it can handle huge amounts of traffic, if it is capable of displaying large amounts of data in an easily understandable manner, the management framework that it provides, and its complexity.

Today, combinations of IDSs and firewalls, called intrusion prevention systems (IPSs), are also available. Rate-based IPSs block traffic flows if they are seen to exceed normal rates. Signature-based IPSs block traffic when signatures of known security attacks are detected. Such systems are part of the intrusion response systems.

Honeypots or Internet traps are systems used to detect and divert security attacks. Such systems look like real resources, perhaps with vulnerabilities. Their value lies in the fact that Oscar may probe them, launch attacks against them, and perhaps compromise some of the systems. Monitoring Oscar's activities using honeypots can help detect other attacks against real systems or design methods of prevention.

2.5 ASSESSMENT AND RESPONSE

It is important to periodically *assess* the security of the network and systems in an organization. Additionally, assessment becomes important after a security incident has been detected and a *response* to the attack has been put in place. In this section, we briefly consider elements of assessment and response. See Northcutt et al. [7], Whitacker and Newman [14], and McNab [15] for more details.

Assessment of a network can be done using external auditors who can perform penetration tests (act essentially like Oscar, but not damage systems), enumerate the entities in the network, discover potential vulnerabilities, and verify if the protection and prevention mechanisms (like firewalls, access control schemes, password management) are working as they are expected. Vulnerability assessment tries to identify the presence of known vulnerabilities that can be and must be patched if patches are available. Since vulnerabilities are often operating system specific, vulnerability scanners may not pick up all vulnerabilities present on hosts in a network. Nessus is a popular open-source vulnerability scanner. Commercial options also exist.

Responding to security attacks when detected is also an important aspect of security. The person in charge of a network needs to be immediately notified if an attack is detected (possibly through redundant means of communication). The security incident must be documented clearly. There must be processes in place to contact vendors and other external help if necessary. Actions to mitigate the impact of the security attack must be taken, followed by eradication of the vulnerability that caused the attack. An assessment of reasons as to why the attack was successful and steps to prevent recurrence must be taken.

2.6 **CONCLUSION**

In this chapter, a high-level overview of network security was provided. The way network communications take place was discussed. Example security attacks were described. Terminology associated with security services was introduced. Protection against attacks using firewalls and prevention mechanisms that make use of cryptography were considered with examples of Kerberos, IPSec, and SSL. Detection of security attacks, security assessment of networks and systems, and response to security incidents were briefly discussed.

REFERENCES

[1] The United States Computer Emergency Readiness Team, at http://www.us-cert.gov.

[2] J. Mirkovic and P. Reiher, "A Taxonomy of DDoS Attack and DDoS Defense Mechanisms," *ACM Computer Communications Review*, 34(2):39–53, April 2004.

[3] D. Moore, C. Shannon, and K. Claffy, "Code Red: A Case Study on the Spread and Victims of an Internet Worm," *Proceedings of the 2nd ACM SIGCOMM Workshop on Internet Measurement (IMW)*, Marseille, France, 2002, pp. 273–284.

[4] Z. Chen, L. Gao, and K. Kwiat, "Modeling the Spread of Active Worms," *Proceedings of IEEE Infocom*, San Franciso, CA, April 2003.

[5] Richard Bejtlich, *The Tao of Network Security Monitoring*. Boston: Addison-Wesley, 2004.

[6] W. Stallings, *Network Security Essentials*, 2nd ed. Englewood Cliffs, NJ: Prentice Hall, 2003.

[7] S. Z. Northcutt, L. Winters, S. Frederick, and K. K. Ritchey, *Inside Network Perimeter Security*. Indianapolis: New Riders, 2005.

[8] W. R. Cheswick, S. M. Bellovin, and A. D. Rubin, *Firewalls and Internet Security*. Boston: Addison-Wesley, 2003.

[9] D. Stinson, *Cryptography: Theory and Practice*, 3rd ed. Boca Raton, FL: Chapman & Hall/CRC Press, 2006.

[10] C. Kaufmann, R. Perlman, and M. Speciner, *Network Security: Private Communication in a Public World*. Englewood Cliffs, NJ: Prentice Hall PTR, 2002.

[11] J. Edney and W. A. Arbaugh, *Real 802.11 Security: Wi-Fi Protected Access and 802.11i*. Englewood Cliffs, NJ: Prentice Hall, 2004.

[12] S. Northcutt and J. Novak, *Network Intrusion Detection: An Analyst's Handbook*. Indianapolis, IN: New Riders, 2001.

[13] E. G. Amoroso, *Intrusion Detection: An Introduction to Internet Surveillance, Correlation, Trace Back, Traps, and Response*. Sparta, NJ: Intrusion.net Books, 1999.

[14] A. Whitaker D. Newman, *Penetration Testing and Network Defense*. Indianapolis, IN: Cisco Press, 2005.

[15] C. McNab, *Network Security Assessment: Know Your Network*. Sebastopol, CA: O'Reilly Books, 2004.

Security and Privacy Architecture

Security and privacy of user, application, device, and network resources and data are increasingly important areas of network architecture and design. Security is integrated within all areas of the network and impacts all other functions on the network. For the proper functioning of security within a network, it is crucial that the relationships among security mechanisms, as well as between the security architecture and other component architectures, be well understood.

Overlaying security onto a developed network was an acceptable approach in the past. Today, however, security must be integrated into the network from the beginning in order for the network to meet the needs of the users and for security to provide adequate protection.

3.1 OBJECTIVES

In this chapter you will learn about various security mechanisms (such as physical security, protocol and application security, encryption/decryption, and perimeter and remote access security), how to determine the relationships both among these mechanisms and between security and the other architectural components, and how to develop the security architecture.

3.1.1 Preparation

To be able to understand and apply the concepts in this chapter, you should be familiar with the basic concepts and mechanisms of security. Some recommended sources of information include:

- *Hacking Exposed: Network Security Secrets & Solutions*, Third Edition, by Stuart McClure, Joel Scambray, and George Kurtz, McGraw-Hill Osborne Media, September 2001.

- *Information Security Architecture: An Integrated Approach to Security in the Organization*, by Jan Killmeyer Tudor, Auerbach, September 2000.

- *Firewalls and Internet Security: Repelling the Wily Hacker*, Second Edition, by William R. Cheswick, Steven M. Bellovin, and Aviel D. Rubin, Addison-Wesley Professional, February 2003.

- *Inside Network Perimeter Security: The Definitive Guide to Firewalls, Virtual Private Networks (VPNs), Routers, and Intrusion Detection Systems*, Second Edition, by Stephen Northcutt, Karen Fredrick, Scott Winters, Lenny Zeltser, and Ronald W. Ritchey, New Riders Publishing, June 2005.

- *Computer Security Handbook*, by Seymour Bosworth and Michel Kabay, John Wiley & Sons, April 2002.

3.2 BACKGROUND

Network security is defined here as the protection of networks and their services from unauthorized access, modification, destruction, or disclosure. It provides assurance that the network performs its critical functions correctly and that there are no harmful side effects. *Network privacy* is a subset of network security, focusing on protection of networks and their services from unauthorized access or disclosure. This includes all user, application, device, and network data. Whenever the term *network security* is used in this book, it includes all aspects of network privacy as well.

There are three classic security considerations: protecting the integrity, the confidentiality, and the availability of network and system resources and data. These considerations are discussed throughout this chapter and are integral to the security architecture. Effective security and privacy combine an understanding of what security means to each of the components of the system—users, applications, devices, and networks—together with the planning and implementation of security policies and mechanisms. Security in the network needs to protect network resources from being disabled, stolen, modified, or damaged. This includes protecting devices, servers, users, and system data, as well as the users' and organization's privacy and image.

Attacks against the system range from seemingly innocuous unauthorized probing and use of resources to keeping authorized users from accessing resources (denial of service), to modifying, stealing, or destroying resources.

This chapter covers how security and privacy may be determined and brought into the network architecture and design. This is an area of great interest and rapid expansion and change in the networking community, so we present concepts and mechanisms that should be valid across a wide range of security requirements. We discuss elements of security administration and various security and privacy mechanisms, consider how to develop a security plan, and examine requirements for security. We also define security policies, perform risk analysis for the architecture and design, and develop a security and privacy plan. We then discuss the security and privacy architecture.

3.3 DEVELOPING A SECURITY AND PRIVACY PLAN

The development of each component architecture is based on our understanding of why that function is needed for that particular network. While one may argue that security is always necessary, we still need to ensure that the security mechanisms we incorporate into the architecture are optimal for achieving the security goals for that network. Therefore, toward developing a security architecture, we should answer the following questions:

1. What are we trying to solve, add, or differentiate by adding security mechanisms to this network?
2. Are security mechanisms sufficient for this network?

While it is likely that some degree of security is necessary for any network, we should have information from the threat analysis to help us decide how much security is needed. As with the performance architecture, we want to avoid implementing (security) mechanisms just because they are interesting or new.

When security mechanisms are indicated, it is best to start simple and work toward a more complex security architecture when warranted. Simplicity may be achieved in the security architecture by implementing security mechanisms only in selected areas of the network (e.g., at the access or distribution [server] networks), or by using only one or a few mechanisms, or by selecting only those mechanisms that are easy to implement, operate, and maintain.

In developing the security architecture, you should determine what problems your customer is trying to solve. This may be clearly stated in the problem definition, developed as part of the threat analysis, or you may need to probe further to answer this question. Some common areas that are addressed by the security architecture include:

- Which resources need to be protected
- What problems (threats) are we protecting against
- The likelihood of each problem (threat)
- This information becomes part of your security and privacy plan for the network. This plan should be reviewed and updated periodically to reflect the current state of security threats to the network. Some organizations review their security plans yearly, others more frequently, depending on their requirements for security.

Note that there may be groups within a network that have different security needs. As a result, the security architecture may have different levels of security. This equates to the security perimeters or zones introduced in the previous chapter. How security zones are established is discussed later in this chapter.

Once you have determined which problems will be solved by each security mechanism, you should then determine if these security mechanisms are sufficient for that network. Will they completely solve the customer's problems, or are they only a partial solution? If they are a partial solution, are there other mechanisms that are available, or will be available within your project time frame? You may plan to implement basic security mechanisms early in the project, and upgrade or add to those mechanisms at various stages in the project.

3.4 SECURITY AND PRIVACY ADMINISTRATION

The preparation and ongoing administration of security and privacy in the network are quite important to the overall success of the security architecture. Like the requirements and flows analyses, understanding what your threats are and how you are going to protect against them is an important first step in developing security for your network. In this section we discuss two important components in preparing for security: threat analysis and policies and procedures.

3.4.1 Threat Analysis

A *threat analysis* is a process used to determine which components of the system need to be protected and the types of security risks (threats) they should be protected from (Figure 3.1). This information can be used to determine strategic locations in the network architecture and design where security can reasonably and effectively be implemented.

A threat analysis typically consists of identifying the assets to be protected, as well as identifying and evaluating possible threats. Assets may include, but are not restricted to:

- User hardware (workstations/PCs)
- Servers
- Specialized devices
- Network devices (hubs, switches, routers, OAM&P)
- Software (OS, utilities, client programs)
- Services (applications, IP services)
- Data (local/remote, stored, archived, databases, data in-transit)

And threats may include, but are not restricted to:

- Unauthorized access to data/services/software/hardware
- Unauthorized disclosure of information

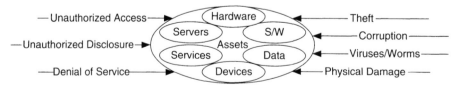

FIGURE 3.1

Potential assets and threats to be analyzed.

- Denial of service
- Theft of data/services/software/hardware
- Corruption of data/services/software/hardware
- Viruses, worms, Trojan horses
- Physical damage

One method to gather data about security and privacy for your environment is to list the threats and assets on a worksheet. This threat analysis worksheet can then be distributed to users, administration, and management, even as part of the requirements analysis process, to gather information about potential security problems.

An example of such a worksheet is presented in Figure 3.2. The results shown in this worksheet were determined during the requirements analysis process and are specific to a particular organization. Depending on the organization, the results of a threat analysis can be quite different from those shown in Figure 3.2. For example, a threat analysis can consist of the information and assets that need to be protected, in terms of confidentiality, integrity, and availability. This analysis can be combined with lists of threats that are currently out there, as well as potential vulnerabilities.

Threat analyses are by their nature subjective. One of the ways to minimize the degree of subjectivity is to involve representatives from various groups of the organization to participate in the analysis process. This helps to get many different

Effect/ Likelihood	User Hardware	Servers	Network Devices	Software	Services	Data
Unauthorized Access	B/A	B/B	C/B	A/B	B/C	A/B
Unauthorized Disclosure	B/C	B/B	C/C	A/B	B/C	A/B
Denial of Service	B/B	B/B	B/B	B/B	B/B	D/D
Theft	A/D	B/D	B/D	A/B	C/C	A/B
Corruption	A/C	B/C	C/C	A/B	D/D	A/B
Viruses	B/B	B/B	B/B	B/B	B/C	D/D
Physical Damage	A/D	B/C	C/C	D/D	D/D	D/D

Effect: Likelihood:
A: Destructive B: Disabling   A: Certain B: Likely
C: Disruptive   D: No Impact   C: Unlikely D: Impossible

FIGURE 3.2

An example of a threat analysis worksheet for a specific organization.

perspectives into the analysis. It is also recommended that you review your threat analysis periodically, such as annually, to identify changes in your environment. As an organization grows and changes, and as the outside world changes, the degrees and types of threats to that organization will also change. A periodic threat analysis ensures that new threats are included and shows where new security mechanisms may be applied to the network. Along with this, a periodic review of security policies and procedures is also recommended. Subsequent reviews may highlight previously overlooked areas in the network, system, and environment.

3.4.2 Policies and Procedures

There are many trade-offs in security and privacy (as with all other architectural components), and it can be a two-edged sword. Sometimes security is confused with control over users and their actions. This confusion occurs when rules, regulations, and security guardians are placed above the goals and work that the organization is trying to accomplish. The road toward implementing security starts with an awareness and understanding of the possible security weaknesses in the network and then leads to the removal of these weaknesses. Weaknesses can generally be found in the areas of system and application software, the ways that security mechanisms are implemented, and in how users do their work. This last area is where educating users can be most beneficial.

Security policies and procedures are formal statements on rules for system, network, and information access and use, in order to minimize exposure to security threats. They define and document how the system can be used with minimal security risk. Importantly, they can also clarify *to users* what the security threats are, what can be done to reduce such risks, and the consequences of not helping to reduce them.

At a high level, security policies and procedures can present an organization's overall security philosophy. Examples of common high-level security philosophies are to deny specifics and accept everything else, or to accept specifics and deny everything else, as in Figure 3.3. The term *specific* refers to well-defined rules about

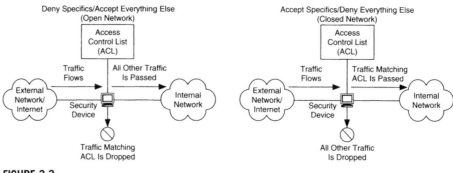

FIGURE 3.3

Example of security philosophies.

who, what, and where security is applied. For example, it may be a list of specific routes that can be accepted into this network, or users that are permitted access to certain resources.

Security that denies specifics and accepts all else reflects an open network philosophy, requiring a thorough understanding of potential security threats, as these should be the specifics to be denied. It can be difficult to verify the security implementation for this philosophy, as it is hard to define "all else."

On the other hand, security that accepts specifics and denies all else reflects a closed network philosophy, requiring a thorough understanding of user, application, device, and network requirements, as these will become the specifics to be accepted. It is easier to validate this security implementation, as there is a finite (relatively small) set of "accepted" uses. Of the two philosophies, accept specifics/ deny all else is the more common philosophy.

When you develop security policies and procedures, remember that, in order for them to be useful, they should be straightforward to implement for your environment (keeping in mind who will be supporting them), enforceable, and have clearly defined areas of responsibility.

Policies and procedures should include:

- Privacy statements (monitoring, logging, and access)
- Accountability statements (responsibilities, auditing)
- Authentication statements (password policies, remote access)
- Reporting violations (contact information, procedures)

Examples of security policies and procedures are acceptable use statements, security incident-handling procedures, configuration-modification policies, and network access control lists (ACLs). Each of these has a place in the security and privacy plan. These policies and procedures should describe not only how network resources can be accessed, used, and modified, but also why, to help users understand the policies they are being asked to accept and work with. Incident-handling procedures can be particularly helpful in making users aware of what to do when a security problem arises, bringing them into the security process rather than just subjecting them to it.

The list of areas for policies and procedures shown below can be used as a starting point to apply to the security architecture:

User Access to the System

- Authorization of use
- Authentication of identity and use of passwords
- Training and acceptance of responsibility for compliance
- Notices that corporate equipment is not private property
- Expectations of the right to privacy

Administrator Skills and Requirements for Certification

- Superusers as well as administrators

System Configuration and Management

- Maintenance
- Virus/Trojan protection
- Patching operating systems and applications
- Monitoring CERT advisories for notices of hacks
- Overseeing who can and cannot connect devices to the network
- Managing notice screens during login or startup
- Establishing what data get backed up
- Establishing what data get saved off-site
- Developing contingency computing plans
- Determining what to do when the system is attacked

3.5 SECURITY AND PRIVACY MECHANISMS

There are several security mechanisms available today and many more on the horizon. However, not all mechanisms are appropriate for every environment. Each security mechanism should be evaluated for the network it is being applied to, based on the degree of protection it provides, its impact on users' ability to do work, the amount of expertise required for installation and configuration, the cost of purchasing, implementing, and operating it, and the amounts of administration and maintenance required.

In this section we cover physical security and awareness, protocol and application security, encryption/decryption, network perimeter security, and remote access security.

3.5.1 Physical Security and Awareness

Physical security is the protection of devices from physical access, damage, and theft. Devices are usually network and system hardware, such as network devices (routers, switches, hubs, etc.), servers, and specialized devices, but can also be software CDs, tapes, or peripheral devices. Physical security is the most basic form of security, and the one that is most intuitive to users. Nevertheless, it is often overlooked when developing a security plan. Physical security should be addressed as part of the network architecture even when the campus or building has access restrictions or security guards.

Ways to implement physical security include the following (see Figure 3.4):

- Access-controlled rooms (e.g., via card keys) for shared devices (servers) and specialized devices
- Backup power sources and power conditioning
- Off-site storage and archival
- Alarm systems (e.g., fire and illegal entry alarms)

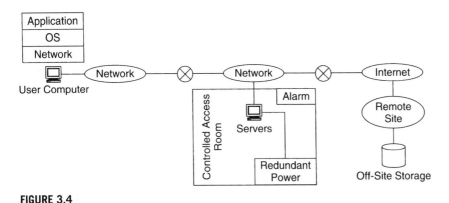

FIGURE 3.4

Areas of physical security.

Physical security also applies to other types of physical threats, such as natural disasters (e.g., fires, earthquakes, and storms). Security from natural disasters includes protection from fire (using alarm systems and fire-abatement equipment), water (with pumping and other water-removal/protection mechanisms), and structural degradation (through having devices in racks attached to floors, walls, etc.). Addressing physical security lays the foundation for your entire network security and privacy plan.

Security awareness entails getting users educated and involved with the day-to-day aspects of security in their network, and helping them to understand the potential risks of violating security policies and procedures. Security awareness can be promoted through providing sessions on security, where users have a chance to discuss the issues and voice their opinions and problems with security mechanisms, policies, and procedures, and potentially offer options for security and privacy; by providing users with bulletins or newsletters (or adding information to the organization's newsletter) on network security and what users can do to help; and by providing users with information on the latest security attacks.

3.5.2 Protocol and Application Security

In this section we consider some common protocol and application security mechanisms: IPSec, SNMP, and packet filtering.

IPSec is a protocol for providing authentication and encryption/decryption between devices at the network layer. IPSec mechanisms consist of authentication header (AH) and encapsulating security payload (ESP). There are two modes that IPSec operates in: transport and tunneling. In transport mode the IP payload is encrypted using ESP, while the IP header is left in the clear, as shown in Figure 3.5.

In tunnel mode (Figure 3.6) IPSec can be used to encapsulate packets between two virtual private network (VPN) gateways (IP$_b$ and IP$_c$ in the figure).

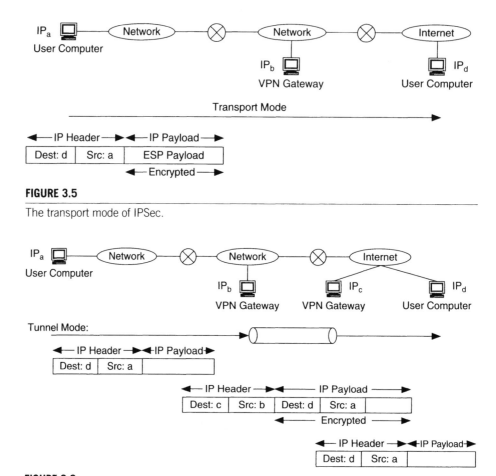

FIGURE 3.5

The transport mode of IPSec.

FIGURE 3.6

The tunnel mode of IPSec.

The tunneling process consists of the following:

- IPSec tunnels are created between VPN gateways IP_b and IP_c in Figure 3.6
- IP packets are encrypted using ESP
- These packets are then encapsulated within another IP packet, and addressed with the ends of the IPSec tunnel (IP_b and IP_c)
- At the end of the tunnel (the VPN gateway serving IP_d), the original packet is unencapsulated and decrypted and sent to its destination (IP_d).

This is an example of *tunneling*, or encapsulating information within protocol headers for the purpose of isolating and protecting that information. Note that this is different from traditional protocol encapsulation, which is used to support varying functions at each protocol layer. Virtual private networks apply this tunneling concept to create multiple isolated networks across a common infrastructure.

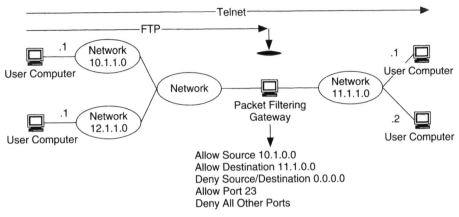

FIGURE 3.7

An example of packet filtering.

Tunneling and VPNs are common methods for building an isolated network across a common infrastructure such as the Internet.

Security for the Simple Network Management Protocol version 3 (SNMPv3) is described in the user-based security model (USM), protecting against modification of information, masquerades, disclosure (eavesdropping), and message stream modification. SNMP Security provides the following security capabilities:

- SNMP message verification (data integrity), user identity verification (data origin authentication), and data confidentiality (via *authProtocol*, *authKey*, *privProtocol*, and *privKey*)

- Detects SNMP messages that have exceeded time thresholds (message timeliness/limited replay) (via *snmpEngineID*, *snmpEngineBoots*, and *snmpEngineTime*)

SNMP security also includes authentication mechanisms *(authProtocol)* and encryption/decryption mechanisms *(privProtocol):*

- HMAC-MD5-96 (128-bit message digest algorithm (MD5) cryptographic hash-function, message authentication codes (HMAC) mode, truncated to 96 bits)

- HMAC-SHA-96 (Secure Hash Algorithm)

- CBC-DES (Cipher Block Chaining Mode Symmetric Encryption/Decryption protocol

SNMP security also provides for modifying MIB views and access modes. For example, it is possible to have different MIB views definable for different groups, and access modes (RO, RW) are also definable for different groups, and are tied to MIB views.

Packet filtering is a mechanism in network devices to explicitly deny or pass packets at strategic points within the network. It is often used to deny packets to or from particular IP addresses or ports (services), as in Figure 3.7.

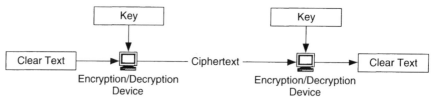

FIGURE 3.8

Encryption/decryption of network traffic.

3.5.3 Encryption/Decryption

While other security mechanisms provide protection against unauthorized access and destruction of resources and information, encryption/decryption protects information from being usable by the attacker. *Encryption/decryption* is a security mechanism where cipher algorithms are applied together with a secret key to encrypt data so that they are unreadable if they are intercepted. Data are then decrypted at or near their destination. This is shown in Figure 3.8.

As such, encryption/decryption enhances other forms of security by protecting information in case other mechanisms fail to keep unauthorized users from that information. There are two common types of encryption/decryption: public key and private key. Software implementations of public key encryption/decryption are commonly available. Examples include data encryption standard (DES) private key encryption, triple DES private key encryption, and Rivest, Shamir, and Adleman (RSA) public key encryption.

Public key infrastructure (PKI) is an example of a security infrastructure that uses both public and private keys. *Public key infrastructure* is a security infrastructure that combines security mechanisms, policies, and directives into a system that is targeted for use across unsecured public networks (e.g., the Internet), where information is encrypted through the use of a public and a private cryptographic key pair that is obtained and shared through a trusted authority. PKI is targeted toward legal, commercial, official, and confidential transactions, and includes cryptographic keys and a certificate management system. Components of this system are:

- Managing the generation and distribution of public/private keys
- Publishing public keys with UIDs as certificates in open directories
- Ensuring that specific public keys are truly linked to specific private keys
- Authenticating the holder of a public/private key pair

PKI uses one or more trusted systems known as Certification Authorities (CA), which serve as trusted third parties for PKI. The PKI infrastructure is hierarchical, with issuing authorities, registration authorities, authentication authorities, and local registration authorities.

Another example is the secure sockets library (SSL). *Secure sockets library* is a security mechanism that uses RSA-based authentication to recognize a party's digital identity and uses RC4 to encrypt and decrypt the accompanying transaction or communication. SSL has grown to become one of the leading security protocols on the Internet.

One trade-off with encryption/decryption is a reduction in network performance. Depending on the type of encryption/decryption and where it is implemented in the network, network performance (in terms of capacity and delay) can be degraded from 15% to 85% or more. Encryption/decryption usually also requires administration and maintenance, and some encryption/decryption equipment can be expensive. While this mechanism is compatible with other security mechanisms, trade-offs such as these should be considered when evaluating encryption/decryption.

3.5.4 Network Perimeter Security

For network perimeter security, or protecting the *external interfaces* between your network and external networks, we consider the use of address translation mechanisms and firewalls.

Network address translation, or NAT, is the mapping of IP addresses from one realm to another. Typically this is between public and private IP address space. Private IP address space is the set of IETF-defined private address spaces (RFC 1918):

- Class A 10.x.x.x 10/8 prefix
- Class B 172.16.x.x 172.16/12 prefix
- Class C 192.168.x.x 192.168/16 prefix

NAT is used to create bindings between addresses, such as one-to-one address binding (static NAT); one-to-many address binding (dynamic NAT); and address and port bindings (network address port translation, or NAPT).

While NAT was developed to address the issues of address space exhaustion, it was quickly adopted as a mechanism to enhance security at external interfaces. Routes to private IP address spaces are not propagated within the Internet; therefore, the use of private IP addresses hides the internal addressing structure of a network from the outside.

The security architecture should consider a combination of static and dynamic NAT and NAPT, based on the devices that are being protected. For example, static NAT is often used for bindings to multiple-user devices such as servers or high-end computing devices, while dynamic NAT is used with generic computing devices.

Firewalls are combinations of one or more security mechanisms, implemented in network devices (routers) placed at strategic locations within a network. Firewalls can be filtering gateways, application proxies with filtering gateways, or devices running specialized "firewall" software.

3.5.5 Remote Access Security

Remote access consists of traditional dial-in, point-to-point sessions, and virtual private network connections, as shown in Figure 3.9. Security for remote access

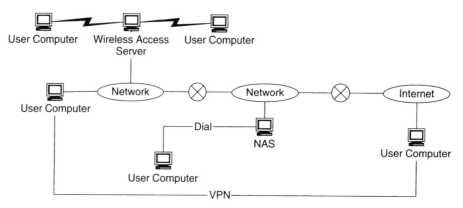

FIGURE 3.9

Remote access mechanisms.

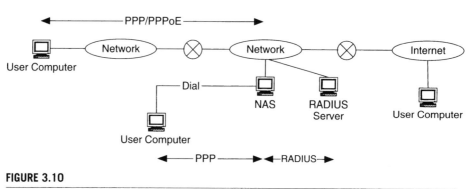

FIGURE 3.10

Remote access considerations.

includes what is commonly known as AAAA: authentication of users; authorization of resources to authenticated users; accounting of resources and service delivery; and allocation of configuration information (e.g., addresses or default route). AAAA is usually supported by a network device such as a network access server (NAS) or subscriber management system (SMS).

Remote access security is common in service-provider networks (see also the service-provider architectural model), but it is evolving into enterprise networks as enterprises recognize the need to support a remote access model for their networks.

Considerations when providing remote access are as follows (see Figure 3.10):

- Method(s) of AAAA
- Server types and placement (e.g., DMZ)
- Interactions with DNS, address pools, and other services

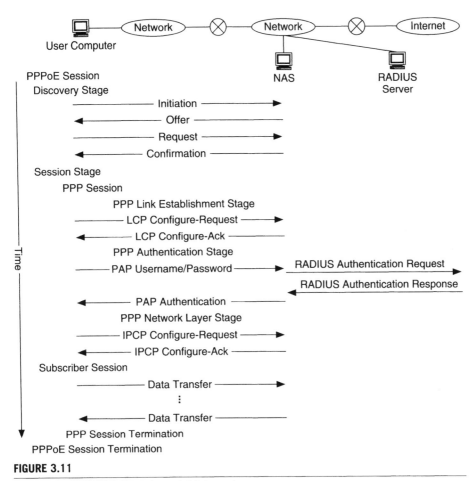

FIGURE 3.11

Process for PPP/PPPoE session establishment.

Figure 3.11 shows the protocol interaction of the point-to-point protocol (PPP), PPP over Ethernet (PPPoE), and remote access dial-in user service (RADIUS) in a remote access network.

This figure shows the process of establishing a PPPoE session, upon which a PPP session is started. PPPoE provides a shim between Ethernet and PPP, supporting the point-to-point nature of PPP sessions over a broadcast Ethernet network. Thus, a PPPoE session starts with a broadcast packet, the PPPoE active discovery initiation (PADI). This packet begins a handshake between the user's computer and NAS, consisting of PADI, PPPoE active discovery offer (PADO), PPPoE active discovery request (PADR), and PPPoE active discovery session (PADS) packets. The PPP session can begin at the completion of this part of the process.

A PPP session has three stages: link establishment, authentication, and network layer. Each stage builds on the previous one to establish the PPP session. Once PPPoE and PPP sessions have been established, the user can begin using the network.

Authentication in a remote access network is typically accomplished via a combination of PPP, PPPoE, PAP, CHAP, and RADIUS protocols. Other authentication mechanisms at the remote access network include tokens, smart cards, digital certificates, and callback. VPNs and tunnels can also be considered as part of the remote access network.

VPNs are an example of what can be considered a subarchitecture. VPNs, by themselves, can require their own set of architectural considerations. This is particularly true when they make an extranet, which is an intranet extended to include access to or from selected external organizations (e.g., customers, suppliers) but not to the general public. Such considerations include equipment types, tunneling protocols and security, VPN locations, policies on VPN provisioning and support, and the use of routing protocols such as the border gateway protocol (BGP) or multi-protocol label switching (MPLS).

Finally, remote access security should also consider wireless communications and portable computing devices using standards such as 802.11 and Homephoneline Networking Alliance (homePNA). Wireless can target a number of environments, such as mobility, portability, and nomadic computing.

3.6 ARCHITECTURAL CONSIDERATIONS

In developing our security architecture we need to evaluate potential security mechanisms, where they may apply within the network, as well as the sets of internal and external relationships for this component architecture.

3.6.1 Evaluation of Security Mechanisms

At this point we have requirements, goals, type of environment, and architectural model(s) and are ready to evaluate potential security mechanisms. As with each component architecture, when evaluating mechanisms for an architecture, it is best to start simple and work toward more complex solutions only when necessary.

Where a security mechanism will apply in a given network depends primarily on where security requirements are located throughout the network, and what the security requirements are, based on the results of the requirements analysis and the security and privacy plan.

Architectural models can help in determining where security mechanisms can be applied in the network. For example, the Access/Distribution/Core architectural model, which separates a network based on function, can be used as a starting point for applying security mechanisms. Using this model, security can be increased at each level, from access network to distribution networks to core

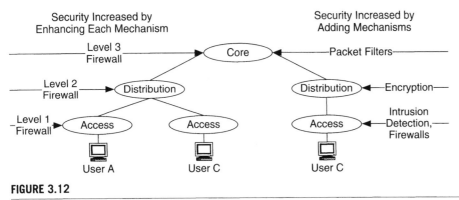

FIGURE 3.12

The Access/Distribution/Core architectural model as a starting point for security.

networks, by either adding security mechanisms or by enhancing the amount of security provided by each mechanism. This is shown in Figure 3.12.

In this figure, security is increased from access to distribution to core areas, either by adding security mechanisms at each area or by increasing the level of security (i.e., enhancing security) at each level. For this architectural model, most traffic flows are sourced/sinked at access networks, and travel across distribution and core networks. By adding mechanisms or enhancing mechanisms at each level, a traffic flow will encounter higher levels of security as it moves from access to distribution to core networks.

In Figure 3.12 traffic flows from User A to User C travel across both access and distribution networks and would encounter two levels of security: Level 1 and Level 2 firewalls, where Level 2 is greater security than Level 1. A Level 2 firewall may have a more complete access control list (ACL), stricter rules for filtering traffic, or greater logging and detection capability.

Traffic flows from User C to User A travel across access, distribution, and core networks. As traffic moves from User C to the core network, it would encounter multiple security mechanisms (intrusion detection, firewalls, encryption/decryption, and packet filters), with security increasing from access to distribution to core. In addition, as traffic moves from the core network to User A, it encounters three levels of firewalls.

In a similar fashion, the service provider and intranet/extranet architectural models can also be used to develop a framework for security in a network.

Security perimeters (i.e., security zones or cells) can be developed within a network, to accommodate multiple levels of security requirements. Two common methods of developing security zones are to increase security as you move deeper into the network (an example of this is shown in Figure 3.12), or to develop zones wherever they are needed in the network, regardless of topology.

When security zones are developed to increase security as you move deeper into a network, they become embedded within each other, as shown in Figure 3.13.

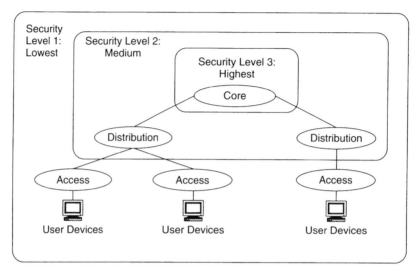

FIGURE 3.13

Security zones embedded within each other.

In a sense the security levels look like the layers of an onion, with the innermost layers having the highest level of security.

Security zones are based on the various security requirements determined during the requirements analysis process and should be described in the security and privacy plan. There may be requirements for different levels of security, coupled to groups of users, their applications, their devices, or devices that are shared among users. Security zones developed to meet such requirements may be scattered throughout the network and may even overlap one another. An example of this is presented in Figure 3.14.

In this figure five security zones are shown, based on different security requirements. The first zone (Security Level 1) covers the entire network and is intended to provide a general level of security for all users, applications, and devices. This may include intrusion detection and logging. The second zone (Security Level 2) provides a higher level of security between this network and all external networks. This may include NAT and firewalls.

The third zone (Security Level 3) provides another level of security for an entire group of users, applications, and/or devices (Group D), whose security requirements are different from the rest of the network. For example, this group may handle financial and/or proprietary information for the company. The fourth zone (Security Level 4) provides security for a subset of users, applications, and/or devices from multiple groups (Groups A and B). These are select users, applications, and/or devices whose security needs are different from others in their groups. For example, they may be working on company-classified projects, producing data that need to be protected from the rest of the groups. The third and fourth zones may apply mechanisms to

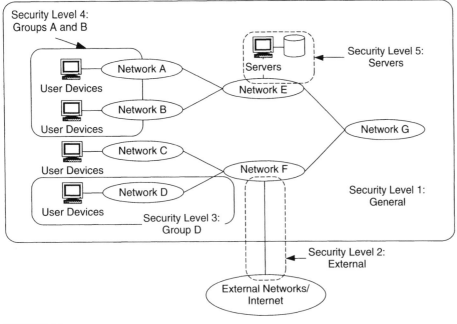

FIGURE 3.14

Developing security zones throughout a network.

protect their data, such as encryption/decryption, and may have access protection via firewalls and/or packet filtering. The fifth zone (Security Level 5) is security for devices used by multiple users, such as servers. This zone may employ monitoring, logging, and authentication to verify user access.

Figures 3.12, 3.13, and 3.14 show how security mechanisms may be applied in a network to achieve multiple security levels or zones.

3.6.2 Internal Relationships

Interactions within the security architecture include trade-offs, dependencies, and constraints among each of the security mechanisms for your network. For example, some security mechanisms require the ability to look at, add to, or modify various information fields within the packet. NAT changes IP address information between public and private address domains. Encryption/decryption mechanisms may encrypt information fields, making them unreadable to other mechanisms.

3.6.3 External Relationships

External relationships are trade-offs, dependencies, and constraints between the security architecture and each of the other component architectures (addressing/

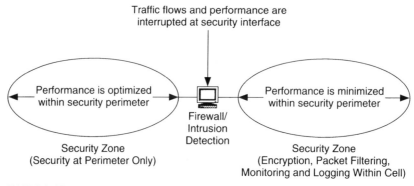

FIGURE 3.15

Security mechanisms may restrict or preclude performance within each zone.

routing, network management, performance, and any other component architectures you may develop). There are some common ones, some of which are presented below.

Interactions between security and addressing/routing. NAT is an addressing mechanism that is often used to enhance security. Therefore, when it is applied for security, it also impacts addressing for the network. In addition, dynamic addressing can interfere with address-specific protective measures and with logging. It is more difficult to determine what is going on when IP addresses are changed frequently.

Interactions between security and network management. Security depends on network management to configure, monitor, manage, and verify security levels throughout the network. In addition, there is a need for maintenance access even during attacks where in-band access to network devices is not available. For example, when devices are not at the same location, using dial-up for out-of-band access is a potential fall-back position to take.

Interactions between security and performance. Security and performance are often at odds, as security mechanisms can impact network performance. The security zones described earlier in this chapter can constrain performance within the areas described by the zones. When security is a high priority, security mechanisms that impact traffic flows may restrict performance mechanisms to operate within security zones, or result in performance being minimized for that zone (Figure 3.15).

When performance is high priority, particularly when there is a need to provision end-to-end performance among select users, applications, or devices, performance mechanisms may preclude the use of intrusive security mechanisms in those areas of the network.

3.7 **CONCLUSION**

In this chapter we discussed various potential security mechanisms for your security architecture, including physical security, protocol and application security, encryption/decryption, and perimeter and remote access security. Based on information from the requirements analysis, we developed input for a security and privacy plan. We also discussed elements of both internal and external relationships for the security architecture.

Network Security Algorithms

From denial-of-service to Smurf attacks, hackers that perpetrate exploits have captured both the imagination of the public and the ire of victims. There is some reason for indignation and ire. A survey by the Computer Security Institute placed the cost of computer intrusions at an average of $970,000 per company in 2000.

Thus there is a growing market for *intrusion detection*, a field that consists of detecting and reacting to attacks. According to IDC, the intrusion-detection market grew from $20 million to $100 million between 1997 and 1999 and is expected to reach $518 million by 2005.

Yet the capabilities of current intrusion detection systems are widely accepted as inadequate, particularly in the context of growing threats and capabilities. Two key problems with current systems are that they are slow and that they have a high false-positive rate. As a result of these deficiencies, intrusion detection serves primarily as a monitoring and audit function rather than as a real-time component of a protection architecture on par with firewalls and encryption.

However, many vendors are working to introduce *real-time* intrusion detection systems. If intrusion detection systems can work in real time with only a small fraction of false positives, they can actually be used to *respond* to attacks by either deflecting the attack or tracing the perpetrators.

Intrusion detection systems (IDSs) have been studied in many forms since Denning's classic statistical analysis of host intrusions. Today, IDS techniques are usually classified as either *signature detection* or *anomaly detection*. Signature detection is based on matching events to the signatures of known attacks.

In contrast, anomaly detection, based on statistical or learning theory techniques, identifies aberrant events, whether known to be malicious or not. As a result, anomaly detection can potentially detect new types of attacks that signature-based systems will miss. Unfortunately, anomaly detection systems are prone to falsely identifying events as malicious. Thus this chapter does *not* address anomaly-based methods.

Meanwhile signature-based systems are highly popular due to their relatively simple implementation and their ability to detect commonly used attack tools.

The lightweight detection system Snort is one of the more popular examples because of its free availability and efficiency.

Given the growing importance of real-time intrusion detection, intrusion detection furnishes a rich source of packet patterns that can benefit from network algorithmics. Thus this chapter samples three important subtasks that arise in the context of intrusion detection. The first is an *analysis* subtask, string matching, which is a key bottleneck in popular signature-based systems such as Snort. The second is a *response* subtask, traceback, which is of growing importance given the ability of intruders to use forged source addresses. The third is an *analysis* subtask to detect the onset of a new worm (e.g., Code Red) without prior knowledge.

These three subtasks only scratch the surface of a vast area that needs to be explored. They were chosen to provide an indication of the richness of the problem space and to outline some potentially powerful tools, such as Bloom filters and Aho–Corasick trees, that may be useful in more general contexts. Worm detection was also chosen to showcase how mechanisms can be combined in powerful ways.

This chapter is organized as follows. The first few sections explore solutions to the important problem of searching for suspicious strings in packet payloads. Current implementations of intrusion detection systems such as Snort (www.snort .org) do multiple passes through the packet to search for each string. Section 4.1.1 describes the Aho–Corasick algorithm for searching for multiple strings in one pass using a trie with backpointers. Section 4.1.2 describes a generalization of the classical Boyer–Moore algorithm, which can sometimes act faster by skipping more bits in a packet.

Section 4.2 shows how to approach an even harder problem—searching for *approximate* string matches. The section introduces two powerful ideas: minwise hashing and random projections. This section suggests that even complex tasks such as approximate string matching can plausibly be implemented at wire speeds.

Section 4.3 marks a transition to the problem of responding to an attack, by introducing the IP traceback problem. It also presents a seminal solution using probabilistic packet marking. Section 4.4 offers a second solution, which uses packet logs and no packet modifications; the logs are implemented efficiently using an important technique called a *Bloom filter*. While these traceback solutions are unlikely to become deployed when compared to more recent standards, they introduce a significant problem and invoke important techniques that could be useful in other contexts.

Section 4.5 explains how algorithmic techniques can be used to extract automatically the strings used by intrusion detection systems such as Snort. In other words, instead of having these strings be installed manually by security analysts, could a system automatically extract the suspicious strings? We ground the discussion in the context of detecting worm attack payloads.

The implementation techniques for security primitives described in this chapter (and the corresponding principles) are summarized in Figure 4.1.

Number	Principle	Used In
P15	Integrated string matching using Aho–Corasick	Snort
P3a, 5a	Approximate string match using min-wise hashing	Altavista
P3a	Path reconstruction using probabilistic marking	Edge sampling
P3a	Efficient packet logging via Bloom filters	SPIE
P3a	Worm detection by detecting frequent content	EarlyBird

FIGURE 4.1

Principles used in the implementation of the various security primitives discussed in this chapter.

Quick Reference Guide

Sections 4.1.1 and 4.1.2 show how to speed up searching for *multiple* strings in packet payloads, a fundamental operation for a signature-based IDS. The Aho–Corasick algorithm of Section 4.1.1 can easily be implemented in hardware. While the traceback ideas in Section 4.4 are unlikely to be useful in the near future, the section introduces an important data structure, called a Bloom filter, for representing sets and also describes a hardware implementation. Bloom filters have found a variety of uses and should be part of the implementor's bag of tricks. Section 4.5 explains how signatures for attacks can be *automatically* computed, reducing the delay and difficulty required to have humans generate signatures.

4.1 SEARCHING FOR MULTIPLE STRINGS IN PACKET PAYLOADS

The first few sections tackle a problem of detecting an attack by searching for suspicious strings in payloads. A large number of attacks can be detected by their use of such strings. For example, packets that attempt to execute the Perl interpreter have *perl.exe* in their payload. For example, the arachNIDS database of vulnerabilities contains the following description.

An attempt was made to execute perl.exe. If the Perl interpreter is available to Web clients, it can be used to execute arbitrary commands on the Web server. This can be used to break into the server, obtain sensitive information, and potentially compromise the availability of the Web server and the machine it runs on. Many Web server administrators inadvertently place copies of the Perl interpreter into their Web server script directories. If perl is executable from the cgi directory, then an attacker can execute arbitrary commands on the Web server.

This observation has led to a commonly used technique to detect attacks in so-called signature-based intrusion detection systems such as Snort. The idea is that a router or monitor has a set of rules, much like classifiers. However, the Snort rules go beyond classifiers by allowing a 5-tuple rule specifying the type of packet (e.g., port number equal to Web traffic) plus an arbitrary string that can appear anywhere in the packet payload.

Thus the Snort rule for the attempt to execute perl.exe will specify the protocol (TCP) and destination port (80 for Web) as well as the string "perl.exe" occurring anywhere in the payload. If a packet matches this rule, an alert is generated. Snort has 300 such augmented rules, with 300 possible strings to search for.

Early versions of Snort do string search by matching each packet against each Snort rule in turn. For each rule that matches in the classifier part, Snort runs a Boyer–Moore search on the corresponding string, potentially doing several string searches per packet. Since each scan through a packet is expensive, a natural question is: Can one search for all possible strings in one pass through packet?

There are two algorithms that can be used for this purpose: the Aho–Corasick algorithm and a modified algorithm due to Commentz-Walter, which we describe next.

4.1.1 Integrated String Matching Using Aho–Corasick

A trie can be used to search for a string that starts at a known position in a packet. Thus Figure 4.2 contains a trie built on the set of two strings "babar" and "barney"; both are well-known characters in children's literature. The trie is built on characters and not on arbitrary groups of bits. The characters in the text to be searched are used to follow pointers through the trie until a leaf string is found or until failure occurs.

The hard part, however, is looking for strings that can start anywhere in a packet payload. The naivest approach would be to assume the string starts at byte 1 of the payload and then traverses the trie. Then if a failure occurs, one could start again at the top of the trie with the character that starts at byte 2.

However, if packet bytes form several "near misses" with target strings, then for each possible starting position, the search can traverse close to the height of the trie. Thus if the payload has L bytes and the trie has maximum height h, the algorithm can take $L \cdot h$ memory references.

For example, when searching for "babar" in the packet payload shown in Figure 4.2, the algorithm jogs merrily down the trie until it reaches the node corresponding to the second "a" in "babar." At that point the next packet byte is a "b" and not the "r" required to make progress in the trie. The naive approach would be to back up to the start of the trie and start the trie search again from the second byte "a" in the packet.

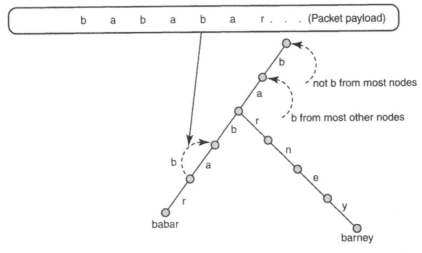

FIGURE 4.2

The Aho–Corasick algorithm builds an alphabetical trie on the set of strings to be searched for. A search for the string "barney" can be found by following the "b" pointer at the root, the "a" pointer at the next node, etc. More interestingly, the trie is augmented with failure pointers that prevent restarting at the top of the trie when failure occurs and a new attempt is made to match, shifted one position to the right.

However, it is not hard to see that backing up to the top is an obvious waste (**P1**) because the packet bytes examined so far in the search for "babab" have "bab" as a suffix, which is a prefix of "babar." Thus, rather than back up to the top, one can precompute (much as in a grid of tries) a failure pointer corresponding to the failing "b" that allows the search to go directly to the node corresponding to path "bab" in the trie, as shown by the leftmost dotted arc in Figure 4.2.

Thus rather than have the fifth byte (a "b") lead to a null pointer, as it would in a normal trie, it contains a failure pointer that points back up the trie. Search now proceeds directly from this node using the sixth byte "a" (as opposed to the second byte) and leads after seven bytes to "babar."

Search is easy to do in hardware after the trie is precomputed. This is not hard to believe because the trie with failure pointers essentially forms a state machine. The Aho-Corasick algorithm has some complexity that ensues when one of the search strings, R, is a suffix of another search string, S. However, in the security context this can be avoided by relaxing the specification (**P3**). One can remove string S from the trie and later check whether the packet matched R or S.

Another concern is the potentially large number of pointers (256) in the Aho-Corasick trie. This can make it difficult to fit a trie for a large set of strings in cache (in software) or in SRAM (in hardware). One alternative is to use, say, Lulea-style encoding to compress the trie nodes.

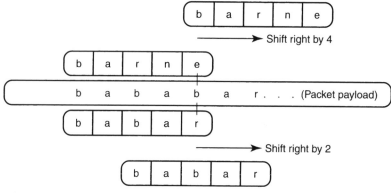

FIGURE 4.3

Integrated Boyer–Moore by shifting a character.

4.1.2 Integrated String Matching Using Boyer–Moore

The famous Boyer-Moore algorithm for *single*-string matching can be derived by realizing that there is an interesting degree of freedom that can be exploited (**P13**) in string matching: One can equally well start comparing the text and the target string from the last character as from the first.

Thus in Figure 4.3 the search starts with the fifth character of the packet, a "b," and matches it to the fifth character of, say, "babar" (shown below the packet), an "r." When this fails, one of the heuristics in the Boyer-Moore algorithm is to shift the search template of "babar" two characters to the right to match the rightmost occurrence of "b" in the template.[1] Boyer-Moore's claim to fame is that in practice it skips over a large number of characters, unlike, say, the Aho–Corasick algorithm.

To generalize Boyer-Moore to multiple strings, imagine that the algorithm concurrently compares the fifth character in the packet to the fifth character, "e," in the other string, "barney" (shown above the packet). If one were only doing Boyer-Moore with "barney," the "barney" search template would be shifted right by four characters to match the only "b" in barney.

When doing a search for both "barney" and "babar" concurrently, the obvious idea is to shift the search template by the smallest shift proposed by any string being compared for. Thus in this example, we shift the template by two characters and do a comparison next with the seventh character in the packet.

Doing a concurrent comparison with the last character in all the search strings may seem inefficient. This can be taken care of as follows. First, chop off all characters in all search strings beyond L, the shortest search string. Thus in Figure 4.3, L is 5 and "barney" is chopped down to "barne" to align in length with "babar."

---

[1]There is a second heuristic in Boyer-Moore, but studies have shown that this simple Horspool variation works best in practice.

Having aligned all search string fragments to the same length, now build a trie starting *backwards* from the last character in the chopped strings. Thus, in the example of Figure 4.3 the root node of the trie would have an "e" pointer pointing toward "barne" and an "r" pointer pointing towards "babar." Thus comparing concurrently requires using only the current packet character to index into the trie node.

On success, the backwards trie keeps being traversed. On failure, the amount to be shifted is precomputed in the failure pointer. Finally, even if a backward search through the trie navigates successfully to a leaf, the fact that the ends may have been chopped off requires an epilogue, in terms of checking that the chopped-off characters also match. For reasonably small sets of strings, this method does better than Aho-Corasick.

The generalized Boyer-Moore was proposed by Commentz-Walter. The application to intrusion detection was proposed concurrently by Coit, Staniford, and McAlerney and Fisk and Varghese. The Fisk implementation has been ported to Snort.

Unfortunately, the performance improvement of using either Aho-Corasick or the integrated Boyer-Moore is minimal, because many real traces have only a few packets that match a large number of strings, enabling the naive method to do well. In fact, the new algorithms add somewhat more overhead due to slightly increased code complexity, which can exhibit cache effects.

While the code as it currently stands needs further improvement, it is clear that at least the Aho-Corasick version does produce a large improvement for *worst-case* traces, which may be crucial for a hardware implementation. The use of Aho-Corasick and integrated Boyer-Moore can be considered straightforward applications of efficient data structures (**P15**).

4.2 **APPROXIMATE STRING MATCHING**

This section briefly considers an even harder problem, that of approximately detecting strings in payloads. Thus instead of settling for an exact match or a prefix match, the specification now allows a few errors in the match. For example, with one insertion "perl.exe" should match "perl.exe" where the intruder may have added a character.

While the security implications of using the mechanisms described next need much more thought, the mechanisms themselves are powerful and should be part of the arsenal of designers of detection mechanisms.

The first simple idea can handle substitution errors. A *substitution error* is a replacement of one or more characters with others. For example, "parl.exe" can be obtained from "perl.exe" by substituting "a" for "e." One way to handle this is to search not for the complete string but for one or more random projections of the original string.

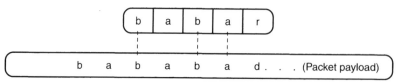

FIGURE 4.4

Checking for matching with a random projection of the target string "babar" allows the detecting of similar strings with substitution errors in the payload.

For example, in Figure 4.4, instead of searching for "babar" one could search for the first, third, and fourth characters in "babar." Thus the misspelled string "babad" will still be found. Of course, this particular projection will not find a misspelled string such as "rabad." To make it hard for an adversary, the scheme in general can use a small set of such random projections. This simple idea is generalized greatly in a set of papers on *locality-preserving hashing*.

Interestingly, the use of random projections may make it hard to efficiently shift one character to the right. One alternative is to replace the random projections by deterministic projections. For example, if one replaces every string by its two halves and places each half in an Aho–Corasick trie, then any one substitution error will be caught without slowing down the Aho–Corasick processing. However, the final efficiency will depend on the number of false alarms.

The simplest random projection idea, described earlier, does not work with insertions or deletions that can displace every character one or more steps to the left or right. One simple and powerful way of detecting whether two or more sets of characters, say, "abcef" and "abfecd," are similar is by computing their *resemblance*.

The resemblance of two sets of characters is the ratio of the size of their intersection to the size of their union. Intuitively, the higher the resemblance, the higher the similarity. By this definition, the resemblance of "abcef" and "abfecd" is 5/6 because they have five characters in common.

Unfortunately, resemblance per se does not take into account order, so "abcef" completely resembles "fecab." One way to fix this is to rewrite the sets with order numbers attached so that "abcef" becomes "1a2b3c4e5f" while "fecab" now becomes "1f2e3c4a5b." The resemblance, using pairs of characters as set elements instead of characters, is now nil. Another method that captures order in a more relaxed manner is to use shingles by forming the two sets to be compared using as elements all possible substrings of size k of the two sets.

Resemblance is a nice idea, but it also needs a fast implementation. A naive implementation requires sorting both sets, which is expensive and takes large storage. Broder's idea is to quickly compare the two sets by computing a random (**P3a**, trade certainty for time) permutation on two sets. For example, the most practical permutation function on integers of size at most $m - 1$ is to compute $P(X) = ax + b \bmod m$, for random values of a and b and prime values of the modulus m.

For example, consider the two sets of integers $\{1, 3, 5\}$ and $\{1, 7, 3\}$. Using the random permutation $\{3x + 5 \bmod 11\}$, the two sets become permuted to $\{8, 3, 9\}$ and $\{8, 4, 3\}$. Notice that the minimum values of the two randomly permuted sets (i.e., 3) are the same.

Intuitively, it is easy to see that the higher the resemblance of the two sets, the higher the chance that a random permutation of the two sets will have the same minimum. Formally, this is because the two permuted sets will have the same minimum if and only if they contain the same element that gets mapped to the minimum in the permuted set. Since an ideal random permutation makes it equally likely for any element to be the minimum after permutation, the more elements the two sets have in common, the higher the probability that the two minimums match.

More precisely, the probability that two minimums match is equal to the resemblance. Thus one way to compute the resemblance of two sets is to use some number of random permutations (say, 16) and compute all 16 random permutations of the two sets. The fraction of these 16 permutations in which the two minimums match is a good estimate of the resemblance.

This idea was used by Broder to detect the similarity of Web documents. However, it is also quite feasible to implement at high link speeds. The chip must maintain, say, 16 registers to keep the current minimum using each of the 16 random hash functions. When a new character is read, the logic permutes the new character according to each of the 16 functions in parallel. Each of the 16 hash results is compared in parallel with the corresponding register, and the register value is replaced if the new value is smaller.

At the end, the 16 computed minima are compared in parallel against the 16 minima for the target set to compute a bitmap, where a bit is set for positions in which there is equality. Finally, the number of set bits is counted and divided by the size of the bitmap by shifting left by 4 bits. If the resemblance is over some specified threshold, some further processing is done.

Once again, the moral of this section is not that computing the resemblance is the solution to all problems (or in fact to any specific problem at this moment) but that fairly complex functions can be computed in hardware using multiple hash functions, randomization, and parallelism. Such solutions interplay principle **P5** (use parallel memories) and principle **P3a** (use randomization).

4.3 IP TRACEBACK VIA PROBABILISTIC MARKING

This section transitions from the problem of *detecting* an attack to *responding* to an attack. Response could involve a variety of tasks, from determining the source of the attack to stopping the attack by adding some checks at incoming routers.

The next two sections concentrate on *traceback*, an important aspect of response, given the ability of attackers to use forged IP source addresses. To understand the traceback problem it helps first to understand a canonical denial-of-service (DOS) attack that motivates the problem.

In one version of a DOS attack, called *SYN flooding*, wily Harry Hacker wakes up one morning looking for fun and games and decides to attack CNN. To do so he makes his computer fire off a large number of TCP connection requests to the CNN server, each with a different forged source address. The CNN server sends back a response to each request R and places R in a pending connection queue.

Assuming the source addresses do not exist or are not online, there is no response. This effect can be ensured by using random source addresses and by periodically resending connection requests. Eventually the server's pending-connection queue fills up. This denies service to innocent users like you who wish to read CNN news because the server can no longer accept connection requests.

Assume that each such denial-of-service attack has a traffic signature (e.g., too many TCP connection requests) that can be used to detect the onset of an attack. Given that it is difficult to shut off a public server, one way to respond to this attack is to trace such a denial-of service back to the originating source point despite the use of fake source addresses. This is the IP traceback problem.

The first and simplest systems approach (**P3**, relax system requirements) is to finesse the problem completely using help from routers. Observe that when Harry Hacker sitting in an IP subnetwork with prefix S sends a packet with fake source address H, the first router on the path can detect this fact if H does not match S. This would imply that Harry's packet cannot disguise its subnetworks, and offending packets can be traced at least to the right subnetwork.

There are two difficulties with this approach. First, it requires that edge routers do more processing with the source address. Second, it requires trusting edge routers to do this processing, which may be difficult to ensure if Harry Hacker has already compromised his ISP. There is little incentive for a local ISP to slow down performance with extra checks to prevent DOS attacks to a remote ISP.

A second and cruder systems approach is to have managers that detect an attack call their ISP, say, A. ISP A monitors traffic for a while and realizes these packets are coming from prior-hop ISP B, who is then called. B then traces the packets back to the prior-hop provider and so on until the path is traced. This is the solution used currently.

A better solution than *manual* tracing would be *automatic* tracing of the packet back to the source. Assume one can modify routers for now. Then packet tracing can be trivially achieved by having each router in the path of a packet P write its router IP address in sequence into P's header. However, given common route lengths of 10, this would be a large overhead (40 bytes for 10 router IDs), especially for minimum-size acknowledgments. Besides the overhead, there is the problem of modifying IP headers to add fields for path tracing. It may be easier to steal a small number of unused message bits.

This leads to the following problem. Assuming router modifications are possible, find a way to trace the path of an attack by marking as few bits as possible in a packet's header.

For a single-packet attack, this is very difficult in an information theoretic sense. Clearly, it is impossible to construct a path of 10 32-bit router IDs from, say, a 2-byte mark in a packet. One can't make a silk purse from a sow's ear.

However, in the systems context one can optimize the expected case (**P11**), since most interesting attacks consist of hundreds of packets at least. Assuming they are all coming from the same physical source, the victim can shift the path computation over time (**P2**) by making each mark contribute a piece of the path information.

Let's start by assuming a single 32-bit field in a packet that can hold a single router ID. How are the routers on the path to synchronize access to the field so that each router ID gets a chance, over a stream of packets, to place its ID in the field?

A naive solution is shown in Figure 4.5. The basic idea is that each router independently writes its ID into a *single* node ID field in the packet with probability p, possibly overwriting a previous router's ID. Thus in Figure 4.5, the packet already has $R1$ in it and can be overwritten by $R3$ to $R1$ with probability p.

The hope, however, is that over a large sequence of packets from the attacker to the victim, every router ID in the path will get a chance to place its ID without being overwritten. Finally, the victim can sort the received IDs by the number of samples. Intuitively, the nodes closer to the victim should have more samples, but one has to allow for random variation.

The two problems with this naive approach are that too many samples (i.e., attack packets) are needed to deal with random variation in inferring order, and the attacker, knowing this scheme, can place malicious marks in the packet to fool the reconstruction scheme into believing that fictitious nodes are close to the victim because they receive extra marks.

To foil this threat, p must be large, say, 0.51. But in this case, the number of packets required to receive the router IDs far away from the victim becomes very large. For example, with $p = 0.5$ and a path of length $L = 15$, the number of packets required is the reciprocal of the probability that the router farthest from the victim sends a mark that survives. This is $p(1 - p)^{L-1} = 2^{-15}$, because it requires the farthest router to put a mark and the remaining $L - 1$ routers not to. Thus the average number of packets for this to happen is $\frac{1}{2^{-15}} = 32{,}000$. Attacks have a number of packets, but not necessarily this many.

The straightforward lesson from the naive solution is that randomization is good for synchronization (to allow routers to independently synchronize access to the single node ID field) but not to reconstruct order. The simplest solution to this

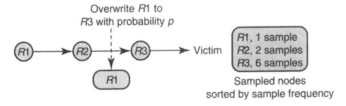

FIGURE 4.5

Reconstructing an attack path by having each router stamp its ID independently, with probability p, into a single node ID field. The receiver reconstructs order by sorting, assuming that closer routers will produce more samples.

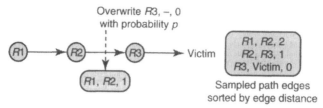

FIGURE 4.6

Edge sampling improves on node sampling by sampling edges and not nodes. This allows trivial order reconstruction based on edge distance and not sample frequency.

problem is to use a hop count (the attacker can initialize each packet with a different TTL, making the TTL hard to use) as well as a node ID. But a hop count by itself can be confusing if there are multiple attacks going on. Clearly a mark of node X with hop count 2 may correspond to a different attack path from a mark of node Y with hop count 1.

The solution provided in the seminal paper avoids the aliasing due to hop counts by conceptually starting with a pair of consecutive node IDs and a hop count to form a triple (R, S, h), as shown in Figure 4.6.

When a router R receives a packet with triple (X, Y, h), R generates a random number between 0 and 1. If the number is less than the sampling probability p, router R writes its own ID into the mark triple, rewriting it as $(R, -, 0)$, where the $-$ character indicates that the next router in the path has still to be determined. If the random number is greater than p, then R must maintain the integrity of the previously written mark. If $h = 0$, R writes R to the second field because R is the next router after the writer of the mark. Finally, if the random number is greater than p, R increments h.

It should be clear that by assuming that every edge gets sampled once, the victim can reconstruct the path. Note also that the attacker can only add fictitious nodes to the start of the path. But how many packets are required to find all edges? Given that ordering is explicit, one can use arbitrary values of p.

In particular, if p is approximately $1/L$, where L is the path length to the farthest router, the probability we computed before of the farthest router sending an edge mark that survives becomes $p(1 - p)^{L-1} \approx p/(1 - p)e$, where e is the base of natural logarithms. For example, for $p = 1/25$, this is roughly $1/70$, which is fairly large compared to the earlier attempt.

What is even nicer is that if we choose $p = 1/50$ based on the largest path lengths encountered in practice on the Internet (say, 50), the probability does not grow much smaller even for much smaller path lengths. This makes it easy to reconstruct the path with hundreds of packets as opposed to thousands.

Finally, one can get rid of obvious waste (**P1**) and avoid the need for two node IDs by storing only the Exclusive-OR of the two fields in a single field. Working backwards from the last router ID known to the victim, one can Exclusive-OR with the previous edge mark to get the next router in the path, and so on. Finally, by viewing each node as consisting of a sequence of a number of "pseudonodes," each with a small fragment (say, 8 bits) of the node's ID, one can reduce the mark length to around 16 bits total.

4.4 IP TRACEBACK VIA LOGGING

A problem with the edge-sampling approach of the previous section is that it requires changes to the IP header to update marks and does not work for single-packet attacks like the Teardrop attack. The following approach, traceback via logging, avoids both problems by adding more storage at routers to maintain a compressed packet log.

As motivations, neither of the difficulties the logging approach gets around are very compelling. This is because the logging approach still requires modifying router forwarding, even though it requires no header modification. This is due to the difficulty of convincing vendors (who have already committed forwarding paths to silicon) and ISPs (who wish to preserve equipment for, say, 5 years) to make changes. Similarly, single-packet attacks are not very common and can often be filtered directly by routers.

However, the idea of maintaining compressed searchable packet logs may be useful as a general building block. It could be used, more generally, for, say, a network monitor that wishes to maintain such logs for forensics after attacks. But even more importantly it introduces an important technique called *Bloom filters*.

Given an efficient packet log at each router, the high-level idea for traceback is shown in Figure 4.7. The victim V first detects an attack packet P; it then queries all its neighboring routers, say, R_8 and R_9, to see whether any of them have P in their log of recently sent packets. When R_9 replies in the affirmative, the search moves on to R_9, who asks its sole neighbor, R_7. Then R_7 asks its neighbors R_5 and R_4, and the search moves backward to A.

The simplest way to implement a log is to reuse one of the techniques in trajectory sampling. Instead of logging a packet we log a 32-bit hash of invariant content (i.e., exclude fields that change from hop to hop, such as the TTL) of the packet. However, 32 bits per packet for all the packets sent in the last 10 minutes is still huge at 10 Gbps. Bloom filters, described next, allow a large reduction to around 5 bits per packet.

4.4.1 Bloom Filters

Start by observing that querying either a packet log or a table of allowed users is a *set membership query*, which is easily implemented by a hash table. For example, in a different security context, if John and Cathy are allowed users and we wish to check if Jonas is an allowed user, we can use a hash table that stores John and Cathy's IDs but not Jonas's.

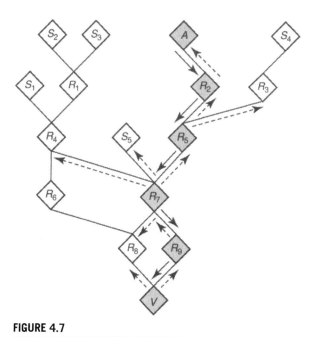

FIGURE 4.7

Using a packet log to trace an attack packet *P* backwards from the victim *V* to the attacker *A* by having the currently traced node ask all its neighbors (the dotted lines) if they have seen *P* (solid line).

Checking for Jonas requires hashing Jonas's ID into the hash table and following any lists at that entry. To handle collisions, each hash table entry must contain a list of IDs of all users that hash into that bucket. This requires at least *W* bits per allowed user, where *W* is the length of each user ID. In general, to implement a hash table for a set of identifiers requires at least *W* bits per identifier, where *W* is the length of the smallest identifier.

Bloom filters, shown in Figure 4.8, allow one to reduce the amount of memory for set membership to a few bits per set element. The idea is to keep a bitmap of size, say, 5*N*, where *N* is the number of set elements. Before elements are inserted, all bits in the bitmap are cleared.

For each element in the set, its ID is hashed using *k* independent hash functions (two in Figure 4.8, *H*1 and *H*2) to determine bit positions in the bitmap to set. Thus in the case of a set of valid users in Figure 4.8, ID John hashes into the second and next-to-last bit positions. ID Cathy hashes into one position in the middle and also into one of John's positions. If two IDs hash to the same position, the bit remains set.

Finally, when searching to see if a specified element (say, Jonas) is in the set, Jonas is hashed using all the *k* hash functions. Jonas is assumed to be in the set if

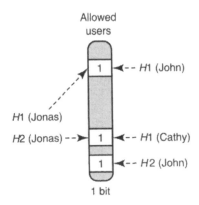

Is Jonas an allowed user?

FIGURE 4.8

A Bloom filter represents a set element by setting k bits in a bitmap using k independent hash functions applied to the element. Thus the element John sets the second (using $H1$) and next-to-last (using $H2$) bits. When searching for Jonas, Jonas is considered a member of the set only if all bit positions hashed to by Jonas have set bits.

all the bits hashed into by Jonas are set. Of course, there is some chance that Jonas may hash into the position already set by, say, Cathy and one by John (see Figure 4.8). Thus there is a chance of what is called a *false positive*: answering the membership query positively when the member is not in the set.

Notice that the trick that makes Bloom filters possible is relaxing the specification (**P3**). A normal hash table, which requires W bits per ID, does not make errors! Reducing to 5 bits per ID requires allowing errors; however, the percentage of errors is small. In particular, if there is an attack tree and set elements are hashed packet values, as in Figure 4.7, false positives mean only occasionally barking up the wrong tree branch(es).

More precisely, the false-positive rate for an m-size bitmap to store n members using k hash functions is

$$(1 - (1 - 1/m)^{kn})^k \approx (1 - e^{kn/m})^k$$

The equation is not as complicated as it may appear: $(1 - 1/m)^{kn}$ is the probability that any bit is *not* set, given n elements that each hashes k times to any of m bit positions. Finally, to get a false positive, all of the k bit positions hashed onto by the ID that causes a false positive must be set.

Using this equation, it is easy to see that for $k = 3$ (three independent hash functions) and 5 bits per member ($m/n = 5$), the false-positive rate is roughly 1%. The false-positive rate can be improved up to a point by using more hash functions and by increasing the bitmap size.

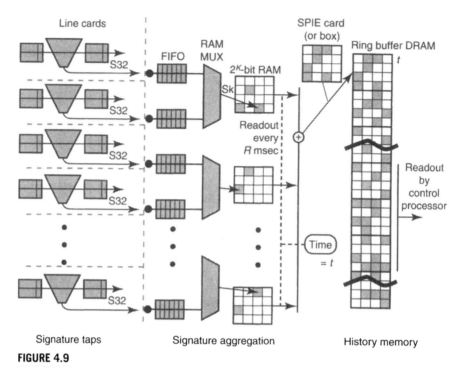

FIGURE 4.9

Hardware implementation of packet logging using Bloom filters. Note the use of two-level memory: SRAM for random read-modify-writes and DRAM for large row writes.

4.4.2 Bloom Filter Implementation of Packet Logging

The Bloom filter implementation of packet logging in the SPIE system is shown in Figure 4.9 (the picture is courtesy of Sanchez et al.). Each line card calculates a 32-bit hash digest of the packet and places it in a FIFO queue. To save costs, several line cards share, via a RAM multiplexor, a fast SRAM containing the Bloom filter bitmap.

As in the case of counters, one can combine the best features of SRAM and DRAM to reduce expense. One needs to use SRAM for fast front-end *random access* to the bitmap. Unfortunately, the expense of SRAM would allow storing only a small number of packets. To allow a larger amount, the Bloom filter bitmaps in SRAM are periodically read out to a large DRAM ring buffer. Because these are no longer random writes to bits, the write to DRAM can be written in DRAM pages or rows, which provide sufficient memory bandwidth.

4.5 DETECTING WORMS

It would be remiss to end this chapter without paying some attention to the problem of detecting worms. A worm (such as Code Red, Nimda, Slammer) begins with an exploit sent by an attacker to take over a machine. The exploit is typically a buffer overflow attack, which is caused by sending a packet (or packets) containing a field that has more data than can be handled by the buffer allocated by the receiver for the field. If the receiver implementation is careless, the extra data beyond the allocated buffer size can overwrite key machine parameters, such as the return address on the stack.

Thus with some effort, a buffer overflow can allow the attacking machine to run code on the attacked machine. The new code then picks several random IP addresses[2] and sends similar packets to these new victims. Even if only a small fraction of IP addresses responds to these attacks, the worm spreads rapidly.

Current worm detection technology is both *retroactive* (i.e., only after a new worm is first detected and analyzed by a human, a process that can take days, can the containment process be initiated) and *manual* (i.e., requires human intervention to identify the signature of a new worm). Such technology is exemplified by Code Red and Slammer, which took days of human effort to identify, following which containment strategies were applied in the form of turning off ports, applying patches, and doing signature-based filtering in routers and intrusion detection systems.

There are difficulties with these current technologies.

1. *Slow Response:* There is a proverb that talks about locking the stable door after the horse has escaped. Current technologies fit this paradigm because by the time the worm containment strategies are initiated, the worm has already infected much of the network.
2. *Constant Effort:* Every new worm requires a major amount of human work to identify, post advisories, and finally take action to contain the worm. Unfortunately, all evidence seems to indicate that there is no shortage of new exploits. And worse, simple binary rewriting and other modifications of existing attacks can get around simple signature-based blocking (as in Snort).

Thus there is a pressing need for a new worm detection and containment strategy that is real time (and hence can contain the worm before it can infect a significant fraction of the network) and is able to deal with new worms with a minimum of human intervention (some human intervention is probably unavoidable to at least catalog detected worms, do forensics, and fine-tune automatic mechanisms). In particular, the detection system should be *content agnostic*. The detection system should not rely on external, manually supplied input of worm signatures.

Instead, the system should *automatically* extract worm signatures, even for new worms that may arise in the future.

---

[2] By contrast, a *virus* requires user intervention, such as opening an attachment, to take over the user machine. Viruses also typically spread by using known addresses, such as those in the mail address book, rather than random probing.

Can network algorithmics speak to this problem? We believe it can. First, we observe that the only way to detect new worms and old worms with the same mechanism is to abstract the basic properties of worms.

As a first approximation, define a worm to have the following abstract features, which are indeed discernible in all the worms we know, even ones with such varying features as Code Red (massive payload, uses TCP, and attacks on the well-known HTTP port) and MS SQL Slammer (minimal payload, uses UDP, and attacks on the lesser-known MS SQL port).

1. *Large Volume of Identical Traffic:* These worms have the property that at least at an intermediate stage (after an initial priming period but before full infection), the volume of traffic (aggregated across all sources and destinations) carrying the worm is a significant fraction of the network bandwidth.
2. *Rising Infection Levels:* The number of infected sources participating in the attack steadily increases.
3. *Random Probing:* An infected source spreads infection by attempting to communicate to random IP addresses at a fixed port to probe for vulnerable services.

Note that detecting all three of these features may be crucial to avoid false positives. For example, a popular mailing list or a flash crowd could have the first feature but not the third.

An algorithmics approach for worm detection would naturally lead to the following detection strategy, which automatically detects each of these abstract features with low memory and small amounts of processing, works with asymmetric flows, and does not use active probing. The high-level mechanisms[3] are:

1. *Identify Large Flows in Real Time with Small Amounts of Memory:* Mechanisms can be described to identify flows with large traffic volumes for any definition of a flow (e.g., sources, destinations). A simple twist on this definition is to realize that the content of a packet (or, more efficiently, a hash of the content) can be a valid flow identifier, which by prior work can identify in real time (and with low memory) a high volume of repeated content. An even more specific idea (which distinguishes worms from valid traffic such as peer-to-peer) is to compute a hash based on the content as well as the destination port (which remains invariant for a worm).
2. *Count the Number of Sources:* Mechanisms can be described using simple bitmaps of small size to estimate the number of sources on a link using small amounts of memory and processing. These mechanisms can easily be used to count sources corresponding to high traffic volumes identified by the previous mechanism.

---

[3]Each of these mechanisms needs to be modulated to handle some special cases, but we prefer to present the main idea untarnished with extraneous details.

3. *Determine Random Probing by Counting the Number of Connection Attempts to Unused Portions of the IP Address:* One could keep a simple compact representation of portions of the IP address space known to be unused. One example is the so-called Bogon list, which lists unused 8-bit prefixes (can be stored as a bitmap of size 256). A second example is a secret space of IP addresses (can be stored as a single prefix) known to an ISP to be unused. A third is a set of unused 32-bit addresses (can be stored as a Bloom filter).

Of course, worm authors could defeat this detection scheme by violating any of these assumptions. For example, a worm author could defeat Assumption 1 by using a very slow infection rate and by mutating content frequently. Assumption 3 could be defeated using addresses known to be used. For each such attack there are possible countermeasures. More importantly, the scheme described seems certain to detect at least all existing worms we know of, though they differ greatly in their semantics. In initial experiments at UCSD as part of what we call the EarlyBird system, we also found very few false positives where the detection mechanisms complained about innocuous traffic.

4.6 CONCLUSION

Returning to Marcus Ranum's quote at the start of this chapter, hacking must be exciting for hackers and scary for network administrators, who are clearly on different sides of the battlements. However, hacking is also an exciting phenomenon for practitioners of network algorithmics—there is just so much to do. Compared to more limited areas, such as accounting and packet lookups, where the basic tasks have been frozen for several years, the creativity and persistence of hackers promise to produce interesting problems for years to come.

In terms of technology currently used, the set string-matching algorithms seem useful and may be ignored by current products. However, other varieties of string matching, such as regular expression matches, are in use. While the approximate matching techniques are somewhat speculative in terms of current applications, past history indicates they may be useful in the future.

Second, the traceback solutions only represent imaginative approaches to the problem. Their requirements for drastic changes to router forwarding make them unlikely to be used for current deployment as compared to techniques that work in the control plane. Despite this pessimistic assessment, the underlying techniques seem much more generally useful.

For example, sampling with a probability inversely proportional to a rough upper bound on the distance is useful for efficiently collecting input from each of a number of participants without explicit coordination. Similarly, Bloom filters are useful to reduce the size of hash tables to 5 bits per entry, at the cost of a small probability of false positives. Given their beauty and potential for high-speed implementation, such techniques should undoubtedly be part of the designer's bag of tricks.

Finally, we described our approach to content-agnostic worm detection using algorithmic techniques. The solution combines existing mechanisms described earlier in this book. While the experimental results on our new method are still preliminary, we hope this example gives the reader some glimpse into the possible applications of algorithmics to the scary and exciting field of network security. Figure 4.1 presents a summary of the techniques used in this chapter, together with the major principles involved.

Concepts in IP Security

5

No topic related to the Internet, with the possible exceptions of the flee availability of pornography and the plague of unwanted spam email, has received more attention in the mainstream media than "*security.*" For the average user the concerns are predominantly viruses that may infect their personal computers, causing inconvenience or damage to their data. Increasingly we also hear about white-collar e-criminals who steal personal financial details or defraud large institutions after illegally gaining entry to their computer systems.

We are also now all familiar with catastrophic failures of parts of the Internet. Although these are sometimes caused by bugs in core components (such as routers) or by the perennial backhoe cutting a cable or fiber, they are increasingly the responsibility of individuals whose sole joy is to pit their wits against those who maintain the Internet. Sometimes known as *hackers*, these people attempt to penetrate network security, or cause disruption through *denial of service attacks* for a range of motives.

Corporate espionage is of relatively little concern to most people, but within every forward-looking company there is a person or a department responsible for keeping the company's secrets safe. At the same time, the populist war against terrorism invokes contradictory requirements—that the government should be able to keep its information private while at the same time examining the affairs of suspects without them being able to hide their communications.

Whatever the rights and wrongs of the politics and sociology, Internet security is a growth industry. This chapter provides an overview of some of the issues and shows the workings of the key security protocols. It introduces the security algorithms without going into the details of the sophisticated mathematics behind encryption algorithms or key generation techniques. For this type of information the reader is referred to the reference material listed at the end of the chapter.

The first sections of the chapter examine the need for security, where within the network it can be applied, and the techniques that may be used to protect data that is stored in or transmitted across the network. There then follows a detailed examination of two key security protocols: IPsec, which provides security at the IP packet level, and Transport Layer Security (TLS), which operates at the transport layer and provides the Secure Sockets Layer (SSL). After a brief discussion of some of the ways to secure Hypertext Transfer Protocol (HTTP) transactions, which are fundamental to the operation of web-based commerce, the chapter describes how hashing and encryption algorithms are used in conjunction with keys to detect modification of data or to hide it completely—the Message Digest Five (MDS) hashing algorithm is presented as the simplest example. The chapter concludes with an examination of how security keys may be securely exchanged across the network so that they may be used to decrypt or verify transmitted data.

5.1 THE NEED FOR SECURITY

It is fair to say that when the Internet was first conceived, security was not given much consideration. In fact, the whole point of the Internet was to enable information to be shared and distributed freely. It is only as a greater number of computers have been connected together, and the sort of information held on computers and distributed across the Internet has grown in quantity and sensitivity, that network security has become an issue.

There are two fundamental issues. First, there is a need to keep information private for access only by authorized parties. Whether it is classified government material, sensitive commercial information, your credit card number, or just a note suggesting that you meet your friend in the bar in half an hour, there is strong motivation to protect any information sent across the Internet from prying eyes. This desire extends beyond protection of data transmitted over the Internet, and should also be considered to cover the safeguarding of files stored on computers attached to the Internet, and access to computing resources and programs. Some of the solutions to this issue can be seen by users on private networks as they are required to log on to their workstations, password protect key documents, and digitally sign their emails.

The second security issue concerns protection of the infrastructure of the Internet. This covers prevention of attacks on the configuration of devices in the network, theft of network resources, and the malicious jamming of nodes or links with spurious data that makes it impossible for legitimate messages to get through.

Somewhere between these two cases comes prevention of unauthorized access to secure locations on computers. This access may be in order to read privileged information, or it may be to replace it with something else, or even simply to delete it. A popular gag among hackers is to replace the content of a web site with slogans or pictures that are neither relevant nor helpful to the cause that the site was promoting.

The Internet has been shown repeatedly to be quite fragile. The accidental misconfiguration of a key router may result in large amounts of data looping or being sent off into a void. Malicious changes to routing information may have a similar effect. At the time of writing, the English-language web site of the Arab news service al-Jazeera is unreachable because someone has stolen its DNS entry on several key servers, resulting in all attempts to reach http://www.aljazeera.net being redirected to another site that displays an American patriotic message. Such intervention in the smooth operation of the Internet, although no doubt a great deal of fun to the perpetrator, is at best an inconvenience for the normal user of the Internet. For the commercial organizations that depend on exchanging information across the Internet or on customers visiting their web sites, these disruptions are a more serious matter.

Various techniques are used to compromise Internet security. The most obvious technique involves simply impersonating another user to access that user's computer. Remote access protocols such as Telnet and FTP make this particularly easy. Of course, data that is sent on the Internet can be examined quite easily using a sniffer, provided access to a computer on the network can be gained or a sniffer can be hooked up to the network at some point.

Even when passwords and authentication or encryption are used, it may be possible for someone to capture a sequence of commands and messages and replay them at a later time to gain access. Such *replay attacks* can at least confuse the receiving application and waste system resources, but may return information such as encryption keys, or may provide access to applications on a remote server.

Denial of service attacks result in degradation of service to legitimate network users. There is no immediately obvious benefit to the perpetrator, although the example in the next section describes how denial of service may be used to trick network operators into giving away their secrets. Denial of service is increasingly a tool of "Internet anarchists" who target organizations with whom they have a disagreement and block access to or from those organizations' private networks.

5.1.1 Choosing to Use Security

On the face of it, it would seem that anyone would be crazy to consider using the Internet without steeping themselves and their computers in the deepest security. Yet most individual users connect their personal computer to the Internet daily without significant consideration of the risks to their data, and only those whose computers are attached to the Internet for prolonged periods of time using high-speed links consider that they are at risk. Even a large proportion of corporations apply only the simplest *gatekeeping* security to prevent unwarranted access into their private networks, and take little or no precautions for the safety of the data that they send across the Internet.

To some extent this is a statistical question: What are the chances of a hacker stumbling across my computer? The answer is that it is currently fairly unlikely, unless you draw attention to yourself, for example, by being a hated multinational corporation with a reputation for polluting the environment, or by writing textbooks on Internet security. The statistical trend, however, may not be in our favor and, just as we have all become aware of the dangers of computer viruses and have equipped ourselves with software to detect and remove viruses, so we will need to protect our computers from hackers who write or use programs that search the Internet for unsecured computers.

There are other trade-offs to consider, too. Not the least of these is price, and although a lot can now be done for the home computer at a very low price, the best corporate Internet security comes at a greater cost. There are also performance costs associated with data encryption and authentication as the algorithms used perform multiple computations on each byte of data that is transmitted. The effect on the rate of data transmission can be reduced by using dedicated security hardware that is optimized for the computations that are needed, but that pushes the price up again. Work is also progressing to develop faster algorithms that are equally secure.

The last consideration is the complexity of a fully secure system. In many cases there are configuration issues to be addressed as security keys must be entered into the system at the sender and receiver—some of these issues can now be solved using key distribution protocols (see Section 5.8). And the complexity of a security system may lead to maintenance problems, with confusion and misjudgment by network operators, as illustrated by the following cautionary (and possibly apocryphal) tale from the early days of networking.

A bank used to transport all its computer data on tape every night from a major branch to its head office. The bank installed a computer link between the sites to make the transfer more efficient and timely. Not being entirely ignorant, it applied a simple encryption algorithm to the data.

As time went by, the bankers became uncomfortable that their encryption algorithm might be too easy to crack, so they bought an upgrade to the software that had a far more sophisticated encryption routine. In due course, they upgraded the software and left the program to run overnight. To their consternation, the next morning they discovered that the data received at the head office was garbled and couldn't be decoded. A quick experiment showed that if they turned off the encryption, the data was transmitted fine, but with encryption enabled the computer at the head office was unable to make sense of the data.

With pressure mounting and the bank due to open, the manager made the obvious decision; the new encryption software was broken and must be disabled for the transmission. So, the data was sent to the head office unencrypted and business went on as usual. The software developers were called but could find nothing wrong with their programs, and so, eventually, hardware engineers came to inspect the leased line between the offices. They, of course, found the point at which the criminals had intercepted the data and mangled everything that was encrypted, allowing through anything that was in the clear. Examination of the bank's records showed that once the nightly transaction had started without encryption, the resourceful thieves had inserted their own records into the data and had siphoned off their share of the money.

5.2 CHOOSING WHERE TO APPLY SECURITY

Security within an IP network can be applied at any or all of a set of different levels. Physical security governs the connectivity and access to private networks; protocol-level security controls and safeguards the essential protocols that make the Internet work; application security can be used to protect sensitive data and to limit access to applications; transport and network layer security is used to protect data flows across public or exposed networks and connections.

Choosing between these options is as much a matter of strategic network planning as it is a requirement for protecting individual pieces of data. Security consultants expend a great deal of effort helping their customers pick exactly the right combination of options to achieve a secure and yet manageable system since it is often the case that increased security is paid for through ever more complex configuration requirements. The consequences of a poorly designed security system extend beyond the problems described in the previous section—an overzealous or badly administered scheme can bar or frustrate legitimate users. The sections that follow briefly outline the levels at which security can be applied.

5.2.1 Physical Security

Perhaps the most obvious and strongest form of security is a physical break in the connectivity. It is very hard for an intruder to gain access to your network or data if there are no connections to the outside world. This approach still forms the foundation of many corporate security models, but as networks grow in size they often include links that are hard to protect (for example, those that run between buildings) and this introduces a vulnerability that a determined outsider may exploit. At the same time, external access to and from the wider Internet and for dial-up connectivity is now almost ubiquitous. Although certain physical connectivity constraints can be applied to both dial-up links and more permanent external links, the gates stand open welcoming the hacker into private networks and offering malicious or just nosy individuals the scope to examine private data exchanges.

Even when there are physical connections from a private network to the outside world, there are some connectivity constraints that can be applied to help bar the doors. On dial-up links caller ID detection or call-back facilities can limit unauthorized access, and permanent links to the Internet are, of course, both few and well known. Nevertheless, such physical security can provide only limited protection for the private network and gives no safeguard for data once it has left the privacy of the corporate network. Software safeguards are needed.

Some simple software configuration control measures can be made at a physical level to enhance security. These techniques are referred to as *Access Control* (see Section 5.3.1) and are used to limit the access available to a node or network by source IP address and by user ID and password.

5.2.2 Protecting Routing and Signaling Protocols

Routing protocols are used to distribute information about links and reachability so that IP packets can be successfully delivered. Although the information distributed by these protocols is not very sensitive (some network providers may want to keep their network topology secret), the protocols themselves are vulnerable to malicious attacks that can cause a break-down in the services provided to end users—a denial of service attack. For example, if someone injected OSPF messages into a network that appeared to advertise a low-cost link from one side of the network to the other, this might find its way into the paths computed by all or most of the nodes in the network, causing traffic to be misrouted and possibly lost entirely.

Similarly, signaling and other IP-based protocols are used to manage network resources and to direct traffic along specific paths. These protocols are also vulnerable to attack, particularly from message replay or spoofing.

Routing and signaling protocols typically offer some security protection through authentication schemes (discussed in Section 5.3.2). These processes allow nodes to verify that a message really was sent by the partner from which it appears to come and, combined with sequence numbering schemes within the protocols themselves, also protect against replay attacks.

In practice, however, authentication is rarely used by deployed routing and signaling implementations. This has something to do with the configuration and management overheads (each node must know a security key for use when authenticating a message from each other node with which it might communicate), and also derives from the fact that network providers are able to apply other security schemes (physical, access control, and network level) to achieve the same ends.

5.2.3 Application-Level Security

For a majority of users the most important aspect of IP security is the protection of their user data as it is transferred across the network. It has been argued that the greatest facilitator of the recent exponential growth of the Internet has been the development of reliable and truly secure techniques for encrypting data. Without these mechanisms it is unlikely that Internet commerce would have become so popular because the sensitive nature of financial details (such as credit card numbers) limits the likelihood of people participating in online transactions across a public network.

Similarly, commercial information is widely regarded as being sufficiently sensitive that it should be protected from prying eyes. The fact that the overwhelming percentage of corporate data is so banal as to be tedious, and that this information outweighs valuable data to such an extent as to hide it quite efficiently, is rightly not considered as an effective security measure. The enthusiastic and determined criminal will be willing to wade through thousands of unimportant emails that set out lunch arrangements or discuss the latest ballgame, in the hope of discovering something of value. Companies, therefore, do not send information "in the clear" across the Internet. Data in file transfers and email exchanges is routinely encrypted as it is transferred between company sites over public networks.

Application security normally takes one of two forms. First, the user can encrypt or password protect the data to be transferred. Many applications such as word processors or file compression tools allow the user to require the use of a password before the file can be opened. This password is usually encrypted and stored within the file so that the receiving application requires the user to enter the same password before the data can be viewed. All nontrivial applications assume that the use of a password also implies that the data should be encrypted—this is wise since the application in question is not the only tool that could be used to examine the file.

The second application security mechanism is embedded in the applications that are used to transfer files or data as distinct from those that the user uses to operate on the data. For example, email programs often allow the user to encrypt individual emails so that the recipient must specify a password before being allowed to read what was sent. An equally important concept is secure exchange of data on web-based transactions—using security extensions to the Hypertext Transfer Protocol (HTTP), it is possible for a user to send and receive sensitive data such as credit card numbers using encryption techniques.

A final concept that is popular, especially in email exchanges, is the digital signature. This technique allows the receiver to verify that the message being read was really sent by the apparent author, and that the message has not been modified by a third party.

Application security has strengths and weaknesses. It allows the user full control of the level of security applied to different transactions, but at the same time it allows the user to make a mistake or simply forget to take appropriate measures. Security modules must be implemented for each application since the rules and methods for applying security within each application protocol differ. Although these modules should be able to share common libraries for encryption and decryption, the applications are developed by different software companies and cannot necessarily rely on the presence of a third-party security library that the consumer would have to purchase and install. So each application may need to include its own security implementation. The alternative to this is offered by applying security across the board to all traffic at a lower layer, as described in the next two sections, but this may mean that more security is used than is actually required, slowing data transfer.

5.2.4 **Protection at the Transport Layer**

Transport protocols are responsible for delivering data on behalf of applications over an IP network. Different transport-layer protocols provide different levels of service, ranging from simple datagram dispatch to guaranteed in-order delivery of data.

The more sophisticated transport protocols include some elements of security that may be used by applications that do not, themselves, include modules that offer secure data transfer. This has the advantage of collecting together all security code in a single place (the transport stack module) and relieving applications from having to include such features. On the other hand, the security enhancements are not available in all transport protocols (for example, the popular User Datagram Protocol), which limits the popularity of transport-layer security.

Perhaps the biggest issue with transport-layer security is that it does not hide or protect important fields in the transport protocol headers. These fields indicate the source and destination of the data and give clues to the purpose of the message exchanges. Additionally, these unprotected fields are fundamental to the successful delivery of the data: if they are modified, the service may be interrupted.

5.2.5 Network-Level Security

The best alternative to application-level security is provided at the network layer where the whole content of IP packets, and even the IP headers themselves, are secured. This solution has many advantages. It is available for all IP traffic between any pair of end points, so it is useful to protect application data and also can be used to secure routing and signaling exchanges.

IP security (IPsec) is the mainstay of network-level security. It is used to authenticate the sender of messages, to verify that message data has not been tampered with, and to hide information from prying eyes. IPsec is used for a wide range of applications, from protecting signaling and routing flows to providing Virtual Private Networks (VPNs) across the public Internet.

5.3 COMPONENTS OF SECURITY MODELS

Security is achieved by building on the three distinct components described in the sections that follow. These are Access Control, in which limits are placed on the ability of a remote system or user to access the local system; authentication, in which the sender's identity and the data he or she sends is authenticated to be genuine and free from modification; and encryption, in which the data is protected by a cipher. These components may be applied at all levels within the network.

5.3.1 Access Control

Access controls provide some of the simpler, but also most widespread, forms of security. Building on the concept of physical security, in which there is no connectivity to the outside world, access controls attempt to limit the users who can connect to a network, host, or application. The most familiar access control comes in the form of user names and passwords; before users can access a given application they must supply their name and password. In many operating systems and applications it is possible to configure user groups that have different privileges—users are assigned to a specific group and this limits what activities they can perform, with only the most privileged user group being able to access the most sensitive data and perform security-related tasks (such as assigning users to groups).

User name and password protection provides a simple lock and key mode of access control, and with it comes the problem of the user who leaves the door open. What happens if a user connects to an application and then walks away from the computer? Couldn't someone else happen by and use the other user's access permissions? To help combat this, many applications automatically log users out after a period of inactivity, and some even prompt users to reenter their password every so often regardless of activity.

But just as someone may lend a friend his or her ATM card and tell the friend the PIN to save a trip to the bank, so user names and passwords may not be treated to particularly high levels of secrecy. In addition, passwords have to be remembered by users who may have accounts on many computers and so they tend to be common words or names. Programs used by hackers to attempt to gain access to computer systems by repeatedly trying user names and passwords take these human failings into account and are coded to try the default password settings first (things like "password") and then run through a series of well-known common passwords, before resorting to words selected from a dictionary. It is an interesting anthropological note that the password "NCC1701D" (the serial number of the starship *Enterprise*) is one of the most common passwords.

A further level of security can be achieved by using a dedicated computer or program known as a *firewall* to provide a security gateway between your private network and the outside world. The firewall is inserted between the private domain and the public network, as shown in Figure 5.1. Normally, access to and from the Internet would be provided by connectivity to a gateway router, but in this case all exchanges between the private network and the Internet also go through the firewall router.

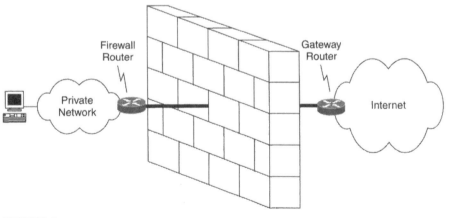

FIGURE 5.1

A firewall gateway provides additional security by filtering packets that are sent between a private network and the Internet.

Firewalls are responsible for applying access control. They filter the IP packets that they forward based on many properties, including source and destination IP address, payload protocol, transport port number, and any other quality that the security manager deems appropriate. The simplest configurations are called *IP Access Lists* and are lists of remote IP addresses that are allowed to source messages that will be passed into the private network through the firewall. Other common filters limit access only to designated hosts (destination IP addresses) and even then restrict incoming packets to those that carry a particular protocol (such as TCP) and target specific port numbers (such as port 80 for web access). Packets that are not allowed through are simply discarded—no special error message is returned because this would surely help a hacker discover a way to penetrate the security.

Filters applied at firewalls can be inclusive or exclusive (or both)—that is, they may be a list of packets that is allowed through, or a list of packets that will be denied access. There are advantages and disadvantages to each approach and a trade-off must be made between the cost of misconfigurations that allow inadvertent access and those that block legitimate use. The latter can normally be fixed quite simply and (provided that the security manager does not panic or overreact when responding to an annoyed user) it is usually considered better to build up a profile of users and packet types that are allowed access than to try to list each of the sources that is not allowed.

A further firewall model inserts an additional computer between the firewall router and the gateway router. This computer serves as an application gateway, and all connections from one side of the firewall to the other are terminated and regenerated at this node, as shown in Figure 5.2. The application gateway can be made additionally secure by applying access control on each side so that the only connections allowed are between the private network and the application gateway, and between the application gateway and the Internet. The application gateway maps connection requests onto connections to real hosts within the private network, hiding those nodes from the outside world—a feature similar to that supplied by HTTP

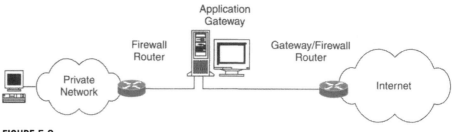

FIGURE 5.2

Application security may be enhanced by the use of an application gateway positioned between two firewall routers.

proxies. Similarly, such gateways may map application protocols or even network protocols, providing access to the Internet for proprietary or nonstandard networks.

Firewall security may actually be condensed to run on a single box so that an application gateway may be combined with a firewall router, or a home computer may run simple access control on its dial-up connection to the Internet.

Firewalls are a popular security solution because they are a simple concept and they provide a single point of security management. This allows the responsibility for security to be placed in the hands of a single person who has only to manage and configure a single computer. Such an approach is also cheap to implement, requiring the addition of only one network element and providing security through a simple software solution. On the other hand, this form of packet filtering may cause an undesirable bottleneck in the path of legitimate data traffic since all packets must pass through the one point of connection and each must be subject to a series of checks against the configured rules.

In the end, however, access control is of only limited efficacy. Malicious users may impersonate others either by stealing their user names and passwords, or by changing their IP addresses to get through the firewall. The very nature of the firewall includes the crack through which an intrusion may occur.

This means that full security must be achieved through more complex techniques described in the sections that follow.

fire wall *n*: a wall constructed to prevent the spread of fire.

5.3.2 **Authentication**

Authentication serves two purposes: it validates that the user or the sender of a message is who he or she claims to be, and it ensures that the message received is genuine and has not been tampered with. At an application level, authentication is usually provided through a user ID and password exchange building on the application access control mechanisms already described. Application-level authentication is most often applied to transactions or sessions (that is, at a relatively high level), although individual components of transactions may be authenticated through the use of digital signatures.

At a per-message level in routing, signaling, and transport protocols, or in IP itself, authentication usually takes the form of a validation process applied to parts or the whole of the message being transported. The sender runs an algorithm over the whole of the message (usually in conjunction with a secret string called a *key*) and includes the output from the algorithm with the message that is sent. The receiver runs the same algorithm over the message using the same key and checks that its result is the same as the one it received. Any attempt by a third party to modify the message will cause the receiver's answer to differ from the one in the message. Since the key is not transmitted, and since it is known only to the sender and the receiver, the attacker cannot patch up the message to defeat the authentication process.

The use of sequence numbers within the protocol messages protected by an authentication scheme helps defeat replay attacks because a replayed message with an incremented sequence number will fail the authentication test, and a replayed message without a change to the sequence number will be rejected by the protocol.

5.3.3 Encryption

Authentication is all very well, but it does not protect the privacy of data that is sent through a public network or over public connections. This data is exposed and may easily be read by anyone using reasonably simple technology. The obvious risks to passwords, financial details, and confidential information require the use of other techniques to hide or encrypt the data that is sent.

Encryption techniques on the Internet are not really that dissimilar to those used in all of the best spy movies. Some formula is applied to the source data to convert it into a stream of apparently meaningless characters. This information can then be safely transmitted across the Internet to the recipient, who applies another formula to decrypt the message and discover the data.

Successful encryption algorithms rely on the fact that someone who intercepts a message cannot readily decrypt it. The first approach to this technique is to keep the encryption and decryption formulae secret—if the algorithms are good, no one will be able to interpret the messages that are exchanged. The problem with this technique is that the algorithm must be well known for the security process to have wide application, which defeats its efficacy as a primary security measure.

The solution is to enhance the encryption algorithms with keys. These keys provide additional input to the encryption and decryption processes, making them unique even when the algorithms are well known. The keys are private to the sender and receiver of the messages.

Encryption may be applied at any level within the network. In many cases, applications or users encrypt all or part of the data they want to send—this is, for example, how credit card details are exchanged during commercial transactions on the World Wide Web. In other circumstances, the transport or network protocols are asked to provide encryption on behalf of the applications—the most widespread encryption and authentication technique at the network layer is provided by IPsec, discussed in the next section.

Authentication and encryption may be applied independently or in combination.

5.4 IPsec

IP security (IPsec) defines a standard way in which IP datagrams may be authenticated or encrypted when they are exchanged between two nodes. The security architecture for IPsec is described in RFC 2401, and RFC 3457 explains some common scenarios in which IPsec may be used. The protocol extensions for IPsec are defined in RFC 2402 (authentication) and RFC 2406 (encryption) and are explained in the sections that follow.

Secure packet exchanges using IPsec occur between a pair of cooperating nodes that establish a *Security Association* (SA). The SA essentially defines the type of security (authentication and/or encryption), the algorithms, and the keys to be applied to all IP packets exchanged between the nodes. As a point of precision, SAs are actually unidirectional, but it would be normal to instantiate them in both directions using the same characteristics with the possible exception of the keys, which might be different for each direction.

IPsec may be deployed end-to-end between host computers or across the network by proxy security servers on behalf of the hosts. That is, the SA may extend from data source to data sink, or may cover only part of the path between the two end points.

5.4.1 Choosing between End-to-End and Proxy Security

Figure 5.3 shows the difference between end-to-end security and the proxy model. In the end-to-end case, the Security Association extends from the source to the destination and packets are fully encrypted or authenticated along the whole length of their path. This is the maximally secure solution.

For proxy security, a node part-way along the data path (a proxy) is responsible for applying IPsec to the IP packets and transferring them to another proxy that validates or decrypts the packets before passing them on to the final destination.

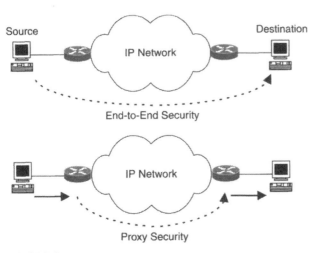

FIGURE 5.3

IPsec may be applied in an end-to-end model or across only part of the network using proxy security.

Proxy security has the obvious drawback that the packets are exposed for part of their path. However, it has many positive points that make it useful and popular. First, it reduces the implementation complexity at the end points—in the proxy model, one proxy may serve multiple end points, allowing the security code to be concentrated just on the proxies. This process extends to allow a single SA to carry traffic belonging to multiple data streams. This is possible if several hosts served by one proxy want to communicate with other hosts served by a second proxy. In this mode of operation, the IP packets from the data streams are grouped together and treated to the same security measures and forwarded to the same remote proxy as if down a *tunnel*.

A final advantage of the proxy model is that, in IPsec, it hides the source and destination IP information as packets traverse the core network. As will be seen in later sections, when packets enter the IPsec tunnel they are completely encapsulated in a new IP packet that flows between proxies—this increases the security by not exposing the end points of the data flows.

End-to-end security is used when individual remote nodes connect into networks (for example, when dialing in through a public network). Proxy security is used when using a public network to connect together networks belonging to the same company to form a virtual private network (VPN).

5.4.2 Authentication

As described in Section 5.3.2, authentication is achieved by processing the message with a key. This is illustrated in Figure 5.4. In IPsec the IP header, data payload, and a key are processed through an authentication algorithm to produce authentication data. This authentication data is placed in an *Authentication*

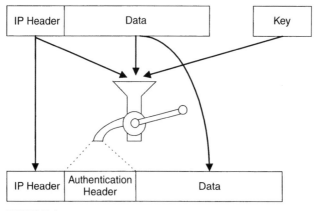

FIGURE 5.4

IPsec authentication is used to verify that the sender of a message is legitimate and that the message has not been tampered with.

Header inserted between the IP header and the payload. The Authentication Header is shown in Figure 5.5.

The hashing algorithm is performed on the whole IP packet to be transmitted—that is, the IP header and the data. The value generated by the hashing process is placed in the Authentication Data field of the Authentication Header and transmitted to the destination. At the destination, the algorithm is performed again on the IP header and the data (but not the Authentication Header) using the same key. The result is compared with the transmitted authentication data to verify that no modification of the packet has occurred. This process and the format of the IPsec Authentication Header are described in RFC 2402.

Any authentication algorithm may be used, and plenty are defined. IPsec places a requirement on implementations that at least the Message Digest Five (MD5) algorithm is supported (see Section 5.7.1). It is (obviously) a requirement that both the sender and the receiver know which authentication algorithm is in use, and the values of the keys. IPsec does not discuss how this information is exchanged or configured, but Section 5.8 describes some possibilities.

One issue should be immediately apparent: some of the values in the IP header may legitimately be modified as the packet traverses the network and this will invalidate the authentication process. To avoid this problem the hashing algorithm is applied to the IP packet with certain key fields (TTL, ToS, checksum, and flags) set to zero. Further, the next protocol field is modified by the insertion of the Authentication Header; it is set to 51 (0x33) to indicate that an Authentication Header is present. The hashing algorithm is applied to the IP packet at the source before the insertion of the Authentication Header, and at the destination it is performed after the removal of the Authentication Header. The Authentication Header, shown in Figure 5.5, carries the payload protocol for restoration into the IP header, and indicates its own length for ease of removal.

One last observation should be made about the insertion of an Authentication Header. The presence of the header may cause the IP packet size to exceed the

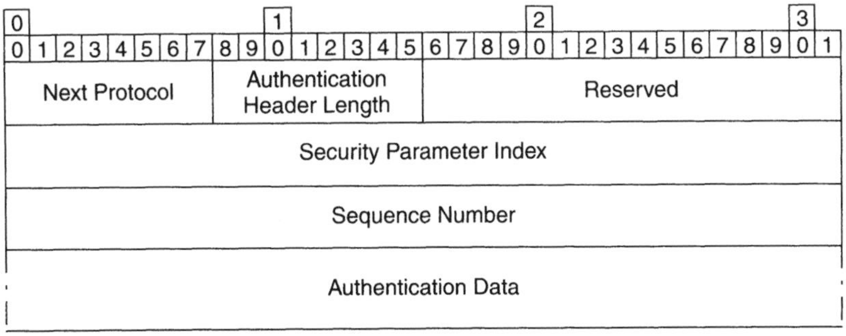

0									1										2										3	
0	1	2	3	4	5	6	7	8	9	0	1	2	3	4	5	6	7	8	9	0	1	2	3	4	5	6	7	8	9	0	1
Next Protocol								Authentication Header Length								Reserved															
Security Parameter Index																															
Sequence Number																															
Authentication Data																															

FIGURE 5.5

The IPsec Authentication Header is inserted into IP packets to carry authentication information.

MTU size for the link into the network. If fragmentation is not allowed, the size of source data packets must be modified before authentication can be used because, otherwise, the packet may be fragmented. Note that fragmentation at the source node is no different from fragmentation within the network—it is performed on the whole IPsec packet, including the Authentication Header (there is no question of one Authentication Header per fragment) and so the fragments must be reassembled at the destination before they can be authenticated.

The Authentication Header (shown in Figure 5.5) includes a Security Parameter Index (SPI) that is used to identify the Security Association that manages this packet. Given a source and destination address pairing, the SPI uniquely identifies the security context, telling the receiver which algorithms and keys to apply. The SPI should be generated randomly to reduce predictability and to limit the chances of a restarting node accidentally reusing an old Security Association. The SPI values 0 through 255 are reserved. A Sequence Number is designed to help prevent denial of service attacks in which malicious parties capture and replay packets or sequences of packets. The sequence number may help the destination node determine that received packets are duplicates or are out of order and discard them without further processing. Finally, the Authentication Header contains the output of the hashing algorithm in a field that will vary in length depending on the algorithm in use.

Authentication can be applied in the end-to-end model or using proxies: in each case the format of the message is the same.

5.4.3 Authentication and Encryption

When data is encrypted an encryption algorithm is fed with a stream of data and an encryption key. The output is a new stream of data that may be longer than the original data. When IPsec encryption is used in end-to-end mode, the data part of the source IP packet is encrypted and transported with the original IP header. The encrypted data is named the *Encapsulated Security Payload* (ESP) and is placed between an ESP header and trailer, as shown in Figure 5.6.

In proxy IPsec encryption the whole source IP packet (header and data) is encrypted as shown in Figure 5.7. A new packet is built with a new IP header that handles the passage down the tunnel from one proxy to the other. The data of this new packet is the encrypted source packet encapsulated between an ESP header and trailer.

Many encryption algorithms exist, and they operate on keys of varying complexity. A massive industry has grown up around the conflicting desires of privacy and transparency, conspiracy and law enforcement. Suddenly, mathematicians who devise these procedures discover that they can be popular if they work in this field. IPsec mandates that implementations must at least support the Data Encryption Standard (DES). This algorithm is discussed in Section 5.7.

The IPsec encryption process is described in RFC 2406. The ESP packet format shown in Figure 5.8 starts off simply enough. After the normal IP header, which

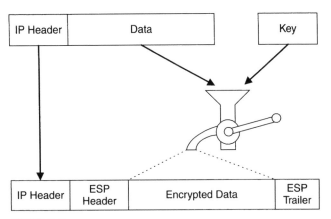

FIGURE 5.6

IPsec encryption may be applied to the IP payload data in the end-to-end security model.

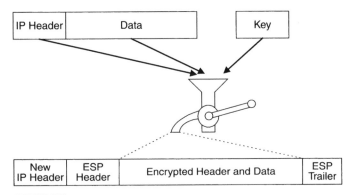

FIGURE 5.7

When IPsec encryption is used in the proxy security model the whole IP packet is encrypted and encapsulated in a new packet.

carries a next protocol value of 50 (0x32) to indicate that an ESP header is present, the ESP header begins with an SPI and Sequence Number that are used in the same way as they are in the authentication process described in the previous section. From here on, however, the packet seems to be a bit of a mess! It is easiest to understand how it is constructed by working from the end toward the beginning.

If authentication is in use in addition to encryption, this will be known to both the source and the destination and a piece of authentication data (the output from the hashing algorithm) with a well-known length will be appended to the packet. In front of this comes a single byte that identifies the protocol of the encrypted payload. In the IP case described here this field does not appear to be necessary— surely we know that the payload is an IP packet?—but there is no reason this method of encryption and encapsulation shouldn't be used to carry non-IP traffic

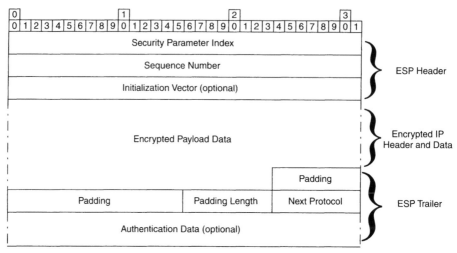

FIGURE 5.8

In IPsec encryption an IP packet is converted into an Encapsulating Security Payload packet.

across an IP network. In our case, if proxy security is in use, the next protocol field is set to 0x04 to indicate IPv4, otherwise the next protocol field is copied from the next header field of the original IP header and indicates the payload type.

Continuing to work backwards through the packet, we reach a count of padding bytes. The padding is present at the end of the encrypted payload data and serves several purposes.

- It may be necessary to ensure that the Next Protocol field ends on a 4-byte boundary, which is an encoding requirement.

- Some encryption algorithms may function over data that is presented only in multiples of a certain number of bytes (such as 4, 8, or 16). Padding is therefore necessary to bring the number of bytes in the IP header and data up to the right number of bytes.

- It may be advantageous to vary the length of packets being sent across a network to better hide the operations being carried out. A trivial example could be the transfer of a password; although the encryption algorithm will hide the password, the packet length could expose the length of the password. Adding padding helps to mask this information.

Working further backwards we reach the encrypted data itself. This is the IP header and data that is being sent across the network. The last field we reach is the optional Initialization Vector. This field is specific to the encryption algorithm and includes any information needed by the decryption algorithm before it can operate—some algorithms include this field directly with the data and others extract specific meanings that guide their operations.

If IPsec is not used to protect the data at the network layer, then the next alternative is to use some form of protection at the transport layer, as described in the next section.

5.5 TRANSPORT-LAYER SECURITY

Transport-layer security is provided by the Transport Layer Security Protocol (TLS) defined in RFC 2246. This protocol is in fact two small protocols designed to run over TCP, being inserted between applications and the transport protocol usually through the use of the *Secure Sockets Layer* (SSL).

The TLS Handshake Protocol is used to correlate what encryption and authentication operations are used on the TCP connection—these may also include data compression. The TLS Record Protocol provides a mechanism for the exchange of handshake messages and is responsible for authentication and encryption of data exchanged over TCP connections. It uses standard algorithms to hash or encode the data that is passed to it over the secure sockets API. The sockets API allows applications to stream data in arbitrary blocks, but most encryption algorithms operate on records of a defined length, so the first thing the TLS Record Protocol must do is buffer data to build up complete records ready for processing. Conversely, large blocks of data must be segmented into records of 2^{14} bytes or less so that they may be properly handled. Figure 5.9 shows how the protocols are arranged and where the Sockets and Secure Sockets APIs fit in.

Annoyingly, the message formats in RFC 2246 are specified in a notation a little like "C" or XDR so that they appear as data structures. For most purposes this may be sufficient because the structures can simply be picked up, made to compile, and used to build and decode messages, but it should be recalled that although structure packing rules may vary by compiler the message formats on the wire must remain constant. The format of the basic TLS record is shown in Figure 5.10. Records are sent as the payload of IP packets with the next header field set to 56

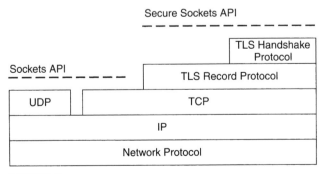

FIGURE 5.9

The Secure Sockets Layer provides an additional level of function above TCP.

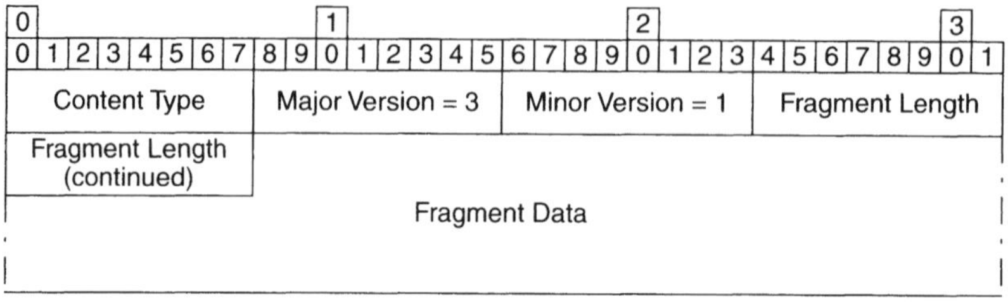

FIGURE 5.10

The Transport Layer Security record format.

Table 5.1 Defined Values for the TLS Record Content Type

Value	Meaning
20	Change of cipher specification
21	TLS alert
22	Handshake message
23	Data

(0x38) to indicate TLS. The Content Type field indicates whether the record is carrying data or is being used to manage the process; the defined values are shown in Table 5.1. The protocol version number is 3.1 and is encoded in two fields (the value 3.1 is historic: TLS is based on a previous protocol called SSL, the protocol that provided the Secure Sockets Layer, which had reached version 3.0 when TLS version 1.0 was invented).

Each TLS Record message may contain a control message or data. If the data (or control message) is too large to fit into one message it must be fragmented and sent in a series of messages. Each fragment may not be larger than 2^{14} bytes after it has been subject to decompression. The use of data compression or data encryption for the payloads of the data messages is selected through configuration or through the use of the TLS Handshake Protocol described in the following section.

5.5.1 The Handshake Protocol

The TLS Handshake Protocol is optional in transport-layer security. It is used to dynamically negotiate and exchange security parameters (algorithms, keys, etc.) for use within the context of a TCP connection. If the Handshake exchanges are not used, security parameters must be exchanged through some other means (for example, manual configuration).

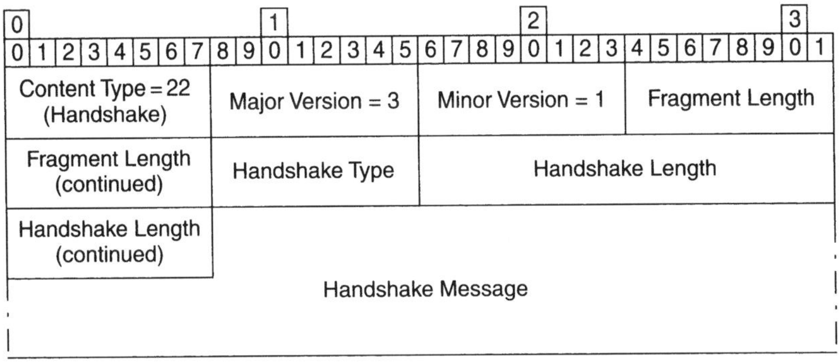

0		1		2		3	
0 1 2 3 4 5 6 7 8 9 0 1 2 3 4 5 6 7 8 9 0 1 2 3 4 5 6 7 8 9 0 1							
Content Type = 22 (Handshake)	Major Version = 3	Minor Version = 1	Fragment Length				
Fragment Length (continued)	Handshake Type	Handshake Length					
Handshake Length (continued)	Handshake Message						

FIGURE 5.11

Transport Layer Security Handshake Protocol messages are carried in TLS records and have a common header.

Handshake messages are carried in TLS Record Protocol exchanges. The record type 23 (handshake) is used, and one or more record fragments may be used to carry the message (note that the maximum handshake message length is 2^{24} and that a fragment can carry only 2^{14} bytes). Each message has a common format, giving the message type and length, and is then followed by message-specific fields. This is shown in Figure 5.11 with the Record Protocol header.

The Handshake Protocol is an end-to-end protocol—the messages are exchanged between the TCP TLS client and server across the network. The basic exchange of messages is initiated by the client sending a Client Hello, as shown in Figure 5.12. The Client Hello indicates the client's desire to establish a security session on this TCP connection, defines a session ID, and lists the security and compression algorithms the client supports and is willing to use.

The server responds with a series of messages that define the server's security parameters. The Server Hello message acknowledges the Client Hello and narrows the lists of security and compression algorithms down to just one of each. The Certificate and Server Key Exchange messages are optional and are used to convey security information (the identity of the server and the server's security keys, respectively) if required. Similarly, the server may optionally send a Certificate Request if it wishes the client to identify itself in a secure way. The server indicates that it has completed this sequence of messages by sending a server Hello Done message.

The client now embarks upon a sequence of messages to pass its certification information to the server. Some of the messages are optional, depending upon whether the server sent an optional request. The Certificate message identifies the client in response to a Certificate Request. The Client Key Exchange message is identical in format to the Server Key Exchange message and reports the client's security parameters. The client confirms that the certificate sent by the server (if one was sent) is acceptable by sending a Certificate Verify message. Now the protocol needs to switch from unencrypted message exchange (which it has used

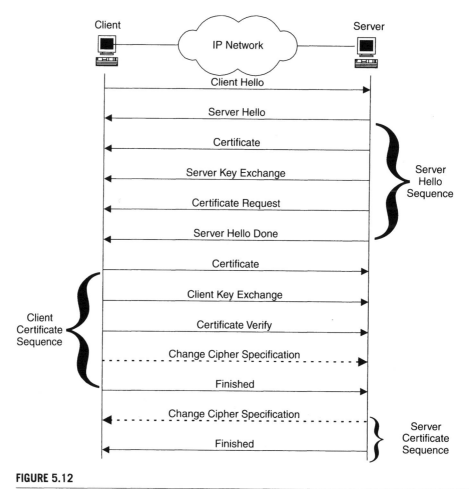

FIGURE 5.12

The TLS handshake message exchange.

so far) to encoded messages. It wants to do this by sending a trigger message so that the receiver also knows that encryption is in use, so it sends a Change Cipher Spec message. But the Change Cipher Spec message is not part of the Handshake Protocol; it is a TLS Record Protocol message. This allows it to be used even when the Handshake Protocol is not in use, for example, when encryption information is configured or exchanged in some other way. Once the use of the cipher has been enabled, the client completes its sequence of messages with a Finished message.

The ball is now back with the server. All that remains for the server to do is enable its own use of encryption for messages sent on the connection. It does this by sending a Change Cipher Spec message followed by a Finished message.

The order of messages shown in Figure 5.12 is important. The only permissible deviation is when an optional message is not included.

The sequence of messages shown in Figure 5.12 may also be reinitiated during the life of a secure TCP connection to renegotiate the security parameters. This may be desirable if the transactions carried on the connection suddenly reach a point at which additional security is needed, or if the connection has been open for a configured time such that the client or server believes it is time to change the key. In this case the client may send a new Client Hello to restart the exchange, or the server may send a Hello Request to trigger the client to send a Client Hello.

Figure 5.13 shows the TLS Handshake Protocol messages converted from their pseudo "C" to byte format. Many of the fields are enumerations of options or types or encryption options and the lists of values can be looked up in RFC 2246. Certificates and the distinguished names of certifying authorities are taken from the ISO's X.509 directory standards. Keys, key information, and signatures are dependent on the encryption algorithms and options selected.

The Finished message bears a little further examination. The message exchange up to and including the Change Cipher Spec message has been in the open (assuming that a lower-layer security system such as IPsec is not in use), which means that it was vulnerable to interception and manipulation. What is needed is a way to verify that the received messages were identical to those sent. The Finish message does this by performing an authentication hashing algorithm on the combined byte stream produced by concatenating together some of the messages and security information already exchanged. The 12-byte authentication data in the Finish message is the output of the Pseudo Random Function (PRF) defined in RFC 2246. The input to the PRF is as follows.

- The Master Secret (a 48-byte secret key shared between the end points).

- A Finished Label (the text string "client finished" or "server finished").

- The output of two distinct hashing algorithms, each applied to the concatenation of all of the Handshake Protocol messages sent by this node on this session up to this point in time (not including this message, not including the Record Protocol headers, and not including the Hello Request message if it was sent).

The two hashing algorithms used are Message Digest Five (MD5) and Secure Hash Algorithm One (SHA-1).

5.5.2 Alert Messages

TLS alert messages have the fragment length set to 2 and carry 2 bytes of error information. The first byte indicates the severity of the error (1 means warning, 2 means fatal), and the second byte indicates the specific error using a value from Table 5.2. When an error is detected on a TLS connection, the node identifying the problem sends an alert message—this may be in response to a message that forms

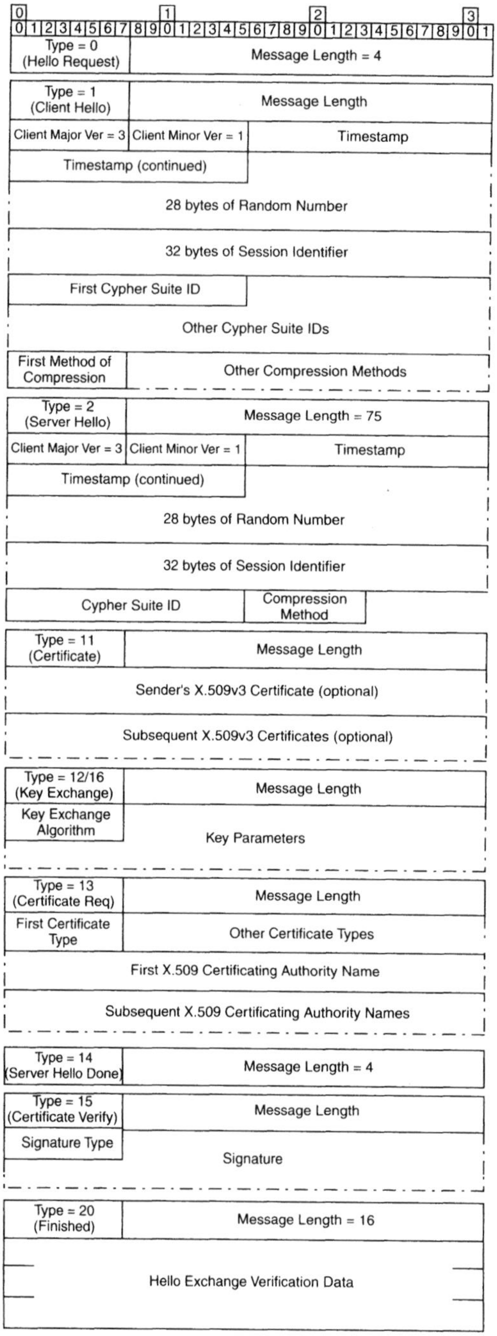

FIGURE 5.13

Transport Layer Security Handshake Protocol messages are specified in RFC 2246 using a notation similar to "C," but may be converted into byte format.

Table 5.2 TLS Alert Messages Carry a Descriptive Error Code

Error Code	Severity	Meaning
0	Warning	close_notify: Notifies the recipient that the sender will not send any more messages (data or control) on this connection. The receiver should respond with a close_ notify to terminate the session. This is a warning message so that the remote node may respond.
10	Fatal	unexpected_message: Indicates a protocol violation.
20	Fatal	bad_record_mac: Authentication of a received record has failed.
21	Fatal	decryption_failed: Decryption failed because of the format of the encrypted data.
22	Fatal	record_overflow: The record length received was too large.
30	Fatal	decompression_failure: Decompression produced an invalid record (for example, the record length was too large after decompression).
40	Fatal	handshake_failure: Could not agree on an acceptable set of connection parameters during the handshake process.
42	Warning	bad_certificate: A certificate was corrupt.
43	Warning	unsupported_certificate: An unsupported certificate type was used.
44	Warning	certificate_revoked: A certificate was revoked by the signer.
45	Warning	certificate_expired: A certificate has expired.
46	Warning	certificate_unknown: A certificate was unusable for some other reason.
47	Fatal	illegal_parameter: Some parameter exchanged during the handshake process was out of range or unknown.
48	Fatal	unknown_ca: A Certificate Authority certificate could not be matched.
49	Fatal	access_denied: The certificate is valid but does not afford the requested access according to local policy.
50	Fatal	decode_error: A message could not be decoded because of an encoding error or a parameter out of range.
51	Warning	decrypt_error: A handshake cryptographic operation failed, including being unable to correctly verify a signature, decrypt a key exchange, or validate a finished message.

(Continued)

Table 5.2 (*Continued*)

Error Code	Severity	Meaning
60	Fatal	export_restriction: An attempt to export a key failed.
70	Fatal	protocol_version: Recognized but unsupported protocol version received.
71	Fatal	insufficient_security: Specific handshake failure when the server requires more security than the client has offered.
80	Fatal	internal_error: An internal programming error or resource shortage has occurred.
90	Warning	user_canceled: Abort the current handshake process. Should be followed by a close_notify.
100	Warning	no_renegotiation: Reject cipher renegotiation for an active session.

part of the handshake procedure, or may report an error with data exchanged on the connection. When a fatal alert message is sent or received, both parties immediately close the connection without sending any further messages and are required to forget any session identifiers, keys, and secrets associated with the connection.

5.6 SECURING THE HYPERTEXT TRANSFER PROTOCOL

Securing the Hypertext Transfer Protocol (HTTP) was an important advance in Internet security that made possible much of today's web-based commerce in a secure environment. Without a solution to security issues in the World Wide Web it is unlikely that the Internet would have grown beyond a giant information base, and online shopping as we know it would never have taken off.

Two strategies have evolved. The first is called the Secure Hypertext Transfer Protocol (S-HTTP) and offers a set of extensions to HTTP. The second approach, called HTTPS, involves running standard HTTP communications over TCP using the Secure Sockets Layer (SSL).

S-HTTP is described in RFC 2660, and is a set of extensions to HTTP. A single new HTTP method is defined; the *Secure* method allows clients to initiate an exchange of encryption and key information so that subsequent data messages may be encrypted or digitally signed. RFC 2617 offers client-server identity authentication functions through additional fields for standard HTTP methods.

S-HTTP is less used than HTTPS because S-HTTP leaves the HTTP message headers exposed. In HTTPS, the entire HTTP communication is packaged within SSL (see Section 5.5) and is completely encrypted. For HTTPS operations, URLs are prefixed with *https://* and port number 443 is used in place of the standard HTTP port 80.

When users start to access a secure web site using HTTPS they usually see a dialog box prompting them to accept the certificate sent from the web server. This implies a close implementation tie-up between the HTTP engine and the protocol stack implementing the SSL.

Securing HTTP communications allows users to build semiprivate web sites, which lets companies provide web-based access to their corporate email systems. This has been developed so that many companies offer their customers selective access to sensitive sites that hold customer-specific details shared between the supplier and consumer (such as databases of reported faults, software patches for download, etc.).

5.7 HASHING AND ENCRYPTION: ALGORITHMS AND KEYS

Hashing and encryption algorithms are used for the most basic authentication procedures and for the highest security encryption of data. Each algorithm takes as input the raw data to be transmitted and a key. A key is a binary value that is used to lock and unlock the data. Keys vary in length from 32 bits to 256 bits or larger—for any specific algorithm it is generally the case that the larger the key, the more difficult it is to crack the encryption code.

As described in the preceding sections, authentication algorithms use the data and key to generate an authentication code. The receiver can run the same algorithm with the same key on the received data and compare the resulting authentication code to the one transmitted with the data. Encryption algorithms use the key to convert the data into a series of apparently meaningless bytes that the receiver must unscramble before they can be used. The data may be unscrambled using a paired algorithm and a partner key corresponding to those used for encryption, or the same algorithm and the same key may be used, depending on the encryption technique employed.

The most basic hashing algorithm is the cyclic redundancy check (CRC). CRC is used in IP to validate that data has not been accidentally modified, for example, by errors during the transmission process. It is valuable for that purpose and will discover a very high proportion of accidental errors, but it is of absolutely no use as an authentication algorithm since there are well-known procedures for modifying the CRC value for any change made to the data. More complex hashing algorithms are used for authentication in conjunction with a security key.

Encryption algorithms tend to be more complex and have longer keys. The standard minimum encryption algorithm is the Data Encryption Standard (DES) described in Section 5.7.2, but many more sophisticated approaches have been developed. There are two keying techniques used in cryptography; the *secret key* model has already been described and functions by the sender and receiver both knowing (and keeping secret) the key so that they can successfully exchange data.

This is a fine procedure, but as already explained it requires some form of key exchange between end points. This is not only insecure, because someone might intercept this key exchange, but it is dependent on the trustworthiness of both the sender and the receiver since, for example, once the receiver knows the sender's key he or she can impersonate the sender or intercept other encrypted data.

Curiously, the solution to this problem is to make the key public knowledge. In *public key* cryptography one algorithm but two keys are used: one to encrypt the data and the other to decrypt it. One of these keys is freely advertised but the other is kept secret. So, for example, a node wishing to receive secret data would advertise the encryption key to use, but would keep secret the decryption key. The remote node would use the advertised (public) encryption key to encode the data and would send it to the recipient where it could be decoded using the secret key. Conversely, a node wishing to prove its identity will advertise a public decryption key, but keep secret its encryption key—in this way anyone can decode its *digital signature* and know that only the owner of the secret encryption key can have sent the message. This technique can be extended to message digest techniques to provide public key authentication.

In practice, algorithms that use two keys (*dual key algorithms*) are more complex and slower to operate since they require each byte of data to be handled many times. This makes them far from ideal for use in bulk data transfer, but fortunately a solution exists. A secret key algorithm is used to encode the data (that is, it is encrypted using an algorithm that can be encoded and decoded using a single key) and the secret key itself is encrypted using a public key algorithm. The encrypted secret key need only be exchanged once for each transaction and can be used to decode all of the data.

5.7.1 Message Digest Five (MD5)

The simplest authentication hashing algorithm in popular use is the Message Digest version 5 (MD5) algorithm described in RFC 1321; RFC 1828 describes how to apply the algorithm to authentication. Support for this algorithm is mandated in several protocols (such as RSVP) and must be supported as a minimum requirement of IPsec. MD5 produces a 16-byte authentication code (the *message digest*) from data of any length with or without a key of any length. Without a key, MD5 can be used like the CRC to detect accidental changes in data. It can be applied to individual messages, data structures, or entire files. But since a hacker could readily recompute the message digest and so mask a malicious change to the data, a key is used (appended or prepended to the data) to make it impossible for a third party to determine the correct MD5 authentication code of a modify packet.

Figure 5.14 shows some sample code to implement the MD5 authentication algorithm by way of evidence that even the simplest authentication algorithms are nontrivial. The guts of the algorithm are the RSA Data Security, Inc. MD5 Message-Digest Algorithm and are copied from RFC 1321. In the code, a top-level function, *MD5( )*, is called with a data buffer and a key; it returns a 16-byte authentication code. This function processes the following strings in turn: the key,

```
/* Function to perform MD5 digest hashing on a buffer with a key */
/* Returns the message digest in a 16 byte string that is supplied */
void MD5 (char *input_buffer, char* input_key, char *output_digest)
{
  u_int32 digest[4];
  u_int32 bit_count[2];
  u_char work_buffer[64];
  u_char pad_buffer[64] ={
          0x80, 0, 0, 0, 0, 0, 0, 0, 0, 0, 0, 0, 0, 0, 0, 0,
             0, 0, 0, 0, 0, 0, 0, 0, 0, 0, 0, 0, 0, 0, 0, 0,
             0, 0, 0, 0, 0, 0, 0, 0, 0, 0, 0, 0, 0, 0, 0, 0,
             0, 0, 0, 0, 0, 0, 0, 0, 0, 0, 0, 0, 0, 0, 0, 0};
  u_char bit_string[8];
  u_int32 _buffer_len=strlen(input_buffer);
  u_int32 key_len=strlen(input_key);
  u_int32 pad_len;
  u_int32 ii, jj;

  /* Pre-initialize the digest to well-known values */
  /* Placing the low order bytes first, the 16 bytes */
  /* should be filled with 0x01 23 45 67 89 ab cd ef */
  /*               0xfe dc ba 98 76 54 32 10 */
  digest[0]=0x67452301;
  digest[1]=0xefcdab89;
  digest[2]=0x98badcfe;
  digest[3]=0x10325476;
  /* initialize the bit counts */
  bit_count[0]=0;
  bit_count[1]=0;

  /* Start the digest with the key */
  if (key_string !=NULL) {
    _MD5_work(&digest, &bit_count, key_string, key_len, &work_buffer);
    /* Pad to the next 64 byte boundary */
    pad_len=key_len % 64;
    if (pad_len !=0)
      _MD5_work(&digest, &bit_count, &pad_buffer, pad_len, &work_buffer);

  /* Perform first pass MD5 calculation on the string */
  _MD5_work(&digest, &bit_count, input_buffer, buffer_len, &work_buffer);

  /* Update the digest with the key (again) */
  if (key_string !=NULL)
    _MD5_work(&digest, &bit_count, key_string, key_len, &work_buffer);

  /* Pad the combined string to a length of 56 modulo 64 */
  /* The value 56 leaves sufficient space for the 8 byte string */
  /* representation of the message length */
  /* Update the digest with the padding */
  pad_len=(bit_count[0]/8) % 64;
  if (pad_len>56)
    pad_len=pad_len - 56;
```

FIGURE 5.14

Code to implement MD5 authentication.

```
   else
     pad_len=56+64 - pad_len;
   if (pad_len ! = 0)
     _MD5_work(&digest, &bit_count, &pad_buffer, pad_len, &work_buffer);

  /* Convert the bit count into a string and add it to the digest */
  /* This fits into the last 8 bytes of the work buffer */
    for (ii=0; ii<2; ii++)
      for (jj=0; jj<4; jj++)
        bit_string[jj+(ii * 4)]=(u_char)((bit_count[ii] >> (jj * 8)) &0xff);
  MD5_work(&digest, &bit_count, &bit_string, 8,&work_buffer);

  /* Move digest data into the output string */
  for (ii=0; ii<4; ii++)
    for (jj=0; jj<4; jj++)
      output_digest[jj+(ii * 4)]=(u_char)((digest[ii] > (jj * 8)) &0xff);

  return;
}

/* Function to process a buffer in 64 byte pieces */
void _MD5_work (u_int32 *digest, u_int32 *bit_count, u_char- *input_buffer,
               u_int32- len, u_char- *work_buffer)

{
  u_int32 bytes_needed;
  u_int32 offset=0;
  /* Is the work buffer partially full? */
  /* If so, how many bytes are needed to fill it up? */
  bytes_needed=64 - ((bit_count[0]/8) % 64);

  /* Update count of number of bits added by this string */
  bit_len=len * 8;
  bit_count [0] +=bit_len;
  if (bit_count[0] < bit_len)
    bit_count[1]++;
  /* Don't forget to handle the case where len * 8 overflows */
  bit_count[1]+=((u_int32)len >> 29);

  /* Try to fill up the work buffer and do the hash */
  while (len > bytes_needed) {
    memcpy(work_buffer[64 - bytes_needed], input_buffer[offset], bytes_needed);
    _MD5_hash(digest, work_buffer);
    len-=bytes_needed;
    offset+=bytes_needed;
    bytes_needed=64;
}

  /* Copy any spare bytes into the work buffer */
  if (len > 0) {
    assert (len < 64);
    memcpy(work_buffer[0], input_buffer[offset], len);
}
```

FIGURE 5.14 (*Continued*)

```
  return;
}

/* Function to do the actual MD5 hashing */
void _MD5_hash (u_int32 *digest, u_char *work_buffer)
{
  u_int32 work_digest [16];
  u_int32 ii, jj;
  u_int32 a = digest [0], b = digest [1], c = digest [2], d = digest [3];

  /* Convert 64 bytes of buffer into integers */

  for (ii=0; ii < 16; ii++)
    for (jj=0; jj < 4; jj++)
      work_digest [ii] +=( (u_int32) (work_buffer[(ii * 4)+jj]) << (jj * 8) );
  /* Now do the ghastly MD5 magic */
  /* The following code is taken from RFC1321 and is copyright RSA Data Security, */
  /* Inc. to which the following copyright notice applies. */
  /* Copyright (C) 1991-2, RSA Data Security, Inc. Created 1991. All rights reserved */
  /* License to copy and use this software is granted provided that it is identified */
  /* as the "RSA Data Security, Inc. MD5 Message-Digest Algorithm" in all material */
  /* mentioning or referencing this software or this function. */
  /* License is also granted to make and use derivative works provided that such */
  /* works are identified as "derived from the RSA Data Security, Inc. MD5 Message */
  /* Digest Algorithm" in all material mentioning or referencing the derived work. */
  /* RSA Data Security, Inc. makes no representations concerning either the */
  /* merchantability of this software or the suitability of this software for any */
  /* particular purpose. It is provided "as is" without express or implied warranty */
  /* of any kind. */
  /* These notices must be retained in any copies of any part of this documentation */
  /* and/or software. */
#define F(x, y, z) (((x) &(y)) | ((~x) &(z)))
#define G(x, y, z) (((x) &(z)) | ((y) &(~z)))
#define H(x, y, z) ((x) ^ (y) ^ (z))
#define I(x, y, z) ((y) ^ ((X) | (~z)))
#define ROTATE_LEFT(x, n) (((x) << (n)) | ((x) >> (32-(n))))
#define FF (a, b, c, d, x, s, ac)                         \
          (a) += F ((b), (c), (d))+(x)+(u_int32) (ac);    \
          (a) = ROTATE_LEFT ((a), (s));                   \
          (a) += (b);
#define GG (a, b, c, d, x, s, ac)                         \
          (a) += G ((b), (c), (d))+(x)+(u_int32) (ac);    \
          (a) = ROTATE_LEFT ((a), (s));                   \
          (a) += (b);
#define HH (a, b, c, d, x, s, ac)                         \
          (a) +=H ((b), (c), (d))+(x)+(u_int32) (ac);     \
          (a) = ROTATE_LEFT ((a) , (s));                  \
          (a) +=(b);
#define II (a, b, c, d, x, s, ac)                         \
          (a) +=I ((b), (c), (d))+(x)+(u_int32) (ac);     \
          (a) = ROTATE_LEFT ((a), (s)),                   \
          (a) +=(b),;
```

FIGURE 5.14 (*Continued*)

```
/* Round 1 */
FF (a, b, c, d, x[ 0],  7, 0xd76aa478);
FF (d, a, b, c, x[ 1], 12, 0xe8c7b756);
FF (c, d, a, b, x[ 2], 17, 0x242070db);
FF (b, c, d, a, x[ 3], 22, 0xc1bdceee);
FF (a, b, c, d, x[ 4],  7, 0xf57c0faf);
FF (d, a, b, c, x[ 5], 12, 0x4787c62a);
FF (c, d, a, b, x[ 6], 17, 0xa8304613);
FF (b, c, d, a, x[ 7], 22, 0xfd469501);
FF (a, b, c, d, x[ 8],  7, 0x698098d8);
FF (d, a, b, c, x[ 9], 12, 0x8b44f7af);
FF (c, d, a, b, x[10], 17, 0xffff5bb1);
FF (b, c, d, a, x[11], 22, 0x895cd7be);
FF (a, b, c, d, x[12],  7, 0x6b901122);
FF (d, a, b, c, x[13], 12, 0xfd987193);
FF (c, d, a, b, x[14], 17, 0xa679438e);
FF (b, c, d, a, x[15], 22, 0x49b40821);

/* Round 2 */
GG (a, b, c, d, x[ 1],  5, 0xf61e2562);
GG (d, a, b, c, x[ 6],  9, 0xc040b340);
GG (c, d, a, b, x[11], 14, 0x265e5a51);
GG (b, c, d, a, x[ 0], 20, 0xe9b6c7aa);
GG (a, b, c, d, x[ 5],  5, 0xd62f105d);
GG (d, a, b, c, x[10],  9, 0x2441453);
GG (c, d, a, b, x[15], 14, 0xd8a1e681);
GG (b, c, d, a, x[ 4], 20, 0xe7d3fbc8);
GG (a, b, c, d, x[ 9],  5, 0x21e1cde6);
GG (d, a, b, c, x[14],  9, 0xc33707d6);
GG (c, d, a, b, x[ 3], 14, 0xf4d50d87);
GG (b, c, d, a, x[ 8], 20, 0x455a14ed);
GG (a, b, c, d, x[13],  5, 0xa9e3e905);
GG (d, a, b, c, x[ 2],  9, 0xfcefa3f8);
GG (c, d, a, b, x[ 7], 14, 0x676f02d9);
GG (b, c, d, a, x[12], 20, 0x8d2a4c8a);

/* Round 3 */
HH (a, b, c, d, x[ 5],  4, 0xfffa3942);
HH (d, a, b, c, x[ 8], 11, 0x8771f681);
HH (c, d, a, b, x[11], 16, 0x6d9d6122);
HH (b, c, d, a, x[14], 23, 0xfde5380c);
HH (a, b, c, d, x[ 1],  4, 0xa4beea44);
HH (d, a, b, c, x[ 4], 11, 0x4bdecfa9);
HH (c, d, a, b, x[ 7], 16, 0xf6bb4b60);
HH (b, c, d, a, x[10], 23, 0xbebfbc70);
HH (a, b, c, d, x[13],  4, 0x289b7ec6);
HH (d, a, b, c, x[ 0], 11, 0xeaa127fa);
HH (c, d, a, b, x[ 3], 16, 0xd4ef3085);
HH (b, c, d, a, x[ 6], 23, 0x4881d05);
HH (a, b, c, d, x[ 9],  4, 0xd9d4d039);
HH (d, a, b, c, x[12], 11, 0xe6db99e5);
HH (b, c, d, a, x[ 2], 23, 0xc4ac5665);
HH (c, d, a, b, x[15], 16, 0x1fa27cf8);
```

FIGURE 5.14 (*Continued*)

```
/* Round 4 */
II (a, b, c, d, x[ 0],  6, 0xf4292244);
II (d, a, b, c, x[ 7], 10, 0x432aff97);
II (c, d, a, b, x[14], 15, 0xab9423a7);
II (b, c, d, a, x[ 5], 21, 0xfc93a039);
II (a, b, c, d, x[12],  6, 0x655b59c3);
II (d, a, b, c, x[ 3], 10, 0x8f0ccc92);
II (c, d, a, b, x[10], 15, 0xffeff47d);
II (b, c, d, a, x[ 1], 21, 0x85845dd1);
II (a, b, c, d, x[ 8],  6, 0x6fa87e4f);
II (d, a, b, c, x[15], 10, 0xfe2ce6e0);
II (c, d, a, b, x[ 6], 15, 0xa3014314);
II (b, c, d, a, x[13], 21, 0x4e0811a1);
II (a, b, c, d, x[ 4],  6, 0xf7537e82);
II (d, a, b, c, x[11], 10, 0xbd3af235);
II (c, d, a, b, x[ 2], 15, 0x2ad7d2bb);
II (b, c, d, a, x[ 9], 21, 0xeb86d391);

/* Finally update the digest and return */
digest [0]+= a;
digest [1]+= b;
digest [2]+= c;
digest [3]+= d;
return;
}
```

FIGURE 5.14 (*Continued*)

padding up to a 64-byte boundary, the data buffer, the key, and more padding. Each string is passed to _MD5_work( ), which chops the data into 64-byte segments and passes them to _MD5_hash( ) to be processed through the algorithm.

MD5 has been discovered to have some security flaws, and work is ongoing to develop fixes and to devise more secure alternatives.

5.7.2 Data Encryption Standard (DES)

The Data Encryption Standard (DES) is the basic encryption algorithm mandated by IPsec. It was standardized by the U.S. National Bureau of Standards as Federal Information Processing Standards Publication 46-2 (superceding FIPS 46-1). DES is a federally approved mathematical algorithm for encrypting and decrypting binary-coded information.

DES uses a minimum 64-bit key of which 56 bits are available to define the key itself, and 8 bits (one per byte) are used to provide error detection on the key itself. The eighth bit in each byte is set to give parity in the byte—that is, it is set so that there are an even number of bits set to 1 within the byte.

Four modes of DES operation are defined, each providing an increased level of complexity and, thus, a better level of security. The Electronic Codebook (ECB) mode is the direct application of the DES algorithm to encrypt and decrypt data, deriving its name from the way secret messages used to be encoded and decoded by hand using a book of codes. The Cipher Block Chaining (CBC) mode is an enhanced mode of ECB that chains together blocks of cipher text to increase the size and therefore complexity of the encoded data. The Cipher Feedback (CFB) mode uses previously generated cipher text together with the message to be encoded as input to the DES algorithm, effectively chaining together the source message with a pseudorandom stream of bytes. The Output Feedback (OFB) mode is identical to CFB except that the previous output of the DES is used as input in OFB.

The DES algorithm is sufficiently complex to warrant its exclusion from this book. For a detailed description of the process refer to the National Institute of Standards and Technology web page listed at the end of this chapter.

5.8 EXCHANGING KEYS

The generation and distribution of keys are fundamental to the operation of security systems. Historically, keys have been "randomly" generated at a central location and distributed to the encryption and decryption sites using the most reliable methods available. Often, this has involved writing the key down on a piece of paper that is then carried to the computers concerned, where it is manually entered into the system. Presumably, the message self-destructed a few seconds later.

Computers have made it possible to achieve a new degree of randomness in key generation and also to distribute keys more freely, but a significant problem is that keys cannot be encrypted when they are transmitted—if they were the user would not be able to interpret them. This means that the most sensitive piece of data, the key to all of the rest of the data, is sent in the open and is easy to intercept.

As described in Section 5.7, dual key cryptography algorithms allow the receiver to tell the sender a public key to use to encode secret data while retaining a separate secret key to decode the data. Since the public key is used only for encryption it does not matter that other users might view it. The secret key that is used to decrypt the messages is never exposed. This method can be used to encrypt other keys that need to be exchanged across public networks—a useful feature since dual key encryption algorithms are considerably more burdensome to operate if applied to all messages.

Key exchange is, therefore, an important aspect of Internet security and is the subject of several protocols. These protocols are also used to allow encryption/decryption partners to negotiate which algorithms and features they will use on the Security Association they maintain.

The Internet Key Exchange (IKE) described in RFC 2409 is the merger of two previous protocols: the OAKLEY key exchange protocol (RFC 2412) and the Internet Security Association and Key Management Protocol (ISAKMP; RFC 2408). The reader might wonder why the merged protocol has a numerically lower RFC number than one of the constituent parts, but this is just an editorial issue as a batch of RFCs were all published at the same time. In all senses, IKE and ISAKMP/OAKLEY are identical.

5.8.1 Internet Key Exchange

ISAKMP provides the necessary negotiation facilities to agree on the level of security required and the algorithms to use. It also allows end points to exchange keys in the most secure fashion possible. It is also important to note that the protocol includes strong authentication of the end points so that a node may know for certain that it is really talking to the correct remote node—otherwise it would be possible for an impostor to participate in a conversation using all of the security techniques and being sent the prized data in a form that it would be able to decrypt.

The first job of ISAKMP is to establish the SA between the end points. This function is taken from ISAKMP and requires a message exchange over TCP or UDP using port number 500 to initiate the SA, negotiate options, exchange public keys, and exchange identity certification information. The elements here are not dissimilar to those described for the Transport Layer Security Handshake protocol in Section 5.5.1, although the message flows are different.

Each ISAKMP message begins with a common message header that identifies the message and the SA to which it applies. The body of the message is made up of a series of payloads. The type of the first payload is indicated in the common header, and each payload announces the type of the subsequent payload if one exists. The format of the payloads depends on their type. Figure 5.15 shows the

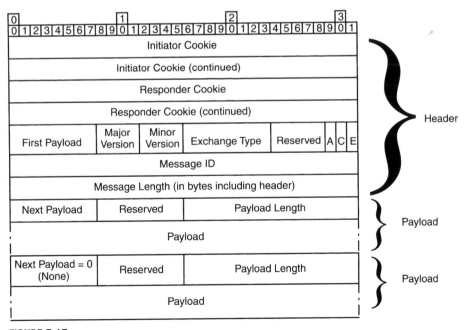

FIGURE 5.15

ISAKMP messages comprise a common header followed by one or more payloads.

ISAKMP common header with two payloads. The initiator and responder cookies identify the SA at the end points. The protocol version defined by RFC 2408 is 1.1. The Message ID is a randomly generated number created by the sender of a request message and echoed in a response, allowing correlation with minimal risk of collision. The Message Length is given in bytes and covers the whole message, including the header. The Exchange Type indicates the ISAKMP mode of operation and so dictates which payloads are required—possible values for this field are shown in Table 5.3. Three flags are used as follows:

A—Authentication Only: The payloads of this message should be subjected to authentication but not encryption.

C—Commit: Used to request (force) a complete message exchange before the contents of a message are put into use.

E—Encrypted: Indicates that the payloads are encrypted using the agreed encryption algorithm.

Table 5.3 ISAKMP Exchange Types Carried in the Common Message Header	
Exchange Type	**Meaning**
0	None.
1	The Base Exchange is designed to allow the Key Exchange and Authentication-related information to be transmitted together. Combining the Key Exchange and Authentication-related information into one message reduces the number of round-trips at the expense of not providing identity protection.
2	The Identity Protection Exchange separates the Key Exchange from the Identity and Authentication-related information providing protection of the identity information at the expense of two additional messages since identities are exchanged under the protection of a previously established common shared secret.
3	The Authentication Only Exchange provides for the transmission of only authentication-related information. This exposes the authentication feature without the extra expense of computing keys. When using this exchange during negotiation, none of the transmitted information will be encrypted.
4	The Aggressive Exchange allows the security association, key exchange, and authentication payloads to be transmitted together in a single message. This reduces the number of round-trips at the expense of not providing identity protection.
5	The Informational Exchange provides a one-way transmission of information that can be used for security association management.

Table 5.4 ISAKMP Payload Types Identify the Components of Messages

Payload Type	Meaning
0	No more payloads.
1	Security Association Parameters. Sets the context for the establishment of a security association by specifying the use to which this association will be put. Contains a Domain of Interpretation (DOI) field that is set to the value 1 to indicate IPsec.
2	The Proposal payload defines the identity of the security association and includes the operational protocol (IPsec, TLS, OSPF, etc.) and the cookies (sometimes known as the Security Parameter Index, or SPI) used in that protocol to represent the association.
3	The Transform payload suggests or agrees on the security processes and algorithms available or chosen for use on the security association.
4	The Key Exchange payload is used to exchange keys.
5	The end points identify themselves using the Identification payload, which is context specific depending on the Domain of Interpretation and the identity type chosen.
6	A Certificate payload provides strong authentication of the identity of an end point using one of a variety of standardized means.
7	The Certificate Request payload can be included in any message and requests that the remote node immediately respond with a message that includes a Certificate payload. (Compare with the Certificate Request in the TLS handshake protocol.)
8	The Hash payload is included in messages if the use of message authentication has been agreed to. The payload contains the output of the hashing algorithm applied to all or part of the message as negotiated using the Transform payload.
9	The transform payload may also negotiate the use of digital signatures. If so, the Signature payload is included in all messages to authenticate their origins.
10	A pseudorandom identifier is included in the Nonce payload to help prevent against replay attacks. The value of this identifier is changed for each instance of the security association, but is constant for the life of one association. Since the Nonce is only present in encrypted messages it is not externally visible and can be verified to be consistent on all messages in one association and a super-security-conscious end node can keep track of previous values to protect against an intruder replaying previous messages.

(Continued)

Table 5.4 (*Continued*)

Payload Type	Meaning
11	The Notification payload contains information data specific to the DOI context.
12	The Delete payload officially "contains a protocol-specific security association identifier that the sender has removed from its security association database and is, therefore, no longer valid." That is to say, it is used to terminate a security association.
13	ISAKMP messages may optionally include Vendor ID payloads to identify the communicating implementations.

The First Payload field of the ISAKMP header indicates the type of the first payload element in the message body. Each payload element also contains a Next Payload field to indicate the type of the next payload. These types are listed in Table 5.4. Each payload also includes a Length field that indicates the length of the payload in bytes, including the Next Payload and Length fields.

The Exchange Types listed in Table 5.4 dictate how the ISAKMP end points exchange information—that is, which payload elements they send in which messages. The main differences are in how the elements are combined and therefore how much protection is available to the information that is sent. In general there is a trade-off between sending a few messages packed with unprotected information, and sending more messages in which the information in the later messages is protected by security negotiated by the earlier messages.

Figure 5.16 illustrates the messages exchanged when an SA is established using the Base Exchange. In step 1 the initiator sends a request carrying the Security Association, Proposal, and Transform payloads to show that it wants to establish a Security Association and to advertise the types of security it wants to apply and the algorithms that it supports. It also includes a Nonce payload to randomize the message. The responder checks that the Nonce is new and, if it is willing to establish a Security Association, responds with the precise subset of security options and algorithms that will be applied (step 2). The initiator then generates keys and sends them together with proof of its identity (step 3) and the responder completes the exchange with its keys and proof that it is who it says it is. The SA is now fully established and data transfer can begin. Note that since the identities and keys are sent on the same message, the identities cannot actually be protected by the security mechanisms.

The Identity Protection Exchange provides protection for the identity exchange. This is achieved by introducing an additional message exchange and sharing out the payloads as shown in Figure 5.17. The Nonce is moved from the initial exchange (steps 1 and 2) to the new exchange (steps 3 and 4) that also swaps keys. Once the

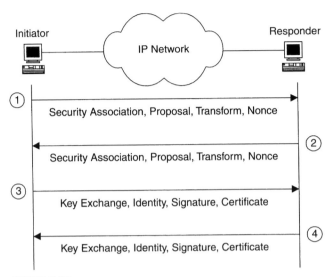

FIGURE 5.16

The ISAKMP messages and payloads exchanged during the establishment of a security association using the Base Exchange.

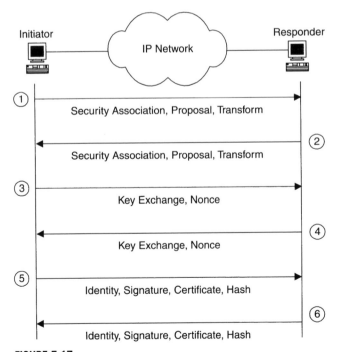

FIGURE 5.17

The ISAKMP Identity Protection Exchange provides additional security during the establishment of a security association.

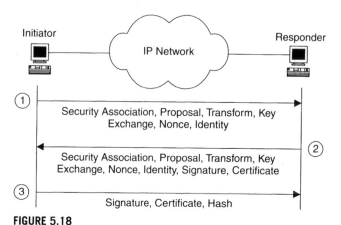

FIGURE 5.18

The number of messages exchanged to set up a security association can be kept down to just three using the Aggressive Exchange.

keys are known they can be applied to all subsequent messages and so the identity exchanges (steps 5 and 6) can be protected by the authentication algorithms and sent along with a Hash payload.

Alternatively, the Aggressive Exchange cuts the number of messages sent to a bare minimum, as shown in Figure 5.18. In this case, the initiator reduces its Proposal and Transform options so that the responder has no choice other than acceptance or refusal. The initiator can therefore generate its keys up front and it sends these on the initial message along with its identity (step 1). The responder replies with all information in one go (step 2), leaving the initiator to certify its identity and maybe use the authentication algorithm to protect this final stage (step 3).

nonce \'nän(t)s\ *n* [**ME** *nanes*, alter. (fr. incorrect division of *then anes* in such phrases as *to then anes* for the one purpose) of *anes* one purpose, irreg. fr. *an* one, fr. **OE** *an*]: the one, particular, or present occasion, purpose, or use <for the ~>.

FURTHER READING

Personal Encryption Clearly Explained, by Pete Loshin (1998). IP Professional. This book provides a comprehensive introduction to the use of security in the Internet and other networks.

Virtual Private Networks—Making the Right Connection, by Dennis Fowler (1999). Morgan Kaufmann. Fowler describes the use of IPsec to provide secure connections between private networks. It also provides a good introduction to user authentication and to key management and exchange.

Applied Cryptography: Protocols, Algorithms, and Source Code in C, by Bruce Schneier (1995). John Wiley & Sons. This is a good starting point for those who want to dig deeper into the way that encryption is made to work.

The following lists show specific RFCs and other standards broken down by topic.

Security Considerations

RFC 1281—Guidelines for the Secure Operation of the Internet
RFC 2411—IP Security—Document Roadmap
RFC 2828—Internet Security Glossary

IPsec

RFC 2401—Security Architecture for the Internet Protocol
RFC 2402—IP Authentication Header
RFC 2406—IP Encapsulating Security Payload (ESP)
RFC 3457—Requirements for IPsec Remote Access Scenarios

Other Security Protocols

1. RFC 2246—The TLS Protocol Version 1.0
2. RFC 2617—HTTP Authentication: Basic and Digest Access Authentication
3. RFC 2660—The Secure HyperText Transfer Protocol
4. RFC 2818—HTTP Over TLS

Algorithms

Data Encryption Standard:[FIPS-46-2], from the U.S. National Bureau of Standards, http://www.itl.nist.gov/div897/pubs/fip46-2.htm

1. RFC 1321—The MD5 Message-Digest Algorithm
2. RFC 1828—IP Authentication Using Keyed MD5
3. RFC 2405—The ESP DES-CBC Cipher Algorithm with Explicit IV

Key Exchange

SKEME: A Versatile Secure Key Exchange Mechanism for Internet, by Hugo Krawcyzk. ISOC Secure Networks and Distributed Systems Symposium, San Diego, 1996.

1. RFC 2408—Intemet Security Association and Key Management Protocol (ISAKMP)
2. RFC 2409—The Internet Key Exchange (IKE)
3. RFC 2412—The OAKLEY Key Determination Protocol

IP Security in Practice

Claims that IPv4 security was neglected by the founders are based on the argument that early IPv4 networks were insecure things strung together on trust between naive but ultimately honorable academicians. However, at the very start the Internet Protocol was defined as a U.S. Department of Defense (DoD) standard, and security was certainly a consideration. Nevertheless, the IETF has given considerably more explicit attention to IPv6 security than was accorded to IPv4 during its early development.

The desirability and utility of authentication and security features at the IP layer have been debated for years. This chapter discusses how authentication and security, including secure password transmission, encryption, and digital signatures on datagrams, are implemented under IP through the *Authentication Header (AH)* and *Encapsulating Security Payload (ESP)* options. Before examining the *IP Security Protocol (IPsec)*, however, we will take a look at the IP security architecture described in RFC 2401, "Security Architecture for the Internet Protocol," and the different pieces of that architecture.

IPv4 as originally designed offered no real security features; it was intended simply as an internetworking protocol. While not necessarily a problem for a networking protocol used largely in research and academic settings, the increase in importance of IP networking to the general business and consumer networking environments makes the potential harm resulting from attacks more devastating than ever. This section examines the following.

- Issues of security for IP
- Security goals defined for IP
- Cryptographic elements of IPsec
- Protocol elements of IPsec
- Implementing IPsec

The next section takes a look at the specifics of IPsec, as well as some of the tools being assembled to achieve these goals.

6.1 IP SECURITY ISSUES

IPsec as defined in RFC 2401 provides a security architecture for the Internet Protocol—*not* a security architecture for the Internet. The distinction is important: IPsec defines security services to be used at the IP layer, both for IPv4 and IPv6. It is often said that IPv6 is "more secure" than IPv4, but the difference is that IPsec is required for all IPv6, whereas it is optional for IPv4 nodes.

The IP Security Protocol (IPsec) provides an interoperable and open standard for building security into the network layer rather than at the application or transport layer. Although applications can benefit from network-layer security, the most important application IPsec enables is the creation of virtual private networks (VPNs) capable of securely carrying enterprise data across the open Internet.

IPsec is often used in conjunction with tunnel management protocols, including the Layer 2 Tunneling Protocol (L2TP), the Layer 2 Forwarding (L2F) protocol designed by Cisco Systems, and Microsoft's Point to Point Tunneling Protocol (PPTP). RFC 2661, "Layer Two Tunneling Protocol 'L2TP,'" defines L2TP as a standards track specification for tunneling packets sent over a PPP link.

While the tunnel management protocols offer access security services, they don't provide authentication or privacy services, so they are often used in conjunction with IPsec—which does provide those services. However, saying that IPsec specifies protocols for encrypting and authenticating data sent within IP packets is an oversimplification and even obscures IPsec's full potential. IPsec enables the following.

Encryption of data passing between two nodes, using strong public and private key cryptographic algorithms

Authentication of data and its source, using strong authentication mechanisms

Control over access to sensitive data and private networks

Integrity verification of data carried by a connectionless protocol (IP)

Protection against *replay* attacks, in which an intruder intercepts packets sent between two IP nodes and resends them after decrypting or modifying them

Limitation of *traffic analysis* attacks, in which an intruder intercepts protected data and analyzes source and destination information, size and type of packets, and other aspects of the data, including header contents that might not otherwise be protected by encryption

End-to-end security for IP packets, providing assurance to users of endpoint nodes of the privacy and integrity of their transmissions

Secure tunneling through insecure networks such as the global Internet and other public networks

Integration of algorithms, protocols, and security infrastructures into an overarching security architecture.

As defined in RFC 2401, "Security Architecture for the Internet Protocol," the goal of the IP security architecture is "to provide various security services for traffic at the IP layer, in both the IPv4 and IPv6 environments." This means security services that have the following features.

Interoperable As with all Internet protocols, interoperability is a fundamental goal. This means that any IP node supporting IPsec can communicate with any other node supporting IPsec. There is a basic set of cryptographic algorithms for encryption and integrity checking, which all IPsec nodes must support, although individual nodes and implementations may support many more, optional, algorithms. Although some nodes are configured to prefer newer or less open algorithms, all nodes are required to support the basic ones.

High quality The baseline for security through IPsec must be set high enough to guarantee a reasonable degree of actual security. Algorithms and key lengths that are to be vulnerable to attack are not acceptable. For example, data encrypted with 40-bit encryption keys can be *brute-forced* or successfully and quickly decrypted by trying every combination. The number of possible keys is $2^{40} - 1$, or roughly 1000 billion; on average, the correct key will be discovered after trying half (about 500 billion) of those combinations. Such attacks are almost trivially easy with commercial off-the-shelf hardware, and thus 40-bit keys are not considered to provide "high-quality" security.

Cryptographically based Cryptographers work with algorithms for encryption, secure hashing, and authentication. Encryption algorithms allow regular data to be transformed into *cyphertext*, data scrambled so that only the entity holding an appropriate *key* can decrypt it. Secure hash algorithms operate on any size chunk of data to generate a fixed-length sequence of bits (the hash). An entity can confirm the integrity of the data by running the hashing algorithm on received data; if the transmitted hash and the calculated hash agree, the data is verified as having been sent without change. Authentication of entities through the use of digital signatures depends on public key algorithms. Data encrypted with the public key of a public/private key pair can be decrypted only by an entity with access to the private key; likewise, if an entity encrypts something (such as the text of a message) with its *private* key, then anyone with access to the public key can decrypt the message and confirm that the sender has access to that key.

By basing IPsec on cryptography rather than on any other mechanisms for security, the protocol designers place limits on the security goals possible to attain through its use while at the same time ensuring that those security goals will be achieved through the use of verifiable and reliable mechanisms.

The IP security architecture allows systems to choose the required security protocols, identify the cryptographic algorithms to use with those protocols, and exchange any keys or other material or information necessary to provide security services.

As may be evident from its highly qualified description, public key cryptography-based mechanisms require that all participants can be confident that public keys are issued only to the entities identified with those keys. When a public key is published purporting to represent Microsoft Corporation, the possibility that the key has been properly issued to Microsoft and not to a computer criminal should approach 100% certainty. Unfortunately, as was demonstrated in early 2001 when it was reported that leading public key infrastructure vendor Verisign, Inc., issued two public key certificates to an impostor claiming to represent Microsoft, this is not always possible.

As a network-layer protocol, IPsec provides security only at the network layer. This means that packets can be protected from the point at which they enter the IP network (the source node's IP interface) to the point at which they leave the IP network (the destination node's IP interface). IPsec cannot substitute for proper application or transport-layer security mechanisms, and IPsec cannot protect against attackers taking control of the source or destination nodes or processes.

6.2 SECURITY GOALS

Computer security can be said to embody three general goals.

Authentication The ability to reliably determine that data has been received as it was sent and to verify that the entity that sent the data is what it claims to be. Successful authentication means preventing attackers from impersonating an authorized entity.

Integrity The ability to reliably determine that the data has not been modified during transit from its source to its destination. Successfully maintaining data integrity means preventing an attacker from modifying authentic data without detection as well as preventing the acceptance of data that has been corrupted somewhere in the network clouds (as happens occasionally).

Confidentiality The ability to transmit data that can be used or read only by its intended recipient and not by any other entity. Successfully maintaining data confidentiality means preventing anyone other than the intended recipient(s) from being able to access private data.

Developments in modern cryptography, specifically in the use of *public key cryptography* (discussed in the next section), make possible the combination of these three goals in one set of functions. These goals—authentication, integrity, and confidentiality—are achieved through three related functions.

Digital signatures unequivocally link the holder of a particular secret with data represented as having been *signed* by that entity.

Secure hashes digitally "summarize" a sequence of data using a repeatable process that will produce identical results only if the data sequence being verified matches the data sequence produced by the sender.

Encryption is the process of performing a reversible transformation on readable data so as to render it unreadable by anyone other than the holder of the appropriate decryption key.

Some or all of these functions are possible in combination or individually in protocols at every layer of the TCP/IP stack, from IP (through IPsec) to the transport layer (through TLS, the Transport Layer Security protocol) to security functions provided through applications.

The goal of IPsec is to provide security mechanisms for all versions of IP.[1] IPsec provides security services at the IP layer, and systems may require other systems to interact with it securely with IPsec and a particular set of security algorithms and protocols. While IPsec mandates support for a basic set of algorithms, it also allows nodes to negotiate acceptably secure interaction with other systems with optional algorithms. IPsec provides the framework within which nodes can negotiate appropriate algorithms, protocols, key lengths, and other aspects of secure communication.

IPsec allows maintenance of the following.

Access control IPsec allows security protocols to be invoked governing the secure exchange of keys, allowing authentication of users for access control purposes.

Connectionless integrity IPsec allows nodes to validate each IP packet independent of any other packet. There is no need to verify sequences of packets or even to have access to other packets exchanged by the same nodes. Connectionless integrity is enabled through use of secure hashing techniques, similar to the use of check digits but with greater reliability and less likelihood of tampering from unauthorized entities.

Data origin authentication Identifying the source of the data contained in an IP packet is another security service provided by IPsec. This function is accomplished through the use of digital signatures.

Defense against packet replay attacks As a connectionless protocol, IP is subject to the threat of replay attacks, where an attacker sends a packet that has already been received by the destination host. Replay attacks can harm system availability by tying up receiving system resources. IPsec provides a packet countermechanism that protects against this ploy.

Encryption Data confidentiality—keeping access to data from anyone but those with proper authorization—is provided through the use of encryption.

Limited traffic flow confidentiality Encrypting data is not always sufficient to protect systems; merely knowing the endpoints of an encrypted

---

[1] IPsec support is mandatory for IPv6 nodes, but optional for IPv4 nodes.

exchange, the frequency of such interaction, or other information about the transmissions can provide a determined attacker with enough information to disrupt or subvert systems. IPsec provides some limited traffic flow confidentiality through the use of IP tunneling, especially when coupled with security gateways.

All of these functions are possible through proper use of the Encapsulating Security Payload (ESP) Header and the Authentication Header (AH). A handful of cryptographic functions is specified for IPsec and is described briefly in the next section.

Public key encryption provides a mechanism for performing almost all of these functions with a single set of processes. AH provides mechanisms for applying authentication algorithms to an IP packet, whereas ESP provides mechanisms for applying any kind of cryptographic algorithm to an IP packet including encryption, digital signature, and/or secure hashes. IPsec is aimed at eliminating certain types of attacks, including the following.

Denial of service (DoS) attacks These occur when an entity uses network transmissions to prevent legitimate users from using network resources. For example, an attacker may flood a host with TCP SYN requests and thereby crash a system, or the attack may consist of repeated transmission of long mail messages with the intention of filling up a user's or site's bandwidth with nuisance traffic.

Spoofing attacks These occur when an entity transmits packets that misrepresent the packets' origins. For example, one type of spoofing attack occurs when the attacker sends a mail message with the From: header indicating the source of the message as, say, the president of the United States. More insidious and almost as easy to engineer are those attacks that occur when packets are sent out with an incorrect source address in the headers.

Man-in-the-middle attacks (MITMs) These occur when an attacker (Alice) positions herself between two communicating entities (call them Bob and Carol) and intercepts all their transmissions. Alice poses as Bob when communicating with Carol, and as Carol when communicating with Bob. Alice, as a result, is able to send whatever data she wants to Bob instead of what Carol wants to send to Bob. MITM attacks are relatively easy when transmissions are not encrypted or authenticated. However, Alice can successfully attack even a protected data stream if she is able to either gain access to Carol's secret keys (or be issued a set of her own public/secret key pairs that is sufficiently similar to Carol's that Bob will be fooled).

This last attack is important because it raises the issue of handling keys. As just noted, encryption and digital signature functions require the use of *keys* to decrypt and/or verify data, and *digital certificates* are one mechanism by which public keys can be distributed. Although all *public key infrastructure* (*PKI*) providers, including Verisign, make their own efforts to validate all applications, the problem is not a matter of technology. As noted earlier, Verisign issued two digital certificates to someone who improperly posed as a representative of Microsoft; a sufficiently motivated attacker will presumably use every possible tactic to get a desired certification. An attacker's ability to forge credentials (from letterhead on which to type a request for a corporate digital certificate to passport, birth certificate, or other documents submitted to support a fraudulent application) may exceed the ability of the PKI provider to detect them.

As a result of this potential vulnerability, IPsec requires a mechanism by which keys can be securely administered and distributed in a way that associates public keys with the entities that are supposed to own them.

As just noted, IPsec secures IP—*not* the Internet and certainly not the systems connected to the Internet or the processes running on those systems. IPsec must be considered only one part of the organizational security strategy. While IPsec-protected traffic may pass unscathed across the global Internet, before it leaves its source and after it arrives at its destination, that traffic will be vulnerable to attacks on local links, local systems, processes, and the protocols used there.

6.3 ENCRYPTION AND AUTHENTICATION ALGORITHMS

Rather than relying on secrecy to protect an encryption or authentication scheme (an approach known as "security through obscurity"), TCP/IP security protocols always specify that cryptographic algorithms be well known and accessible. This is done for several reasons, not the least of which is that as an open protocol suite, TCP/IP protocol specifications must be published freely. The most important reason, however, is that secrecy is a poor safeguard over security.

Attempting to keep an encryption algorithm secret is almost impossible, particularly if it is being used by anyone other than the person who knows the secret. Attackers have many cryptanalysis tools at their disposal for breaking codes, and they need only have access to ciphertexts to break them. Having access to the software used to encrypt and/or decrypt data with the secret algorithm makes the task much easier: the attacker must only determine what the software does to the data to figure out how to reverse the operation.

The greatest advantage that published algorithms provide is the benefit of scrutiny by researchers and others seeking to find ways to further improve or break the algorithms. The more trained experts examine an algorithm, the less likely they are to overlook an "obvious" attack.

Security algorithms and protocols are hard to design because there are so many different ways to attack them—and designers can't always imagine them all. Although national security organizations as well as corporations may have their own top-secret codes, secrets are hard to keep. Spies and other criminals are well known for their skill at motivating (through bribery, extortion, or other means) people who know secrets to share them.

The prevailing wisdom in security holds that a good encryption or authentication algorithm should be secure even if an attacker knows what algorithm is being used. This is particularly important for Internet security, since an attacker with a sniffer will often be able to determine exactly what kind of algorithm is being used by listening as systems negotiate their connections.

In this section we'll cover five types of important cryptographic functions.

- Symmetric encryption
- Public key encryption
- Key exchange
- Secure hashes (message digests)
- Digital signature

6.3.1 Symmetric Encryption

Most people are familiar with *symmetric encryption*, if only at a visceral, intuitive level: Plaintexts are encrypted with a secret key and some set of procedures, and they are decrypted with the same key and the same set of procedures. If you have the key, you can decrypt all data that has been encrypted with that key. Sometimes known as *secret key encryption*, symmetric encryption is computationally efficient and it is the most frequent type of encryption for network transmission of volumes of data.

In October 2000, the National Institute of Standards and Technology (NIST) announced that the *Rijndael*[2] data encryption algorithm had been selected for the *Advanced Encryption Standard (AES)*, replacing the outdated *Data Encryption Standard (DES)* algorithm originally developed during the 1970s by IBM. DES uses 56-bit keys, although a variation called *triple DES* encrypts data three times with the DES algorithm, providing improved security.

Using a secure encryption requires using sufficiently long keys. Shorter keys are vulnerable to brute-force attacks, in which an attacker uses a computer to try all the different possible keys. Key lengths on the order of 40 bits, for example, are considered insecure because they can be broken by brute-force attacks in very short order by relatively inexpensive computers. Single-DES has been brute-forced as well; in general, 128-bit and longer keys are likely to be secure against such attacks for the immediate future.

Symmetric encryption algorithms can be vulnerable to other types of attacks. Most applications that use symmetric encryption for Internet communications use session keys, meaning that the key is used for only a single-session data transmission (sometimes several keys are used in one session). Loss of a session key thus compromises only the data that was sent during that session or portion of a session.

---

[2]According to an FAQ at the NIST Web site, "The algorithm's developers have suggested the following pronunciation alternatives: 'Reign Dahl,' 'Rain Doll,' and 'Rhine Dahl.'" The AES home page is http://csrc.nist.gov/encryption/aes/.

These are some of the other symmetric encryption algorithms that have been or are currently being used for Internet applications.

RC2/RC4 These commercial symmetric encryption algorithms were developed and marketed by the cryptography firm RSA.

CAST Developed in Canada and used by Nortel's Entrust products, CAST supports up to 128-bit keys.

IDEA The International Data Encryption Algorithm supports 128-bit keys. It was patented by Swiss firm Ascom, which granted permission for IDEA to be used for free noncommercial use in the seminal and open source encryption program Pretty Good Privacy (PGP), written by Philip Zimmermann and published for a time by Network Associates, Inc.

GOST This algorithm was reportedly developed by a Soviet security agency.

Blowfish This algorithm was developed by Bruce Schneier and released to the public domain.

Twofish This was Bruce Schneier's submission to the AES competition.

Skipjack This algorithm was developed by the National Security Agency for use with the Clipper chip's escrowed key system.

6.3.2 Public Key Encryption

Public key encryption, also called *asymmetric encryption*, uses pairs of keys: One, the *public key*, is associated with the other, the *secret key*. The public key is intended to be made public. Any data encrypted with the public key can only be decrypted with the secret key and any data encrypted with the secret key can be decrypted with the public key.

Anyone can get a public key and encrypt some data with it. That data can be decrypted only by the holder of the secret key. As long as an entity can keep its secret key a secret, other entities can be sure that any data encrypted with the public key will be accessible only to the holder of the associated secret key. The holder of the secret key can encrypt something using that secret key and make it available to another entity. That entity can verify the first entity as holding the secret key of a particular public key pair by decrypting the data with the public key.

Public key encryption tends to be computationally intensive and is most often used to encrypt session keys for network transmissions as well as for digital signatures.

The most commonly used type of public key encryption is the *RSA* algorithm developed by Ron Rivest, Adi Shamir, and Len Adleman. RSA defines a mechanism for choosing and generating the secret/public key pairs, as well as for the actual mathematical function to be used for encryption.

6.3.3 Key Management

One of the most complex issues facing Internet security professionals is how to manage keys. This includes not only the actual distribution of keys through a key exchange protocol but also the negotiation of key length, lifetime, and cryptographic algorithms between communicating systems.

An open channel (an open communication medium over which transmissions can be overheard) like the global Internet complicates the process of sharing a secret. This process is necessary when two entities need to share a key to be used for encryption. Some of the most important cryptographic algorithms relate to the process of sharing a key over an open channel securely, in a way that keeps the secret from anyone but the intended recipients.

Diffie-Hellman key exchange is an algorithm that allows entities to exchange enough information to derive a session encryption key. Alice (the customary entity name for the first participant in a cryptographic protocol) calculates a value using Bob's public value and her own secret value (Bob is the second participant in cryptographic protocols). Bob calculates his own value and sends it to Alice; they each then use their secret values to calculate their shared key. The mathematics are relatively simple (but outside the scope of this book); the bottom line is that Bob and Alice can send each other enough information to calculate their shared key but not enough for an attacker to be able to figure it out.

Diffie-Hellman is often called a public key algorithm, but it is not a public key *encryption* algorithm. Diffie-Hellman is used to calculate a key, but that key must be used with some other encryption algorithm. Diffie-Hellman can be used for authentication, though, and is also used by PGP.

Key exchange is integral to any Internet security architecture, and candidates for the IPsec security architecture include the *Internet Key Exchange (IKE)* protocol and the *Internet Security Association and Key Management Protocol (ISAKMP)*.

ISAKMP is an application protocol, using UDP as its transport, which defines different types of messages that systems send to each other to negotiate the exchange of keys. The mechanisms and algorithms for doing the actual exchanges, however, are not defined in ISAKMP—it is a framework to be used by the specific mechanisms. The mechanisms, often based on Diffie-Hellman key exchange, have been defined in a number of different proposals over the years. These are some of them.

Photuris Based on Diffie-Hellman, *Photuris* adds the requirement that the requesting node send a *cookie*, a random number that is used as a sort of session identifier. The cookie is sent first, and the server acknowledges the request by returning the cookie. This reduces the risk from denial of service attacks made by attackers forging their source addresses. Photuris also requires all parties to sign their negotiated key to reduce the risk of a man-in-the-middle attack (in which an attacker pretends to be Bob to one system's Alice, while pretending to be Alice to the other system's Bob).

SKIP Sun Microsystems' *Simple Key-management for Internet Protocols* (*SKIP*) is also based on Diffie-Hellman key exchange, but rather than requiring parties to use random values to calculate their keys, SKIP calls for the use of a secret table that remains static. The parties look up secret values in this table and then transmit calculated values based on some secret value from the table.

OAKLEY Although this mechanism shares some features with Photuris, it provides different modes of key exchange for situations where denial of service attacks are not a concern.

By defining a separate protocol, ISAKMP, for the generalized formats required to do key and Security Association exchanges, it can be used as a base to build specific key exchange protocols. The foundation protocol can be used for any security protocol, and it does not have to be replaced if an existing key exchange protocol is replaced.

It should be noted that manual key management is an important option and in many cases is the *only* option. This approach requires individuals to personally deliver keys and configure network devices to use them. Even after open standards have been firmly determined and implemented, particularly as commercial products, manual key management will continue to be an important choice.

As more research is done with IPsec, work on an IKE successor protocol (sometimes called *Son-of-IKE*) is ongoing, with IKEv2 one candidate protocol that (as of 2002) is a work in progress.

6.3.4 Secure Hashes

A hash is a digital summary of a chunk of data of any size. Simple types of hashes include check digits; secure hashes produce longer results (often 128 bits or longer). Good secure hashes are extremely difficult for attackers to reverse-engineer or subvert in other ways. Secure hashes can be used with keys or without, but their purpose is to provide a digital summary of a message that can be used to verify whether some data that has been received is the same as the data sent. The sender calculates the hash and includes that value with the data; the recipient calculates the hash on the data received. If the results match the attached hash value, the recipient can be confident in the data's integrity.

Commonly used hashes include the MD2, MD4, and MD5 message digest functions published by Network Associates. The *Secure Hash Algorithm* (*SHA*) is a digest function developed as a standard by NIST. Hashes may be used on their own or as part of digital signatures.

6.3.5 Digital Signature

Public key encryption, as noted previously, relies on key pairs. Digital signatures rely on the property of public key encryption that allows data encrypted with an entity's secret key to be decrypted with the public key of the pair. The sender calculates a secure hash on the data to be signed and then encrypts the result using a secret key. The recipient calculates the same hash and then decrypts the encrypted value attached by the sender. If the two values match, the recipient knows that the owner of the public key was the entity that signed the message and that the message was not modified during transmission.

The RSA public key encryption algorithm can be used for digital signatures: The signing entity creates a hash of the data to be signed and then encrypts that hash with its own secret key. The certifying entity then calculates the same hash on the data being received, decrypts the signature using the signing entity's public key, and compares the two values. If the hash is the same as the decrypted signature, then the data is certified.

Digital signatures carry with them several implications.

- A signature that can be certified indicates that the message was received without any alteration from the time it was signed to the time it was received.

- If a signature cannot be certified, then the message was corrupted or tampered with in transit, the signature was calculated incorrectly, or the signature was corrupted or tampered with in transit. In any case, an uncertifiable signature does not necessarily imply any wrongdoing but does require that the message be resigned and resent in order to be accepted.

- If a signature is certified, it means that the entity associated with the public key was the *only* entity that could have signed it. In other words, the entity associated with the public key cannot deny having signed the message. This is called *nonrepudiation* and is an important feature of digital signatures.

There are other mechanisms for doing digital signatures, but RSA is probably the most widely used one and is implemented in the most popular Internet products.

6.4 IPSEC: THE PROTOCOLS

IPsec is a security tunneling protocol, defining a mechanism that allows a node to encrypt and/or authenticate packets and encapsulate the secured packets (which may now be literally indecipherable, having been encrypted) into new packets. Figure 6.1 illustrates the basic idea behind IPsec and other security tunneling protocols.

IPsec depends on the use of *security gateways*, which encapsulate IP packets on behalf of their clients. In Figure 6.1, the security gateway labeled "X" serves, among others, hosts A', B', and C'; "Y" serves hosts A, B, and C. The PC off on the side has its own, software, security gateway. In this example, the tunnel from X to Y carries all secured traffic between the two pictured Internets. In this case, each security gateway integrates all traffic for its local network and encrypts and/or

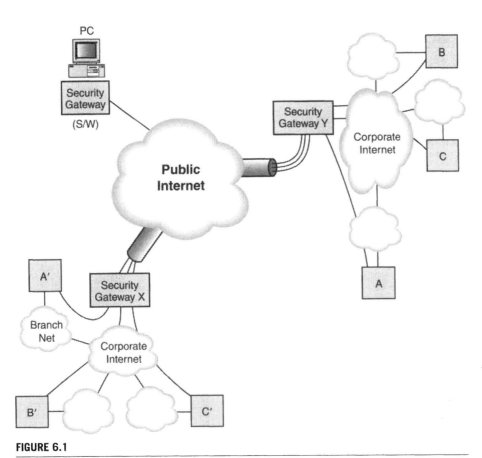

FIGURE 6.1

Security tunneling across a hostile network.

authenticates all of it between itself and the security gateway at the other end. If all traffic is being encrypted (a good bet), then any attacker sitting inside the public Internet could intercept these packets but would get relatively little information from them. At best, the attacker would discover that there is a secure tunnel between X and Y, but she would likely learn only how much traffic was being sent between the two security gateways.

The security gateways create secure tunnels, as shown in Figure 6.2, by accepting IP packets sent from one node (A) to another (B). A sends off the packets as if they were going to be delivered directly to B; the security gateway X then takes those packets (along with any others from the same network) and treats them as raw data to be sent to security gateway Y. The packets sent by A are shown as open envelopes to signify that they have not been encrypted, while the packets sent from X are shown as sealed envelopes to indicate that they contain the encrypted packets sent from A.

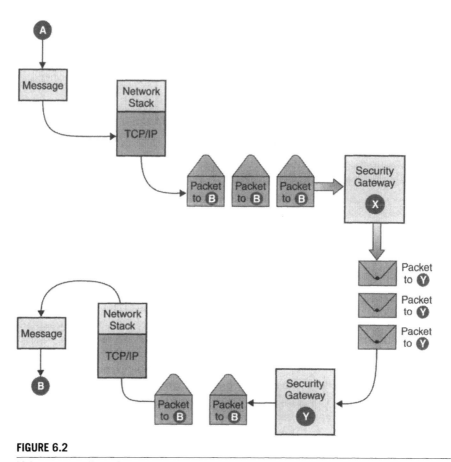

FIGURE 6.2

Using a secure tunnel.

The original IPsec specifications define security protocols for the Authentication Header (AH) and the Encapsulating Security Payload (ESP) IP options, as header options (for IPv4) or header extensions (for IPv6). As their names imply, AH provides an authentication mechanism, whereas ESP provides an encryption ("encapsulated security") mechanism for privacy.

6.5 IP AND IPSEC

IPsec provides security services for either IPv4 or IPv6, but the way it provides those services is slightly different in each. When used with IPv4, IPsec headers are inserted after the IPv4 header and before the next-layer protocol header.

IPv6 simplifies header processing: Every IPv6 packet header is the same length, 40 octets, but any options can be accommodated in extension headers that follow the IPv6 header. IPsec services are provided through these extensions.

The ordering of IPsec headers, whether within IPv4 or IPv6, has significance. For example, it makes sense to encrypt a payload with the ESP Header and then use the Authentication Header to provide data integrity on the encrypted payload. In this case, the AH Header appears first, followed by the ESP Header and encrypted payload. Reversing the order, by doing data integrity first and then encrypting the whole lot, means that you can be sure of who originated the data but not necessarily certain of who did the encryption.

6.5.1 Security Associations

The *Security Association (SA)* is a fundamental element of IPsec. RFC 2401 defines the SA as "a simplex 'connection' that affords security services to the traffic carried by it." This rather murky definition is clarified by a description; an SA consists of three things.

- A Security Parameter Index (SPI)
- An IP destination address
- A security protocol (AH or ESP) identifier

As a simplex connection, the SA associates a single destination with the SPI; thus, for typical IP traffic there will be two SAs: one in each direction that secure traffic flows (one each for source and destination host). SAs provide security services by using either AH or ESP but not both (if a traffic stream uses both AH and ESP, it has two—or more—SAs).

The *Security Parameter Index (SPI)* is an identifier indicating the type of IP header the security association is being used for (AH or ESP). The SPI is a 32-bit value identifying the SA and differentiating it from other SAs linked to the same destination address. For secure communication between two systems, there would be two different security associations, one for each destination address.

Each security association includes more information related to the type of security negotiated for that connection, so systems must keep track of their SAs and what type of encryption or authentication algorithms, key lengths, and key lifetimes have been negotiated with the SA destination hosts.

6.5.2 Using Security Associations

As mentioned earlier, ISAKMP provides a generalized protocol for establishing SAs and managing cryptographic keys within an Internet environment. The procedures and packet formats needed to establish, negotiate, modify, and delete SAs are defined within ISAKMP, which also defines payloads for exchanging key generation and authentication data. These formats provide a consistent framework for transferring this data, independent of how the key is generated or what type of encryption or authentication algorithms are being used.

ISAKMP was designed to provide a framework that can be used by any security protocols that use SAs, not just IPsec. To be useful for a particular security protocol, a *Domain of Interpretation*, or *DOI*, must be defined. The DOI groups related protocols for the purpose of negotiating security associations—security protocols that share a DOI all choose protocol and cryptographic transforms from a common namespace. They also share key exchange protocol identifiers, as well as a common interpretation of payload data content.

While ISAKMP and the IPsec DOI provide a framework for authentication and key exchange, ISAKMP does not actually define how those functions are to be carried out. The IKE protocol, working within the framework defined by ISAKMP, does define a mechanism for hosts to perform these exchanges.

The sending host knows what kind of security to apply to the packet by looking in a *Security Policy Database (SPD)*. The sending host determines what policy is appropriate for the packet, depending on various selectors (for example, destination IP address and/or transport-layer ports), by looking in the SPD. The SPD indicates what the policy is for a particular packet: Either the packet requires IPsec processing of some sort—in which case it is passed to the IPsec module for processing—or it does not—in which case it is simply passed along for normal IP processing.

Outbound packets must be checked against the SPD to see what kind (if any) of IPsec processing to apply. Inbound packets are checked against the SPD to see what kind of IPsec service should be present in those packets.

Another database, called the *Security Association Database (SAD)*, includes all security parameters associated with all active SAs. When an IPsec host wants to send a packet, it checks the appropriate selectors to see what the SAD says is the security policy for that destination/port/application. The SPD may reference a particular SA, so the host can look up the SA in the SAD to identify appropriate security parameters for that packet.

6.5.3 Tunnel and Transport Mode

IPsec defines two modes for exchanging secured data: *tunnel mode* and *transport mode*. IPsec transport mode protects upper-layer protocols and is used between end nodes. This approach allows end-to-end security because the host originating the packet is also securing it, and the destination host is able to verify the security, either by decrypting the packet or certifying the authentication.

Tunnel mode IPsec protects the entire contents of the tunneled packets. The tunneled packets are accepted by a system acting as a security gateway, encapsulated inside a set of IPsec/IP headers, and forwarded to the other end of the tunnel, where the original packets are extracted (after being certified or decrypted) and then passed along to their ultimate destination.

The packets are only secured as long as they are "inside" the tunnel, although the originating and destination hosts could be sending secured packets themselves, so that the tunnel systems are encapsulating packets that have already been secured.

Transport mode is good for any two individual hosts that want to communicate securely; tunnel mode is the foundation of the *Virtual Private Network*, or *VPN*. Tunnel mode is also required any time a *security gateway* (a device offering IPsec services to other systems) is involved at either end of an IPsec transmission. Two security gateways must always communicate by tunneling IP packets inside IPsec packets; the same goes for an individual host communicating with a security gateway. This occurs any time a mobile laptop user logs into a corporate VPN from the road, for example.

Tunneling, shown in Figure 6.3, allows two systems to set up SAs to enable secure communications over the Internet. Network traffic originates on one system, is encrypted and/or signed, and is then sent to the destination system. On receipt, the datagram is decrypted or authenticated, and the payload is passed along up the receiving system's network stack where it is finally processed by the application using the data. This is a *transparent mode* use of security associations, because the two hosts could be communicating just as easily without security headers—and because the actual IP headers of the datagrams must be exposed to allow them to be routed across the Internet.

An SA can also be used to tunnel secure IP through an internetwork. Figure 6.4 shows how this works. All IP packets from system A are forwarded to the security gateway X, which creates an IP tunnel through the Internet to security gateway Y, which unwraps the tunneled packets and forwards them. Security gateway Y might forward those packets to any of the hosts (B, C, or D) within its own local intranet, or it could forward them to an external host, like M. It all depends on where the originating host directs those packets. Whenever an SA destination node is a security gateway, it is by definition a tunneled association. In other words, tunneling can be done between two security gateways (as shown in Figure 6.4), or it can be done between a regular node and a security gateway. Thus, host M could create a tunneled connection with either security gateway, X or Y. It is tunneled by virtue of the fact that datagrams sent from M are passed first to the security gateway, which then forwards them appropriately after decrypting or authenticating.

A   Encryption/Authentication Header   Internet   B

FIGURE 6.3

A pair of hosts using IPsec to communicate transparently across the Internet.

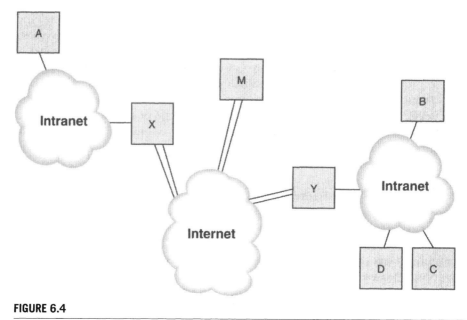

FIGURE 6.4

IP security tunneling.

6.5.4 Encapsulating Security Payload (ESP)

Specified in RFC 2406, "IP Encapsulating Security Payload (ESP)," the ESP Header allows IP nodes to exchange datagrams whose payloads are encrypted. The ESP Header is designed to provide several different services (some overlapping with the Authentication Header), including the following.

- Confidentiality of datagrams through encryption
- Authentication of data origin through the use of public key encryption
- *Antireplay services* through the same sequence number mechanism as provided by the Authentication Header
- Limited traffic flow confidentiality through the use of security gateways

The ESP Header can be used in conjunction with an Authentication Header. In fact, unless the ESP Header uses some mechanism for authentication, it is recommended that the Authentication Header be used with the ESP Header.

The ESP Header must follow any headers that need to be processed by nodes intermediate to the destination node—all data that follows the ESP Header will be encrypted, with the encrypted payload beginning directly after the last ESP Header field (see following).

ESP can be used in tunnel or transport mode, similar to the Authentication Header. In transport mode, the IP Header and any Hop-by-Hop, Routing, or Fragmentation Extension Headers precede the Authentication Header (if present), followed by the ESP Header. Any Destination Options Headers can either precede or follow the ESP Header, or even both; any Headers that follow the ESP Header are encrypted.

The result appears, in many respects, to simply be a regular IP datagram transmitted from source to destination, with an encrypted payload. This use of ESP in transport mode is appropriate in some cases, but it allows attackers to study traffic between the two nodes, noting which nodes are communicating, how much data they exchange, when they exchange it, and so forth. All this information may potentially provide the attacker with some information that helps defeat the communicating parties.

An alternative is to use a security gateway, much as just described for the Authentication Header. A security gateway can operate directly with a node or can link to another security gateway. A single node can use ESP in tunnel mode by encrypting all outbound packets and encapsulating them in a separate stream of IP datagrams that are sent to the security gateway. That gateway then can decrypt the traffic and resend the original datagrams to their destinations.

When tunneling, the ESP Header encapsulates the entire tunneled IP datagram and is an extension to the IP Header directing that datagram to a security gateway. It is also possible to combine ESP Headers with Authentication Headers in several different ways; for example, the tunneled datagram may have a Transport-Mode Authentication Header.

The following ESP Header format (taken from RFC 2406) includes the Next Header field, which appears near the end of the ESP Header and indicates the presence (and identity) of any other headers (such as AH) that may follow. The rest of the ESP Header consists of the following.

Security Parameter Index (SPI) This is the same 32-bit value referred to in the section on the Authentication Header. This value is used by the communicating nodes to refer to a security association, which can be used to determine how the data should be encrypted.

```
 0                   1                   2                   3
 0 1 2 3 4 5 6 7 8 9 0 1 2 3 4 5 6 7 8 9 0 1 2 3 4 5 6 7 8 9 0 1
+-+-+-+-+-+-+-+-+-+-+-+-+-+-+-+-+-+-+-+-+-+-+-+-+-+-+-+-+-+-+-+-+ ----
|               Security Parameters Index (SPI)                 | ^Auth.
+-+-+-+-+-+-+-+-+-+-+-+-+-+-+-+-+-+-+-+-+-+-+-+-+-+-+-+-+-+-+-+-+ |Cov-
|                    Sequence Number                            | |erage
+-+-+-+-+-+-+-+-+-+-+-+-+-+-+-+-+-+-+-+-+-+-+-+-+-+-+-+-+-+-+-+-+ | ----
|                   Payload Data (variable)                     | |   ^
~                                                               ~ |   |
|                                                               | |Conf.
+               +-+-+-+-+-+-+-+-+-+-+-+-+-+-+-+-+-+-+-+-+-+-+-+-+ |Cov-
|               |        Padding (0-255 bytes)                  | |erage
+-+-+-+-+-+-+-+-+               +-+-+-+-+-+-+-+-+-+-+-+-+-+-+-+-+ |   |
|               |               | Pad Length  |  Next Header    | v   v
+-+-+-+-+-+-+-+-+-+-+-+-+-+-+-+-+-+-+-+-+-+-+-+-+-+-+-+-+-+-+-+-+ ------
|                 Authentication Data (variable)               |
~                                                               ~
|                                                               |
+-+-+-+-+-+-+-+-+-+-+-+-+-+-+-+-+-+-+-+-+-+-+-+-+-+-+-+-+-+-+-+-+
```

Sequence Number This 32-bit value is set to zero to start and is incremented by one with each datagram sent. As just described for the Authentication Header, the sequence number can be used to protect against replay attacks, and a new security association must be set up before this value cycles through all 2^{32} values.

Payload Data This is a variable-length field and actually contains the encrypted portion of the datagram, along with any supplementary data necessary for the encryption algorithm (e.g., initialization data). The payload begins with an *initialization vector*, a value that must be sent in plaintext; encryption algorithms need this value to decrypt the protected data.

Padding The encrypted portion of the header (the payload) must end on the appropriate boundary, so padding may be necessary.

Padding Length This field indicates how much padding has been added to the payload data.

Next Header This field operates as it normally does with other IPv6 extension headers; it just appears near the end of the header (where it can be given confidentiality protection) rather than at the beginning so that the next layer protocol can be hidden from any unauthorized third parties.

Authentication Data This is an *Integrity Check Value* (*ICV*) calculated on the entire ESP Header (except for the authentication data). This authentication calculation is optional. The ICV is discussed at greater length following.

6.5.5 Authentication Header

The Authentication Header can be used to do the following.

- Provide strong integrity services for IP datagrams, which means the AH can be used to carry content verification data for the IP datagram.

- Provide strong authentication for IP datagrams, which means that the AH can be used to link an entity with the contents of the datagram.

- Provide nonrepudiation for IP datagrams, assuming that a public key digital signature algorithm is used for integrity services.

- Protect against replay attacks through the use of the sequence number field.

The Authentication Header can be used in tunnel mode or in transport mode, which means that it can be used to authenticate and protect simple, direct datagram transfers between two nodes, or it can be used to encapsulate an entire stream of datagrams that is sent to or from a security gateway.

AH is specified in RFC 2402, "IP Authentication Header," and the header is shown on page 115 (taken from RFC 2402).

In transport mode, the Authentication Header protects the payload of the original IP datagram as well as the parts of the IP Header that do not change from hop to hop (e.g., the Hop Limit field or Routing Headers). Figure 6.5 shows what happens to a transport mode IP datagram as the Authentication Header is calculated and added to it (the Destination Options Header may also appear before the Authentication Header). The destination IP address and extension headers are protected only insofar as they do not change from hop to hop.

When the Authentication Header is used in tunnel mode, however, it is used differently. Figure 6.6 shows the difference. The original destination IP address, along with the entire original IP datagram, is encapsulated into an entirely new IP datagram that is sent to the security gateway. Thus, the entire original IP datagram is fully protected, as are the portions of the encapsulating IP Headers that don't change.

AH header fields include the following.

> **Payload length** This 8-bit field indicates the entire length of the Authentication Header in units of 32-bit words, minus 2.

As originally defined, the Authentication Header consisted of 64 bits of header, with the rest devoted to authentication data (see the following). Thus, the payload length field merely indicated the length (in 32-bit words) of the authentication data. With the addition of the Sequence Number field (see the following), this value now equals the length of the authentication data plus the length of the Sequence Number field.

```
Datagram prior to calculating AH
------------------------------------------------
| dest IP hdr | ext headers | TCP | Data |
------------------------------------------------

Datagram after inserting AH
----------------------------------------------------------------
| dest IP hdr | ext headers | AH | dest options | TCP | Data |
----------------------------------------------------------------
| <------- authenticated except for fields that change ---------->|
```

FIGURE 6.5

Adding an Authentication Header to an IP datagram in transport mode.

```
Original IP datagram
---------------------------------------------
| orig IP hdr | ext hdrs | TCP | Data |
---------------------------------------------

IP datagram for tunneling to security gateway (GW)
--------------------------------------------------------------------------
| GW IP hdr | ext hdrs | AH | orig IP hdr | ext hdrs | TCP | Data |
--------------------------------------------------------------------------
```

FIGURE 6.6

Adding an Authentication Header to an IP datagram in tunnel mode.

Reserved The next 16 bits are reserved for future use; at present, they must be set to all zeros.

Security Parameter Index (SPI) This 32-bit value is an arbitrary number. Together with the destination IP address and security protocol (in this case, AH to indicate the Authentication Header), the SPI uniquely identifies the security association to be used for the Authentication Header. An SPI value of zero is for local use only and should never be transmitted; values from 1 through 255 are reserved by the Internet Assigned Numbers Authority (IANA) for future use.

Sequence Number This 32-bit value is a mandatory counter; it is also included by the sender, although it may not always be used by the recipient. Starting from zero, this counter is incremented with every datagram sent and is used to prevent replay attacks. When the recipient is using it for antireplay purposes, it will discard any datagrams that duplicate a sequence number that has already been received. This means that when the counter is ready to cycle through (when 2^{32} datagrams have been received), a new security association must be negotiated—otherwise, the receiving system will discard all datagrams once the counter is reset.

Authentication Data This field contains the Integrity Check Value (ICV), which is the heart of the Authentication Header. The contents must be a multiple of 32 bits in length and may contain padding to attain that length. Calculation of this value is discussed in the next section.

6.5.6 Calculating the Integrity Check Value (ICV)

The Authentication Data fields in the AH and ESP Headers are variable-length fields, each of which contains an Integrity Check Value (ICV). The field is variable length to accommodate variations from ICV algorithms, and the length is specified by the selected function. This is an optional field: It is included only when an authentication service is in use for the SA that corresponds to the header, and information about the ICV function in use is maintained along with the rest of the SA data.

The ICV calculation is a bit tricky in that some of the data being authenticated may be modified en route, such as IP header hop counts. According to RFC 2402 the AH ICV is computed on the IP header fields that either don't change in transit or whose values on arrival can be predicted, the AH header itself (though the Authentication Data field is set to zero for the calculation), and the upper-level protocol data that is being authenticated (this is assumed to be unchanged in transit).

The ESP ICV, according to RFC 2406, is computed on the entire ESP packet, excluding the Authentication Data field. This includes the SPI, Sequence Number, Payload Data, Padding (if present), Pad Length, and Next Header; the last four fields will be in ciphertext form, since encryption is performed prior to authentication.

These are the suggested algorithms for ICV.

Message Authentication Codes (MACs), the results of which are then encrypted with an appropriate symmetric encryption algorithm (for example, AES)

Secure hash functions, such as MD5 or SHA-1 (an updated version of SHA)

To comply with the standard, implementations must support MD5 and SHA-1 keyed hashing, at least.

6.5.7 IPsec Headers in Action

IPsec security services are provided through the AH and ESP Headers in conjunction, of course, with appropriate and relevant key management protocols. The AH protocol is specified in RFC 2402, "IP Authentication Header"; ESP is specified in RFC 2406, "IP Encapsulating Security Payload (ESP)."

Either security header may be used by itself, or both may be used together in various combinations of transport or tunnel modes. When used together with AH encapsulating ESP, packet authentication can be checked prior to decrypting the ESP Header payload. These headers can also be nested when using IPsec tunneling: An originating node can encrypt and digitally sign a packet, and then send it to the local security gateway. That gateway may then reencrypt and resign the packet as it sends it off to another security gateway.

The ESP and AH authentication services are slightly different: ESP authentication services are ordinarily provided only on the packet payload, whereas AH authenticates almost the entire packet including headers.

The Sequence Number field is mandatory for all AH and ESP Headers and is used to provide antireplay services. Every time a new packet is sent, the Sequence Number is increased by one (the first packet sent with a given SA will have a Sequence Number of 1).

When the receiving host elects to use the antireplay service for a particular SA, the host checks the Sequence Number: If it receives a packet with a Sequence Number value that it has already received, that packet is discarded.

The Authentication Data field contains whatever data is required by the authentication mechanisms specified for that particular SA to authenticate the packet. The ICV may contain a keyed Message Authentication Code (MAC) based on a symmetric encryption algorithm (such as AES or Triple-DES) or a one-way hash function such as MD5 or SHA-1.

The most obvious difference between ESP and AH is that the ESP Header's Next Header field appears at the end of the security payload. Of course, since the header may be encapsulating an encrypted payload, you don't need to know what next header to expect until after you've decrypted the payload—thus, the ESP Next Header field is placed after rather than before the payload.

ESP's authentication service covers only the payload itself, not the IP headers of its own packet as with the Authentication Header. And the confidentiality service covers only the payload itself; obviously, you can't encrypt the IP headers of the packet intended to deliver the payload and still expect any intermediate routers to be able to process the packet. Of course, if you're using tunneling, you can encrypt everything, but only everything in the tunneled packet itself.

6.6 IMPLEMENTING AND DEPLOYING IPSEC

IP-layer security protects IP datagrams. It does not necessarily have to involve the user or any applications. This means users may be merrily using all of their applications without ever being aware that all their datagrams are being encrypted or authenticated before being sent out to the Internet (of course, that situation will only occur as long as all the encrypted datagrams are properly decrypted by hosts at the other end).

As a result, one question that comes up is how to implement IPsec. RFC 2401 suggests several strategies for implementing IPsec in a host or in conjunction with a router or firewall.

Integrated implementation Integrate IPsec into the native IP implementation. This approach is probably the best, but also the most difficult, as it requires rewriting the native IP implementation to include support for IPsec. Integrating IPsec into the IP stack adds security natively and makes it an integral part of any IP implementation. However, it also requires that the entire stack be updated to reflect the changes.

"Bump-in-the-stack" (BITS) Implement IPsec "beneath" the IP stack and above the local network drivers. The IPsec implementation monitors IP traffic as it is sent or received over the local link, and IPsec functions are performed on the packets before passing them up or down the stack. This works reasonably well for individual hosts doing IPsec.

This approach inserts special IPsec code into the network stack just below the existing IP network software and just above the local link software. In other words, this approach implements security through a piece of software that intercepts datagrams being passed from the existing IP stack to the local link layer interface. This software then does the necessary security processing for those datagrams and hands them off to the link layer. This approach can be used to upgrade systems to IPsec support without requiring that their IP stack software be rewritten.

"Bump-in-the-wire" (BITW) Implement IPsec in a hardware cryptographic processor. The crypto processor gets its own IP address; when used for individual hosts, the bump-in-the-wire acts much like a BITS implementation, but when the same processor provides IPsec services to a router or firewall, it must behave as a security gateway—meaning that it must do IPsec security protocols in tunnel mode.

This approach uses external cryptographic hardware to perform the security processing. The device is usually an IP device that acts as a sort of a router or, more accurately, security gateway for all IP datagrams from any system that sits behind it. When such a device is used for a single host, it works very much like the BITS approach, but implementation can be more complex when a single BITW device is used to screen more than one system.

These options differ more in terms of where they are appropriate than in subjective terms. Applications that require high levels of security may be better served with a hardware implementation. Applications that run on systems for which new IPsec-compliant network stacks are not available may be better served by the BITS approach.

6.7 CONCLUSION

Network security is probably the subject of as many books and chapters within technical books as IP. This chapter provides a concise introduction to IP security issues and security goals, starting with the definition of the challenges facing security managers and the tools at their disposal. IPsec provides authentication services through the use of public key encryption, digital signature, and secure hashing tools; it provides privacy services through the use of public and secret key encryption as well.

On top of these cryptographic tools, however, IPsec requires additional protocols to handle the secure and verifiable distribution and management of encryption keys. IPsec combines these cryptographic and security protocols with IP, using security associations to link packets with hosts and a pair of optional IP security headers (ESP and AH) to transmit IP packets securely.

IPsec is often linked to IPv6 because while IPsec support in IPv4 is optional, it is mandatory for all IPv6-capable hosts. Although some cite "security" as a reason to prefer IPv6 over IPv4, to a great degree the same level of security is possible if IPsec were mandatory for all IPv4 nodes.

Security in Wireless Systems

7.1 INTRODUCTION

Although radio has existed for almost 100 years, most of the population uses wireline phones. Only over the last 30 years have large numbers of people used wireless or cordless phones. With this exposure, users of wireless phones and the news media have challenged two bedrocks of the telecommunications industry: privacy of conversation and billing accuracy.

The current concepts of privacy of communications and accuracy of billing are based on the telephone company's ability to route an individual pair of wires to each residence and office. Thus, when a call is placed on a pair of wires, the telephone company can correctly associate the call on a wire with the correct billing account [1–4]. Similarly, since there is a pair of wires from a home to the telephone company central office, no one can easily listen to the call. For most people, a wiretap is an abstract concept that only concerns someone who is involved in illegal activities.

Communications on shared media can be intercepted by any user of the media. When the media are shared, anyone with access to the media can listen to or transmit on the media. Thus, communications are no longer private. In shared media, the presence of a communication request does not uniquely identify the originator, as it does in a single pair of wires per subscriber. In addition, all users of the network can overhear any information that an originator sends to the network and can resend the information to place a fraudulent call. The participants of the phone call may not know that their privacy is compromised (see Figure 7.1). When the media are shared, privacy and authentication are lost unless some method is established to regain it. Cryptography provides the means to regain control over privacy and authentication [5].

In the past, there have been attempts to control privacy and authentication through noncryptographic means. These have failed thus far. The designers of the original cellular service in the United States implemented authentication of the mobile telephone using a number assignment module (NAM) and an electronic serial number (ESN). The NAM would be implemented in a programmable read only memory (PROM) for easy replacement when the phone number changed.

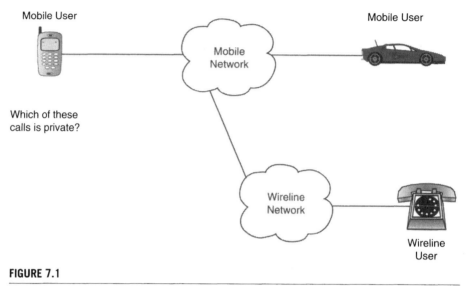

FIGURE 7.1

Mobile system privacy.

The ESN would be implemented in a tamper-resistant module that could not be changed without damaging the cellular telephone. In practice, many manufacturers implement the NAM and the ESN in either battery-backed random access memory (RAM) or electrically erasable PROM (EEPROM). The manufacturer and the installer place the data in the phone via external programming.

Similarly, the designers assumed that privacy of cellular communications would occur because 900-MHz scanners would be difficult and too expensive to build. When those scanners became easily available, the U.S. Congress passed the Electronic Communications Privacy Act in 1986, and in 1992 the FCC banned the importation and manufacture of scanners covering cellular phone bands. In practice, the laws do not help since there are millions of scanners in existence today. Furthermore, cellular test equipment is easy to build or buy, and most cellular phones can be placed in a maintenance mode that allows them to monitor any channel. Any cellular phone can be easily converted to a cellular scanner.

To provide the proper privacy and authentication for a mobile station, a cryptographic system is essential. Some of the cryptographic requirements are in the air interface between the mobile station and base station. Other requirements are on databases stored in the network and on information shared between systems in the process of handoff to provide service for roaming units.

In this chapter we examine the requirements needed for privacy and authentication of wireless systems, and then we discuss how each of the cellular and personal communications services (PCS) systems supports these requirements. The chapter discusses four levels of voice privacy. We then identify requirements in the areas of privacy, theft resistance, radio system requirements, system lifetime, physical requirements as implemented in mobile stations, and law enforcement needs. We will examine different methods that are in use to meet these needs.

7.2 SECURITY AND PRIVACY NEEDS OF A WIRELESS SYSTEM

7.2.1 Purpose of Security

Most frauds result in a loss to the service provider. It is important to recognize that this loss may be in terms of:

- No direct financial loss, but results in lost customers and an increase in use of the system with no revenue.

- Direct financial loss, where money is paid out to others, such as other network carriers and operators of value-added networks such as a premium rate service line.

- Potential loss of business, where customers may move to another service provider because of the lack of security.

- Failure to meet legal and regulatory requirements, such as license conditions, or data protection legislation.

The objective of security for most wireless systems is to make the system as secure as the public switched telephone network. The use of radio as the transmission medium allows a number of potential threats from eavesdropping on the transmissions. It was soon apparent in the threat analysis that the weakest part of the system was the radio path, as this can be easily intercepted.

The technical features for security are only a small part of the security requirements; the greatest threat is from simpler attacks such as disclosure of the encryption keys, an insecure billing system, or corruption. A balance is required to ensure that these security processes meet these requirements. At some point in time judgment must be made of the cost and effectiveness of the security measure limitation.

7.2.2 Privacy Definitions

When most people think of privacy, they think of either of two levels [6,13]: none, and privacy that is used by military users.

However, as we describe here, there are four levels of privacy that need to be considered.

- **Level 0: None.** With no privacy enabled, anyone with a digital scanner could monitor a call.

- **Level 1: Equivalent to wireline.** As discussed earlier, most people think wireline communications are secure. Anyone in the industry knows that they are not, but the actions to tap a line often show the existence of the tap. With wireless communications, the tap can occur without anyone's knowledge. Therefore, the actions to tap a wireline call must be translated into a different requirement for a wireless system. With this level of security, the types of conversations that would be protected are the routine everyday conversations of most people. These types of communications would be personal discussions that most people would not want exposed to the general public—for example, details of a recent operation or other medical procedure, family financial matters, mail order using a credit card, family discussions, request for emergency services (911), and discussions of vacation plans (thus revealing when a home will be vacant).

- **Level 2: Commercially secure.** This level would be useful for conversations in which the participants discuss proprietary information—for example, stock transactions, lawyer-client discussions, mergers and acquisitions, or contract negotiations. A cryptography system that allows industrial activities to be secure for about 10–25 years would be adequate. If one particular conversation was broken, the same effort would be needed to break other conversations.

- **Level 3: Military and government secure.** This is the level that an average person thinks of when cryptography is discussed. This would be used for the military activities of a country and nonmilitary government communications. The appropriate government agency would define requirements for this level.

7.2.3 Privacy Requirements

In this section we discuss the privacy needs of a wireless telephone user. Figure 7.2 is a high-level diagram of a wireless system that shows areas where intruders can compromise privacy. A user of a mobile system needs privacy in the following areas:

- **Privacy of call setup information.** During a call setup, the mobile station will communicate information to the network. Some of the information that a user or mobile station could send includes calling number, calling card number, or type of service requested. The system must send all this information in a secure fashion.

- **Privacy of speech.** The system must encrypt all spoken communications so that intruders cannot intercept the signals by listening on the airwaves.

- **Privacy of data.** The system must encrypt all user communications so that intruders cannot intercept the data by listening on the airwaves.

- **Privacy of user location.** A user should not transmit information that enables an eavesdropper to determine the user's location. The usual method

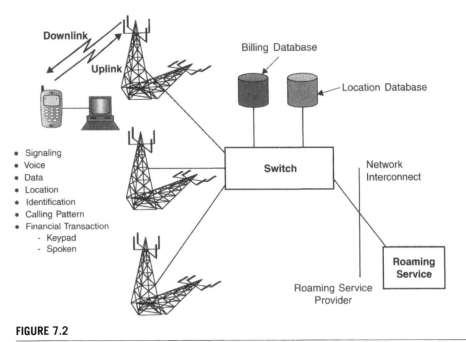

- Signaling
- Voice
- Data
- Location
- Identification
- Calling Pattern
- Financial Transaction
    - Keypad
    - Spoken

FIGURE 7.2

Privacy requirements.

to meet this requirement is to encrypt the user ID. Three levels of protection are often needed:

1. Eavesdropping of radio link
2. Unauthorized access by outsiders to the user location information stored in the network visitor location register (VLR) and home location register (HLR)
3. Unauthorized access by insiders to the user location information stored in the network. This level is difficult to achieve, but not impossible

- **Privacy of user identification.** When a user interacts with the network, the user ID is sent in a way that does not show user identification. This prevents analysis of user calling patterns based on user ID.

- **Privacy of calling patterns.** No information must be sent from a mobile that enables a listener of the radio interface to do traffic analysis on the mobile user. Typical traffic analysis information is:
    - Calling number
    - Frequency of use of the mobiles
    - Caller identity
    - Privacy of financial transactions

If the user transmits credit card information over any channel, the system must protect the data. Users may order items from mail order houses via a telephone that is wireless. Users may choose to voice their credit card numbers rather than dialing them via touch-tone phone.

Users may access bank voice response systems, where they send account data via tone signaling. Users may access calling card services of carriers and may speak or use tone signaling to send the card number.

All these communications need to be private. Since the user can send the information on any channel—voice, data, or call control—the system must encrypt all channels.

7.2.4 Theft Resistance Requirements

The system operator may or may not care if a call is placed from a stolen mobile station as long as the call is billed to the correct party. The owner of a mobile station will care if the unit is stolen.

The mobile terminal design should reduce theft of the mobile station by making reuse of a stolen mobile station difficult. Even if the mobile station is registered to a new legitimate account, the use of the stolen mobile station should be stopped. The mobile station design should also reduce theft of services by making reuse of a stolen mobile station unique information difficult. Requirements needed to accomplish the reduction in theft are:

- **Clone-resistant design.** In the current wireless systems, cloning of mobile stations is a serious problem; methods must be put in place to reduce or eliminate fraud from cloning. To achieve fraud reduction, mobile station unique information must not be compromised by any of the following means:

  1. Over the air: Someone listening to a radio channel should not be able to determine information about the mobile station and then program it into a different mobile station.

  2. From the network: The databases in the network must be secure. No unauthorized person should be able to obtain information from those databases.

  3. From network interconnect: Systems will need to communicate with each other to verify the identity of roaming mobile stations. A system operator could perpetrate fraud by using the security information about roaming mobile stations to make clone mobile stations.

  4. The communication scheme used between systems to validate roaming mobile stations should be designed so that theft of information by a fraudulent system does not compromise the security of the mobile station.

  5. Thus, any information passed between systems for security checking of roaming mobile stations must have enough information to authenticate

the roaming mobile station. It must also have insufficient information to clone the roaming mobile station.

6. From users cloning their own mobile station: Users can perpetrate fraud on the system. Multiple users could use one account by cloning mobile stations. The requirements for reducing or eliminating this fraud are the same as those to reduce repair and installation fraud described below.

■ **Installation and repair fraud.** Theft of service can occur when the service is installed or when a terminal is repaired. Multiple mobile stations can be programmed with the same information (cloning). The cryptographic system must be designed so that installation and repair cloning is reduced or eliminated.

■ **Unique user ID.** More than one person may use a handset. It is necessary to identify the correct person for billing and other accounting information. Therefore, the user of the system must be uniquely identified in the system.

■ **Unique mobile station ID.** When all security information is contained in a separate module (smart card), the identity of the user is separate from the identity of the mobile station. Stolen mobile stations can then be valuable for obtaining service without purchasing a new (full price) mobile station. Therefore, the mobile station should have unique information contained within it that reduces or eliminates the potential for stolen mobile stations to be registered with a new user.

7.2.5 Radio System Requirements

When a cryptographic system is designed, it must function in a hostile radio environment characterized by bit errors caused by:

■ **Multipath fading and thermal noise.** The characteristics of the radio channel affect the choice of cryptographic algorithms. The radio signals will take multiple diverse routes from the mobile station to the base station. The effect of multiple diverse routes that can be severe and cause burst errors is fading. Although the system may be interference limited, there may be conditions when the limiting factor on performance is thermal noise. The choice of cryptographic modes must include both of these channel characteristics.

■ **Interference.** The mobile systems may initially share a radio spectrum with other users. The modulation scheme and cryptographic system must be designed so that interference with shared users of the spectrum does not compromise the security of the system.

■ **Jamming.** Although usually thought about only in the context of military communications, civilian systems can also be jammed. As wireless communication becomes ubiquitous, jamming of the service can also be a method of breaking the security of the system. Therefore, cryptographic systems must work in the face of jamming.

- **Support of handoff.** When the call handoff occurs to another radio port in the same or adjacent mobile system, the cryptographic system must maintain synchronization.

7.2.6 System Lifetime Requirements

It has been estimated that computing power doubles every 18 months. An algorithm that is secure today may be breakable in 5 to 10 years. Since any system being designed today must work for many years after design, a reasonable requirement is that the procedures must last at least 20 years. The algorithm must have provisions to be upgraded in the field.

7.2.7 Physical Requirements

Any cryptographic system used in a mobile station must work in the practical environment of a mass-produced consumer product. Therefore, the cryptographic system must meet the following requirements:

- **Mass production.** It can be produced in mass quantities (million of units per year).

- **Exported and/or imported.** The security algorithm must be capable of being exported and imported. Two problems are solved with export and import restrictions lifted:
  1. It can be manufactured anywhere in the world.
  2. It can be carried on trips outside the United States.
    As an alternative, if an import/export license for the algorithm cannot be obtained, the following restrictions must apply:
    - Either only U.S. manufacturing or two-stage manufacturing
    - All mobile stations must be made in the United States or all mobile stations made outside the United States will have final assembly in the United States
    - All mobile stations must be impounded on leaving the United States

- **Basic handset requirements.** Any cryptographic system must have minimum impact on the following mobile station requirements:
  - Size
  - Weight
  - Power drain
  - Heat dissipation
  - Microprocessor speed
  - Reliability
  - Cost

■ **Low-cost level 1 implementation.** Level 1 implementation would be expected as a baseline for most mobile systems. Therefore, level 1 implementation must be low cost. Designers obtain low-cost solutions by implementations that can be done either in software or in low-cost hardware. Software solutions are attractive. Often mobile stations have spare read only memory (ROM), RAM, and central processing unit (CPU) cycles in microprocessors.

7.2.8 Law Enforcement Requirements

When a valid court order is obtained in the United States, current telephones (either wired or wireless) are relatively easy to tap by the law enforcement community. The same requirements described in this chapter to ensure privacy and authentication of wireless mobile communications make it more difficult to execute legitimate court wiretap orders.

The law enforcement community can wiretap mobile stations after properly obtaining court orders. When an order is obtained, there are several ways a mobile system operator can meet the needs of the order. Any method used must not compromise the security of the system. Figure 7.3 shows possible approaches to tapping the call. The tap can be done over the air or at a central switch.

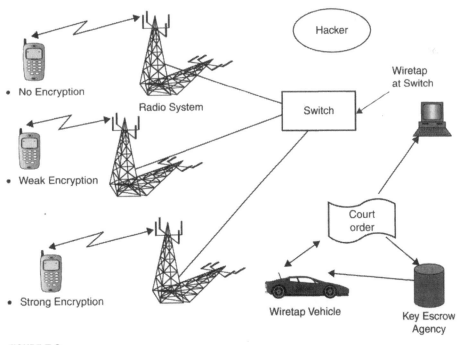

FIGURE 7.3

Law enforcement requirements.

This discussion assumes that only the radio portion of the link is encrypted and the call appears in the clear in the wired portion of the network. If end-to-end encryption is used, other means must be considered to obtain the information since the call never appears clear except at the end points.

Over-the-Air Tap

When the tap is done over the air, a wiretap van is required. The van is driven to inside the cell where the call is placed. A centrally located base station (BS) receives interference from mobile stations in many cells or may not be able to receive a low-power mobile station at all.

In a large-cell mobile system, wiretap stations could be deployed in each cell, but in a small cell system, the number of tap points would be too high. Therefore, a wiretap van is needed and is driven to the correct cell where the call is placed.

After the van is driven to the correct cell, it needs to be close to the mobile station. A van might have an antenna that is a maximum of 6 to 10 feet high versus a BS antenna that has a height of 25 to 100 feet or more. Thus, the van must be closer to the mobile station than a cell radius. A quick rule of thumb for the wiretap van is that if the mobile station is in line of sight, then the wiretap van can receive the mobile station transmission.

If a wiretap van is used, then the transmissions of the mobile station must be decrypted. The following are possibilities:

- **No encryption:** This approach makes tapping the easiest; if no encryption is used, anyone can listen to a call over the airwaves. Thus, law enforcement personnel can listen to and record a call, and so can anyone else.

- **Breakable algorithms:** If the algorithm is weak enough, law enforcement agencies can break the algorithm when permitted to do so by an appropriate court order. Unfortunately, given the proliferation of desktop/laptop personal computers, any algorithm that can be easily broken by the law enforcement community will also be quickly broken by anyone else.

- **Strong encryption:** Strong encryption makes it difficult, if not impossible, for the wiretap van to decrypt the transmission. One method to resolve this dilemma is to use a key escrow system where all cryptographic keys would be available from an appropriate key escrow agency. With a court order, the information could be obtained by law enforcement agencies so that they could listen to and record a call.

Wiretap at Switch

Since all mobile calls must be routed through a central switch, those calls that use radio-link-only encryption can be tapped at the central switch under a court order.

This is the preferred method for low-power wireless calls. This method leaves it to the user and system provider to have appropriate levels of security in the wireless portion of the call.

7.3 REQUIRED FEATURES FOR A SECURED WIRELESS COMMUNICATIONS SYSTEM

For wireless communications to be secure the following features must be available [8-12]:

- **User authentication** proves that the users are who they claim to be.

- **Data authentication** consists of data integrity and data origin authentication. With data integrity the recipient can be sure that the data has not changed. Data origin authentication proves to the recipient that the stated sender has originated the data.

- **Data confidentiality** means the data is encrypted so that it is not disclosed while in transit.

- **Nonrepudiation** corresponds to a security service against denial by either party of creating or acknowledging a message.

- **Authorization** is the ability to determine whether an authenticated entity has the permission to execute an action.

- **Audit** is a history of events that can be used to determine whether anything has gone wrong and, if so, what it was, when it went wrong, and what caused it.

- **Access control** enables only authorized entities to access resources.

- **Availability** ensures that resources or communications are not prevented from access or transmission by malicious entities.

- **Defense against denial of service** is the attack corresponding to the security service of availability.

7.4 METHODS OF PROVIDING PRIVACY AND SECURITY IN WIRELESS SYSTEMS

North American and European cellular and PCS systems support a variety of air interface protocols. They include:

- The Advanced Mobile Phone System (AMPS)
- The IS-54/IS-136 TDMA protocol
- The IS-95 CDMA
- The cdma2000
- The Global System for Mobile communications (GSM)
- The Wideband CDMA (WCDMA) system

Across these protocols, there are four security models that have been used for cellular/ PCS phones in the United States and Europe.

1. **MIN/ESN:** The original AMPS used a 10-digit mobile identification number (MIN) and a 32-bit ESN. All data is sent in clear text. Data is shared between systems with bad (incorrect) MINs, ESNs, and MIN/ESN pairs. When a mobile station (MS) roams into a system, first the bad list is checked, and then a message is sent to the home system to validate the MIN/ESN pair. The intersystem communications are sent via Signal System 7 (SS7) using an ANSI IS-41 protocol.

   As an improvement to this approach, some systems require that a user enter a PIN before placing the calls. The main advantage of the personal identification number (PIN) is that it can be changed in the network when it is compromised, and the user can continue to have the same phone number. Cellular phones that are cloned must have their phone number (MIN) changed to stop the fraudulent use.

2. **Shared secret data (SSD):** The TDMA and CDMA systems in the United States use SSD stored in the network and the mobile phone. At service initiation time, a secret key is stored in the phone and the network. AMPS, IS-95 CDMA, IS-54/IS-136 TDMA, and cdma2000 all support SSD. The intersystem communications are sent via SS7 using an ANSI IS-41 protocol.

   All mobile stations are assigned an ESN at the time of manufacturing. They are also assigned a 15-digit international mobile subscriber identity (IMSI) that is unique worldwide, an A-key, and other data at the time of service installation. When the MS is turned on, it must register with the system. When it registers, it sends its IMSI and other data to the network. The VLR in the visiting system then queries the HLR for the security data and service profile information. The VLR then assigns a temporary mobile subscriber identity (TMSI) to the MS. The MS uses the TMSI for all further access to that system. The TMSI provides anonymity of communications since only the MS and the network know the identity of the MS with a given TMSI. When the MS roams into a new system, some air interfaces use the TMSI to query the old VLR and then assign a new TMSI; other air interfaces request that the MS send its IMSI and then assign a new TMSI.

   Each time an MS places or receives a call, a call counter (CHCNT) is incremented. The counter is also used for clone detection since clones will not have a call history identical to the legitimate phone.

3. **Security triplets (token based):** GSM uses its own unique algorithm and does not share secrets between cellular or PCS systems. It uses a token-based authentication scheme. When an MS roams into a system, a message is sent to the home system asking for sets (3 to 5 typically) of triplets (unique challenge, response to the challenge, and a voice privacy key derived from the challenge). Each call that is placed or received uses one triplet. After all triplets are used up, the visited system must send a new message to the home system to get another set of triplets. The intersystem communications use the CCITT SS7 and GSM mobile application part (MAP) protocol.

Each system operator can choose its own authentication method. The MS and the HLR each support the same method and have common data. Each MS sends a registration request; then the network sends a unique challenge. The MS calculates the response to its challenge and sends a message back to the network. The VLR contains a list of triplets; the network compares a triplet with responses it receives from the MS. If the response matches, the MS is registered with the network. The just-used triplet is discarded.

4. **Public key:** The public key system is analogous to the lock and its combinations. A public key algorithm relies on two cryptographic keys, intimately related to each other but each not derivable from the other. Public key systems do not need communications to the home system to validate the MS. The intersystem communications are still needed to validate the account and get user profile information.

7.5 WIRELESS SECURITY AND STANDARDS

The National Institute of Standards and Technology (NIST) expects that future IEEE 802.11 (and possibly other wireless technologies) products will offer advanced encryption standard (AES)-based data link-level cryptographic services that are validated under the U.S. Federal Information Processing Standard (FIPS) 140-2 [7]. As these will mitigate most concerns about wireless eavesdropping or active wireless attacks, their use is strongly recommended when they become available.

- **IEEE 802.11—WLAN.** Data security using encryption is an optional functionality of medium access control (MAC). The functionality is called wired equivalent privacy (WEP). Encryption is only supplied between stations and not on an end-to-end basis. No key management is specified. Authentication is performed by assigning an Extended Service Set ID (ESSID) to each access point (AP) in the network and by using the ESSID in a challenge-response authentication scheme. WEP was shown to have severe security weaknesses. Wi-Fi protected access (WPA) was introduced by the Wi-Fi Alliance as an intermediate solution to WEP insecurities. WPA implemented a subset of IEEE 802.11i specifications, which will be discussed in the following section.

- **European and North American Systems.** Almost all information being sent between an MS and the network is encrypted, and sensitive information is not transmitted over a radio channel.

7.6 IEEE 802.11 SECURITY

The IEEE 802.11 Wi-Fi wireless local area network (WLAN) standard addressed security with the WEP protocol, which proved relatively easy to crack and was shown to have major security weaknesses. IEEE 802.11i, also known as Wi-Fi protected access 2 (WPA2), is an improved security protocol for IEEE 802.11. IEEE 802.11i includes stronger encryption, authentication, and key management strategies that go a long way toward guaranteeing data and system security.

The new data-confidentiality protocols in 802.11i are the *temporal key integrity protocol* (TKIP) and *counter-mode/block chaining message authentication code protocol* (CCMP). 802.11i also uses an 802.1X key distribution system to control access to the network. Because 802.11 handles unicast and broadcast traffic differently, each traffic type has different security concerns. 802.11i uses a negotiation process to select the correct confidentiality protocol and key system for each traffic type. Other features introduced in 802.11i include key caching and preauthentication.

The TKIP is a data confidentiality protocol, which improves the security of products using WEP. Among WEP's numerous flaws are its lack of a message integrity code and its insecure data-confidentiality protocol. The message integrity code enables devices to authenticate that the packets are coming from the claimed source. This authentication is important in a wireless system where traffic can be easily injected. The TKIP uses a mixing function to defeat weak-key attacks. The mixing function creates a per frame key to avoid the WEP weaknesses.

The CCMP is a data-confidentiality protocol to handle packet authentication as well as encryption. For confidentiality CCMP uses AES in counter mode. For authentication and integrity, CCMP uses a cipher block chaining message authentication code (CBC-MAC). In 802.11i, CCMP uses a 128-bit key. The block size is 128 bits. The CBC-MAC size is 8 octets, and nonce size is 48 bits. There are two bytes of 802.11 overhead. The CBC-MAC, the nonce, and the 802.11 overhead make the CCMP packet 16 octets larger than an unencrypted 802.11 packet. Although slightly slower, the larger packet is not a bad exchange for increased security.

The CCMP protects some fields that are not encrypted. The additional parts of the 802.11 frame that are protected are known as additional authentication data (AAD). AAD includes the packet source and destination and protects against attackers replaying packets to different destinations.

The 802.1X provides a framework to authenticate and authorize devices connecting to the network. It prevents access to the network until such devices pass authentication. The 802.1X also provides a framework to transmit key information between authenticator and supplicant. For 802.11i, the access point takes the role of the authenticator and the client card the role of supplicant. The supplicant authenticates with the authentication server through the authenticator. In 802.1X, the authenticator enforces authentication. The remote authentication dial-in user service (RADIUS) protocol (see Section 7.9) is typically used between authenticator and authentication server. Once the authentication server concludes authentication with the supplicant, the authentication server informs the authenticator of the successful authentication and passes established keying material to the authenticator. At that point, the supplicant and authenticator share established key material through extensive authentication protocol over LANs (EAPOL)-key exchange. If all exchanges have been successful, the authenticator allows traffic to flow through the controlled port giving the client access to the network.

The 802.11i EAPOL-key exchange uses a number of keys and has a key hierarchy to divide initial key material into useful keys. The two key hierarchies are: pairwise key hierarchy and group key hierarchy. In the 802.11i specification, these exchanges are referred to as the 4-way handshake and the group key handshake. The 4-way handshake does several things:

- Confirms the pairwise master key (PMK) between the suppliant and authenticator
- Establishes the temporal keys to be used by the data-confidentiality protocol
- Authenticates the security parameters that were negotiated
- Performs the first group key handshake
- Provides keying material to implement the group key handshake

Wireless clients often roam back and forth between access points. This has a negative effect on the system performance. Key caching reduces the load on the authentication server and reduces the time required to get connected to the network. The basic concept behind the key caching is for a client and access point to retain a security association when the client roams away from the access point. When the client roams back to the access point, the security association can be restarted.

Preauthorization enables a client to establish a PMK security association to an access point with which the client has yet not been associated. Preauthorization provides a way to establish a PMK security association before a client associates. The advantage is that the client reduces the time that it is disconnected from the network. Preauthorization has limitations. Clients performing preauthorization will add load to the authorization server. Also, since preauthorization is done at the IEEE 802 layer, it does not work across IP subnets.

7.7 SECURITY IN NORTH AMERICAN CELLULAR/ PCS SYSTEMS

The ANSI-41 authentication features are independent of the air-interface protocol used to access the network, and subscribers are never involved in the process. A successful outcome of authentication occurs when it can be shown that the MS and the network possess identical results of a calculation performed in both the MS and the network. The authentication center (AC) is the primary functional entity in the network responsible for performing this calculation, although the serving system (i.e., the VLR) may also be allocated certain responsibilities. The authentication calculations are based on a set of algorithms, collectively known as the *cellular authentication and voice encryption* (CAVE) algorithm.

The authentication process and algorithm are based on the following two secret numbers:

1. Authentication key (A-key) (64-bit)
2. Shared secret data (SSD) (128-bit)

The A-key is a 64-bit secret number that is the permanent key used by the authentication calculations in both the MS and the AC. The A-key is permanently installed into the MS and is securely stored at the AC in the network when a new subscription is obtained.

Once the A-key is installed in the MS, it should not be displayed or retrievable. The MS and the AC are the only functional entities ever aware of the A-key; it is never transmitted over the air or passed between systems. The primary function of the A-key is as a parameter used in calculation to generate the SSD.

The COUNT is a 6-bit parameter that is intended to provide additional security in case the A-key or SSD is compromised. The current value of the COUNT is maintained by both the MS and the authentication controller. The respective counts should generally be the same—they may not always match exactly due to radio transmission problems or system failures in the network. If the respective counts differ by a large enough range, or frequently do not match, the AC may assume that a fraudulent condition exists and take corrective action. Note that a COUNT mismatch detection does not conclusively indicate that the particular MS accessing the system is fraudulent—only that a clone may exist.

7.7.1 Shared Secret Data Update

The SSD is a 128-bit secret number that is essentially a temporary key used by authentication calculations in both the MS and the AC. The SSD may also be shared with the serving system via a number of ANSI-41 messages. The SSD is a semipermanent value. It can be modified by the network at any time, and the network can command the MS to generate a new value.

The SSD is obtained from calculations using the A-key, the ESN, and a random number shared between the MS and the network. SSD calculation results in two separate 64-bit values, SSD_A and SSD_B. SSD_A is the value used for the authentication process, whereas SSD_B is used for encryption algorithms for privacy and to encrypt and decrypt selected messages on the radio traffic channel. Figure 7.4 shows the SSD generation process. At any time, the network can order the MS to update the SSD by generating the new SSD with a new SSD random number for security purposes.

7.7.2 Global Challenge

For a global and unique challenge authentication process, the ANSI-41 standard is used [8, 9]. In a global challenge the serving system presents a numeric

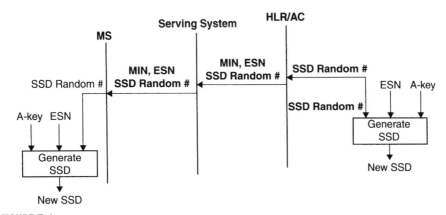

FIGURE 7.4

SSD generation.

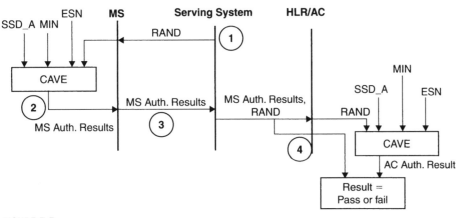

FIGURE 7.5

Global challenge authentication process (no SSD sharing with the serving system).

authentication challenge to all mobile stations that are using a particular radio control channel. The ANSI-41 AC verifies that the numeric authentication response from an MS attempting to access the system is correct. This is called a *global challenge* because the challenge indicator and random number used for the challenge are broadcast on the radio control channel and are used by all mobile stations accessing that control channel.

The authentication process flow diagram (when SSD is not shared with the serving system) is given in Figure 7.5.

1. The serving system generates a random number (RAND) and sends it to the MS in the overhead message on the control channel.

2. MS calculates an authentication result using CAVE and transmits that result back to the serving system when it accesses the system for registration, call origination, or paging response purposes.

3. The serving system forwards the authentication result and the random number to AC.

4. The AC independently calculates an authentication result and compares it to the result received from the MS. If the results match, the MS is considered successfully authenticated. If the results do not match, the MS may be considered fraudulent and service may be denied.

If the SSD is shared, then the serving system performs the calculations.

7.7.3 Unique Challenge

In the ANSI-41 unique challenge, the authentication controller directs the serving system to present a numeric authentication challenge to a single MS that either is requesting service from the network or is already engaged in a call. The serving system presents the numeric authentication challenge to the MS and verifies that the numeric authentication response provided by the MS is correct. The unique challenge is so named because the challenge indicator and the random number used for the challenge are directed to a particular MS, whereas a global challenge is required by each MS. Figure 7.6 shows the basic unique challenge procedure for authentication when SSD is not shared.

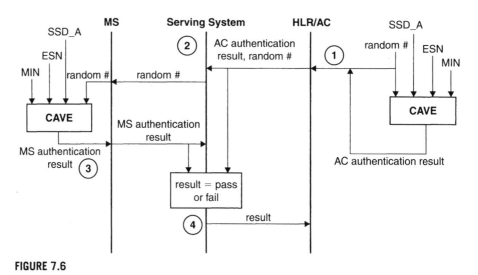

FIGURE 7.6

Basic unique challenge authentication process when SSD is not shared.

1. The AC generates a random number and uses it to calculate an authentication result. The AC sends both the random number and authentication result to the serving system.

2. The serving system forwards the random number to the MS.

3. The MS calculates an authentication result and sends it to the serving system.

4. The serving system compares the result from the AC with the result from the MS. If the results match, the MS is considered to have successfully responded to the challenge. If they do not match, the MS may be considered fraudulent and service may be denied. Either way, the serving system reports the results to the AC.

If SSD is shared, the serving system may initiate the unique challenge process and would report a failure to the AC.

7.8 SECURITY IN GSM, GPRS, AND UMTS

7.8.1 Security in GSM

GSM allows three-band phones to be used seamlessly in more than 160 countries. In GSM, security is implemented in three entities:

- **Subscriber identity module** (SIM) contains IMSI, TMSI, PIN, MSISDN, authentication key K_i (64-bit), ciphering key (K_c) generating algorithm A8, and authentication algorithm A3. SIM is a single chip computer containing the operating system (OS), the file system, and applications. SIM is protected by a PIN and owned by an operator. SIM applications can be written with a SIM tool kit.

- **GSM handset** contains ciphering algorithm A5.

- **Network** uses algorithms A3, A5, A8; K_i and IDs are stored in the authentication center.

Both A3 and A8 algorithms are implemented on the SIM. The operator can decide which algorithm to use. Implementation of an algorithm is independent of hardware manufacturers and network operators.

A5 is a stream cipher. It can be implemented very efficiently on hardware. Its design was never made public. A5 has several versions: A5/1 (most widely used today), A5/2 (weaker than A5/1; used in some countries), and A5/3 (newest version based on the Kasumi block cipher).

The authentication center contains a database of identification and authentication information for subscribers including IMSI, TMSI, location area identity (LAI), and authentication key (K_i). It is responsible for generating (RAND), response (RES), and ciphering key (K_c), which are stored in HLR/VLR for authentication and encryption processes. The distribution of security credentials and encryption algorithms provides additional security.

GSM uses information stored on the SIM card within the phone to provide encrypted communications and authentication. GSM encryption is only applied to communications between a mobile phone and the base station. The rest of the transmission over the normal fixed network or radio relay is unprotected, where it could easily be eavesdropped or modified. In some countries, the base station encryption facility is not activated at all, leaving the user completely unaware of the fact that the transmission is not secure.

GSM encryption is achieved by the use of a shared secret key. If this key is compromised it will be possible for the transmission to be eavesdropped and for the phone to be cloned (i.e., the identity of the phone can be copied). The shared secret key could easily be obtained by having physical access to the SIM, but this would require the attacker to get very close to the victim. However, it has been shown by research that the shared secret key can be obtained over the air from the SIM by transmitting particular authentication challenges and observing the responses.

If the base station can be compromised then the attacker will be able to eavesdrop on all the transmission being received. The attacker will also have access to the shared secret keys of all the mobile phones that use the base station, thus allowing the attacker to clone all of the phones.

Authentication in the GSM system is achieved by the base station sending out a challenge to the mobile station. The MS uses a key stored on its SIM to send back a response that is then verified. This only authenticates the MS, not the user.

A 64-bit key is divided to provide data confidentiality. It is not possible to encrypt all the data; for example, some of the routing information has to be sent in clear text.

GSM Token-Based Challenge

The security-related information consisting of triplets of RAND, signature response (SRES), and K_c is stored in the VLR. When a VLR has used a token to authenticate an MS, it either discards the token or marks it used. When a VLR needs to use a token, it uses a set of tokens that is not marked as used in preference to a set that is marked used.

When a VLR successfully requests a token from the HLR or an old VLR, it discards any tokens that are marked as used. When an HLR receives a request for tokens, it sends any sets that are not marked as used. Those sets shall then be deleted or marked as used. The system operator defines how many times a set may be reused before being discarded. When HLR has no tokens, it will query the authentication center for additional tokens.

The token-based challenge can be integrated into various call flows (e.g., registration, handoff). It is described separately here for clarity. Figures 7.7 and 7.8 show the call flows of token-based challenges.

1. The serving system sends a RAND to the MS.
2. The MS computes the SRES using RAND and the authentication key (K_i) in the encryption algorithm.

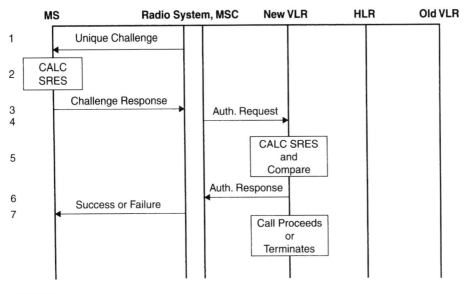

FIGURE 7.7

GSM token-based unique challenge.

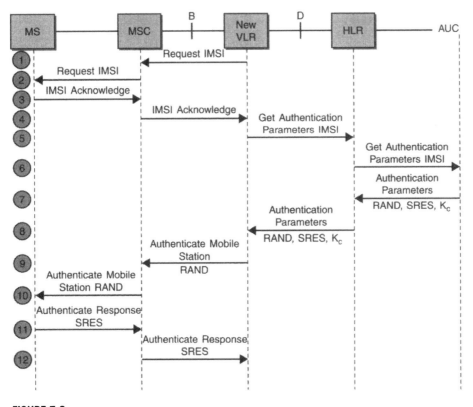

FIGURE 7.8

GSM token-based unique challenge with ciphering.

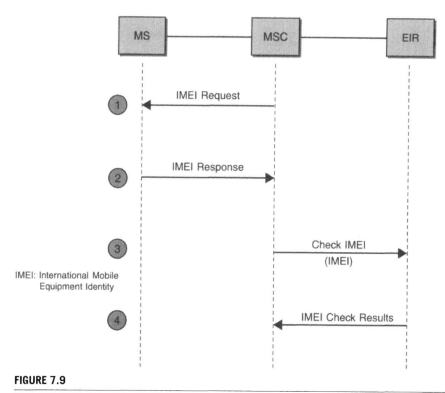

FIGURE 7.9

Equipment identity check.

3. The MS transmits the SRES to the serving system.
4. The MSC sends a message to the VLR requesting authentication.
5. The VLR checks the SRES for validity.
6. The VLR returns the status to the MSC.
7. The MSC sends a message to the MS with a success or failure indication.

Both GSM and North American systems use the international mobile equipment identity (IMEI) stored in the equipment identity register (EIR) to check malfunctions and fraudulent equipment. The EIR contains a valid list (list of valid mobiles), a suspect list (list of mobiles under observation), and a fraudulent list (list of mobiles for which service is barred) (see Figure 7.9 for call flow).

7.8.2 Security in GPRS

The general packet radio service (GPRS) allows packet data to be sent and received across a mobile network (GSM). GPRS can be considered an extension to the GSM network to provide 3G services. GPRS has been designed to allow users to connect to the Internet, and as such is an essential first step toward 3G networks for all mobile operations. In GPRS, TMSI is replaced by P-TMSI and P-TMSI signature as alternative identities. The HLR GPRS register maps between internet protocol (IP) addresses and IMSI.

GPRS security functionality is equivalent to the existing GSM security. Authentication and encryption setting procedures are based on the same algorithms, keys, and criteria as in GSM systems.

GPRS provides identity confidentiality to make it difficult to identify the user. This is achieved by using a temporary identity where possible. When possible, confidentiality also protects dialed digits and addresses. As in GSM, the device is authenticated by a challenge-response mechanism. This only verifies that the smart card within the device contains the correct key. GPRS does not provide end-to-end security so there is a point where the data is vulnerable to eavesdropping or attack. If this point can be protected, e.g., in a physically secure location, this is not a problem. However, if end-to-end security is required, there are other standards that can be used over GPRS; such as the wireless application protocol (WAP) and Internet protocol security (IPSec).

In GPRS authentication is performed by serving GPRS support node (SGSN) instead of VLR. The encryption is not limited to radio part, but it is up to SGSN. An IP address is assigned after authentication and ciphering algorithm negotiation.

7.8.3 Security in UMTS

The security in universal mobile telecommunications services (UMTS) is built upon the security of GSM and GPRS. UMTS uses the security features from GSM that have proved to be needed and robust. UMTS security tries to ensure compatibility with GSM in order to ease interworking and handoff between GSM and UMTS. The security features in UMTS correct the problems with GSM by addressing its real and perceived security weaknesses. New security features are added as necessary for new services offered by UMTS and to take into account the changes in network architecture. In UMTS the SIM is called UMTS SIM (USIM).

UMTS uses public keys. In UMTS mutual authentication between the mobile and BS occurs; thus there is no fake BS attack. UMTS has increased key lengths and provides end-to-end security. The other security features of UMTS are listed below:

- Subscriber individual key K.
- Authentication center and USIM share
  - User-specific secret key K;
  - Message authentication functions f_1, f_2; and
  - Key generating functions f_3, f_4, f_5.
- The authentication center has a random number generator.
- The authentication center has a scheme to generate fresh sequence numbers.
- USIM has a scheme to verify freshness of received sequence numbers.
- Authentication functions f_1, f_2 are:
  - MAC (XMAC); and
  - RES (XRES).

- Key generating functions f_3, f_4, f_5 are:
  - f_3: ciphering key CK (128 bit);
  - f_4: integrity key IK (128 bit); and
  - f_5: anonymity key AK (128 bit).
- Key management is independent of equipment. Subscribers can change handsets without compromising security.
- Assure the user and network that CK/IK have not been used before.
- For operator-specific functions, UMTS provides an example called Milenage based on the Rijndael block cipher.
- Integrity function f_9 and ciphering function f_8 are based on the Kasumi block cipher.

7.9 DATA SECURITY

The primary goals in providing data security are confidentiality, integrity, and availability. Confidentiality deals with the protection of data from unauthorized disclosures of customers and proprietary information. Integrity is the assurance that data has not been altered or destroyed. Availability is to provide continuous operations of hardware and software so that parties involved can be assured of uninterrupted service.

In this section, we focus upon commonly used data security methods including firewalls, encryption, and authentication protocols.

7.9.1 Firewalls

Firewalls have been used to prevent intruders from securing Internet connection and making unauthorized access and denial of service attacks to the organization network. This could be for a router, gateway, or special purpose computer. The firewalls examine packet flowing into and out of the organization network and restrict access to the network. There are two types of firewalls: (1) packet filtering firewall, and (2) application-level gateway.

The packet filter examines the source and destination address of packets passing through the network and allows only the packets that have acceptable addresses. The packet filter also examines IP addresses and TCP (transmission control protocol) ports. The packet filter is unaware of applications and what an intruder is trying to do. It considers only the source of data packets and does not examine the actual data. As a result, malicious viruses can be installed on an authorized user computer, giving the intruder access to the network without authorized user knowledge.

The application-level gateway acts as an intermediate host computer between the outside client and the internal server. It forces everyone to log in to the gateway and allows access only to authorized applications. The application-level gateway separates a private network from the rest of the Internet and hides individual computers on the network. This type of firewall screens the actual data. If the message is deemed safe, then it is sent to the intended receiver. These firewalls require more processing power than packet filters and can impact network performance.

7.9.2 Encryption

Encryption is one of the best methods to prevent unauthorized access of an intruder. Encryption is a process of distinguishing information by mathematical rules. The main components of an encryption system are: (1) plaintext (not an encrypted message), (2) encryption algorithm (works like a locking mechanism to a safe), (3) key (works like the safe's combination), and (4) ciphertext (produced from a plaintext message by an encryption key).

Decryption is the process that is the reverse of encryption. It does not always use the same key or algorithm. Plaintext results in decryption. The following types of keys are used in encrypting data.

Secret Key (symmetric encryption)

Both sender and recipient share a knowledge of the same secret key. The scrambling technique is called encryption. The message is referred to as plaintext or clear text, and the encrypted version of it is called ciphertext. The encryption of a plaintext x into a ciphertext y using a secret key e_k is given as (see Figure 7.10):

$$y = e_k(x) \text{ Ciphertext}$$

The corresponding decryption yields

$$x = d_k(y) \text{ Plaintext}$$

where d_k is the decryption key.

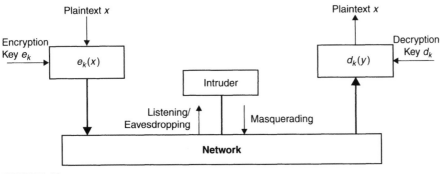

FIGURE 7.10

Encryption using a secret key.

Ideally, the encryption scheme should be such that it cannot be broken at all. Because there are no practical methods of achieving such an unconditional security, encryption schemes are designed to be computationally secure. The encryption and decryption algorithms use the same key, and, hence, such algorithms are called *symmetric key algorithms*. The symmetric key algorithm is vulnerable to interception and key management is a challenge. The strength of this algorithm depends upon the length of the key. Longer keys are more difficult to break. If the length of a secret key is n bits, at least 2^{n-1} steps would be required to break the encryption.

The data encryption standard (DES) defined by US NIST performs encryption in hardware thereby speeding up the encryption and decryption operation. Additional features of DES are:

1. DES is a block cipher and works on a fixed-size block of data. The message is segmented into blocks of plaintext, each comprising 64 bits. A unique 56-bit key is used to encrypt each block of plaintext into a 64-bit block of ciphertext. The receiver uses the same key to perform the decryption operation on each 64-bit data block it receives, thereby reassembling the blocks into a complete message.

2. The larger the key, the more difficult it is for someone to decipher it. DES uses a 56-bit key and provides sufficient security for most commercial applications. Triple-DES is the extended version of DES, which applies DES three times with two 56-bit keys.

International data encryption algorithm (IDEA) is a block cipher method similar to DES. It operates on 64-bit blocks of plaintext and uses a 128-bit key. The algorithm can be implemented either in hardware or software. It is three times faster than DES and is considered superior to DES.

The key sizes used in current wireless systems are not sufficiently large enough for good security. IS-136 uses a 64-bit A-key that is secure, but is still considered to be weak.

Public Key (or asymmetric encryption)

Public key encryption uses longer keys than does symmetric encryption. The key management problem is greatly reduced because the public key is publicized and the private key is never distributed. There is no need to exchange keys.

In a public key system, two keys are used, one for encrypting and one for decrypting. The two keys are mathematically related to each other but knowing one key does not divulge the other key. The two keys are called the "public key" and the "private key" of the user. The network also has a public key and a private key.

The sender uses a public key to encrypt the message. The recipient uses its private key to decrypt the message. Public key infrastructure (PKI) is a set of hardware, software, organizations, and policies to public key encryption work on the Internet. There are security firms that provide PKI and deploy encrypted channels

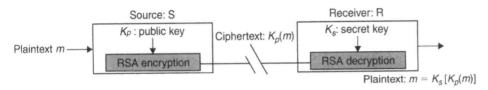

FIGURE 7.11

RSA algorithm operation.

to identify users and companies through the use of certificates—VeriSign Inc. Xcert offers products based on PKI.

Public Key Algorithms

Rivet-Shamir-Adleman (RSA) Algorithm The RSA algorithm [7] is based on public key cryptography. The pretty good privacy (PGP) version of RSA is a public domain implementation available for noncommercial use on the Internet in North America. It is often used to encrypt e-mail. Users make their public keys available by posting them on web pages. Anyone wishing to send an encrypted message to that person copies the public key from the web page into the PGP software and sends the encrypted message using the person's public key.

Two interrelated components of the RSA are (see Figure 7.11):

1. Public key and the private key
2. The encryption and decryption algorithm

Steps in the RSA algorithm are:

- Choose two large prime numbers, p and q (RSA labs recommend that the product of p and q be on the order of 768 bits for personal use and 1024 bits for corporate use).

- Compute $n = pq$ and $z = (p - 1) \times (q - 1)$.

- Choose a number, e, less than n, which has no common factors (other than 1) with z (in this case e and z are the prime numbers).

- Find a number d such that $ed - 1$ is exactly divisible by z.

- The public key available to the world is the pair of numbers (n, e), and the private key is the pair of numbers (n, d).

$$\text{Encrypted value} \qquad m^e \bmod(n) = C \qquad\qquad (7.1)$$

$$\text{Plaintext} \qquad m = C^d \bmod(n) \qquad\qquad (7.2)$$

Example 7.1

Using the prime numbers $p = 5$ and $q = 7$, generate public and private keys for the RSA algorithm.

Solution

$n = pq = 5 \times 7 = 35$, $z = (p - 1) \cdot (q - 1) = 4 \times 6 = 24$
choose $e = 5$, because 5 and 24 have no common factors except 1
choose $d = 29$ since $ed - 1 = 5 \times 29 - 1 = 144$. This is exactly divisible by z (24).
Public key (35, 5)
Private key (35, 29)

If the sender sends a letter e that has a numeric representation of 5, show that the receiver gets the letter e. The calculations are shown below.

Sender:

Plaintext letter	m: numeric representation	m^e	ciphertext: $C = m^e$ mod n
e	5	$5^5 = 3125$	10

Receiver:

Ciphertext	c^d	$m = c^d$ mod n	Plaintext letter
10	10^{29}	5	e

Diffie-Hellman (DH) Algorithm The Diffie-Hellman key exchange algorithm was proposed in 1976. It is a widely used method for key exchange and is based on cyclic groups. In practice, multiplicative groups of prime field Zp or the group of an elliptic curve are most often used. If the parameters are chosen carefully, the DH protocol is secure against passive (i.e., an attacker can only eavesdrop) attacks. The DH key exchange is a cryptographic protocol that allows two parties that have no prior knowledge of each other to jointly establish a shared secret key over an insecure communications channel. This key can then be used to encrypt subsequent communications using a symmetric key cipher. The implementation of protocol uses the multiplicative groups of integers modulo p, where p is prime and g is primitive mod p.

The algorithm works as follows (see Figure 7.12):

1. Ron and Mike agree to use a prime number p and base g.
2. Mike chooses a secret integer $a \in \{2, 3, 4, ..., p - 1\}$ and sends Ron g^a mod p.
3. Ron chooses a secret integer $b \in \{2, 3, 4, ..., p - 1\}$ and sends Mike g^b mod p.
4. Ron computes $(g^a \bmod p)^b \bmod p = K$.
5. Mike computes $(g^b \bmod p)^a \bmod p = K$.
6. Mike and Ron use K as the secret key for encryption.

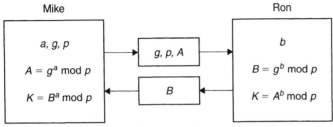

$$K = A^b \bmod p = (g^a \bmod p)^b \bmod p = (g^b \bmod p)^a \bmod p = B^a \bmod p$$

FIGURE 7.12

Diffie-Hellman key exchange algorithm.

It should be noted that only a, b and $g^{ab} = g^{ba}$ are kept secret. All other values are sent in clear. Once Mike and Ron compute the shared secret key they can use it as an encryption key, known to them only, for sending messages across the same open communications channel.

Example 7.2

Determine the secret encrypting key, K, using the Diffie-Hellman key exchange algorithm, if two parties agree to use a prime number $p = 23$ and base $g = 5$. Party A selects its secret number $a = 6$ and party B chooses its secret number $b = 15$.

Solution

Party A sends to party B $g^a \bmod p = 5^6 \bmod 23 = 8$.
Party B sends to party A $g^b \bmod p = 5^{15} \bmod 23 = 19$.
Party A computes $(g^b \bmod p)^a \bmod p = 19^6 \bmod 23 = 2$.
Party B computes $(g^a \bmod p)^b \bmod p = 8^{15} \bmod 23 = 2$.
Parties A and B use $K = 2$ as the secret key for encryption.

One-Time Key Method

The one-time key method is based on the generation of a new key every time data is transmitted. A single-use key is transmitted in a secure (encoded) mode and, once used, becomes invalid. In some implementations, the central system does not issue a key for a new connection until the user supplies the previously used key.

Elliptic Curve Cryptography (ECC)

The features of the ECC are discussed below:

- ECC is a public key encryption technique that is based on elliptic curve theory.
- ECC can be used in conjunction with most public key encryption methods, such as RSA and Diffie-Hellman.
- ECC can yield a level of security with a 164-bit key, while other systems require a 1024-bit key.

- Because ECC helps to establish equivalent security with lower computing power and battery resources, it is widely used for mobile applications.
- Many manufacturers (3COM, Cylink, Motorola, Pitney Bowes, Siemens, TRW, and VeriFone) have included support for ECC in their products.

Digital Signature

A digital signature provides a secure and authenticated message transmission (enabled by public key enabling (PKE)). It provides proof identifying the sender. The digital signature includes the name of the sender and other key contents (e.g., date, time, etc.). The features of the digital signature method are discussed below:

- A digital signature can be used to ensure that users are who they claim to be.
- The signing agency signs a document, m, using a private decryption key, d_B, and computes a digital signature $d_B(m)$.
- The receiver uses the agency's public key, e_B, and applies it to the digital signature, $d_B(m)$, associated with the document, m, and computes $e_b[d_b(m)]$ to produce m.
- This algorithm is very fast, especially with hash functions.
- It is only used in message authentication codes when a secure channel is used to transmit unencrypted messages, but needs to verify their authenticity.
- It is also used in the secure channels of a secure socket layer (SSL).

7.9.3 Secure Socket Layer

SSL is a protocol that uses a session-level layer in the Internet to provide a secure channel. SSL is widely used on the web. In SSL, the server sends its public key and encryption technique to be used to the browser. The browser generates a key for the encryption technique and sends it to the server. Communications between server and browser are encrypted using the key generated by the browser.

The features of SSL are:

- Negotiate cipher suite, which is a collection of encryption and authentication algorithms.
- Bootstrapped secure communication, which eliminates the need for third parties, and uses unencrypted communications for initial exchanges.
- Public key crypto for secret keys and secret key crypto for data.

7.9.4 IP Security Protocol (IPSec)

IPSec is a widely used protocol that can be employed with other application-layer protocols (not just for web applications such as SSL). The operations of IPSec between A and B involve:

- A and B generate and exchange two random keys using Internet key exchange (IKE).

- A and B combine the two numbers to create an encryption key to be used between them.
- A and B negotiate the encryption technique to be used such as DES or 3DES.
- A and B then begin transmitting data using either the transport mode, in which only the IP payload is encrypted or tunnel mode, in which the entire IP packet is encrypted.

7.9.5 **Authentication Protocols**

Authentication of a user is used to ensure that only the authorized user is permitted into the network and into the specific resource inside the network. Several methods used for authentication are user profile, user account, user password, biometrics, and network authentication.

The user profile is assigned to each user account by the manager. The user profile determines the limits of a user in accessing the network (i.e., allowable login day and time of day, allowable physical locations, allowable number of incorrect login attempts). The user profile specifies access details such as data and network resources that a user can access and type of access (e.g., read, write, create, delete). The form of access to the network may be based on the password, card, or one-time password. With a biometric-based form of access, the user can gain access based on finger, hand, or retina scanning by a biometric system. It is convenient and does not require remembering a password. Biometric-based methods are used in high-security applications.

Network authentication requires a user to log in to an authentication server, which checks the user ID and password against a database, and issues a certificate. The certificate is used by the user for all transactions requiring authentications. Kerberos is one of many commonly used authentication protocols. Two other authentication protocols that have been used are remote authentication dial-in user service (RADIUS) and terminal access controller access control system + (TACACS+).

Kerberos is a secret key network authentication protocol that uses a DES cryptographic algorithm for encryption and authentication. It was designed to authenticate requests for network resources. Kerberos is based on the concept of a trusted third party that performs secure verification of users and services. The primary use of Kerberos is to verify that users and the network services they use really are who and what they claim to be. To accomplish this, a trusted Kerberos server issues tickets to users. These tickets, which have a limited life span, are stored in a user's credential cache. The tickets are used in place of standard user name and password authentication mechanisms.

RADIUS is a distributed client/server system that secures the network against unauthorized access. In the Cisco implementation, RADIUS clients run on Cisco routers and send authentication requests to a server. The central server contains all user authentication and network service access information. RADIUS is the only security protocol supported by wireless authentication protocol.

TACACS+ (improved TACAS) is a security application that provides centralized validation of users attempting to gain access to a router or network access server. TACACS+ services are maintained in a database on a TACACS+ daemon running on a UNIX, Windows NT, Window 2000 workstation. TACACS+ provides for separate and modular authentication, authorization, and accounting facilities.

A network administrator may allow remote users to have network access through public services based on remote-access solutions. The network must be designed to control who is allowed to connect to it, and what they are allowed to do once they get connected. The network administrator may find it necessary to configure an accounting system that tracks who logs in, when they log in, and what they do once they have logged in.

Authentication, authorization, and accounting (AAA) security services provide a framework for these kinds of access control and accounting functions. The user dials into an access server that is configured with challenge handshake authentication protocol (CHAP). The access server prompts the user for a name and password. The access server authenticates the user's identity by requiring the user name and password. This process of verification to gain access is called *authentication*. The user may now be able to execute commands on that server once it has been successfully authenticated.

The server uses a process for authorization to determine which commands and resources should be made available to that particular user. Authorization asks the question, what privileges does this user have? Finally, the number of login attempts, the specific commands entered, and other system events can be logged and time-stamped by the accounting process. Accounting can be used to trace a problem, such as a security breach, or it may be used to compile usage statistics or billing data. Accounting asks questions such as: What did this user do and when was it done? The following are some of the advantages in using AAA:

- AAA provides scalability. Typical AAA configurations rely on a server or group of servers to store user names and passwords. This means that local databases don't have to be built and updated on every router and access server in the network.

- AAA supports standardized security protocols—TACACS+, RADIUS, and Kerberos.

- AAA lets the administrator configure multiple backup systems. For example, an access server can be configured to consult a security server first and a local database second.

- AAA provides an architectural framework for configuring three different security features: authentication, authorization, and accounting.

7.10 AIR INTERFACE SUPPORT FOR AUTHENTICATION METHODS

The various air interfaces used for PCS and cellular systems in Europe and North America support one or more of the different authentication methods. Only the

Table 7.1 Summary of Authentication Methods for PCS and Cellular Systems in Europe and North America

Air Interface	MIN/ESN	Type of Authentication SSD	Token-Based	Public Key	Type of Voice Privacy Supported
AMPS	X				None
CDMA IS-95		X			Strong
TDMA IS-136		X			Strong
GSM			X		Strong
cdma2000		X			Strong
UMTS			X		Strong

older AMPS supports MIN/ESN as the authentication method. All of the digital systems in North America, except for GSM1900, support SSD. GSM supports only token-based authentication. UMTS supports token-based authentication along with some advanced security features. cdma2000 supports SSD. Table 7.1 summarizes this information.

7.11 SUMMARY OF SECURITY IN CURRENT WIRELESS SYSTEMS

Each of the security methods satisfies the security needs for a wireless system in different ways. The older AMPS has poor security. The digital systems using either SSD or tokens meet most of the security needs of the wireless systems except full anonymity. The public key-based security system meets all the requirements, including anonymity, but is not yet fully implemented. Privacy of communications is maintained via encryption of signaling, voice, and data for the digital systems. The AMPS sends all data in the clear and has no privacy unless the user adds it to the system. The following is a summary of the support for security requirements for the PCS and cellular systems in North America and Europe (see Table 7.2).

7.11.1 Billing Accuracy

Since AMPS phones can be cloned from data intercepted over the radio link, billing accuracy for AMPS is low to none. For other systems, when authentication is done, billing accuracy is high. If a system operator gives service before authentication or even if authentication failure occurs, then billing accuracy will be low.

Table 7.2 Summary of Support for Security Requirements for PCS and Cellular Systems in Europe and North America

Feature	MIN/ESN (AMPS)	SSD	Token-Based	Public Key
Privacy of Communication				
■ Signaling	None	High: messages are encrypted	High: messages are encrypted	High: messages are encrypted
■ Voice	None	High: voice is encrypted	High: voice is encrypted	High: voice is encrypted
■ Data	None	High: data is encrypted	High: data is encrypted	High: data is encrypted
Billing Accuracy				
■ Accuracy	None: phones can be cloned	High: if authentication is done	High: if authentication is done	High: if authentication is done
Privacy of User Information				
■ Location	None	Moderate: using IMSI/ TMSI	Moderate: using IMSI/ TMSI	High: public key provides full anonymity
■ User ID	None	Moderate: using IMSI/ TMSI	Moderate: using IMSI/ TMSI	High: public key provides full anonymity
■ Calling Pattern	None	High: using TMSI and encryption	High: using TMSI and encryption	High: public key provides full anonymity
Theft Resistance of MS				
■ Over the Air	None	High	High	High
■ From Network	Depends on system design	Depends on system design	Depends on system design	Depends on system design
■ From Interconnection	Depends on system design	Depends on system design	Depends on system design	Depends on system design
■ Cloning	None	High	Medium	High

(*Continued*)

Table 7.2 (*Continued*)

Feature	MIN/ESN (AMPS)	SSD	Token-Based	Public Key
Handset Design	Algorithm run in micro-processor of handset	Algorithm run in micro-processor of handset	Algorithm run in microprocessor of handset	Micro-processor speed may be fast enough for some algorithms
Law Enforcement Needs	Easily met on the air interface (if van is nearby to MS or at the switch)	Must wiretap at the switch	Must wiretap at the switch	Must wiretap at the switch

7.11.2 Privacy of Information

Privacy of user information is high for the public key system, moderate for the SSD and token-based systems (since sometimes IMSI is sent in cleartext), and low for the AMPS.

7.11.3 Theft Resistance of MS

MS theft resistance is high over-the-air transmission for all systems except the AMPS. Since the token-based system in GSM doesn't support a call history count, it has a lower resistance to cloning than the SSD or public key systems. Earlier AMPS phones using MIN/ESN have no resistance to cloning, but now they support SSD. The resistance of stealing data from network interconnects or from operations systems (OS) in the network depends on the system design.

7.11.4 Handset Design

All of the authentication and privacy algorithms easily run in a standard 8-bit microprocessor used in mobile stations, except the public key systems.

7.11.5 Law Enforcement

The AMPS is relatively easy to tap at the air interface. The digital systems will require a network interface since privacy is maintained over the air interface.

The network requirements currently meet most of the needs of the law enforcement community doing legal wiretaps.

7.12 CONCLUSION

In this chapter, we discussed the requirements for strong privacy and authentication of wireless systems, and outlined how each of the cellular and PCS systems supports these requirements. Four levels of voice privacy were presented. We then identified requirements in the areas of privacy, theft resistance, radio system requirements, system lifetime, physical requirements as implemented in mobile stations, and law enforcement needs. We also examined different methods of authentication that are in use to satisfy these needs.

The chapter described the requirements that any cryptographic system should meet to be suitable for use in a ubiquitous wireless network. We also examined security models and described how they met security requirements.

REFERENCES

[1] D. M. D'Angelo, B. McNair, and J. E. Wilkes, "Security in Electronic Messaging Systems," *AT&T Technical Journal*, 73(3), May/June 1994.

[2] JTC(AIR)/94.03.25-257R1. "Minimum Requirements for PCS Air Interface Privacy and Authentication."

[3] T. Karygiannis and L. Owens, *Wireless Network Security*. NIST Special Publication, 800-48, November 2002.

[4] L. Owens and D. Crowe, *Wireless Security Perspectives*. Calgary, Canada: Cellular Networking Perspectives Ltd., 1999–2001.

[5] Paar, C. *Lectures Notes—Applied Cryptography and Data Security,* version 2.5, January 2005.

[6] Report of the Joint Experts Meeting on Privacy and Authentication for PCS. Phoenix, Arizona, November 8–12, 1993.

[7] R. L. Rivet, A. Shamir, and L. Adleman, "A Method for Obtaining Digital Structures and Public-Key Crypto Systems," *Communications ACM*, 21(2):120–127, February 1978.

[8] R. A. Snyder and M. D. Gallagher, *Wireless Telecommunications Networking with ANSI-41*, second edition. New York: McGraw-Hill, 2001.

[9] TIA Interim Standard, IS-41 C, "Cellular Radio Telecommunication Intersystem Operations."

[10] TR-46 P&A ad hoc/94.04.17.01R5, "TR-46 PCS Privacy and Authentication, Volume 1, Common Requirements," Version 6, November 1994.

[11] TR-46 P&A ad hoc/94.04.17.02R4, "TR-46 PCS Privacy and Authentication, Volume 2, PCS1900 Based Requirements."

[12] TR-46 P&A ad hoc/94.04.17.02R3, "TR-46 PCS Privacy and Authentication, Volume 3, Shared Secret Data Requirements."

[13] J. E. Wilkes, "Privacy and Authentication Needs of PCS," *IEEE Personal Communications*, 2(4), August 1995.

Mobile Security and Privacy

The phenomenal growth of the Internet has given rise to a variety of network applications and services that are pervading our daily life at a staggering pace. This trend is being boosted by myriad mobile devices that essentially make it possible to access network resources anywhere, anytime. In parallel, security and privacy issues have surfaced in almost every aspect of the mobile computing paradigm, from wireless communication security to network denial of service (DoS) attacks, to secure network protocols, and to mobile privacy. Furthermore, the inherent characteristics of mobile computing have imposed greater challenges on mobile security and privacy solutions than on general wired network security approaches.

This chapter explores a wide range of mobile security and privacy issues, presents a big picture of this broad area, and offers some insight into the fundamental security problems surrounding the design of secured mobile wireless systems and applications. The chapter begins with a security primer summarizing a set of basic network security concepts and security schemes, followed by an in-depth coverage of security issues in cellular networks, wireless LAN, Bluetooth, and other emerging mobile wireless systems. When presenting each topic, we introduce technical aspects of each problem and discuss some proposed approaches for solving them. When possible, we then outline some real-world solutions to the underlying problems. Readers will be able to quickly obtain a solid understanding of key mobile security and the related privacy issues.

The security issues surrounding mobile wireless networks and applications can be categorized as follows:

Message confidentiality
Message integrity
Message authentication
Nonrepudiation
Access control

When discussing differences between security and privacy, we consider this list to be comprised of security problems, whereas identity and location anonymity are topics relevant to mobile privacy.

8.1 SECURITY PRIMER

Let us first consider a typical scenario in a mobile computing paradigm, where it is possible to use a mobile device (e.g., cell phone, PDA, smart phone, laptop computer) to access a network service using a variety of wireless communication technologies, such as a wireless local area network (LAN) or cdma2000. This operation involves utilizing some type of hardware (i.e., the mobile device being used), one or more wireless network devices, a back-end wired or wireless network infrastructure, and software, such as the application and supporting mobile operating system of the mobile device, operational and management software on wireless devices, and application software on destination servers. The scenario becomes much more complicated when group communication is being performed. Nevertheless, the fundamental question is how we can secure the entire communication environment. This problem can be approached from several different perspectives:

- *End user's perspective*—An end user may use the mobile device for many purposes, including online shopping, online banking, and personal communication with friends and colleagues, or the end user may utilize such services as online maps, weather forecasts, or online gaming. Because in many cases sensitive information is sent back and forth, the end user's major concerns are likely to include data confidentiality and integrity, as well as authenticity of the other party with which the user is connected.

- *Service provider's perspective*—A service provider has to provide a secure network infrastructure for various mobile applications and services that directly interface to end users. This implies secured communication over wireless networks and wired networks. The service provider and the end user have to authenticate each other, and the computing platform should guarantee that no information will be divulged during the communication between them. The service provider also has to protect the network infrastructure against attacks.

- *Employer's perspective*—Enterprise networks must be able to ensure the security of corporate assets. This is particularly crucial when the enterprise network provides both wired and wireless access. A well-defined, highly secured wired enterprise network may be completely open to attackers if a wireless access extension to the enterprise network is not secured. For example, a rogue access point in an enterprise network may essentially provide a means to bypass corporate firewalls and directly access network resources.

Many technical notions, terms, and technologies have been introduced to address security problems in common network environments. Table 8.1 provides a brief summary of this terminology.

Depending on the nature of security problems encountered in the mobile wireless world, they can be addressed in one or more layers of the network protocol stack. Radio modulation techniques such as FHSS (Frequency Hopping Spread

Table 8.1 Security Terminology

Term	Description
Encryption	The transformation of some information (*cleartext* or *plaintext*) into a form (*ciphertext*) that is only readable by intended recipients who hold some decryption keys
Confidentiality	A security function that ensures that no one except the intended recipient who holds some key is able to obtain the message being transferred between the sender and the recipient
Integrity	A security function that allows the intended recipient to detect any modification to a message from a sender performed by a third party
Authentication	A security function that enables verification of the identity of a person, a data object, or a system
Nonrepudiation	A security function that ensures that a message sender cannot deny a message it sends previously
Cryptography	Mathematical foundations of security mechanisms facilitating the four security functions: confidentiality, integrity, authentication, and nonrepudiation
Secret key cryptography	A type of cryptographic mechanism that enables the sender and the intended recipient to use the same shared key for security functions
Public key/private key cryptography	Another type of cryptographic mechanism in which two keys are used by an entity—a public key that is made available to anyone and a private key derived from the public key and known only to the owner and sometimes some trusted parties
Symmetric key encryption	An encryption mechanism that allows the sender and recipient to use the same secret shared key to encrypt and decrypt a message; also called *secret key encryption*
Asymmetric key encryption	An encryption mechanism in which the message sender uses the intended recipient's public key to encrypt a message and the recipient uses his or her private key to decrypt it
Cipher	The mathematical algorithm that is used to encrypt cleartext
Message digest	Fixed-size output of a one-way hash function applied to a message of arbitrary size
Message authentication code (MAC)	A code of a message that is computed based on the message and a secret key such that the intended recipient who holds the secret key can verify the integrity of the message
Hash MAC (HMAC)	A MAC that is computed using a one-way cryptographic hash function such as MD5 and SHA-1 and a key

(*Continued*)

Table 8.1 (*Continued*)

Term	Description
Digital signature	A code that is computed based on the message or a hash code of the message and the private key of the sender such that anyone can verify the integrity of the message using the sender's public key; the sender "signs" the message (digital signature is the public key equivalent of MAC)
Digital certificate	A form of electronic certificate document issued by a generally trusted certificate authority (CA) to certify someone's public key; a digital certificate, signed by the CA, contains the owner's identity, the owner's certified public key, the name of the issuer (the CA that issued the digital certificate), certificate expiration date, and some other information; a CA's public key is often distributed with software packages such as web browsers and e-mail software
Public key infrastructure (PKI)	A public-key-based architecture that uses digital certificate signed by a CA to create, manage, distribute, and verify public keys and their associated identity information
Pretty good privacy (PGP)	A technique developed by Phil Zimmermann that uses asymmetric key encryption for e-mail encryption and authentication between two entities
Authorization	The process of granting and denying specific services to an entity based on its identity and established policy

Spectrum) can be used to provide wireless signal transmission security at the physical layer. Link encryption is often used in wireless networks where an access point or master serves as the gateway for everyone. Internet protocol security (IPSec) is an example of a network layer security mechanism. End-to-end security can be addressed at the transport layer. Applications usually have to deal with user authentication and access control. This chapter focuses on security solutions at the data link layer and above which invariably leverage cryptographic principles as building blocks.

A cryptographic system is the realization of a cryptographic scheme or mechanism that can be integrated into a general computer or network system to provide specific security services. The two types of a cryptographic system are *symmetric key systems* and *asymmetric public key systems*. Symmetric key systems such as the Data Encryption Standard (DES) and Advanced Encryption Standard (AES) use the same *secret key* for encryption and decryption, thus requiring a secured way to distribute the key; for example, the Diffie–Hellman key exchange protocol (explained later in Section 8.1.4) specifies a method for symmetric key distribution. In contrast, public key systems use two different keys for encryption

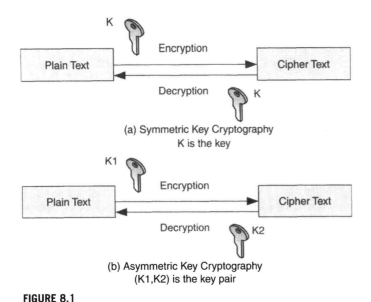

FIGURE 8.1

Symmetric cryptography and asymmetric cryptography.

and decryption: a *public key*, which is known to the public, and a corresponding *private key*, which is known only to the owner of the key pair. The public/private key pair generation algorithm ensures that it is mathematically impossible to deduce the private key based on a public key. An important characteristic of public key cryptographic systems is that the two keys are mathematically related in such a way that data encrypted by a public key can only be decrypted using the corresponding private key, and vice versa. Figure 8.1 depicts both symmetric key cryptography and asymmetric public key cryptography. Public key systems essentially provide a foundation for various security solutions to the problems listed earlier. The basic idea of these approaches is that a message from a sender can be encrypted using its private key and the recipient can verify that the message is, in fact, from the sender (sender authentication). Conversely, by using the recipient's public key to encrypt data, the sender can be assured that only the intended recipient is able to decrypt the scrambled data (recipient authentication). As discussed below, very often a public/private key pair is used in combination with other techniques to provide secure communication during a session. In order to ensure public key authenticity while it is being distributed in a network, the public key infrastructure (PKI) can be used (explained later in Section 8.1.3).

Public key cryptography was first proposed in 1976 by Whitfield Diffie and Martin Hellman as an encryption scheme. Public key cryptographic systems have been widely used to provide confidentiality and authentication between senders and recipients and to secure transmission of some negotiated secret such as a session key between them. In the latter case, the cryptographic system is a hybrid system combining both asymmetric cryptography and symmetric cryptography. Popular public key cryptographic systems include RSA and elliptic curve cryptography (ECC).

8.1.1 Ciphers and Message Confidentiality

The first issue in message security is to encrypt the message such that no one except the intended recipient is able to recover the message content. In the context of symmetric key cryptography, this is often done by a block cipher using some secret key. A block cipher takes a fixed length of information (for example, a 128-bit block of cleartext) and uses a secret key to produce ciphertext, usually of the same length as the cleartext block. A block cipher also supplies a decryption function that takes the cipher text and the secret key and then produces the original cleartext. For messages that are larger than block size, a cipher may employ a particular mode to deal with the message. A mode defines the way a cipher is applied to cleartext. An important concept in data encryption is the well-known Kerckhoffs' principle, which states that an encryption scheme should be secure even if the algorithm used is known to the public. This means that an attacker is well aware of the algorithm and the ciphertext of a message but not the secret key.

Asymmetric encryption algorithms use public/private key pairs for encryption and decryption, thus they do not require the two parties involved to share the same secret key. A good cipher should make it computationally difficult for an attacker to decrypt a message without knowing the key (i.e., the shared secret key or the private key being used for encryption). Popular symmetric block ciphers are DES/Triple-DES and AES, whereas well-known asymmetric ciphers include RSA and ECC. Generally, asymmetric ciphers are much slower than symmetric ones in terms of encryption speed. In addition to the common ciphers introduced below, a number of technology-specific ciphers such as the A5 algorithm are used in global system for mobile (GSM)/general packet radio service (GPRS) systems. Following is a brief introduction to these ciphers:

- Data Encryption Standard (DES) and Triple-DES—DES uses a 56-bit secret key to encrypt message blocks of 64 bits. There are 16 identical stages of processing, called *rounds*, and an initial and final permutation. The Feistel function determines how data are processed throughout those rounds using carefully generated subkeys for each round. DES has been a federal standard of data encryption for years but was finally superseded by AES in 2002, due to its weakness of using short 56-bit keys. In fact, as a result of the fast advancement in computing power, DES has been broken by brute force attacks in one to two days with the help of some powerful computers. Triple-DES is a relatively improved DES in that it uses three DES operations sequentially to compute the ciphertext. It performs a DES encryption, then a DES decryption, and then a DES encryption again. Triple-DES is generally considered a better cipher than DES. Its main drawback is computation overhead incurred by the three DES procedures.

- Advanced Encryption Standard (AES)—AES has a fixed block size of 128 bits and a key size of 128, 192, or 256 bits. A data block is organized into a 4×4 array, or *state*. AES may require 10 to 14 rounds of computation, depending on the key size. Because many operations in a single round can be performed in parallel, AES is comparatively easier to implement in both hardware and software and can be done much faster than DES. The real name of the cipher is Rijndael, a combination of the two designer's names: Joan Daemen and Vincent Rijmen. Rijndael was chosen by the National Institute of Standards and Technology (NIST) to be the government standard. As of this writing, no attack has broken AES.

- Blowfish and Twofish—Blowfish is yet another block cipher developed by Bruce Schneier in 1993. It uses a key up to 448 bits over blocks of 64 bits. Blowfish has 16 rounds following the Feistel function. Blowfish is generally regarded as a compact and fast replacement of DES. Twofish specifies block size of 128 bits and uses a key size up to 256 bits. Twofish also made it to the final list of the AES contest but lost to Rijndael. There is no reported successful attack over Blowfish and Twofish.

Other well-known block ciphers are CAST-128, CAST-256, RC5, and RC6, among others. It is important to remember that, with regard to data encryption on mobile devices, computational overhead becomes a much more severe problem than on desktop computers; hence, while choosing a cipher to encrypt packets in a wireless network, those ciphers with low overhead such as RC5 will be advantageous.

In addition to block ciphers, another type of cipher is the stream cipher. Unlike block ciphers, a stream cipher encrypts one bit or one byte at a time. The two types of stream ciphers are synchronous and self-synchronizing ciphers. Synchronous stream ciphers require a key to produce a keystream, which in turn is used to compute the ciphertext. The computation is done by XORing (exclusive OR operation) the keystream with the cleartext. Decryption follows in the same manner. Self-synchronizing stream ciphers do not require a key. Instead, they use some bits of the previous ciphertext to produce the keystream. Stream ciphers are primarily used to secure network data transmission where the cleartext is a stream of bits rather than a static data block.

RC4 is the most widely used stream cipher, although it has been shown that RC4 is not always secure. RC4 was designed by Ron Rivest of RSA Security in 1987. RC4 (Rivest Cipher 4) is one of the four ciphers that Rivest developed. In RC4, a variable-length key is first used to perform a permutation of one byte according to a key scheduling algorithm. The result, along with two index pointers, is fed into a pseudo-random generation algorithm (PRGA) to produce the keystream, which will be XORed with the cleartext to obtain the cipher. RC4 has been found to have serious vulnerability in the key scheduling algorithm that in some special cases may enable an attacker to recover the encryption key [1]. This weakness has been leveraged by some researchers to break wireless equivalent privacy (WEP) encryption, the security mechanism of IEEE 802.11b wireless LAN, which uses RC4 for data encryption. Details regarding this WEP vulnerability are provided in Section 8.3.

Most commercial security software supports a list of block or stream ciphers from which users can choose. A well-known opensource cipher implementation is the *libcrypto* library in the OpenSSL package (http://www.openssl.org/). Both Java and Microsoft .Net provide a package of these ciphers. In addition, they are also supported in the mobile platforms J2ME and .Net Compact Framework. Cryptographic schemes discussed in the rest of this section, such as hashing algorithms, digital signatures, and digital certificates, are generally supported by these libraries.

8.1.2 Cryptographic Hash Algorithms and Message Integrity

Aside from message confidentiality, another security problem is how to ensure message integrity—that is, how to protect data from being modified between the two parties. One-way hashing was introduced for this purpose. Simply put, a one-way hash algorithm, sometimes referred to as a *message digest algorithm*, makes sure that any modification to a message can be detected. A cryptographic hash algorithm or message digest algorithm in this regard must possess the following security properties:

- *Fixed-length output*—Given any size of message, it must produce a fixed size result, which is the hash code.

- *One-way*—Given a message m and a hash algorithm h, it is easy to compute $h(m)$; however, given a hash code x and hash algorithm h, it is computationally impossible to find m such that $h(m) = x$.

- *Collision resistance*—Because a hash algorithm is effectively a mapping between a large code space to a considerably smaller code space, collisions are bound to happen, meaning that brute force attacks are theoretically possible. The challenge is how to find collisions within a reasonable amount of time, given a state-of-the-art computing facility. The two types of collision resistance are strong collision resistance and weak collision resistance. Strong collision resistance means it is computationally impossible to find two different messages that can be hashed into the same code, whereas weak collision resistance means it is impossible to find a message that can be hashed into the same hash code of another given message.

Depending on how a hash algorithm operates, the two types of cryptographic hash algorithms are keyed and keyless. Keyed hash algorithms take a message and a key to compute the hash code, while keyless hash algorithms simply use the message to compute the hash code. Keyless hash algorithms are used to detect modifications to a message, assuming that the hash code of the original message is correctly transmitted to the recipient. Because of the collision resistance property, any change to the transmitted message can be detected immediately; however a problem arises when an attacker modifies the intercepted message, generates a hash code, and sends the tampered message and its hash code to the recipient. In this case, a hash code produced by a keyless hash algorithm fails to ensure message integrity. Message authentication code (MAC) algorithms solve this problem by including a key (either a symmetric secret key or the private key of the sender) in the computation of the hash code; thus, attackers are unaware that the key cannot generate the correct hash code for a modified message. Hash algorithms can also be used in digital signatures (introduced in the next section). Following is a list of widely used cryptographic hash algorithms:

- *Message digests 4 and 5 (MD4 and MD5)*—MD5 splits a message into blocks of 512 bits and then performs four rounds of hashing to produce a 128-bit hash code. MD4 is a weaker hash algorithm that only performs three rounds of hashing. In August 2004, collisions for MD5 were announced by Wang et al. [2]. Their attack technique was reported to take only an hour; on a fairly powerful computer they were able to find an alternative message for a given message, yet both created the same hash code, proving that MD5 is vulnerable to a weak collision attack. Using the same technique, they also devised a method to manually attack MD4 and two other hash algorithms, HAVAL-128 and RIPEMD. MD5 is still widely used in existing systems, ranging from digital signature to file checksum; however, neither MD4 nor MD5 should be considered for future systems due to the collision problem, especially for systems utilizing MD5 to generate digital signatures and digital certificates.

- *Secure hash algorithm 1 (SHA-1)*—SHA-0 was initially proposed in 1993 as a hashing standard by the National Security Agency (NSA) and was standardized by NIST. Later, in 1995, SHA-0 was replaced by SHA-1 after the NSA found a weakness in SHA-0. The weakness was also discovered by Chabaud and Joux. Based on MD4, SHA-1 works on blocks of 512 bits and produces a 160-bit hash code. SHA-1 adds an additional circular shift operation that appears to have been specifically intended to address the weaknesses found in SHA-0. The 160-bit hash code of SHA-1 may not be sufficiently strong against brute force attacks. It has been reported that the same team of Chinese researchers who broke MD5 has found a way to significantly reduce the computational complexity of discovering collisions in SHA-1. As it turns out, the problem of SHA-1 is the hash code size. NIST published three SHA hash algorithms that produce larger hash codes: SHA-256, SHA-384, and SHA-512. These hash algorithms are able to generate hash codes of 256 bits, 384 bits, and 512 bits, respectively. Not surprisingly, they are significantly slower than SHA-1.

- *RACE integrity primitives evaluation message digest –160 (RIPEMD)*—RIPEMD-160 was developed in 1996 by Dobbertin et al. It is an improved version of the original RIPEMP, which was developed in the framework of the EU project RIPE (RACE Integrity Primitives Evaluation, 1988–1992). There are also variants of RIPEMD supporting hash code length of 128 bits, 160 bits, 256 bits, and 320 bits. RIPEMD collisions were reported in 2004 [2], and RIPEMD is not used as often as SHA-1.

- *Message digest and MAC (Message Authentication Code)*—Message digest ensures that if someone in the middle alters a message, the recipient will detect it. On the sender side, the sender will hash a message or a file (for checksum computation) to be downloaded using a one-way hashing algorithm (such as MD5 or SHA-1, described above), attach the result (the message digest) to the message, and send it out. Upon receiving the message, the recipient will apply the same hash algorithm to the received message body and compare the result with the received message digest. If they match, the message has been transmitted intact; otherwise, the message has been changed in some way on its way to the recipient, and the recipient may simply reject the message.

If an attacker forges a hash code of a modified message, the hashing algorithm may utilize a cryptographic key as part of the input in addition to the message being transmitted. More generally, a MAC that is computed based on the message and a cryptographic key can be used to guarantee message integrity. If the computation is done using a hash algorithm, such a technique is referred to as HMAC, which essentially uses a keyless hash algorithm and a key to implement the algorithm of a keyed hash algorithm. Well-known HMAC algorithms include HMAC-MD5, HMAC-SHA1, and HMAC-RIPEMD. MAC can also be computed using symmetric block ciphers such as DES; for example, a message can be encrypted using the DES CBC (Cipher Block Chaining) mode. The ciphertext can then be used as MAC. Furthermore, to prevent tampering of the message digest itself, the sender can encrypt the message digest using its own private key so the recipient, with the sender's public key at hand, can be assured that this message has come from the sender. This scheme is referred to as *digital signature* and will be discussed in the next subsection.

As a last note, an attacker may launch a message reply attack by simply resending a number of legitimate messages previously captured. The recipient may be fooled by such legitimate messages. To counteract these attacks, the sender can use a sequence number for each message that is contained in the integrity-protected part of the message. The sequence number keeps increasing so replayed messages will not be accepted.

8.1.3 Authentication

Common authentication mechanisms are digital signature, digital certificate, and PKI, which are described in the following text.

Digital Signature

Digital signature is designed to assure recipients that the senders of messages are really who they claim to be and the messages have not been modified along the way. Similar to a signature in the real world, the sender digitally signs a message, and the receipt is able to verify the authenticity of the message by looking at the digital signature. In other words, digital signature offers authentication of the sender and message integrity.

Digital signing and verification between two parties are conducted as shown in Figure 8.2. The sender:

- Prepares cleartext to send (e.g., an e-mail or a packet).

- Hashes the data using a cryptographic hash algorithm to generate a message digest; hashing is not reversible.

- Encrypts the message digest with the sender's private key, which generates the digital signature that uniquely identifies the sender.

- Appends the digital signature to the original cleartext and sends it to the recipient. Of course, the cleartext can be encrypted using symmetric or asymmetric ciphers.

The recipient:

- Uses the sender's public key to decrypt the digital signature; the result is used in the next step.

- Hashes the received message body with the same algorithm used by the sender.

- Compares the decrypted message digest with the computation result from the previous step; if they are the same, the message must be originated from the sender, and the message has not been altered.

Now let's see if an attacker can impersonate the sender. Without the sender's private key, the attacker has no way to create a valid digital signature for the message because on the recipient side, after the message is hashed, the result will never be

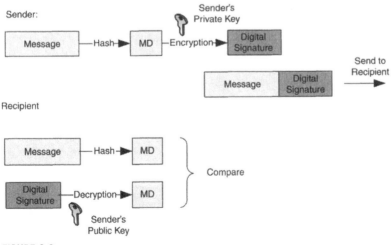

FIGURE 8.2

Digital signature.

the same as the result after decryption of the digital signature. On the other hand, an attacker who chooses to tamper with the sender's message body will also fail, as the hash code of the received message will become inconsistent with that carried in the digital signature.

PKI and Digital Certificate

Asymmetric cryptographic systems (introduced above) assume that a party knows the other's public key. A problem with public authenticity is how someone holding the public key of someone else can be sure that the key does, indeed, belong to that person. What if the distribution of public keys is not at all secure? For example, an attacker could generate and publish bogus public keys of some victims.

The general architecture to address this issue is public key infrastructure (PKI). In a PKI system, the certificate authority (CA) has a public key but its private key is not known to everyone in the system. A single CA PKI is depicted in Figure 8.3(a). To join the PKI system, a user must generate his or her own public/private key pair and ask the CA to certify the public key. The CA will then verify the identity and the associated public key. The CA then signs a digital document stating that the public key really does belong to the person in question. This digital document is a *digital certificate* and should be sent to a recipient whenever the person is about to communicate with some party with public key encryption or digital

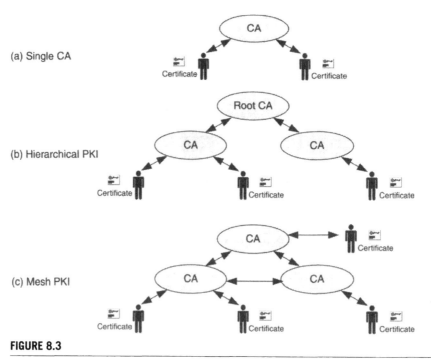

FIGURE 8.3

PKI architecture.

signing. Because everyone in the PKI system knows the public key of the CA, they can check the authenticity of the certificate and thus the public key of the sender. The certificate usually contains the owner's identity, a signature of the CA, and an expiration date. Table 8.2 shows common fields in a digital certificate. The X.509 standard defines the format of a digital certificate.

In reality, a PKI system is organized into multiple levels in a hierarchy to distribute certificate generation and verification among a number of CAs, as shown in Figure 8.3(b). On the top of the tree is the root CA, who is trusted by every user and every other CA. In effect, a chain-of-trust relationship can be established regardless of which low-level CA a user selects, as those CAs can always find a common high-level CA within the hierarchy. Verification is done in the same way as DNS (Domain Name Server) resolution. For example, in a two-level CA system, the public key certificate of a user consists of two parts: (1) a message issued by a high-level CA to certify a low-level CA and (2) a message issued by the low-level CA who will eventually certify the public key of the user. This forms a trust chain of two CAs, and path validation can be conducted. Thus, any party who elects to receive a user certificate (as well as the certificate of the CA certifying the user certificate) must first compute the public key of the low-level CA serving that user and then obtain the user certificate. As the number of levels increases, certificate verification requires more computation. A variance of hierarchical PKI is a trust list architecture, in which some high-level CAs maintain a list of trusted CAs in another hierarchy. A trust chain is therefore established with the trust list instead of a root CA.

A third PKI architecture, mesh PKI, is shown in Figure 8.3(c). There is no publicly trusted root CA in a mesh PKI. A CA in a mesh PKI may choose to trust a subset

Table 8.2 Field in a Digital Certificate	
Field	**Description**
Version	Version number
Serial number	Unique ID of the certificate
Certificate signature algorithm	Encryption and hashing algorithms used to create the signature in the certificate
Issuer	ID of the issuing CA
Validity	Duration for which the certificate is valid
Subject	Owner information
Subject public key info	Subject's public key algorithm (RSA, for example) and public key
Extensions	Additional information regarding the certificate
Certificate Signature Value	Signature of the CA

of other CAs. Users always trust the CA issuing the certificates. Path validation of a user certificate may involve a means to discover the path itself. A bridge CA can be used to link a hierarchical PKI to a mesh PKI. It is not a root CA trusted by everyone; rather, it serves as a common intermediate CA in a trust chain.

8.1.4 Key Management

Key management refers to the process of creating, distributing, and verifying cryptographic keys. It determines how an entity binds to a key. Here, we introduce the Diffie–Hellman (DH) key exchange protocol, RSA, and ECC.

Diffie–Hellman Key Exchange Protocol

The DH key exchange protocol provides a means for two parties to agree on the same secret key over an insecure communication channel. In its simplest form, each party send to the other a number that is computed with a chosen secret number respectively. The same secret key is thus determined based on the number received from the other party; however, if the two numbers are transmitted over an insecure channel, it is computationally difficult for any third party to recover the secret key. The DH key exchange protocol uses a pair of publicly available numbers (p and g) along with the user's random variables for the computation of a secret number. In this case, p is a large prime number and g is an integer less than p, where p and g satisfy the following property: For any number n between 1 and $p - 1$ inclusive, there is a number m such that $n = g^m \bmod p$. Each of the two parties engaging in the DH key exchange protocol will first generate a private random variable. Let's say the variables are a and b. Each party proceeds to compute $g^a \bmod p$ and $g^b \bmod p$ and they exchange results. Then, the shared secret key (k) can be obtained by computing $k = [(g^b) \bmod p]^a \bmod p$ and $[(g^a) \bmod p]^b \bmod p$ at each party. Note that $[(g^b) \bmod p]^a \bmod p = [(g^a) \bmod p]^b \bmod p = (g^{ab}) \bmod p$. No one other than the two communicating parties will know a and b, so it is not computationally feasible to compute k using p, q, and the two public values $g^a \bmod p$ and $g^b \bmod p$.

Note that, although both sides are able to agree on a secret key, there is no way for each of them to be sure that the other side is indeed the person with whom they want to communicate, meaning that no authentication is being performed during the key exchange process. This opens up the protocol to a man-in-the-middle attack, in which an attacker is able to read and modify all messages between the two parties. Digital signature can be applied in this case to prevent man-in-the-middle attacks.

RSA

Designed by Ron Rivest, Adi Shamir, and Len Adleman [3], RSA is a public key algorithm that provides both digital signature and public key encryption. RSA is the public key algorithm used in pretty good privacy (PGP). Key generation in RSA is based on the fact that factoring very large numbers is computationally impossible.

RSA keys are typically 1024 to 2048 bits long, much larger than the largest factored number ever. A message is encrypted using the public key of the recipient. To decrypt the ciphertext, one must know the private key corresponding to that public key. Given the public key and the cipher text, an attacker must factor a large number in the public key into two prime numbers so as to deduce the private key. In addition to message encryption, RSA also provides a digital signature that allows senders to sign a message digest using their private keys. Thus, no one is able to forge a message from the sender unless he or she knows the private key. RSA was patented in the United States in 1983; the patent expired in 2000.

Elliptic Curve Cryptography

An alternative to RSA, elliptic curve cryptography (ECC) is another approach to public key cryptography. It was independently proposed by Victor Miller and Neal Koblitz in the mid-1980s. ECC is based on the property of elliptic curve in algebraic geometrics. An elliptic curve is defined by a set of points (x, y) over a two-dimensional space such that $y^2[+x \cdot y] = x^3 + a \cdot x^2 + b$, where the term in the square bracket can be optional. ECC allows one to choose a secret number as a private key, which is then used to choose a point on a nonsecret elliptic curve. A nice property of an elliptic curve is that it enables both parties to compute a secret key solely based on its private key (the number chosen) and the other's public key. The secret key specific to these two parties is a product of those two private keys and a public base point. A third party cannot easily derive the secret key. NIST has published a recommendation of five different symmetric key sizes (80, 112, 128, 192, 256). ECC is generally used as an asymmetric scheme that allows for smaller key sizes than RSA. The drawback of ECC is the computation overhead associated with the elliptic curve.

Key management in symmetric cryptographic systems poses a different problem. Using stream ciphers, communication between two parties can be encrypted with a secret key only known to the two parties. Naturally it would be better to allow the two parties to frequently change the secret key to reduce the risk of message replay attacks and cipher breaks. For example, the two parties may agree on a new secret key for each new session between them. This secret key is referred to as a session key. In a network environment where many nodes have to communicate with others, a session key can be issued by a trusted third party every time two nodes are about to communicate. This simple scheme requires a node to have only one secret key shared with the trusted third party, relieving it from maintaining a secret key for every other node in the network. An example of such systems is Kerberos (http://web.mit.edu/kerberos/www/).

As a last note in the authentication section, GSP/GPRS systems employ a technology-specific authentication mechanism (the A3 algorithm) for authentication between a base station and a mobile station. The A3 algorithm, along with the A5 encryption algorithm and A8 key management algorithm, are introduced in Section 8.2.

8.1.5 **Nonrepudiation**

Nonrepudiation refers to a security function of a system that produces evidence to prove that an operation has been performed by an entity. For example, a message recipient should hold a piece of electronic documentation for the message such that the sender cannot deny message transmission. Conversely, the sender must be able to show that the recipient did indeed receive the message. Nonrepudiation of origin proves that the message was sent, and nonrepudiation of delivery proves that the message was received.

Nonrepudiation is generally considered a facet of the security function in electronic transaction settings, as neither sender nor recipient can repudiate a transaction after it is committed. A digital signature appended to a message sent by a sender or an acknowledgement generated by the recipient can be used to provide nonrepudiation. In this case, the digital signature serves as the evidence for nonrepudiation of origin and delivery. Because only the owner of the digital signature knows his or her private key, that person cannot deny transmission of any messages signed by his or her digital signature. One-time passwords are another scheme to realize the nonrepudiation function.

8.1.6 **Network Security Protocols**

We have discussed security schemes for message confidentiality, message integrity, and message authentication. Those schemes are generally used to secure a communication channel between two parties. Another level of authentication is concerned with user authentication (i.e., verifying the identity of an entity to prevent unintended data access or impersonation). Recall that cryptographic keys are invariably used in those message-centric security mechanisms. Now, let us assume that point-to-point communication channels are secured and look at a network consisting of more than two nodes in which user authentication is associated with proper authorization with respect to data access. For example, in a typical setting, a user elects to log in to a system (a group of machines) in order to read or write a file physically stored somewhere in the system. A user must be authenticated against some security tokens managed at a log-in server before the desired access is granted.

Password

Each account in a multiple-user system is assigned a password. Users can change their passwords but must obey some password creation guidelines to avoid the use of passwords that are too simple. For any network security protocols, cleartext passwords should never be sent over a network. This is the reason why the once popular Telnet protocol has been abandoned in today's networks. On a log-in server, users' passwords are usually hashed. A good password policy should force a user to change passwords once in a while. In addition, other means of human identity can be used to replace passwords. Recent developments in biometrics suggest that fingerprints, voices, faces, and irises can be utilized to identify humans with much better security. The term *biometrics* refers to systems and techniques that make use of features of a person's body for verification and identification. Features of a person include fingerprint, facial pattern, hand geometry, iris, retina, voice pattern, and signature.

Challenge and Response

For challenge and response schemes, the log-in server of a system sends a random message (the challenge) to a user who is willing to authenticate the system. The user applies a security function to the challenge and sends the result back to the log-in server, which performs the same security function and compares its results with those from the user. The challenge and response scheme can be applied in various settings. For example, it can be used to implement a one-time password, in which each password becomes invalid right after it is used. Additionally, the security function itself can be the secret. In effect, no password is transmitted over the network, and the messages subject to interception are different every time, thereby reducing the likelihood of success of an eavesdropping attack.

Kerberos

Kerberos (http://web.mit.edu/kerberos/www/) is a secret key-based network authentication protocol (Figure 8.4). The name *Kerberos* comes from Greek mythology (Kerberos was the three-headed dog that guarded the entrance to Hades).

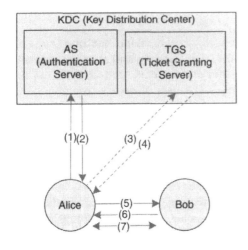

(1) Alice is authenticated by AS

(2) AS generates TGT (Ticket Granting Ticket)

(3) Alice sends TGT and her identity encrypted by the session key to TGS

(4) TGS verifies Alice's request and then generates a new session key for communication between Alice and Bob, and a service ticket for Alice to pass to Bob

(5) Alice sends the service ticket to BOB and identity encrypted by the new session key

(6) Bob verifies Alice's identity with the service ticket

(7) Alice and Bob start to communicate using the new session key

FIGURE 8.4

Kerberos (version 5).

Kerberos can be viewed as a distributed authentication service that allows a computer program (a client) running on behalf of a principal (a user) to prove its identity to a verifier (a server). In the heart of Kerberos is the key distribution center (KDC), which consists of two logically independent components: an authentication server (AS) and a ticket-granting server (TGS). A user (Alice) who wants to communicate with another user (Bob) must first be authenticated by the AS. To do this, Alice must use her secret key (e.g., her password) to encrypt a challenge sent from the AS. The AS generates a ticket-granting ticket (TGT), which is comprised of (1) a session key encrypted by Alice's secret key (password) for the upcoming communication between Alice and the TGS and (2) a secured temporal credential used to identify Alice's request to the TGS encrypted by the TGS' secret key (which is unknown to Alice) and the session key. Alice then sends the TGT along with an authenticator (i.e., Alice's identity encrypted by the session key of Alice and the TGS) to the TGS. It is the TGS that eventually generates a session key for the upcoming communication between Alice and Bob, after verifying the data in the ticket and the authenticator. At the same time, a service ticket (encrypted by Bob's secret key) for Alice to pass to Bob is also generated.

Finally, Alice sends the service ticket and a corresponding authenticator (her identity encrypted by their session key) to Bob, who verifies if the identity in the service ticket and Alice's authenticator match. If yes, Bob and Alice can begin to communicate with the session key. If Bob is a log-in server of a network system such as in a Windows domain, Kerberos is used to authenticate a user to access shared resources in the network. Kerberos relies on time-stamps and lifespan parameters to prevent message replay attacks. This requires clock synchronization among the participating machines.

Internet Protocol Security

Internet protocol security (IPSec) is a suite of protocols and mechanisms that collectively provides message confidentiality, message integrity, and message authentication at the IP layer. Depending on whether end systems support IPSec, an IP packet can be delivered in one of the two modes: transport mode or tunnel mode. In transport mode, the IP payload is secured in terms of message integrity and authentication when the authentication header (AH) protocol is used or confidentiality when the encapsulating security payload (ESP) protocol is used; but the IP header is not protected. In tunnel mode, a new IP header is used, followed by the encrypted IP packet.

IPSec provides ESP and AH protocols for message security, as shown in Figure 8.5. The AH protocol determines how an IPSec system uses the AH header, which is a hash code of all immutable fields in the IP packet, for message integrity and origin authentication. In contrast, the ESP protocol provides message confidentiality in addition to message integrity and authentication. In transport mode, an ESP header is inserted after the original IP header, and the original IP payload is encrypted. In tunnel mode, a new IP header is used for tunneling, followed by an ESP header and by the encrypted IP packet. In both cases, message integrity and

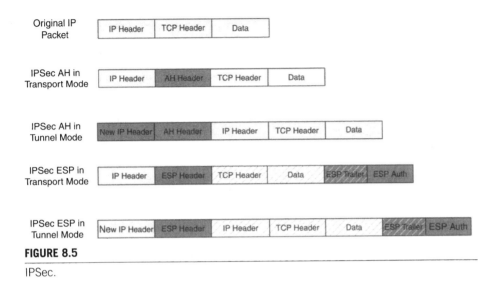

FIGURE 8.5

IPSec.

authentication are provided by an ESP authentication field appended to the end of the packet.

In addition, the Internet key exchange (IKE) protocol is supplied for symmetric key management. The IKE protocol is a hybrid of three key management protocols: Internet Security Association and Key Management Protocol (ISAKMP), Oakley, and SKEME (Versatile Secure Key Exchange Mechanism for Internet). These protocols work together to allow dynamic negotiation of cryptographic keys using the DH key exchange algorithm. IPSec is widely used to implement virtual private networks (VPNs), which enable secure access to a remote network via the public Internet.

Secure Socket Layer

Unlike IPSec, which works at the IP layer, secure socket layer (SSL) and its successor, transport layer security (TLS), are network security protocols at the transport layer. SSL and TLS support any connection-oriented application layer protocols such as HTTP (HyperText Transport Protocol), LDAP (Lightweight Directory Access Protocol), IMAP (Internet Message Access Protocol), and NNTP (Network News Transport Protocol). In reality, SSL and TLS are mainly used in conjunction with HTTPS protocol to secure communication between a web server and a web client, and TLS is being increasingly used with other application protocols such as POP3 (Post Office Protocol 3) and SMTP (Simple Mail Transfer Protocol). The default HTTPS port number on an SSL-enabled web server is 443. SSL requires a server certificate such that the server can be authenticated by a client or a browser according to an RSA public/private key encryption scheme. Subsequent web traffic is encrypted with a 128-bit or longer session key generated by a symmetric cipher such as DES, 3DES, RC2, or RC4. SSL can also be used to authenticate the client, in which case the client must obtain a public/private key pair and a digital certificate.

8.1.7 General Considerations of Mobile Security and Privacy

Mobile security and privacy essentially possess sets of unique characteristics that separate them from wired network security, such as open-air transmission of wireless signals, comparatively low computing power of mobile devices, high error rate of wireless signal transmission, security management for mobility, and location-sensitive security concerns. The need for security is much stronger than in wired networks, yet to build a secure mobile wireless system one must address a variety of constraints unique to the mobile wireless environment. Some security solutions such as those cryptographic ciphers and security network protocols may not be applicable to a mobile computing environment. For example, computationally intensive ciphers may not work on mobile devices, and in many cases the stable network connection required by many network authentication schemes is not always available.

Even if some security mechanisms can be ported to a mobile wireless system, they must be enhanced with sophisticated components so as to provide confidentiality, integrity, authentication, and nonrepudiation in highly varying mobile wireless settings. In addition, many network protocols are designed without security in mind and must be augmented with security considerations. For example, routing protocols in *ad hoc* networks must offer some security to prevent eavesdropping and message tampering. The following is a list of threats in mobile wireless networks:

- *Loss and theft of mobile devices*—Every year hundreds of thousands of mobile devices are lost in airports, hotels, restaurants, etc. This is probably by far the most serious threat to enterprise data and individual privacy.

- *Channel eavesdropping*—An attacker may capture messages transmitted in a wireless channel without being detected.

- *Identity masquerading*—An attacker may impersonate a legitimate user or service provider.

- *Message replay*—An attacker may capture a series of messages between two parties and send them to someone later.

- *Man-in-the-middle attack*—An attacker may intercept and modify messages being sent between two parties or inject new messages without being detected.

- *Wireless signal jamming and interference*—An attacker may use powerful antennas to transmit noisy signals with appropriate modulation in order to disrupt the normal operation of radio receivers.

- *Denial of service*—An attacker may use rogue access points, mobile stations, or specific frequency jamming devices to generate a huge amount of network traffic toward a target computer.

- *War-driving and unauthorized access*—An attacker may use special radio equipment to pinpoint unsecured wireless access points in an area while driving around. Those unsecured wireless LANs, many of which are linked to corporate networks, are wide open to unauthorized users.

- *Virus and wireless spamming*—Small, malicious programs may propagate among mobile device users via short message service (SMS) messages or the wireless Internet. SMS spamming could be another big issue, as subscribers have to pay for that.

In the following sections, security issues in specific wireless networks are discussed in detail.

8.2 CELLULAR NETWORK SECURITY

As more mobile applications are being delivered to cell phone users, the security mechanism employed by underlying traditional cellular systems must be redesigned to adapt to various new network settings. Moreover, because of the extensive use of cell phones and smart phones, a security breach or a network attack may have an enormous impact on every aspect of the modern society, far beyond the scope of the Internet. Emerging cellular systems have provided the means to secure wireless data transmission and e-commerce transactions, in addition to providing a more general authentication, authorization, and accounting (AAA) solution.

8.2.1 Secure Wireless Transmission

Data transmission in a cellular network can be categorized as user traffic or signaling traffic. Four security issues with regard to cellular traffic are user traffic confidentiality, signaling traffic confidentiality, user identity authentication, and user identity anonymity. For user traffic between subscribers and the back-end system, encryption is necessary to ensure confidentiality. Aside from radio layer frequency hopping modulation and code-division multiple access (CDMA) coding schemes, GSM/GPRS, CDMA, universal mobile telecommunications system (UMTS), and cdma2000 all employ some encryption for user traffic to achieve end-to-end security. For user authentication, authentication schemes generally utilize some sort of identity module on the cell phone. We use GPRS and CDMA as examples to show how end-to-end security is implemented in cellular networks. GSM/GPRS (later Third Generation Partnership Project, or 3GPP) defined an encryption protocol based on an A5 algorithm (GEA3 for GPRS), an authentication protocol based on an A3 algorithm, and a cryptographic key management protocol based on an A8 algorithm. Table 8.3 provides a summary of these algorithms.

In a GSM/GPRS network, a subscriber is identified by a unique international mobile subscriber identity (IMSI) stored in the subscriber identity module (SIM) along with the handset (the phone). The SIM also has a secret key (K_i) associated with the IMSI. On the network side, IMSI and its K_i are stored in an authentication center (AuC). The subscriber authentication is carried out in a challenge-and-response fashion, whereby a random number as a challenge is generated and sent to the mobile station by a serving GPRS service node (SGSN). The mobile station uses its K_i to produce a code as the response according to the A3 algorithm. The encryption key (K_c) is derived from the same random number and K_i by the A8 algorithm. On the mobile station, this is performed by the SIM module. Data and voice traffic are encrypted using K_c by applying the A5 algorithm, a stream cipher. It is said that the K_c is 40 bits long, but no official document reveals its actual length. When the mobile station moves around, a temporary mobile subscriber identity (TMSI) is issued by the network to track the mobile station. Whenever a mobile station changes its associated mobile switching center (MSC), it will obtain a new TMSI that is only valid within the location area of the MSC in charge. A TMSI is encrypted with K_c as part of a TMSI reallocation request message and sent to the mobile station. After applying the A5 algorithm with K_c, the mobile station then confirms reception of the TMSI by replying with a TMSI reallocation confirmation message. Thus, the TMSI reallocation process is again a challenge-and-response scheme.

The universal mobile telecommunications system (UMTS)/wideband CDMA (WCDMA) improved GPRS mobile security by introducing large cipher keys of 128

Table 8.3 GSM/GPRS (3GPP) Security Algorithms

Type	Algorithm	Description
Key management	A8	Uses a 128-bit RAND and a 128-bit K_i to produce a 64-bit K_c.
Challenge and response authentication	A3	Uses 1280-bit RAND (the challenge) and a 128-bit authentication key K_i (allocated during user subscription) to produce 32-bit expected response SRES. Implemented on MS SIM and HLR or AuC.
Symmetric encryption	A5	Uses 22-bit COUNT (TDMA frame number) and 64-bit cipher key K_c to produce 140-bit cipher blocks on both BSS and MS for encryption and decryption, respectively.

bits and providing data integrity. Signaling messages and data messages are protected by a KASUMI block cipher protocol that uses the 128-bit cipher key. The same algorithm generates a 64-bit message authentication code to ensure data integrity. Unlike proprietary algorithms used in GSM/GPRS, KASUMI is publicly available for cryptanalytic review.

The Third Generation Partnership Project (3GPP) has formed a working group TSG SA (i.e., Technical Specification Group: Services and Systems Aspects) WG3 Security responsible for the investigation of security issues, and setting up security requirements and frameworks for overall 3GPP systems. The SA WG3 has published a number of technical specifications (TSs) and technical reports (TRs) of security issues ranging from 3G security threats to cryptographic algorithm requirements and specific algorithms to 3GPP and wireless LAN Internet security.

cdma2000 1x uses a 64-bit authentication key (A Key) and an electronic serial number (ESN) to derive two encryption keys for signaling messages and data messages, respectively. The encryption algorithm is AES. cdma2000 1x EVDO uses a 128-bit A Key derived from a DH key exchange. The authentication protocol in cdma2000 networks is cellular authentication and voice encryption (CAVE). Table 8.4 shows a summary of algorithms in CDMA networks. The 128-bit SSD generated by the CAVE algorithm has two equal-length parts: SSD_A and SSD_B. Using

Table 8.4 CDMA Security Algorithms

Type	Algorithm	Description
Key Management	Cellular authentication and voice encryption (CAVE)	Uses a 64-bit reprogrammable authentication key (A Key, allocated with the handset); the electronic serial number (ESN), and a home location register (HLR)/authentication center (AC)-generated random number are used to derive a 128-bit subkey called the shared secret data (SSD), known to the mobile station and its MSC.
Challenge and Response Authentication	CAVE	Uses SSD- and MSC-generated random number (the challenge) to produce an 18-bit authentication signature and a key to replace a well-known value used for voice encoding.
Symmetric Encryption	Cellular message encryption algorithm (CMEA), ORYX, and AES	Uses 64-bit CMEA key derived from part of SSD for signaling message encryption. ORYX is a stream cipher for data messages.

CAVE with SSD_A and a random number (the challenge) generated by the MSC, a mobile station is able to generate an 18-bit authentication signature (the response) and send it to the base station. A mobile station also uses SSD_B to generate a secret key that will be used to scramble the voice. In addition, using the CAVE algorithm, a mobile station can also generate a 64-bit CEMA key and a 32-bit data key. The CEMA key is used to encrypt signaling traffic, and the data key is used to encrypt and decrypt data traffic.

Authentication, authorization, and accounting (AAA) are an integral part of 3G cellular systems. In cdma2000, AAA functionalities are provided by home AAA servers and visited AAA servers along with other mobile IP components. The packet data service node (PDSN) (foreign agent) in a visited network forwards usage data of a mobile station to the home AAA, possibly through a broker AAA. In UMTS, the CN has a home agent and an AAA server. Using serving GPRS service nodes (SGSNs) and gateway GPRS support nodes (GGSNs) as gateways, a mobile station's visited AAA server can communicate with its home AAA server for usage updates, roughly the same procedure as for location updates with the exception that the data being transmitted are related to AAA functions.

8.2.2 Secure Wireless Transaction

Mobile applications are primarily deployed in a heterogeneous network environment in which wireless and wired networks, secured enterprise networks, and wide open home wireless networks coexist and interconnect. One cannot count solely on wireless communication security even though the underlying wireless network is highly secure. Higher layer (network layer or beyond) security mechanisms are invariably required when user traffic is exposed to the unsecured Internet or wireless networks fail to provide the desired security functions. In the following, the wireless transport layer security (WTLS) and WAP (Wireless Application Protocol) identification module (WIM) of WAP and IPSec or SSL VPNs are introduced as the most widely used security protocols on today's mobile devices. Note that they can also be used in other wireless networks, such as wireless LANs and Bluetooth.

Wireless Transport Layer Security

Wireless transport layer security (WTLS), as defined in WAP 2.0, provides message confidentiality, message integrity, and unidirectional or mutual authentication at the transport layer. It is logically identical to SSL/TLS but has been adapted to the wireless environment. Message encryption is performed using RC4, DES, and triple-DES or 3-DES. Message integrity is guaranteed using HMAC. Authentication is based on PKI, using RSA, ECC, or DH. A WAP server (also called WAP gateway) uses a WTLS certificate, a particular form of an X.509 certificate. A WAP client may also use a digital certificate obtained from a CA for authentication, although it is uncommon. The following is a description of session establishment for the case when the WAP server must be authenticated (class 2 service of WTLS).

When a client and a server begin a handshake, they first exchange two random numbers in the "hello" messages. When the public key of the server has been verified with a certificate, the client sends a pre-master secret key encrypted by the server's public key. This pre-master secret key and the random numbers exchanged will be used on both sides to compute a 160-bit master secret key. For data encryption, an encryption key block is calculated based on the master secret key, a sequence number, random numbers exchanged, and a string indicating the party of the calculation. This key block will be eventually used to derive encryption keys for an algorithm such as RC4, DES, or triple-DES that has been negotiated during the "hello" message exchange.

WTLS specifies keyed hashing algorithms such as SHA-1 and MD5 for the computation of MAC over compressed data. For mobile devices with limited computing power, a light overhead SHA_XOR_40 algorithm is also provided in an earlier version of WTLS. The key used during MAC computation, also known as the MAC secret, is also derived from the encryption key block. In order to make denial of service attacks more difficult to accomplish, the WTLS specification suggests that a WAP server should not allow an attacker to break up an existing connection or session by sending a single message in plaintext from a forged address.

Figure 8.6 depicts the WTLS architecture. At its heart is the record protocol, which interfaces with the wireless datagram protocol (WDP) and the wireless transport protocol (WTP) and is responsible for data encryption and integrity verification. The handshake protocol defines the negotiation of cryptographic parameters such as algorithms, authentication schemes, and compression methods. When the negotiation is complete, the change cipher spec protocol is performed, indicating that the party is ready to use the negotiated mechanism. After that application, data can be exchanged according to the application data protocol.

An earlier version of WTLS is not secure, as researchers have found some security problems [4]. For example, in WTLS predicable initialization vectors (IVs) may lead to encryption key breach, and the SHA_XOR_40 algorithm does not provide

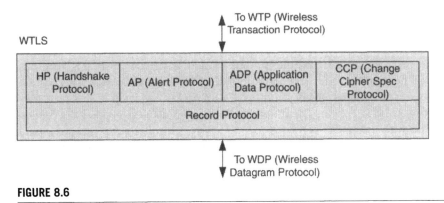

FIGURE 8.6

WTLS architecture.

message integrity if stream ciphers are used. In light of these problems, the latest version of WTLS (version 06-Apr-2001) has made significant changes; for example, the SHA_XOR_40 algorithm has been removed.

WAP Identification Module

In order to seamlessly integrate WAP into an e-commerce environment, a WAP client must be authenticated with respect to mobile device identity. A tamperproof WIM module can be embedded into a WAP client device for this purpose. It could be a component of the SIM card or an external smart card containing the following information: a public/private key pair of the device for signing and another pair for authentication, manufacturer's certificates, and user certificates or their URLs. A WIM module implements the WTLS class 3 service, allowing the WAP client associated with it to be authenticated. This class of service specifies that, in addition to server authentication during the handshake, the client must generate a digital signature using one of its public/private key pairs stored in the WIM module, enabling nonrepudiation of client messages.

As a similar wireless web platform, iMode also provides SSL-based server authentication, message encryption, and integrity. Because iMode is a proprietary architecture, details of its security mechanisms are not publicly available. Other wireless web platforms have been developed by Japanese companies, such as EZWeb (KDDI) and J-Sky (J-Phone). Although internals of those systems are not revealed to the public, it is commonly believed that they offer the same set of security services based on SSL or TLS.

IPSec/SSL VPNs

IPSec/SSL VPNs are widely used in mobile wireless networks to allow for secure remote network access. These protocols are transparent to the underlying radio technologies used for wireless communication. As long as a network is IP based, theoretically IPSec will work without a problem, although in reality there are some problems with respect to the nature of wireless transmission and mobility. For example, a VPN tunnel may be interrupted during handoff. Unlike IPSec VPNs, which provide secure access to a network, SSL VPNs enables secure remote access to an application inside a network.

Mobile VPN is particularly useful when a mobile device is used by a salesperson, field engineer, or other type of mobile worker wishing to remotely access an enterprise network via the Internet. A mobile VPN, based on either IPSec or SSL, could solve the problem. Aside from a VPN client on the mobile device, a VPN gateway must be set up for client authentication and data encryption/decryption. A problem with using VPN is related to U.S. export control on cryptography, which basically imposes strict control over the export of cryptographic software and hardware for national security considerations. Strong cryptographic systems such as 128-bit key VPNs are not allowed to be exported unless certain licenses have been obtained. Worldwide corporate networks are at risk when VPN clients in overseas offices use 40-bit encryption.

Aside from these two protocols, smart phones running an advanced operating system such as Windows Smartphone allow for normal SSL to be used within a mobile web browser. It is expected that higher layer security protocols will be directly ported onto relatively powerful mobile devices such as smart phones.

8.3 WIRELESS LAN SECURITY[*]

Because more cell phones and smart phones are being equipped with Wi-Fi interfaces, related security problems of IEEE 802.11 wireless LANs have become a hot topic, especially after numerous serious vulnerabilities of wired equivalent privacy (WEP), the security mechanism of 802.11, were discovered. Understandably, when the 802.11 wireless LAN standard was developed, security was apparently not a top priority. The "wired equivalence" design rationale essentially led to some earlier versions of wireless LAN security solutions that clearly failed to deliver security functions they were supposed to provide. Many Wi-Fi products in use are based on these flawed protocols and mechanisms. Fortunately, the IEEE 802.11 working group has offered several new standards with enhanced security. Wireless LAN products often incorporate enhanced security as an option in addition to wide-open configurations. For example, WAP has been required in all new Wi-Fi certified products since 2004, and WPA2 (for 802.11i) was required for Wi-Fi certification beginning in 2005.

Security risks in wireless LANs include eavesdropping, unauthorized access, masquerading, man-in-the-middle attacks, denial of service (DoS), and rogue access points:

■ *Eavesdropping*—Eavesdropping is highly possible because the coverage of wireless signals is quite difficult to determine, and anyone within the range with an appropriate interface will be able to pick up the signal and intercept ongoing data transmissions at will. Weak encrypted signals can be cracked with modest effort. Powerful tools such as AirSnort and Kismet made wireless eavesdropping on unsecured wireless LANs much easier.

■ *Unauthorized access*—Unauthorized access happens when a home or enterprise wireless LAN operates in default configuration mode, which permits anyone to use its Internet access as well as other resources shared in the network.

■ *Masquerading*—Many wireless LANs use wireless adaptor's MAC address (physical address) as filters. Thus, attackers may masquerade themselves by spoofing MAC addresses. This can be done in conjunction with eavesdropping.

---

[*]Here, we use the most popular wireless LAN standard (IEEE 802.11) for discussion.

- *Man-in-the-middle attacks*—Wireless LANs are designed to allow an access point to authenticate a station but not the other way around; hence, a station cannot be sure that the access point in question is what it claims to be. Attackers may pretend to be an access point sitting between a station and a real access point to intercept, modify, and forge packets.

- *Denial of service (DoS)*—DoS is very common on the wired Internet. Many machines are organized to attack a single website, making it unable to service legitimate users. In wireless LANs, attackers may use rogue APs, their own stations, or other non-802.11 spectrum jammers to send a large amount of forged 802.11 management or control frames or broad-spectrum noise. The IEEE 802.11 MAC protocol also has been shown to be vulnerable to DoS attack [5].

- *Rogue access points*—Due to the ease of network setup and configuration, one may quickly build a small insecure wireless LAN and make it work instantly by connecting it to the wired back-end; hence, the entire wired network may become insecure because of the rogue wireless LAN.

8.3.1 Common 802.11 Security Myths

In practice, wireless LANs are often wide open without any access control or simply employ a MAC-based (here MAC refers to the adapter's physical address) access control list (ACL) to authenticate legitimate mobile stations. An ACL is essentially a list of MAC addresses that are permitted to access the network. Those data frames not originating from legitimate MAC addresses will be rejected by the access point without going through further authentication. As in a wired LAN, a MAC address in a frame header is always transmitted in cleartext regardless of the encryption method in use, allowing anyone to gather a list of MAC addresses of stations associated with an access point. An attacker can forge data frames that use those authorized MAC addresses and gain access to the network; therefore, contrary to common belief, the MAC base access control solution does not solve the problem.

Another common security myth associated with 802.11 is the use of an extended service set identifier (ESSID). Because an ESSID identifies an access point, many believe that by disabling beacon messages containing the ESSID of an access point an attacker will not be able to determine the ESSID and thus cannot associate to the access point. In fact, this does not prevent an attacker from getting the ESSID because it is still sent in probe messages when a client associates to an access point; also, many wireless LANs use default, well-known ESSIDs.

Given the fact that a large number of wireless LAN access points are being used and there is no effective way to prevent wireless LAN signals from traveling far, it is tempting to get free access to adjacent wireless LANs while walking, driving, or even flying by using appropriate wireless LAN equipment. In an effort to detect wireless LANs in a regional area, some people have been intensively engaged in activities known as war walking, war driving, and war flying [6]. In all cases, a PDA or a laptop computer with a wireless LAN interface and a global positioning system (GPS) receiver, a handy software tool such as Net Stumbler (http://www.netstumbler.com/) or Air Magnet (http://www.airmagnet.com/), and an optional high-gain antenna are all it takes to produce a so-called wireless access point (WAP) map of access points, either secured (using WEP/WPA/WPA2 or higher layer security measured) or unsecured. With a powerful antenna, a war driver could be many miles away from the physical location of a wireless LAN yet still manage to pick up its signals. Figure 8.7 is a Wi-Fi map of Seattle made by students at the University of Washington (http://depts.washington.edu/wifimap). The dots in the figure represent 802.11 access points (secured and unsecured) within reach of the war drivers. Unsecured wireless LANs detected by war driving not only offer war drivers a free ride on the Internet but also invite attackers to obtain remote access to a network without being filtered by firewalls or detected by intrusion-detection systems.

8.3.2 **WEP Vulnerability**

The service set identifier (SSID)-based access control indeed does not offer any security functions. Besides, it is common sense that wireless communication should be encrypted and properly authenticated. WEP is the first security mechanism for wireless LANs. A shared secret key of 40 or 104 bits is used by all participating stations within a BSS (Basic Service Set) bounded to the same access point. The encryption algorithm is RC4. For every packet sent between a station and the associated access point, a 32-bit integrity check value (ICV) is computed according to a CRC-32 algorithm. Then RC4 uses a 64-bit key to encrypt the data and the

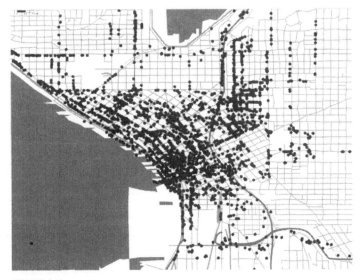

FIGURE 8.7

A Wi-Fi map of Seattle, WA (Courtesy of University of Washington).

ICV. The encryption key is composed of a 24-bit randomly generated initialization vector (IV) and a 40-bit shared secret key, as shown in Figure 8.8(a). Using the 64-bit encryption key, the pseudo-random generation algorithm (PRGA) of RC4 computes a keystream, which will be XORed with a plaintext message (see Figures 8.8(b) and (c)). To let the other party know the IV, it is added to the encrypted payload data as part of the packet (the ciphertext), as shown in Figure 8.8(d).

Wired equivalent privacy (WEP) is known to have numerous security problems. The first problem is the lack of key management, such as the DH key exchange protocol. The secret key must be distributed by other means of communication and is subject to social engineering attacks, where attackers trick legitimate users of a system in order to obtain passwords, addresses, or other sensitive information. As the network grows, more stations must be informed of the same secret key, and

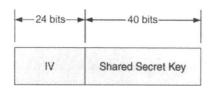

(a) WEP Encryption Key

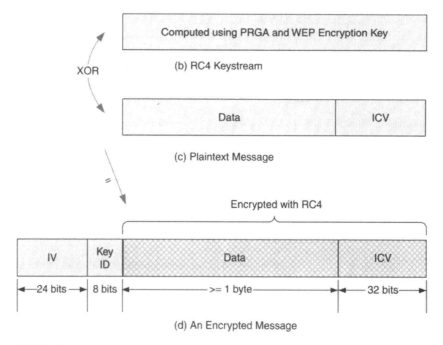

FIGURE 8.8

WEP encryption.

it would be quite cumbersome to change the secret key for security reasons. Very often the secret key is not secret any more after some time.

The second problem with WEP is the 24-bit IV. Because each packet transmitted has an IV, it is possible that the same IV will be used again after some time. (The code space of IV will exhaust after 2^{24} packets have been sent.) On the other hand, RC4 has been found by Fluhrer et al. [1] to have a severe weakness in its key scheduling algorithm; when an encryption key is constructed by the above-mentioned method, an attacker will be able to derive the 40-bit secret part of the encryption key by analyzing those packets that share the same encryption key (secret key + IV) [1]. This attack is referred to as the FMS attack. It has been shown that a WEP key can be cracked in a matter of several hours.

The third problem with WEP is the CRC-32 algorithm used to calculate the ICV [7]. CRC in itself is a simple mechanism for detecting random errors; it was not designed to detect deliberate data falsification. In fact, it has been shown that it is possible to modify the encrypted payload of an 802.11b message without disrupting the checksum (ICV). Furthermore, the CRC-32 algorithm does not involve any keying function, such as HMAC. Thus, an attacker who knows a keystream that corresponds to an IV can safely inject forged packets into the BSS.

8.3.3 **802.11 Authentication Vulnerabilities**

The IEEE 802.11 wireless LAN specification defines two authentication modes: open and shared key authentication. The default open authentication imposes no authentication on a station that wants to communicate with the access point. In the shared key mode, a challenge-and-response scheme is used. Upon receiving an authentication request from a station identified by its MAC address, the access point responds with a 128-byte randomly generated challenge text in cleartext. The station then encrypts the challenge text with a shared key using RC4 and sends the result back to the access point. The access point uses the same shared key to decrypt the response. If the decrypted value matches the challenge text, the station is authenticated and can proceed to send and receive messages in the BSS; otherwise, the station is rejected.

As mentioned earlier, the problem of this authentication mechanism stems from RC4, stated in a paper by Fluhrer et al. [8]. An attacker who obtains a large number of challenge-and-response authentication sequences corresponding to WEP encryption keys (the same IV) can easily deduce the keystreams produced by RC4 by leveraging those weaknesses described in the previous section. From that point, the attacker can authenticate himself to the access point by correctly responding to any challenge texts using the keystream without knowing the shared secret key. Even worse, with the keystream, the cleartext of those messages being analyzed can be revealed by simply XORing the ciphertext against the keystream, exactly the same operation that the associated access point should perform. Using tools such as WEPCrack (http://wepcrack.sourceforge.net/) or AirSnort (http://airsnort .shmoo.com/), it would not take long to crack a WEP key.

8.3.4 802.1X, WPA, and 802.11i

To address the security issues of WEP, one method suggested is to build security overlay on top of the insecure wireless LAN. VPN is often used in practice. 802.11i, which was complete in 2004, was designed to address wireless LAN security issues. 802.1X is a security standard for a more general LAN environment. The Wi-Fi protected access (WPA) protocol has been developed by the Wi-Fi Alliance as an interim solution for 820.11i; hence, 802.11i includes WPA features and some new features, such as AES, CCMP (see discussion below), preauthentication, and key caching for fast handoff.

The IEEE 802.1X standard enables port-based mutual authentication and flexible key management in an IEEE 802 local area network. It does not specify a single authentication method but uses the extensible authentication protocol (EAP) as the underlying authentication framework to support various authentication methods such as smart cards, one-time passwords, and certificates. When an unauthenticated supplicant (a client) attempts to connect to an authenticator (a wireless access point), the authenticator opens a port for the supplicant to pass only EAP authentication messages to the back-end authenticator server, which could be, for example, a remote dial-in user service (RADIUS) server. Initially designed for authentication and authorization of dial-in modem access, RADIUS as a protocol (standardized in RFC 2058) has been augmented to facilitate any form of secure remote access with respect to authentication, authorization, and accounting. The supplicant submits its identity to the authentication server, which makes the decision as to whether or not the supplicant should be granted access to the LAN. The authentication server will send either "accepted" or "rejected" to the authenticator. If the result is "accepted," the authenticator will change the client's port to an authorized state, meaning that the port can be used to pass any other additional traffic. As shown in Figure 8.9, 802.1X can be integrated with an existing AAA infrastructure such as RADIUS to provide user-based centralized authentication.

Wireless protected access (WPA) is an interim solution to wireless LAN security that is required by the Wi-Fi Alliance. WPA is backward compatible with WEP in place on widely deployed wireless LAN devices; WPA only requires software or firmware upgrades to existing systems. Each station using WPA will use a different 128-bit encryption key for RC4 data encryption, which can be "refreshed" frequently. The protocol enabling these features is temporal key integrity protocol (TKIP). Key elements of TKIP are listed as follows [9]:

- *Michael*—Michael is a message integrity code (MIC) algorithm that uses a 64-bit key, called the MIC key, to produce a 64-bit tag (a MAC) for a packet, in addition to ICV. Michael is designed to impose dramatically lowered computational overhead on a mobile station than are other MAC algorithms.

- *Per-packet key mixing*—TKIP employs a key mixing function that takes the base WEP key, source MAC address, and packet sequence number as inputs

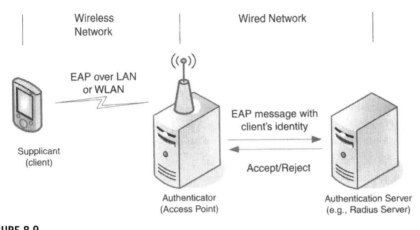

FIGURE 8.9

802.1X in a wireless LAN setting.

and produces a new 128-bit WEP key for each individual packet. The mixing function is carried out in two phases to reduce computational overhead.

- *Packet sequencing*—Each packet has a 48-bit sequence number, which will be further used to compute the encryption key. This feature defeats message replay attacks.

WPA adopted IEEE 802.1X to provide both authentication and key management. For enterprise networks where a separate AAA server such as a RADIUS is in place, WPA can be integrated with the AAA server for authentication and key distribution. In WPA and WPA2-Enterprise (WPA2 is the product certification available through the Wi-Fi Alliance for 802.11i compatible products. Both WPA and WPA2 have two authentication modes: Enterprise and Personal), the AAA server authenticates individual users and then delivers per-session pairwise master keys (PMKs). In WPA and WPA2-Personal, all stations and the AP have the same pre-shared secret key (PSK) used for both group authentication and PMK. In both cases, the PMK is not used for encryption; it is mixed with the station's MAC and an IV to derive a pairwise temporal key (PTK), which in turn will be used to deduce the AES encryption key.

The encryption key and MIC key used by TKIP are derived from a master key generated by 802.1X. Frequent key changes enabled by 802.1X allow the encryption key and MIC key used by the TKIP to be refreshed every once in a while, thus reducing the risk of key breach due to eavesdropping. Created by the Wi-Fi Alliance, WPA is supported by a large number of device vendors.

Because WPA serves as a quick patch to WEP, it effectively makes it more difficult to compromise a wireless LAN. The downside of WPA is that it is rather complicated to implement, which could give rise to more security risks. It is also not efficient to introduce an additional MIC key other than the encryption key and use both ICV and MIC for message integrity. Unlike WPA, 802.11i is designed to provide a long-term solution to 802.11 security. Like WPA, it employs 802.1X as the underlying authentication mechanism. Other key features of 802.11i are:

- Countermode–CBC–MAC protocol (CCMP)—Like TKIP, CCMP provides message confidentiality and integrity but uses AES as the cipher instead of RC4. The cipher block chaining message authentication code (CBC–MAC) protects both header and data integrity. The 128-bit encryption key is also used for computation of the 64-bit MAC. The IV is still 48 bits.

- *Pairwise key hierarchy*—802.11i does not compute an encryption key for each packet; instead, the same PMK generated by the 802.1X authentication procedure is used for all packets during an association. PMK is first used to derive a PTK by the access point and the station after proper handshakes between them. The AES encryption key is further deduced from PTK.

- *Key caching and preauthentication*—A user's credentials are kept on the authentication server; thus, when the user leaves and returns shortly, it is not necessary to prompt the user for log-in information; the reauthentication is done transparently. Preauthentication enables a station to be authenticated to an AP before moving to it. Both schemes are designed to speed up authentication in supporting fast handoff.

It should be noted TKIP is also part of 802.11i, but it should only be considered as a short-term solution. Table 8.5 presents a comparison of the three security protocols for 802.11 wireless LAN.

Table 8.5 802.11 Security Protocols Comparison			
	WEP	**WPA**	**802.11i**
Stage	Initial security mechanism; insecure	Intermediate solution (a snapshot of 802.11i taken in 2002)	Long-term solution (completed in 2004) (WPA2 certifies 802.11i products)
Encryption Algorithm	RC4	Enhanced RC4	AES
Key Length	40 bits	128 bits refreshable	128 bits
Key Management	None	802.1X EAP	802.1X EAP
Message Integrity	CRC-32	Michael (including header)	CCMP (including header)
Logical Equivalence	None	802.1X + TKIP + RC4	802.1X + CCMP + AES

8.4 BLUETOOTH SECURITY

As a simple personal area network (PAN) solution, Bluetooth has become the *de facto* standard interface on cell phones and PDAs. People use Bluetooth to transmit files between a mobile device and a desktop computer or between two Bluetooth-enabled devices. Bluetooth earphones enable voice over Bluetooth channels within a short range. Even though the Bluetooth signal can travel only a very limited distance (usually less than 10 m), there are still security issues with respect to data confidentiality and authentication. The Bluetooth SIG (Special Interest Group) has incorporated a security architecture into the official Bluetooth specification.

8.4.1 Bluetooth Security Architecture

Recall that the Bluetooth specification defines a number of "profiles" for different types of typical usages, such as a dial-up networking profile, fax profile, headset profile, LAN access profile, file transfer profile, and synchronization profile. Each profile has been specified with a set of protocols suitable for those applications falling into the profile. In providing security for various applications, the Bluetooth SIG has defined a number of profile security policies, each of which specifies recommended baseband security options and protocols for different usage models and profiles. Aside from frequency hopping, the basic Bluetooth baseband security mechanisms are listed below:

- *Challenge-and-response authentication*—If device A wishes to be authenticated by device B, device B will send a 128-bit random number (RAND) to device A upon being requested to do so by device A, which uses a 128-bit secret authentication key (link key), RAND, and its 48-bit device address (BD_ADDR) to compute a response according to an algorithm called E_1. When the response is received at device B, device B performs the same computation and compares the result with the response. If they match, then device B is authenticated. Bluetooth devices in a piconet of multiple devices use a shared link key for mutual authentication between two devices. The same link key is also used to derive the encryption key.

- *Per-packet encryption using* E_0—Bluetooth devices may use an encryption key of length 4 to 128 bits, subject to an individual country's regulations. The encryption key is generated by an E_3 algorithm each time the device enters encryption mode. Because communication is always between a slave and a master, the master should initiate the encryption sequence by sending a RAND to the slave. On the slave side, it performs the E_0 algorithm that takes the encryption key, the device address of the master, current clock value, and RAND to compute a keystream. The keystream is then XORed with the packet payload to produce to ciphertext.

In a Bluetooth piconet, a session refers to the period of time a device stays in a piconet. A link key can be either a semipermanent key or a temporary key, depending on the application.

A semipermanent link key allows a device to use the same link key to connect to other devices in a piconet after a session is over. This is useful when some devices must communicate frequently once in a while. A temporary link key is valid only within a session and will be discarded when the session is over. For different scenarios, four different types of link keys are defined. Below is a summary of these keys and when they should be used:

- *Combination link* key is used for each new pair of Bluetooth devices if they decided to use this type of link key. The procedure to establish a combination link key between two devices is called pairing, in which both devices generate a random number and use it to produce a key. They then exchange those random numbers and compute the combination key. It is used for multiple connections from a single device.

- *Unit link* key is specific to a single device and is stored in nonvolatile memory. It is used in installation or when the device is first activated and is never changed afterwards. A device can use another device's unit key as a link key. Which link key should be used is determined during initialization. It is used for communication between two trusted devices.

- *Master link* key is a temporary link key generated by a master device to replace the current link key. It is used for point-to-multipoint communication such as a master broadcasting to its slaves.

- *Initialization link* key is generated using a shared PIN code and device address. The PIN code must be entered to both devices. It is used only to protect initialization parameter transmission when no other keys are available during Bluetooth pairing.

Bluetooth security profile policies have provided general recommendations as to what protocols and algorithms as well as keys should be used in different settings. For specific applications, however, care must be taken to ensure that desired security functions or countermeasures to possible attacks are implemented.

8.4.2 Bluetooth Weakness and Attacks

The use of a PIN code during pairing presents some security risks [10]. The length of a PIN can be between 8 and 128 bits. It could come with the device or can be selected by the user. Prior to link key exchange, an initialization key will first be computed, which in turn uses the PIN code. An attacker may make an exhaustive search over all possible PINs up to a specific length. To verify its guess, the attacker only needs to eavesdrop on the communication channel between two victims to capture random numbers in cleartext and perform the initialization key algorithm. When the PIN code is obtained, the attacker can compute the initialization key and the link key. Eventually, the encryption key can also be obtained, and the communication between those two devices is completely compromised. For this reason, longer PIN codes are strongly suggested by the Bluetooth SIG. An even better countermeasure to PIN attacks is to conduct initialization of two devices in a private and closely secured environment where no wireless communication can be eavesdropped.

The nature of the Bluetooth technology allows mobile device manufacturers to choose a set of configurations optimized for a specific application model. Although this does offer some flexibility to mobile device manufacturers and effectively promotes the technology, it also results in security risks to some extent because in some cases security mechanisms are not well implemented or not taken into account, even if the security building blocks are clearly specified in Bluetooth specification. The five types of attacks targeting Bluetooth implementation problems are:

- Bluesnarfing
- Bluebugging
- Bluejacking
- Back-door attack
- Virus and battery draining attack

In a Bluesnarfing attack, an attacker uses modified Bluetooth equipment and directional antennae to capture data from some Bluetooth devices that could be a mile away. The weakness being leveraged in this case is a default insecure mode enabled by some mobile device manufacturers (see below for details). After successful Bluesnarfing, everything on the device is exposed to the attacker.

In a Bluebugging attack, an attacker may remotely control a Bluetooth device, intercepting or rerouting communication without a trace. Bluesnarfing and Bluebugging attacks are mainly targeting cell phones with a Bluetooth interface. They usually require the victim devices to be in "discoverable" mode; that is, the device will respond to discovery queries sent from other Bluetooth devices. It turns out that many cell phones are in this mode by default, which makes them susceptible to these attacks. Worse, a brute force MAC address scan could possibly discover those devices that are not in "discoverable" mode, aided by tools such as RedFang and Bluesniff (http://bluesniff.shmoo.com/); thus, Bluetooth war walking or war driving (i.e., the activity of discovering Bluetooth devices in the proximity) are also possible using these tools.

Bluejacking involves sending unsolicited messages to a Bluetooth cell phone utilizing a security vulnerability in the Bluetooth handshake protocol when two devices are pairing for mutual authentication. During the handshake, the other party's device name will be displayed. Thus, by manipulating the device name, an attacker can send anonymous messages or broadcast messages (proximity spamming) among visible devices. Contrary to public perception, Bluejacking does not imply hijacking of a Bluetooth device. Personal data on a device remain secure and the device is still under the total control of the user, but it does make the victim worry about the security of the device because unwanted messages from someone are being displayed on the device.

A back-door attack allows an attacker to take advantage of a secretly estab-lished trusted "pairing" relationship such that the target Bluetooth device can be remotely monitored and controlled without the user's notice. Not only can per-sonal data such as phone books, business cards, calendar, pictures, and e-mail be downloaded from the target device, but also all services available on the device, such as the cellular network connection, built-in camera, audio recorder, or music player, may be accessed and surreptitiously controlled.

The insecure "discoverable" mode of Bluetooth provides a vehicle for mobile virus and worm propagation. Although today's mobile operating systems have imposed strict security mechanisms whereby users are prompted when any installation of programs is about to occur, most people do not even bother to read the warning message and simply click "OK." Worms such as the Cabir worm have certainly demonstrated that cell phones can easily be infected by a mobile virus. Several variants of the Cabir worms have spread among smart phones running Symbian OS with Bluetooth configured in the "discoverable" mode. As a worm, the program tries to propagate by scanning for vulnerable cell phones using Bluetooth and then sends itself to those victims. A side effect of this worm is that the device's battery drains quickly while the worm is constantly scanning for other devices. Other forms of battery draining attacks use some properly pow-ered attacking Bluetooth device to query a victim repetitively, effectively disabling the device after some time. Code signing is a defending technique against these threats. Only those programs developed by trust vendors will be registered and digitally signed, so users have the chance to reject any unsigned downloaded code.

It is clear that, in fighting with mobile viruses, users have to bear the respon-sibility to be alert to any suspicious programming. Mobile antivirus software may also help users detect any possible infections.

8.5 *AD HOC* NETWORK SECURITY

Security issues in mobile *ad hoc* networks encompass a much broader range of challenges, in addition to secured routing at the network layer. As communica-tion in a MANET involves one-hop link layer protocols between two directly con-nected nodes and multihop packet routing protocols across a set of nodes, the security mechanism in MANET should also take into account both the link layer and network layer accordingly, assuming the wireless physical layer is properly secured.

8.5.1 Link Layer *Ad Hoc* Security

For a MANET application, end-to-end security service can be provided by authen-tication and encryption, which in turn rely on lower layer security protocols to function. IEEE 802.11 WEP is an example of a link layer security mechanism that unfortunately fails to protect one-hop communication between a mobile station and an access point. As discussed earlier, 802.11i has been designed to address the problem of WEP. Specifically, in the distribution coordination function (DCF) mode, when a node senses the channel and finds out it is used by other transmissions, it will initiate a binary exponential back-off procedure waiting until the next try. This scheme does not guarantee any fairness over channel access. In fact, it favors the last node among contending nodes. Therefore, one heavily loaded node may keep occupying the channel whereas a lightly loaded node may have to back off many times. Modifications to the back-off scheme have been proposed, mainly to penalize those misbehavior nodes with a large back-off value.

The principle idea of protocols is to add security extensions to traditional *ad hoc* routing protocols. Note that secured *ad hoc* routing protocols can be categorized as "proactive" security services that are based on node authentication and message confidentiality [11] and the assumption that a node will forward messages according to its routing table or routing mechanism. When a node is compromised and does not forward messages as expected, "reactive" schemes such as ACK (Acknowledgement)-based malicious node detection and coordinated rating are needed.

8.5.2 Key Management

Node authentication in MANET is much more complicated than in a fixed network because of the nature of transient network organization and dynamically changing network topology. Indeed, there is hardly a centralized trusted authority in MANET. And, even when there is, it may not constantly be accessible to every node in the network. Thus, a PKI-based authentication scheme is not directly applicable to MANET. To provide authentication among mobile nodes in such a distributed environment, threshold cryptography can be used.

Threshold cryptography essentially distributes cryptographic functions of an individual node to each node in a group, thus eliminating central authority. It is based on the idea that, even if some individual nodes may be compromised, the majority of a group can always be trusted. In its simplest form, in the context of CA, each node in a group of n nodes holds a distinct piece of the group's private key, and any t nodes can work together to perform the security function as a whole for the group, but any $t - 1$ nodes cannot. This scheme can be used to distribute the security function (i.e., providing a certificate for a node's public key) of a single CA over a number of servers [12]. Each server (a fairly stable node in an *ad hoc* network) holds a share of the private key (k). It computes a public key corresponding to its private key share. The public key (K) corresponding to the private key (k) is known to each server. To sign a digital certificate, each server generates a partial digital signature using its private key share. A combiner (a server that directly interfaces a service requester) needs to gather t such partial signatures in order to produce a signed digital certificate. Hence, compromised servers will not affect the digital signature service provided by these servers as a whole because they can only generate at most $t - 1$ partial digital signatures. A combiner also verifies the combination using its public key. Tampered partial signatures from compromised servers will be detected by the combiner.

Constructing partial signatures for CA certification is highly computationally intensive and cannot be performed on mobile devices with inherent resource constraints. To adapt threshold cryptography to MANET, a scheme that combines ID-based cryptography and threshold cryptography has been introduced [13]. An ID-based cryptosystem provides public/private key encryption using node ID to derive the effective public key of each node. An ID-based encryption scheme consists of four algorithms as follows:

- *Setup* takes an input security parameter and returns a master public/private key pair for the system. Every node in the system knows the master public key but not the private key.

- *Encrypt* takes the master public key, the identity of the recipient, and a plaintext message and returns a ciphertext. Note that in normal encryption, the recipient's public key and the plaintext are fed into a cipher.

- *Extract* takes the master private key and an ID (an identity string, such as a MAC address) and produces a personal private key to the identity. Every node must obtain its private key from a private key generation (PKG) service.

- *Decrypt* takes the master public key, a cipher text, and a personal private key and returns the plaintext.

It is obvious that an attacker cannot decrypt an intercepted message without knowing the master private key or personal private key of the node to which the message is headed. The combined key management approach aims at leveraging ID-based public/private key pair generation to reduce computational overhead. It works as follows. First, the initial participating nodes decide on a set of security parameters, such as threshold t, and their identities. Then a threshold PKG is performed by these initial nodes to compute a master public/private key pair in a distributed fashion. The master public key is known to everyone. The personal private key of each node is generated based on the node's identity conforming to t-out-of-n threshold cryptography such that fewer than t nodes cannot recover the master private key. Nodes joining the system later must communicate with at least t nodes serving the PKG to obtain t shares of the personal private keys (not the private keys) and compute the personal private key. Because node ID is commonly available in a message header, this approach does not require any specific public key propagation mechanism, as is the case in the CA approach. Another way to introduce low-overhead asymmetric cryptography to mobile devices is using ECC. To this end, some ECC-based distributed key generation schemes have been proposed, such as that of Boneh–Franklin [14].

8.5.3 **Wireless Sensor Network Security**

Wireless sensor networks have been used in a number of application scenarios, including wild habitat monitoring, lighting and temperature control of a building, and glacial monitoring. More wireless sensor applications that closely relate to our daily life are on the way. As a consequence, security problems of wireless sensor networks have surfaced in response to concerns that potential data interception or tampering could result in serious damage to a system.

The principle challenge of security in a wireless sensor network is the seriously constrained sensor hardware that cannot facilitate generally used security mechanisms on regular desktop computers. Below is a summary of the hardware capability of a Smart Dust node developed at the University of California, Berkeley (see Table 8.6) [15]. It is worth noting that new wireless sensor modules tend to have significantly improved hardware components as a result of the rapid advancements in wireless sensor technology but still lag behind regular desktop computers and even PDAs.

A wireless sensor is generally expected to operate for years without battery replacement, thus reducing power consumption is always a key design objective. Even if it is possible to incorporate powerful processors and communication capabilities into sensor nodes, their power consumption may exceed what a small battery can support. Consequently, given such a hardware configuration, it would be impractical to use traditional security mechanisms in a wireless sensor network, as they usually require a large amount of memory during operation and impose significant communication and computing overhead on the sensor nodes; for example, asymmetric digital signatures for authentication are too expensive for sensor nodes because they may drain a battery too quickly. One way to provide authentication is to employ symmetric key cryptographic systems between sensor nodes, each sharing a secret key with the central trusted base station. To establish a new key, two nodes use the base station as a trusted third party to set up a secured communication channel.

Table 8.6 Characteristics of Prototype Smart Dust Nodes	
CPU	**8-Bit, 4 MHz**
Storage	8-KB instruction flash 512-bytes RAM 512-bytes EEPROM
Communication	916-MHz radio
Bandwidth	10 Kbps
Operating system	TinyOS
Operating system code space	3500 bytes
Available code space	4500 bytes

Another security problem in this domain is secured routing in both static wireless sensor networks and future mobile wireless sensor networks. *Ad hoc* routing protocols such as DSR (Dynamic Source Routing) or AODV (Ad hoc On-Demand Distance Vector) are again unsuitable for wireless sensor networks because of the communication overhead and requirement for state maintenance at each node. In addition, message routing in a wireless sensor network often follows a pattern of many-to-one, meaning that many sensor nodes communicate back to a base station, and, as opposed to routing in *ad hoc* networks of mobile devices, in-networking processing (intermediate nodes processing messages being forwarded) for data aggregation makes secured routing in a wireless sensor network more challenging. Commonly used end-to-end security mechanisms cannot be applied in this case because the contents of messages are subject to modification. Karlof and Wagner [16] compiled a list of attacks on sensor network routing:

- Spoofed, altered, or replayed routing information

- Selective forwarding (a sensor node does not forward messages faithfully)

- Sinkhole attacks (a compromised node spoofs messages to attract traffic from adjacent nodes according to the routing algorithm)

- Sybil attacks (a compromised node pretends to be multiple nodes, thereby confusing routing algorithms and resulting in potential identity theft)

- Wormholes (multiple compromised nodes can collude to establish out-of-band channels, effectively disrupting network topology)

- "Hello" flood attacks (a node simply broadcasts bogus "hello" messages or overheard messages in the network hoping to manipulate topology)

- Acknowledgment spoofing (a node sends spoofed link layer acknowledges to senders of overheard messages)

Among these types of attacks, bogus routing information, Sybil attacks, "hello" floods, and acknowledgment spoofing can be defeated by employing link layer encryption and authentication along with identity verification and authenticated broadcast. Multipath routing can be used to defeat selected forwarding attacks. In order to provide symmetric key cryptography, the network must ensure that no other nodes can impersonate the trusted base station, as each node will obtain a symmetric key from the trusted base station, which also initiates an authenticated broadcast to perform a query. Asymmetric authentication is needed to make sure compromised nodes cannot perform authenticated broadcasts. One way to achieve this is to use delayed disclosure of a series of keys derived from a one-way symmetric key chain [15], which requires the base station and nodes to be loosely synchronized. The base station uses a secret key (K_n) as the last key in the key chain and computes K_{n-1} using a one-way function $F: K_{n-1} = F(K_n)$. Then, it uses $K_1, K_2, \ldots$ during a specific time period subsequent to computing the MAC

(Message Authentication Code) of packets sent within that time slot. Nodes receiving those packets can verify the integrity as well as authenticity of those packets later when the base station discloses keys in the same order as they were used to compute the MAC.

8.6 MOBILE PRIVACY

As in wired networks, security issues in a mobile computing environment are closely related to privacy issues. Generally, the notion of privacy encompasses two types of problems. One is data privacy: the protection of sensitive user information that by all means should be secured during transmission or in storage, such as a credit card number being transmitted over a secure socket layer (SSL) connection, or Social Security numbers stored in a database on disks and tapes. These problems also fall into the mobile security domain, and various security mechanisms to ensure data privacy have already been discussed in this chapter. The second type of privacy issue—namely, privacy services—is primarily concerned with adjustable privacy exposure and enabling mechanisms. The key challenge to this type of security issue is the conflict between more pervasive mobile applications utilizing the sensitive information of users and the need for privacy protection in a computing environment of many such applications. Three approaches have been proposed to offer general privacy-related services in a pervasive mobile computing environment [17]:

- *Increasing awareness of potential privacy breach*—Let the system notify the user whenever sensitive information is being revealed to an external service or system that the user cannot control. For example, a smart phone user should be notified when the user's location and identity are being tracked by a location-based service.

- *Maintaining an audit trail*—The system keeps an audit log of all privacy-related information exposure, interactions, and data exchanges. This does not prevent privacy violation but at least provides some record of what information has been exposed, how, and when.

- *Intelligent alert*—In some cases a user's privacy is exposed not by the system but by an adversary; for example, a smart phone user engaging in a Bluetooth data transmission may be detected by someone nearby and the identity of the user may be revealed because of the data transmission. In this case, ideally the system should be able to detect such a privacy breach even if it is directly involved.

Mobile privacy is more complicated than mobile security because you cannot just draw a line between what information can be used or shared and what cannot, whereas in security we know that a set of security functions should be implemented in a system. Moreover, legislation is very often involved, because privacy is indeed surrounded by sensitive legal issues. Because a system may surreptitiously detect, use, expose, distribute, or abuse people's privacy-related information, it seems quite reasonable to regulate the use of personal data by credit card companies, telecoms, banks, etc. For example, laws pertaining to privacy include the Privacy Act of 1974, Electronic Communications Privacy Act (1986), and No Electronic Theft (NET) Act (1997). Also, in response to security challenges on the web, W3C has been working on a project called P3P (Platform for Privacy Preference Project, http://www.w3.org/P3P), aimed at developing a framework of protocol for an international privacy policy.

Technologically, the fundamental challenge in this domain is to provide more new services to improve productivity and the user's experience while still guaranteeing a minimal, satisfactory level of privacy exposure. Below we introduce two major mechanisms in this field: identity privacy and location privacy.

8.6.1 Identity and Anonymity

Anonymity in the context of computing refers to a service that prevents the disclosure of the identity of someone who is engaged in network communication or interaction to a system. Anonymity is not always a priority; in many cases, we are not particularly concerned that when we surf the web our travels on the Internet are being logged by nearly all web servers. In some cases, however, anonymity is required, such as:

- Users do not want to be censored when accessing some websites. Information censorship is largely due to political reasons.

- Users do not want to reveal information about operations such as file sharing being performed with a computer or a cell phone.

- Users do not want to expose personal information to an untrustworthy online community or they simply do not want to be traced in a network.

- Users want to remain anonymous to prevent identity theft.

Many people think that the Internet offers anonymity. This was reflected by a now-famous cartoon in an issue of *The New Yorker* magazine published in 1993. It showed a dog sitting at a computer, talking to another one: "On the Internet, no one knows you are a dog." Unfortunately, without using a specially designed privacy-enhancing system, nearly every action of a user, as well as the user's identity, is traceable as long as interested parties such as law enforcement agencies, Internet service providers (ISPs), and network administration authorities consider it worth the time and money to do so. In the mobile wireless world, we are well aware that every phone call is logged and can be tapped, and technically every bit can be traced back to the sender. Thus, the challenge of mobile privacy lies in the fact that a mobile system must provide both privacy and accountability.

When there is a direct logical mapping between the user's identity and network location such as IP address, cell phone number, or processor identifier, the goal of anonymity is thus reduced to protecting the network location from being exposed to unintended parties. A simple solution is to introduce a proxy between the user and the place of interest (a website, for example) to hide the network location of the user. An example of such a proxy-based anonymity system is Anonymizer (http://www.anonymizer.com). A user always goes through the proxy (the anonymizer) in order to reach the destination using a URL such as http://www.anonymizer.com:8080/www.yahoo.com. The proxy acts on behalf of the user when visiting a website. Although a user's identity is hidden from the visited server, this approach does not protect the anonymity of the server. To this end, a proxy for the server could be a solution, which hides the real URL of the server and simply exposes a cryptic URL to users. Rewebber (http://www.rewebber.de/) is an example of such a system. In both user–proxy and server–proxy setups, a user has to trust the proxy, and communication between a user and the proxy is not protected in terms of privacy. For this reason, cryptographic mechanisms are introduced in some systems such as Mix-Net and Onion Ring.

A mix network is a set of router nodes (mixes) that allow for anonymous message transfer using a layered public key encryption. They have been used to maintain privacy during e-mailing, web surfing, electronic voting, and electronic payment. The idea of mix networks as a solution to e-mail privacy was first proposed by David Chaum in 1981. In its initial design, a computer (called a *mix*) processes each e-mail (or any type of data item) before it is delivered. A sender may choose intermediate mix nodes to form a path across a mix network, or the mix network can enforce a path for every message. The latter approach is referred to as a *cascade*. Figure 8.10 depicts the logical architecture of a cascade. Depending on the number of mix nodes a message will traverse, a message (M) is encrypted first using the public key of the recipient (K_a) and a random number (R_1). The result is then appended with the address of the recipient and further encrypted using the public key of the last mix node along the path (K_n). Each intermediate mix node decrypts the message using its private key and forwards the result to the next mix node. Output messages at a mix node are also permutated to disguise the order of

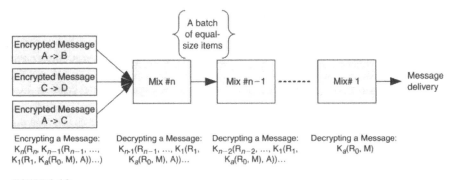

FIGURE 8.10

A cascade mix network.

arrival. In effect, no single mix node knows both the sender address and recipient address. Input messages to a mix node are reordered; therefore, correspondence between items in its input and those in its output at a mix node is protected. The downside of a mix network is that it requires mix nodes to trust each other, meaning that everyone will perform normally. Later improvements to the approach have employed credit-based mix node selection and threshold cryptography to relax this requirement while still ensuring message anonymity.

A similar idea—namely, Onion Routing (http://www.onion-router.net)—is designed to use a collection of widely distributed routers (Tor nodes) to create random paths for the sender such that no individual server knows the complete path. Before sending data over an anonymous path, the first Tor router adds a layer of encryption for each subsequent one in the path. As the message traverses the network, each Tor router removes one layer of encryption.

Unlike Mix-Net and Onion Ring operating at the network layer, Crowds [18] is an application layer protocol designed for web traffic anonymity, utilizing a crowd of proxies to hide the network location of a message. The basic idea is to blend a user's traffic with that of many others such that it is not possible to trace a single web request or reply back to the sender. Any user willing to participate in the crowd could be a proxy in the crowd. The user's traffic will first be forwarded to the crowd along a probabilistic virtual path before going to the public Internet.

Freenet is an example of a peer-to-peer-based anonymity network (http://freenet .sourceforge.net/). It allows anybody to publish and read information with complete anonymity. Freenet achieves this by pooling the nodes' storage for data replication services while the true origin or destination of the data remains completely anonymous. In Freenet, shared files are mapped into a key space. Aside from locally stored files, a node maintains a local key routing table allowing the node to forward a query message from one neighbor (the predecessor) to another appropriate neighboring node on behalf of that predecessor, in case the key in question is not locally served. Note that, unlike IP routing, where the source IP address is always forwarded hop-by-hop as part of the IP header, query routing messages in Freenet do not carry the request's identity along the path. Therefore, requester (a node querying a file) anonymity is preserved because a node forwarding or replying to a query does not know the requester's identity (a node ID in Freenet). In order to maintain the inserter's anonymity (or, more precisely, key anonymity, as a file is identified by a routable key), Freenet employs a variation of the mix network approach for inserter (a node that shares a file in the network) anonymity: Messages between a sender and a recipient must go through a chain of prerouting nodes, each acting as a mix to impose public key-based encryption over links along the chain. After going through the mix network, a message is disguised as if it is originated from the last mix. Then the message is sent to Freenet for normal routing.

In the context of mobile wireless services, identity anonymity is sometimes necessary in mobile payment, mobile trading, and information sharing. Considering the amount of web traffic in current mobile Internet and wireless network applications, an application layer anonymity system is preferable to network layer solutions. For example, we can use a set of WAP proxies acting like a crowd to mix WAP traffic from many mobile users. Alternatively, depending on the requirements of a specific mobile service, a service anonymizer can be introduced as part of the back-end system by a mobile service provider. The predominant task of a service anonymizer in an m-commerce environment is hiding one user's real identity from the other during a transaction. In addition, a service anonymizer can be integrated with an authentication system. An example of such systems used for mobile micropayment is described in Hu et al. [19].

8.6.2 Location Privacy

A particularly significant class of privacy issues is location privacy in a mobile wireless environment. Location privacy refers to the capability of a mobile application or service to prevent unintended parties from obtaining a person's current or past location. The fact that more location-based services, including GPS, Wi-Fi, radiofrequency identification (RFID), and wireless sensor network technologies, will have the capability to monitor a user's location has led to increasing concerns as to how to protect the location information from unintended access. Here, we focus on a subsystem in a location-aware system that enables location privacy.

There are three categories of problems surrounding location privacy for a mobile system, each solving the problem from a different viewpoint:

- *Category I*—Location information security (secure location data gathering and transmission with respect to privacy requirement)

- *Category II*—Identity pseudonym (applying identity anonymity schemes to location service)

- *Category III*—Location information policy (building interactive social and legal privacy aware framework)

The first category, location information security, is mainly concerned with the formatting and secure transmission of location information in order to protect user privacy. The IEEE Work Group Geographic Location/Privacy (Geopriv) [20] has provided a location privacy framework that is independent of the underlying location determination mechanism. The framework defines a location object that conveys location information and possibly privacy rules to which Geopriv security mechanisms and privacy rules are to be applied. Geopriv recommends the use of security mechanisms of the location object itself, such as MAC (Message Authentication Code) and encryption as part of the location object. In addition, secure transport of location objects should be used whenever possible in protocols carrying location objects to ensure appropriate distribution, protection, usage, retention, and storage of location objects based on the rules that apply to those location objects. One example of such a privacy-preserving communication protocol is Mist [21]. This approach is based on an overlay network in the form of a hierarchy of Mist routers that perform limited PKI-secured handle-based routing to hide the location of a connection (here, location is the addresses of the source and the destination). A handle is an ID that uniquely identifies an upward Mist router in the hierarchy. Intermediate Mist routers are unaware of the endpoints of a connection (source and destination addresses). The protocol effectively prevents insiders, system administrators, and the system itself from tracking a user's location without affecting normal secured communication.

The second category, identity pseudonym, hides the user's identity by making network traffic anonymous in a location-based application. A broad range of anonymity techniques used in wired network applications could be adopted to location-based applications. For example, Beresford and Stajano [22] have designed a privacy-protecting framework based on frequently changing pseudonyms, thereby effectively mapping the problem of location privacy onto that of anonymous communication. An anonymizing proxy is introduced to leverage the idea of mix networks in the general anonymity service domain to delay and reorder messages when users exit mix zones.

The last category of solutions, location information policy, focuses on building a framework of privacy policies and mechanisms that allows users to interact with location-based applications to control location information release with respect to corresponding privacy policies. Privacy solutions in this category in essence rely on respect and social and legal norms to enforce privacy. The most notable effort in this direction includes the Privacy Preference Project (P3P) [23] and pawS [24], which provide an industry standard of privacy policies that websites can use to announce their specific privacy practices. The goals of P3P include simplifying the process of reading privacy policies, minimizing latency delays, and making policies conforming to the law. The P3P architecture consists of user agents, privacy reference files, and privacy policies. User agents can be part of a web browser or a browser plug-in. A user agent automatically fetches the P3P policies of a website when the user visits the site and checks these policies against the user's predetermined preferences. A policy reference file is used to collect the P3P policies of certain regions of a website (such as a web page), portions of a website, or the entire website. P3P employs an XML encoding scheme for P3P policies. pawS [24] is a similar approach. Both P3P and pawS are specifically designed to address privacy issues on the Web. A more general approach utilizing the same basic idea has been proposed to protect privacy when arbitrary location-based applications request a user's location [25].

8.7 CONCLUSION

Mobile security and privacy are by all means interrelated issues that must be addressed as a whole. Because of the potentially pervasive nature of future mobile computing applications, people are far more concerned with these issues than common security risks in a wired network environment. A mobile wireless system must take security and privacy into account at the very beginning of the design phase and utilize appropriate security service building blocks to provide data confidentiality, integrity, authentication, and nonrepudiation, as well as efficient access control. Different mobile wireless systems and applications may employ a set of security mechanism at different layers, due to the intrinsic restrictions of the underlying network and mobile devices. In this chapter, we have explored security issues in some widely deployed mobile wireless systems, such as cellular networks, wireless LAN, and Bluetooth. We also introduced interesting yet challenging security issues in emerging mobile *ad hoc* networks. 3G cellular networks by design provide strong low layer security for mobile applications and services. On the other hand, wireless LAN is an excellent example of bad design strategy to demonstrate that security has to be considered a high priority when it comes to designing a mobile wireless system. The well-known WEP vulnerabilities have largely hindered the widespread implementation of 802.11 wireless LAN in business organizations and government agencies. The IEEE 802.11 working group has designed a new standard, called 802.11i, to address these weaknesses. Bluetooth security concerns grew significantly after researchers demonstrated that they could use Bluetooth equipment to hack into a Bluetooth cell phone up to a mile away. Although this particular security problem is merely an implementation issue rather than a serious protocol design issue, some researchers have pointed out several weaknesses in the official Bluetooth specifications that may lead to personal information breaches and device compromise. The Bluetooth specification was largely based on the assumption that within its limited signal range of $<10\,m$ security was not a significant problem. This turned out to be a false assumption. Security services in *ad hoc* networks lead to new challenges due to the absence of a fixed network infrastructure in MANET.

Problems such as secured routing, link layer security, and key management were examined. We introduced two problems in the domain of mobile privacy: anonymity and location privacy. Anonymity is a critical problem because people are seeking technological ways to ensure freedom over the Internet. Location privacy is particularly important to mobile users who wish to take advantage of emerging location-based services but do not want to be traced for whatever reasons. Technical, social, and legal solutions have been proposed to address this problem to some extent.

Aside from wireless network security mechanisms, many of the security and privacy problems discussed in this chapter are closely related to requirements of the underlying mobile applications and services such as location-based services, mobile commerce, and instant messaging.

FURTHER READING

3GPP SA3 Security Working Group, http://www.3gpp.org/TB/SA/SA3/SA3.htm (3GPP technical specifications).

3GPP2's Security Working Group (3GPP2 TSG-S Working Group 4), http://www.3gpp2.org/Public_html/specs/tsgs.cfm.

AES/Rijndael, csrc.nist.gov/CryptoToolkit/aes/rijndael/.

EEF DES Cracker, http://www.eff.org/Privacy/Crypto/Crypto_misc/DESCracker/.

For a list of practical ways to protect a Wi-Fi network, see http://www.wi-fi.org/OpenSection/secure.asp? TID = 2 (the site also introduces WPA2, a Wi-Fi certified security solution based on 802.11i).

IEEE AAA Working Group, http://www.ietf.org/html.charters/aaa-charter.html.

IETF Geographic Location/Privacy Working Group, http://www.ietf.org/html.charters/geopriv charter.html; Geopriv Requirement, http://www.ietf.org/rfc/rfc3693.txt.

IETF Internet Key Exchange, http://www.ietf.org/rfc/rfc2409.txt.

IETF IPSec Working Group, http://www.ietf.org/html.charters/ipsec-charter.html.

IETF PKI (X.509) Working Group, http://www.ietf.org/html.charters/pkix-charter.html.

REFERENCES

[1] S. R. Fluhrer, I. Mantin, and A. Shamir, "Weaknesses in the key scheduling algorithm of RC4," in *Proc. of the Eighth Annual Workshop on Selected Areas in Cryptography*, August 2001.

[2] X. Wang, D. Feng, X. Lai, and H. Yu, "Collisions for Hash Functions MD4, MD5, HAVAL-128, and RIPEMD," in *Proc. the 24th Annual International Cryptology Conference (Crypto'04)*, Santa Barbara, CA, 2004.

[3] R. Rivest, A. Shamir, and L. Adleman, "A method for obtaining digital signatures and public-key cryptosystems," *Commun. ACM.*, 21(2):120–126, 1978.

[4] M.-J. Saarinen, "Attacks against the WAP WTLS Protocol," in *Proc. Proceedings of the IFIP TC6/TC11 Joint Working Conference on Secure Information Networks: Communications and Multimedia Security*, Leuven, Belgium, 1999.

[5] H. Berghel, "Wireless infidelity I: War driving," *Commun. ACM.*, 47(9):21–26, 2004.

[6] S. Fluhrer, I. Mantin, and A. Shamir, "Weaknesses in the key schedule algorithm of RC4," in *Proc. the 4th Annual Workshop on Selected Areas of Cryptography*, August 2001.

[7] N. Borisov, I. Goldberg, and D. Wagner, "Intercepting mobile communications: The insecurity of 802.11," in *Proc. the 7th Annual International Conference on Mobile Computing and Networking (MOBICOM'01)*, Rome, Italy, 2001.

[8] N. Cam-Winget, R. Housley, D. Wagner, and J. Walker, "Security flaws in 802.11 data link protocols," *Commun. ACM*, 46(5):35–39, 2003.

[9] M. Jakobsson and S. Wetzel, "Security weakness in Bluetooth," in *Proc. RSA Conference 2001*, San Francisco, CA, 2001.

[10] V. Gupta, S. Krishnamurthy, and M. Faloutsos, "Denial of Service Attacks at the MAC Layer in Wireless Ad Hoc Networks," in *Proc. IEEE Military Communications Conference (MILCOM)*, Anaheim, CA, 2002.

[11] H. Yang, H. Luo, F. Ye, S. Lu, and L. Zhang, "Security in mobile *ad hoc* networks: Challenges and solutions," *IEEE Wireless Commun.*, 11(1):38–47, 2004.

[12] L. Zhou and Z. J. Haas, "Securing *ad hoc* networks," *IEEE Network Mag.*, 13(6):24–30, 1999.

[13] A. Khalili, J. Katz, and W. A. Arbaugh, "Toward secure key distribution in truly *ad hoc* networks," in *Proc. 2003 Symposium on Applications and the Internet Workshops (SAINT'03 Workshops)*, Orlando, FL, January 27–31, 2003.

[14] D. Boheh and M. Franklin, "Identity-based encryption from the Weil pairing," *SIAM J. Computing.*, 32(3):586–615, 2003.

[15] A. Perrig, R. Szewczyk, V. Wen, D. Culler, and J. D. Tygar, "SPINS: Security Protocols for Sensor Networks," in *Proc. the 7th Annual International Conference on Mobile Computing and Networking (MOBICOM'01)*, Rome, Italy, 2001.

[16] C. Karlof and D. Wagner, "Secure routing in wireless sensor networks: Attacks and counter-measures," in *Proc. of the First IEEE International Workshop on Sensor Network Protocols and Applications*, Anchorage, AK, May 2003.

[17] M. Satyanarayanan, "Privacy: The Achilles heels of pervasive computing?," *IEEE Pervasive Comput.*, 2(1):2–3, 2003.

[18] M. K. Reiter and A. D. Rubin, "Anonymous web transactions with crowds," *Commun. ACM.*, 42(2):32–48, 1999.

[19] Z.-Y. Hu, Y.-W. Liu, X. Hu, and J.-H. Li, "Anonymous Micro-payments Authentication (AMA) in Mobile Data Networks," in *Proc. the 23rd Annual Joint Conference of the IEEE Computer and Communications Societies (INFOCOM'04)*, Hong Kong, 2004.

[20] IEEE Geographic Location/Privacy, http://www.ietf.org/html.charters/geopriv-charter.html, 2004.

[21] J. Al-Muhtadi, R. Campbell, A. Kapadia, M. D. Mickunas, and S. Yi, "Routing through the mist: Privacy preserving communication in ubiquitous computing environment," in *Proc. of the 22nd International Conference on Distributed Computing Systems (ICDCS'02)*, Vienna, Austria, July 2002.

[22] A. R. Beresford and F. Stajano, "Location privacy in pervasive computing," *IEEE Pervasive Comput.*, 2(1):46–55, 2003.

[23] Platform for Privacy Preference 1.0 (P3P1.0) specification, World Wide Web Consortium, http://www.w3.org/TR/2002/REC-P3P-20020416/, 2002.

[24] M. Langheinrich, "Privacy by design: Principles of privacy-aware ubiquitous systems," in G. D. Abowd, B. Brumitt, and S. A. Shafer (Eds.), *Proc. of the 3rd International Conference on Ubiquitous Computing*, Atlanta, GA: Springer–Verlag, 2001.

[25] G. Myles, A. Friday, and N. Davies, "Preserving privacy in environments with location-based applications," *IEEE Pervasive Comput.*, 2(1):56–64, 2003.

Optical Network Survivability

9

Providing resilience against failures is an important requirement for many high-speed networks. As these networks carry more and more data, the amount of disruption caused by a network-related outage becomes more and more significant. A single outage can disrupt millions of users and result in millions of dollars of lost revenue to users and operators of the network.

As part of the service-level agreement between a carrier and its customer leasing a connection, the carrier commits to providing a certain *availability* for the connection. A common requirement is that the connection be available 99.999% (five 9s) of the time. This requirement corresponds to a connection downtime of less than 5 minutes per year.

A connection is routed through many nodes in the network between its source and its destination, and there are many elements along its path that can fail. The only practical way of obtaining 99.999% availability is to make the network *survivable*, that is, able to continue providing service in the presence of failures. *Protection switching* is the key technique used to ensure survivability. These protection techniques involve providing some redundant capacity within the network and automatically rerouting traffic around the failure using this redundant capacity. A related term is *restoration*. Some people apply the term *protection* when the traffic is restored in the tens to hundreds of milliseconds, and use the term *restoration* to schemes where traffic is restored on a slower time scale. However, we do not distinguish between protection and restoration in this chapter.

Protection is usually implemented in a distributed manner without requiring centralized control in the network. This is necessary to ensure fast restoration of service after a failure.

We will be concerned with failures of network links, nodes, and individual channels (in the case of a WDM network). In addition, the software residing in today's network elements is immensely complex, and reliability problems arising from software bugs have become a serious issue. This is something that is usually dealt with by using proper software design and is hard to protect against in the network.

In most cases failures are triggered by human error, such as a backhoe cutting through a fiber cable, or an operator pulling out the wrong connection or turning off the wrong switch. Links fail mostly because of fiber cuts. This is the most likely failure event. There were 136 such failures reported by U.S. carriers to the Federal Communications Commission in 1997. Fiber that is deployed inside of oil and gas pipelines is less likely to be cut than fiber that is buried directly in the ground or strung on poles. For instance, Williams Communications, which runs fiber beside oil pipelines, has experienced only a single fiber cut since 1986.

The next most likely failure event is the failure of active components inside network equipment, such as transmitters, receivers, or controllers. In general, network equipment is designed with redundant controllers. Moreover, failure of controllers doesn't affect traffic but only impacts management visibility into the network.

Node failures are another possibility to be reckoned with. Entire central offices can fail, usually because of catastrophic events such as fires or flooding. These events are rare, but they cause widespread disruption when they occur. Examples include the fire at the Hinsdale central office of Illinois Bell in 1988 and the flooding of several central offices due to Hurricane Floyd in 1999.

Protection schemes are also used extensively to allow maintenance actions in the network. For example, in order to service a link, typically the traffic on the link is switched over to an alternate route using the protection scheme before it is serviced. The same technique is used when nodes or links are upgraded in the network.

In most cases, the protection schemes are engineered to protect against a single failure event or maintenance action. If the network is large, we may need to provide the capability to deal with more than one concurrent failure or maintenance action. One way to handle this is to break up the network into smaller subnetworks and restrict the operation of the protection scheme to within a subnetwork. This allows one failure per subnetwork at any given time. Another way to deal with this issue is to ensure that the mean time to repair a failure is much smaller than the mean time between failures. This ensures that, in most cases, the failed link will be repaired before another failure happens. Some of the protection schemes that we will study do, however, protect the network against some types of simultaneous multiple failures.

The restoration times required depend on the application/type of data being carried. For SONET/SDH networks, the maximum allowed restoration time is 60 ms. This restoration time requirement came from the fact that some equipment in the network drops voice calls if the connection is disrupted for a period significantly longer than 60 ms. Over time, operators have gotten used to being able to achieve restoration on these time scales. However, in a world dominated by data, rather than voice traffic, the 60 ms number may not be a hard requirement, and operators may be willing to tolerate somewhat larger restoration times, particularly if they see other benefits as a result, such as higher bandwidth efficiency, which in turn would lead to lower operating costs. On the other hand, another point of view is that the restoration time requirements could get more stringent as data rates in the network increase. A downtime of 1 second at 10 Gb/s corresponds to losing over a gigabyte of data. Most IP networks today provide services on a best-effort basis and do not guarantee availability; that is, they try to route traffic in the network as best as they can, but packets can have random delays through the network and can be dropped if there is congestion.

Survivability can be addressed within many layers in the network. Protection can be performed at the physical layer, or layer 1, which includes the SONET/SDH and the optical layers. Protection can also be performed at the link layer, or layer 2, which includes the ATM layer and the MPLS layer that are part of IP networks. Finally, protection can also be performed at the network layer, or layer 3, such as the IP layer. There are several reasons why this is the case. For instance, each layer can protect against certain types of failures but probably not protect against all types of failures effectively. We will focus primarily on layer 1 restoration in this chapter, but also briefly discuss the protection techniques applicable to layers 2 and 3.

The rest of this chapter is organized as follows. We start by outlining the basic concepts behind protection schemes. Many of the protection techniques used in today's telecommunication networks were developed for use in SONET and SDH networks, and we will explore these techniques in detail. We will also look at how protection is implemented in today's IP networks. Following this, we will look at protection functions in the optical layer in detail, and then discuss how protection functions in the different layers of the network can work together.

9.1 BASIC CONCEPTS

A great variety of protection schemes are used in today's networks. We will talk about *working* paths and *protect* paths. Working paths carry traffic under normal operation; protect paths provide an alternate path to carry the traffic in case of failures. Working and protection paths are usually diversely routed so that both paths aren't lost in case of a single failure.

Protection schemes are designed to operate over a range of network topologies. Some work on point-to-point links. Ring topologies are particularly popular in SONET/SDH. A ring is the simplest topology offering an alternate route around a failure. In the optical layer, many protection schemes have been designed to operate over true mesh topologies.

Protection may be *dedicated* or *shared*. In dedicated protection, each working connection is assigned its own dedicated bandwidth in the network over which it can be rerouted in case of a failure. In shared protection, we make use of the fact that not all working connections in the network fail simultaneously (for example, if they are in different parts of the network). Therefore, by careful design, we can make multiple working connections share protection bandwidth among themselves. This helps reduce the amount of bandwidth needed in the network for protection. Another advantage of shared protection is that the protection bandwidth is available to carry low-priority traffic under normal conditions. This low-priority traffic is discarded in the event of a failure when the bandwidth is needed to protect a connection.

Protection schemes can either be *revertive* or *nonrevertive*. In both schemes, if a failure occurs, traffic is switched from the working path to the protect path. In a nonrevertive scheme, the traffic remains on the protect path until it is manually switched back onto the original working path, usually by a user through the network management system. In a revertive scheme, once the working path is repaired, the traffic is automatically switched back from the protect path onto the working path. Reversion allows the network to return to its original state once the failure is restored. Dedicated protection schemes may be revertive or nonrevertive; however, shared protection schemes are usually revertive. Since multiple working connections share a common protection bandwidth, the protection bandwidth must be freed up as soon as possible after the original failure has been repaired, so that it can be used to protect other connections in the event of another failure occurring.

To confuse terminology further, the protection switching can be *unidirectional* or *bidirectional*. This is not to be confused with unidirectional transmission or bidirectional transmission over a fiber. Figure 9.1 illustrates the two

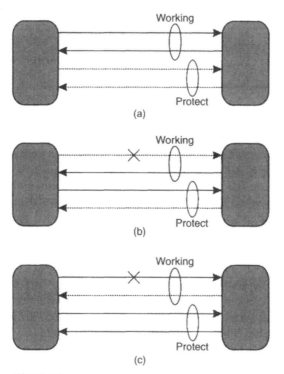

FIGURE 9.1

Unidirectional and bidirectional protection switching. (a) The link is shown under normal operation. (b) Unidirectional protection switching. After a unidirectional fiber cut, only the affected direction of traffic is switched over to the protection fiber. (c) Bidirectional protection switching. After a undirectional fiber cut, both directions of traffic are switched over to the protection fibers.

schemes for the case where two fiber pairs are used on the point-to-point link, with each fiber carrying traffic in one direction (unidirectional transmission). In unidirectional protection switching, each direction of traffic is handled independent of the other. Thus in the event of a single fiber cut, only one direction of traffic is switched over to the protection fiber and the other direction remains on the original working fiber. In bidirectional switching, both directions are switched over to the protection fibers. For the case where bidirectional transmission is used, the switching mostly becomes bidirectional by default because both directions of traffic are lost when a fiber is cut (both directions may not be lost if there is an equipment failure, rather than a fiber cut).

Unidirectional protection switching is used in conjuction with dedicated protection schemes since it can be implemented very easily by switching the traffic at the receiving end from the working to the protect path, without requiring a signaling protocol between the receiver and the transmitter. For example, in Figure 9.1, if a fiber carrying traffic from left to right is cut, without affecting the fiber carrying traffic from right to left, the transmitter on the left is not aware that there has been a failure. In the case of unidirectional dedicated protection, if traffic is transmitted simultaneously on the working and protect paths, the receiver at the end of the paths simply selects the better of the two arriving signals. However, if bidirectional switching is required, the receiver needs to inform the transmitter that there has been a cut. This requires a signaling protocol, called an *automatic protection-switching* (APS) protocol.

A simple APS protocol works as follows: if a receiver in a node detects a fiber cut, it turns off its transmitter on the working fiber and then switches over to the protection fiber to transmit traffic. The receiver at the other node then also detects the loss of signal on the working fiber and then switches its traffic over to the protection fiber. Actual APS protocols used in SONET and optical networks are quite a bit more complicated because they have to deal with many different possible scenarios than the one described here.

In a bidirectional communication system, where traffic is transmitted in both directions over a single fiber, a fiber cut will be detected by both the source and the destination. While no APS protocol is required to deal with fiber cuts, an APS protocol will still be needed to deal with unidirectional equipment failures and to support other maintenance functions.

In the case of shared protection schemes, an APS protocol is required to coordinate access to the shared protection bandwidth. Therefore most shared protection schemes use bidirectional protection switching because it is easier to control and manage in a more complex network than unidirectional switching.

There is also the question of how and where the traffic is rerouted in the event of a failure. Here we distinguish between *path* switching, *span* switching, and *ring* switching. Figure 9.2 illustrates these concepts. In path switching (Figure 9.2(b)), the connection is rerouted end to end from its source to its destination along an alternate path. In span switching (Figure 9.2(c)), the connection is rerouted on a spare link between the nodes adjacent to the failure. In ring switching

(Figure 9.2(d)), the connection is rerouted on a ring between the nodes adjacent to the failure.

Finally, different protection schemes operate at different layers in the network (for example, SONET/SDH, ATM, MPLS, IP) and at different sublayers within a layer. For example, there are schemes that protect one connection at a time, as well as schemes that protect all connections on a failed fiber together. In SONET/SDH networks, the former schemes operate at the path layer, and the latter schemes operate at the line (multiplex section in SDH) layer. In many cases, path layer schemes operate end to end, rerouting traffic along an alternate path all the way from the source to the destination. In contrast, line layer schemes are almost all localized— that is, they reroute traffic around the failed link. Similarly, in the optical layer, we have schemes operating either at the optical channel layer or the optical multiplex section layer.

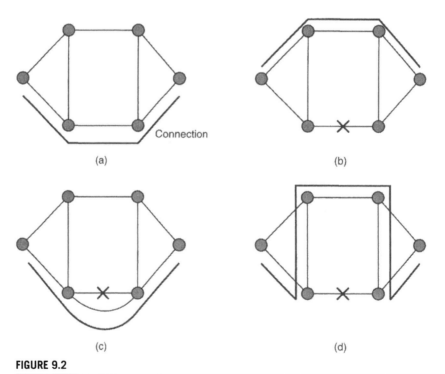

FIGURE 9.2

Path, span, and ring switching. (a) Working path for the connection under normal operation. (b) Path switching, where the connection is rerouted end to end on an alternate path. (c) Span switching, where the connection is rerouted on a spare link between the nodes adjacent to the failure. (d) Ring switching, where the connection is rerouted on a ring between the nodes adjacent to the failure.

9.2 PROTECTION IN SONET/SDH

A major accomplishment of SONET and SDH network deployment was to provide a significant improvement in the availability and reliability of the overall network. This was done through the use of an extensive set of protection techniques. Similar schemes are used in both SONET and SDH, but their nomenclature is different. We will specify both nomenclatures but use the SONET nomenclature for the most part.

A taxonomy of the different protection schemes is given in Table 9.1. We will start by describing the different types of protection mechanisms that are used for simple point-to-point links, and then discuss how these can be applied for networks. Each protection scheme can be associated with a specific layer in the network. The SONET layer includes a *path* layer and a *line* layer. Both path layer and line layer protection schemes are used in practice. Equivalently, SDH networks use both *channel* layer and *multiplex section* (MS) layer protection schemes. A path layer protection scheme operates on individual paths or connections in the network. For example, in an OC-48 (2.5 Gb/s) ring supporting STS-1 (51 Mb/s) connections, a path layer scheme would treat each STS-1 connection independently and switch them independently of each other. A line layer scheme, on the other hand, operates on the entire set of connections at once and generally does not distinguish between the different connections that are part of the aggregate signal. In the former example, a line layer protection scheme in an OC-48 ring would switch all the connections within the OC-48 together. (There are some exceptions to this statement. The bidirectional line-switched rings (BLSRs) that we will study later do allow bits to be set for each connection. In the event of a failure, only those connections that are specified are switched. This is needed to ensure that some

Table 9.1 A Summary of Protection Schemes in SONET and SDH. *N* denotes the number of working interfaces that share a single protection interface. The schemes operate either in the path layer or in the SONET line layer/SDH multiplex section (MS) layer. Path layer ring schemes include unidirectional path-switched ring (UPSR) or $1 + 1$ subnetwork connection protection (SNCP). Line layer ring schemes include bidirectional line-switched ring (BLSR) or, equivalently, multiplexed section-shared protection ring (MS-SPRing)

			Protection Scheme		
SONET Term	$1 + 1$	I:N	UPSR		BLSR
SDH Term	$1 + 1$	I:N		SNCP	MS-SPRing
Type	Dedicated	Shared	Dedicated	Dedicated	Shared
Topology	Point-point	Point-point	Ring	Ring/mesh	Ring
Layer	Line/MS	Line/MS	Path/–	–/path	Line/MS

connections can be left unprotected if so desired, and also to handle node failures, as we will see in Section 9.2.4.)

9.2.1 Point-to-Point Links

Two fundamental types of protection mechanisms are used in point-to-point links: $1 + 1$ protection and 1:1 or, more generally, 1:N protection, as shown in Figure 9.3. Both operate in the line or multiplex section layer.

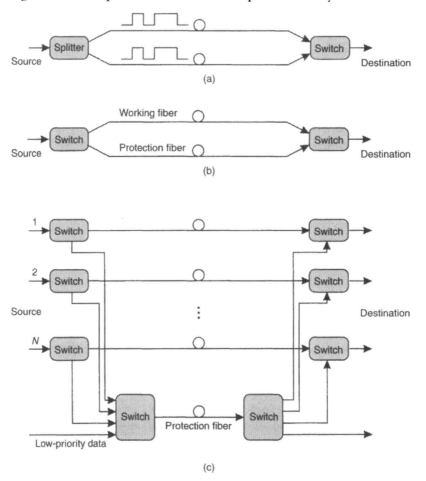

FIGURE 9.3

Different types of protection techniques for point-to-point links: (a) $1 + 1$ protection, where the signal is simultaneously transmitted over two paths; (b) 1:1 protection, where the signal is transmitted over a working path under normal conditions but switched to a protect path after a failure; and (c) 1:N protection, which is a more generalized form of 1:1 protection, where N working paths share a single protection path.

In $1+1$ protection, traffic is transmitted simultaneously on two separate fibers (usually over disjoint routes) from the source to the destination. Assuming unidirectional protection switching, the destination simply selects one of the two fibers for reception. If that fiber is cut, the destination simply switches over to the other fiber and continues to receive data. This form of protection is very fast and requires no signaling protocol between the two ends. Note that since connections are usually full duplex, there is actually a pair of fibers between the two nodes, say, node A and node B for the working traffic. One fiber carries traffic from A to B, and the other carries traffic from B to A. Likewise there is another pair of fibers for protection traffic. Node A's receiver and node B's receiver can make the switching decisions independently.

In 1:1 protection, there are still two fibers from the source to the destination. However, traffic is transmitted over only one fiber at a time, say, the working fiber. If that fiber is cut, the source and destination both switch over to the other protection fiber. As we discussed earlier, an APS protocol is required for signaling between the source and destination. For this reason, 1:1 protection is not as quick as unidirectional $1+1$ protection in restoring traffic because of the added communication overhead involved. However, it offers two main advantages over $1+1$ protection. The first is that under normal operation, the protection fiber is unused. Therefore, it can be used to transmit lower-priority traffic. This lower-priority traffic must be discarded if the working fiber is cut. SONET and SDH equipment in the field does provide support for this lower-priority or *extra traffic*. This capability is not widely used today, but carriers in the past have used this capability on occasion to carry "lower-priority" data traffic or even voice traffic, when their networks are temporarily over capacity. This is likely to change in the future with the advent of data services, as we shall see in Section 9.4. Best-effort data services, in particular, can use this capability.

Another advantage is that the 1:1 protection can be extended so as to share a single protection fiber among many working fibers. In a more general 1:N protection scheme, N working fibers share a single protection fiber. This arrangement can handle the failure of any single working fiber. Note that in the event of multiple failures, the APS protocol must ensure that only traffic on one of the failed fibers is switched over to the protection fiber.

In the previous discussion we talked about how the protection is done, but skimmed over what the triggers are for initiating protection switching. In SONET/SDH, the incoming signal is continuously monitored. Protection switching is initiated if a signal fail or a signal degrade condition is detected on the line. A signal fail represents a hard failure and is detected typically as a loss of signal or as a loss of the SONET/SDH frame. Out of the 60 ms allowed for restoration, detecting the failure and initiating protection switching must be performed within 10 ms.

9.2.2 Self-Healing Rings

Ring networks have become very popular in the carrier world as well as in enterprise networks. A ring is the simplest topology that is *2-connected*, that is, provides two separate paths between any pair of nodes that do not have any nodes or links in common except the source and destination nodes. This allows a ring network to be resilient to failures. Rings are also efficient from a fiber layout perspective—multiple sites can be interconnected with a single physical ring. In contrast, a hubbed approach would require fibers to be laid between each site and a hub node, and would require two disjoint routes between each site and the hub, which is a more expensive proposition.

Much of the carrier infrastructure today uses SONET/SDH rings. These rings are called *self-healing* since they incorporate protection mechanisms that automatically detect failures and reroute traffic away from failed links and nodes onto other routes rapidly. The rings are implemented using SONET/SDH add/drop multiplexers (ADMs). These ADMs selectively drop and add traffic from/to the ring as well as protect the traffic against failures.

The different types of ring architectures differ in two aspects: in the directionality of traffic and in the protection mechanisms used. A *unidirectional* ring carries working traffic in only one direction of the ring (say, clockwise), as shown in Figure 9.4. Working traffic from node A to node B is carried clockwise along the ring, and working traffic from B to A is also carried clockwise, on a different set

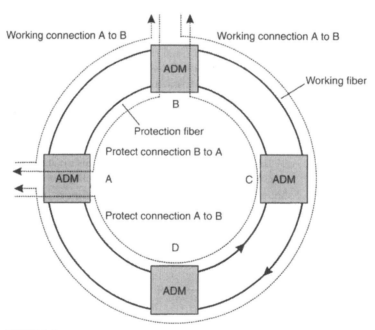

FIGURE 9.4

A unidirectional path-switched ring (UPSR). One of the fibers is considered the working fiber and the other the protection fiber. Traffic is transmitted simultaneously on the working fiber in the clockwise direction and on the protection fiber in the counterclockwise direction. Protection is done at the path layer.

of links in the ring. A *bidirectional* ring carries working traffic in both directions. Figure 9.5 shows a four-fiber bidirectional ring. Working traffic from A to B is carried clockwise, and working traffic from B to A is carried counterclockwise along the ring. Note that in both unidirectional and bidirectional SONET/SDH rings, all connections are bidirectional and use up the same amount of bandwidth in both directions. The two directions of a connection are routed differently based on the type of ring, as we discussed earlier.

The SONET/SDH standards dictate that in SONET/SDH rings, service must be restored within 60 ms after a failure. This time includes several components: the time needed to detect the failure, for which 10 ms is allocated; the time needed to signal to other nodes in the network (if needed), including the propagation delays; the actual switching time; and the time to reacquire the frame synchronization after the switch-over has occurred.

Three ring architectures have been widely deployed: two-fiber unidirectional path-switched rings (UPSR), four-fiber bidirectional line-switched rings (BLSR/4), and two-fiber bidirectional line-switched rings (BLSR/2). In SDH, the $1+1$ path protection has been defined to operate in a more general mesh topology and is called subnetwork connection protection (SNCP). SDH multiplex section shared protection ring/4 (MS-SPRing/4) and MS-SPRing/2 are similar to BLSR/4 and BLSR/2,

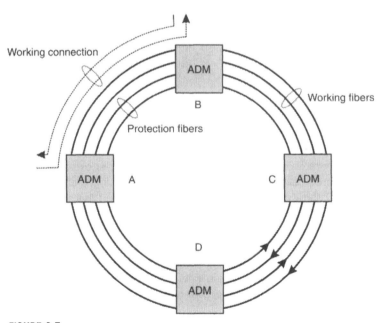

FIGURE 9.5

A four-fiber bidirectional line-switched ring (BLSR/4). The ring has two working fibers and two protection fibers. Traffic between two nodes is transmitted normally on the shortest path between them, and either span or ring switching is used to restore service after a failure.

Table 9.2 Comparison of Different Types of Self-Healing Rings

Parameter	UPSR SNCP	BLSR/4 MS-SPRing/4	BLSR/2 MS-SPRing/2
Fiber pairs	1	2	1
TX/RX pairs/node	2	4	2
Protection type	Dedicated	Shared	Shared
Protection capacity	= Working capacity	= Working capacity	= Working capacity
Link failure	Path switch	Span/ring switch	Ring switch
Node failure	Path switch	Ring switch	Ring switch
Restoration speed	Faster	Slower	Slower
Implementation	Simple	Complex	Complex

respectively. Table 9.2 summarizes the features of the different architectures, which we will discuss in detail in the following sections.

9.2.3 Unidirectional Path-Switched Rings

Figure 9.4 shows a UPSR. One fiber is used as the working fiber and the other as the protection fiber. Traffic from node A to node B is sent simultaneously on the working fiber in the clockwise direction and on the protection fiber in the counterclockwise direction. The protection is performed at the path layer for each connection as follows. Node B continuously monitors both the working and protection fiber and selects the better signal between the two for each SONET connection. Under normal operation, suppose node B receives traffic from the working fiber. If there is a link failure, say, of link AB, then B will switch over to the protection fiber and continue to receive the data. Note that the switch-over is done on a connection-by-connection basis. Observe that this is essentially like the 1 + 1 scheme that we studied earlier, except that it is operating at the path layer in a ring rather than at the line layer in a point-to-point configuration.

Note that this protection scheme easily handles failures of links, transmitters/ receivers, or nodes. It is simple to implement and requires no signaling protocol or communication between the nodes. The capacity required for protection purposes is equal to the working capacity. This will turn out to be the case for the other ring architectures as well.

The main drawback with the UPSR is that it does not spatially reuse the fiber capacity. This is because each (bidirectional) connection uses up capacity on every link in the ring and has dedicated protection bandwidth associated with it. Thus, there is no sharing of the protection bandwidth between connections. For example, suppose each connection requires 51 Mb/s (STS-1) of bandwidth and the ring operates at 622 Mb/s (OC-12). Then the ring could support a total of twelve 51 Mb/s connections. The BLSR architectures that we will study next do incorporate spatial reuse and can support aggregate traffic capacities higher than the transmission rate.

UPSRs are popular topologies in lower-speed local exchange and access networks, particularly where the traffic is primarily hubbed from the access nodes into a hub node in the carrier's central office. In this case, we will see that the traffic carrying capacity that a UPSR can support is the same as what the more complicated ring architectures incorporating spatial reuse can support. This makes the UPSR an attractive option for such applications due to its simplicity and, thus, lower cost. Typical ring speeds today are OC-3 (STM-1) and OC-12 (STM-4). There is no specified limit on the number of nodes in a UPSR or on the ring length. In practice, the ring length will be limited by the fact that the clockwise and counterclockwise paths taken by a signal will have different delays associated with them, which in turn will affect the restoration time in the event of a failure.

A UPSR is essentially $1 + 1$ protection implemented at the path layer in a ring.

9.2.4 Bidirectional Line-Switched Rings

BLSRs are much more sophisticated than UPSRs and incorporate additional protection mechanisms, as we will see below. Unlike a UPSR, they operate at the line or multiplex section layer. The BLSR equivalent in the SDH world is called a multiplex section shared protection ring (MS-SPRing).

Figure 9.5 shows a four-fiber BLSR. Two fibers are used as working fibers, and two are used for protection. Unlike a UPSR, working traffic in a BLSR can be carried on both directions along the ring. For example, on the working fiber, traffic from node A to node B is carried clockwise along the ring, whereas traffic from B to A is carried counterclockwise along the ring. Usually, traffic belonging to both directions of a connection is routed on the shortest path between the two nodes in the ring. However, in certain cases [[1]Kha97, [2]LC97], traffic may be routed along the longer path to reduce network congestion and make better use of the available capacity.

A BLSR can support up to 16 nodes, and this number is limited by the 4-bit addressing field used for the node identifier. The maximum ring length is limited to 1200 km (6 ms propagation delay) because of the requirements on the restoration time in the case of a failure. For longer rings, particularly for undersea applications, the 60 ms restoration time has been relaxed.

A BLSR/4 employs two types of protection mechanisms: *span switching* and *ring switching*. In span switching, if a transmitter or receiver on a working fiber fails, the traffic is routed onto the protection fiber between the two nodes on the same link, as shown in Figure 9.6. (Span switching can also be used to restore traffic in the event of a working fiber cut, provided the protection fibers on that span are routed separately from the working fibers. However, this is usually not

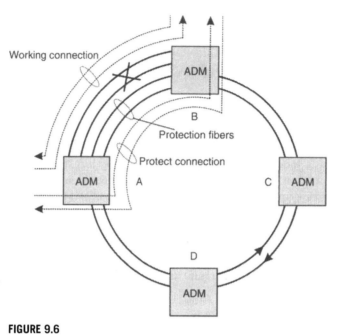

FIGURE 9.6

Illustrating span switching in a BLSR/4. Traffic is switched from the working fiber pair to the protection fiber pair on the same span.

the case.) In case of a fiber or cable cut, service is restored by ring switching, as illustrated in Figure 9.7. Suppose link AB fails. The traffic on the failed link is then rerouted by nodes A and B around the ring on the protection fibers. Ring switching is also used to protect against a node failure.

A BLSR/2, shown in Figure 9.8, can be thought of as a BLSR/4 with the protection fibers "embedded" within the working fibers. In a BLSR/2, both of the fibers are used to carry working traffic, but half the capacity on each fiber is reserved for protection purposes. Unlike a BLSR/4, span switching is not possible here, but ring switching works in much the same way as in a BLSR/4. In the event of a link failure, the traffic on the failed link is rerouted along the other part of the ring using the protection capacity available in the two fibers. As with 1:1 protection on point-to-point links, an advantage of BLSRs is that the protection bandwidth can be used to carry low-priority traffic during normal operation. This traffic is preempted if the bandwidth is needed for service restoration.

BLSRs provide spatial reuse capabilities by allowing protection bandwidth to be shared between spatially separated connections. The spatial reuse achievable in a best-case scenario is illustrated in Figure 9.9. As in the UPSR example above, consider a BLSR/2 operating at 622 Mb/s (OC-12), supporting 51 Mb/s STS-1 connections. The figure shows a ring with four nodes and STS-1 connections between each pair of adjacent nodes. Note that all four of these connections can be protected by

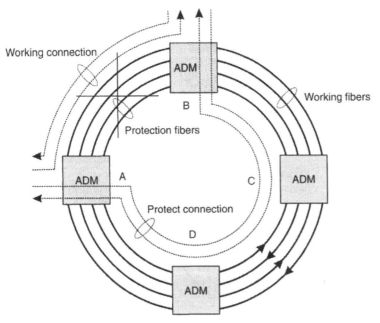

FIGURE 9.7

Illustrating ring switching in a BLSR/4. Traffic is rerouted around the ring by the nodes adjacent to the failure.

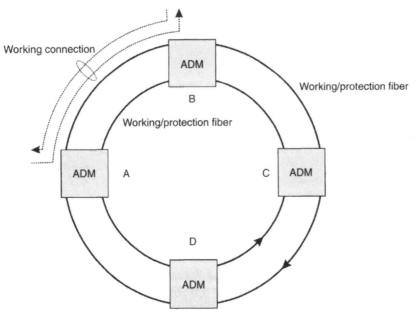

FIGURE 9.8

A two-fiber bidirectional line-switched ring (BLSR/2). The ring has two fibers and half the bandwidth. Ring switching is used to restore service after a failure.

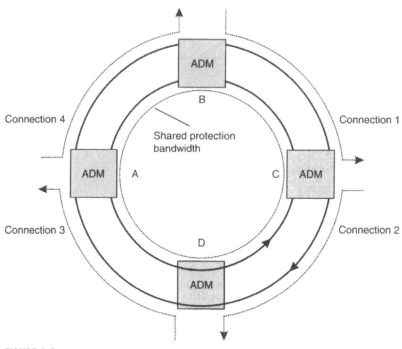

FIGURE 9.9

Spatial reuse in a BLSR. Multiple working connections can share protection bandwidth around the ring as long as they do not overlap on any link.

dedicating 51 Mb/s of bandwidth around the ring that is shared by all these connections. This is because these connections do not overlap spatially and thus do not need to be restored simultaneously, as long as we are dealing with only single-failure conditions. In this example, the 622 Mb/s ring could thus support a total of 24 such 51 Mb/s connections (6 connections per link; note that only half the capacity is available for working traffic, over four links), as compared to just 12 for an equivalent UPSR. This capacity increases as the number of nodes in the rings increases. An 8-node OC-12 BLSR/2 could support 48 STS-1 connections in the example above.

Thus BLSRs are more efficient than UPSRs in protecting distributed traffic patterns. Their efficiency comes from the fact that the protection capacity in the ring is shared among all the connections, as we saw above. For this reason, BLSRs are widely deployed in long-haul and interoffice networks, where the traffic pattern is more distributed than in access networks. Today, these rings operate at OC-12 (STM-4), OC-48 (STM-16), and OC-192 (STM-64) speeds. Most metro carriers have deployed BLSR/2s, while many long-haul carriers have deployed BLSR/4s. BLSR/4s can handle more failures than BLSR/2s. For example, a BLSR/4 can simultaneously handle one transmitter failure on each span in the ring. It is also easier to service than a BLSR/2 ring because multiple spans can be serviced independently without

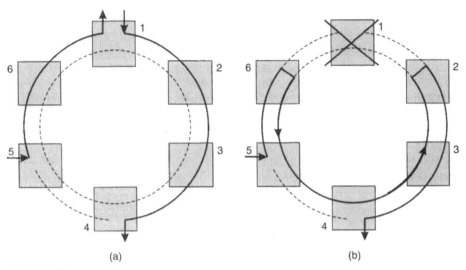

FIGURE 9.10

Erroneous connections due to the failure of a node being treated by its adjacent nodes as link failures. (a) Normal operation, with a connection from node 5 to node 1 and another connection from node 1 to node 4. (b) After node 1 fails, nodes 6 and 2 invoke ring switching independently. This causes a connection to be set up erroneously between node 5 and node 4. This problem can be prevented by first identifying the failed node and then not restoring any connections that originate or terminate at the failed node.

taking down the ring. However, ring management in a BLSR/4 is more complicated than in a BLSR/2 because multiple protection mechanisms have to be coordinated.

BLSRs are significantly more complex to implement than UPSRs. They require extensive signaling between the nodes for many reasons, as we will see below. This signaling is done using the K_1/K_2 bytes in the SONET overhead.

Handling Node Failures in BLSRs

So far, we have dealt primarily with how to handle failures of links, such as those occurring from a fiber cut. Failures of nodes are usually less likely because, in many cases, redundant configurations (such as dual power supplies and switch fabrics) are used. However, nodes may still fail because of some catastrophic events or human errors. Handling node failures complicates the BLSR restoration mechanism. The failure of a node is seen by all its adjacent nodes as failures of the links that connect them to the failed node. If each of these adjacent nodes performs restoration assuming that it is a single link failure, there can be undesirable consequences. One example is shown in Figure 9.10. Here, when node 1 fails, nodes 6 and 2 assume it is a link failure and attempt to reroute the traffic around the ring (ring switching) to restore service. This causes erroneous connections, as shown in the figure. The only way to prevent such occurrences is to ensure that the nodes performing the restoration determine the type of failure before invoking their restoration mechanisms. This would require exchanging messages between the nodes in the network. In the preceding example, nodes 6 and 2 could first try to exchange messages around the ring to determine if they have both recorded link failures and, if so, invoke the appropriate restoration procedure. This restoration procedure can avoid these misconnections by not attempting to restore any traffic that originates or terminates at the failed node. This is called *squelching*. Thus each node in a BLSR maintains squelch tables that indicate which connections need to be squelched in the event of node failures. The price paid for this is a slower restoration time because of the coordination required between the nodes to determine the appropriate restoration mechanism to be invoked.

Low-Priority Traffic in BLSRs

Just as we saw with 1:1 protection earlier, BLSRs can use the protection bandwidth to carry low-priority or extra traffic, under normal operation. This extra traffic is lost in the event of a failure. However, this feature requires additional signaling between the nodes in the event of a failure to indicate to the other nodes that they should operate in protection mode and throw away the low-priority traffic.

9.2.5 Ring Interconnection and Dual Homing

A single ring is only a part of the overall network. The entire network typically consists of multiple rings interconnected with each other, and a connection may have to be routed through multiple rings to get to its destination. The interconnection of these rings is thus an important aspect to be considered. The simplest way for rings to interoperate is to connect the drop sides of two ADMs on different rings back to back, as shown in Figure 9.11. The interconnection is done using signals typically at lower bit rates than the line bit rate. For instance, two OC-12 UPSRs may be interconnected by DS3 signals. In many cases, a digital crossconnect is interspersed between the two rings to provide additional grooming and multiplexing capabilities.

The problem with the approach above is that if one of the ADMs fails, or there is a problem with the cabling between the two ADMs, the interconnection is broken. A way to deal with this problem is to use *dual homing*. Dual homing makes use of two hub nodes to perform the interconnection, as shown in Figure 9.12. For traffic going between the rings, connections are set up between the originating node on one ring and both the hub nodes. Thus if one of the hub nodes fails, the other node can take over, and the end user does not see any disruption to traffic. Similarly, if there is a cable cut between the two hub nodes, alternate protection paths are now available to restore the traffic.

Rather than set up two separate connections between the originating node and the two hub nodes, the architecture uses a multicasting or *drop-and-continue* feature present in the ADMs. Consider the connection shown between an

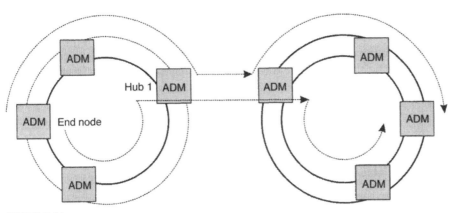

FIGURE 9.11

Back-to-back interconnection of SONET/SDH rings. This simple interconnection is vulnerable to the failure of one of the two nodes that form the interconnect, or of the link between these two nodes.

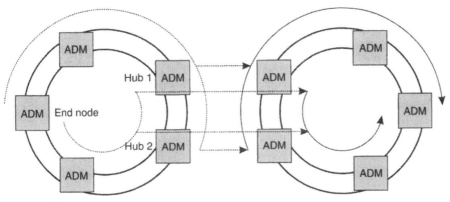

FIGURE 9.12

Dual homing to handle hub node failures. Each end node is connected to two hub nodes so as to be able to recover from the failure of a hub node or the failure of any interconnection between the hub nodes. The ADMs in the nodes have a "drop-and-continue" feature, which allows them to drop a traffic stream as well as have it continue onto the next ADM.

end node and the two hub nodes (hub 1 and hub 2) in Figure 9.12. In the clockwise direction of the ring, the ADM at hub 1 drops the traffic associated with the connection but also simultaneously allows this traffic to continue along the ring, where it is again dropped at hub 2. Likewise, along the counterclockwise direction, the ADM at hub 2 uses its drop-and-continue feature to drop traffic from this connection as well as pass it through to hub 1. Note that additional bandwidth is used up between the two hub nodes on each ring to support this capability.

Dual homing is being deployed in business access networks to interconnect access UPSRs with interoffice BLSRs as well as to interconnect multiple BLSRs. It can also be applied to interconnections between two subnetworks, not necessarily two rings (although rings are the major application). In general, for dual homing to work, the dual node interconnect itself must be a protected subnetwork, so that alternate paths are available if any of the hub nodes or the links interconnecting them fails.

9.3 PROTECTION IN IP NETWORKS

The IP layer has historically provided best-effort services. IP, by its very nature, uses dynamic, hop-by-hop routing of packets. Each router maintains a routing table of the next-hop neighbor for each destination, and incoming packets are routed based on this table. If there is a failure in the network, the intradomain routing protocol (OSPF or IS-IS) operates in a distributed manner and updates these routing tables at each router within the domain. In practice, it can take seconds after the failure is detected before the routing tables at all the routers converge and have consistent routing information. During this process, packets continue to be routed based on the current versions of the routing tables at the routers, which can be inconsistent and incorrect. This causes packets to be routed incorrectly and possibly loop within the network. Potentially, packets could therefore be lost or undergo long delays on the order of seconds after a failure is detected. Even if a router decides to route a packet along an alternate route, following the detection of a failure, packets could still loop within the network, as shown in Figure 9.13. In this example, consider packets destined for router D. Suppose link CD fails. Node C would then attempt to route packets destined for D to router B, hoping to find an alternate path to reach router D. Router B, however, still thinks that the best way to get to router D is through router C and would route that packet back to router C. This is the case until the routing tables at the routers have all converged.

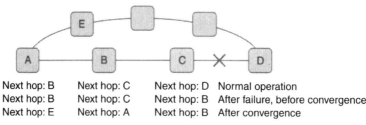

Next hop: B	Next hop: C	Next hop: D	Normal operation
Next hop: B	Next hop: C	Next hop: B	After failure, before convergence
Next hop: E	Next hop: A	Next hop: B	After convergence

FIGURE 9.13

An example to illustrate routing loops in an IP network after a failure. It takes many interations before the routing tables at the nodes converge to the correct routes. In the meantime, there can be routing loops.

The slow recovery from failures is due to the fundamental nature of IP routing—the fact that it is distributed, next-hop-based dynamic routing. Providing faster restoration times requires some way to nail down paths and have packets follow a known path through the network. This capability is provided by multi-protocol label switching (MPLS). MPLS allows label-switched paths (LSPs) to be set up between nodes. All packets belonging to an LSP are routed along the same path. This allows several protection schemes to be implemented within the MPLS layer (which can be viewed as a link layer under the IP network layer). For example, upon detecting a link failure, we could set up alternate LSPs for all the LSPs currently using that link, and reroute packets on the newly set up LSPs. This could be done locally to route around a failed link, or it could be done at the ends of the LSPs. A variety of protection schemes, such as $1 + 1$, ring, or shared mesh, could be implemented using this approach and are being developed currently.

The other aspect of protection in the IP layer has to do with the time taken by the IP layer to detect failures in the first place. In a typical implementation used in intradomain routing protocols [3][AJY00], adjacent routers exchange periodic "hello" packets between themselves. If a router misses a certain number of these packets, it declares the link to have failed and initiates rerouting. By default, the routers send hello packets every 10 seconds and declare the link down if they miss three successive hello packets. Thus it could take up to 30 seconds to detect a failure. The process can be speeded up by exchanging hello packets more frequently; however, the minimum interval is currently specified to be 1 second. More typically, core routers detect failures in about 10 seconds. Alternatively, a separate set of packets can be exchanged periodically for this purpose [4][HYCG00]. However, these packets can get queued up in buffers if there are a lot of other packets waiting and so may have to be processed at higher priority levels than regular packets.

Another option is to rely on the underlying SONET or optical layer to detect the failure and inform the IP layer. This can be done by having the line card inside a router look at the framing and communicate failure detection information up into the routing protocol. However, this is not usually architected into today's routers.

9.4 WHY OPTICAL LAYER PROTECTION

The optical layer provides lightpaths for use by its client layers, such as the SONET, IP, or ATM layers. (Recall that the layers that use the services provided by the optical layer are called client layers of the optical layer.) We have seen that extensive protection mechanisms are available in the SONET layer, and there is some degree of protection possible in the other client layers as well. These layers were all designed to work independently of each other and not rely on protection mechanisms available in other layers. We will see below that there is a strong need for protection in the optical layer, despite the existence of protection mechanisms in the client layers.

- SONET/SDH networks incorporate extensive protection functions. However, other networks such as IP, ATM, and ESCON networks do not provide the same level of protection. As we saw in Section 9.3, IP traffic for the most part is "best-effort" traffic. However, as carrier networks become more data centric, there is an increasing expectation from both carriers and their customers that these networks will need to provide the same level of availability as SONET and SDH networks.

- One way for realizing this capability is to develop additional protection mechanisms within the IP, ATM, or other client layers, as we saw in Section

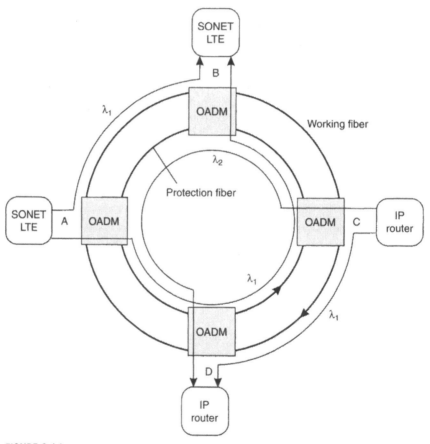

FIGURE 9.14

A WDM ring built using optical add/drop multiplexers (OADMs), supporting two interconnected SONET line terminals (LTEs) and two interconnected IP routers using protection provided by the SONET and IP layers, respectively. The SONET and IP boxes do not share protection bandwidth.

9.3. Another way to protect data networks is to rely on optical layer protection, which can be quite cost-effective and efficient.

■ Significant cost savings can be realized by making use of optical layer protection instead of client layer protection. We illustrate this with two examples.

Consider an example of a WDM ring network with lightpaths carrying higher-layer traffic. Figure 9.14 illustrates an example where there is no optical layer protection. Two SONET line terminals (LTEs) are connected to each other through lightpaths provided by the optical layer, as are two IP routers. For simplicity we look at a undirectional lightpath from LTE A to LTE B and another lightpath from router C to router D. These two lightpaths are protected by the SONET and IP layers, respectively, using $1 + 1$ protection. The working connection from LTE A to LTE B is established on wavelength λ_1 along the shortest path in the ring, and the other protection connection is established, say, on the same wavelength λ_1 around the ring. Likewise, the working connection from router C to router D may be established on λ_1 on the shortest path. However, the protection connection from router C to router D, which needs to be routed around the ring, must be allocated another wavelength, say, λ_2. Thus two wavelengths are required to support this configuration.

Figure 9.15 shows what can be gained by having the optical layer do the protection instead. Now we can eliminate the individual $1 + 1$ protection for the SONET LTEs and the IP routers and make them share a common protection wavelength around the ring. Only a single wavelength is required to support this configuration. Note, however, that only a single link cut can be handled by this arrangement, whereas the earlier arrangement of Figure 9.14 can handle some combinations of multiple fiber cuts (see Problem 9.11). Likewise, the arrangement of Figure 9.14 can support two simultaneous transmitter failures, whereas the arrangement of Figure 9.15 can support only a single such failure. Nevertheless, if we are primarily interested in handling one failure at any given time, the optical layer protection scheme of Figure 9.15 offers a clear savings in capacity.

Consider what would happen if we had to support N such pairs (N being the number of links in the ring), with each of them being adjacent on the ring. Without optical layer protection, N protection wavelengths would be required.

With optical layer protection, only one wavelength would be needed. Optical layer protection is more efficient because it shares the protection resources across multiple pairs of client layer equipment. In contrast, client layer protection mechanisms cannot share the protection resources between different or independent clients.

Another example of an IP network operating over WDM links is shown in Figure 9.16. Consider two network configuration options. Figure 9.16(a) shows the IP routers interconnected by two diversely routed WDM links. In this case, no protection is provided by the optical layer, and the protection against fiber cuts as well as equipment failures (for example, router port failure) is handled completely by the IP layer. Note that the configuration shown requires three working ports and three protect ports on each router.

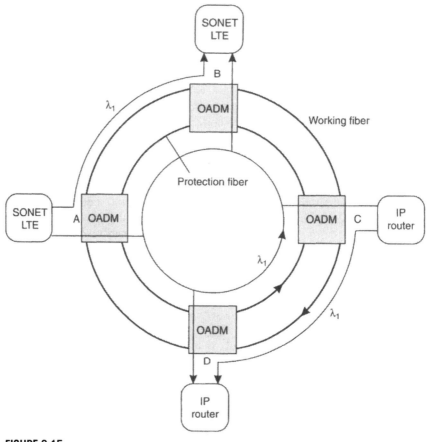

FIGURE 9.15

Benefit of optical layer protection. The configuration is the same as that of Figure 9.14. However, the optical layer now uses a single wavelength around the ring to protect both the SONET and IP connections.

Figure 9.16(b) shows a better way of realizing a network with the same capabilities, by making use of protection within the optical layer. In this case, fiber cuts are handled by the optical layer. A simple bridge-and-switch arrangement is used to connect two diversely routed fiber pairs in a single WDM system. In general, it is more efficient to have fiber cuts handled by the optical layer, since a single switch then takes care of restoring all the channels, instead of having each individual IP link take care of the restoration by itself. More importantly, this arrangement can result in a significant savings in equipment cost. In contrast with the previous configuration, this configuration requires each router to have only a single protect port instead of three. If one of the working ports in the router fails, the router

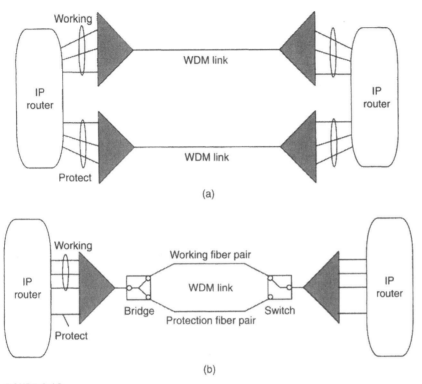

FIGURE 9.16

Example showing the benefit of optical layer protection compared to protecting at the IP layer. (a) All the protection is handled by the routers. Two diversely routed WDM links are used. Each IP router uses three working ports and three protect ports to protect against both fiber cuts and equipment failures. (b) A single WDM line system is deployed, with protection against fiber cuts handled by the optical layer. Equipment failures are handled by the IP layer. The IP routers now use three working ports and an additional protect port in case one of the working ports fails.

directs the traffic onto the protect port. Note that this type of failure cannot be handled by the optical layer.

This example also brings out another value of optical layer protection. Generally the cost of a router port is significantly higher than the cost per port of optical layer equipment. Therefore it is cheaper to reserve protection bandwidth in the optical layer (effectively reserve ports on optical layer equipment), rather than have additional ports in IP routers for this purpose.

- The optical layer can handle some faults more efficiently than the client layers. A WDM network carries several wavelengths of traffic on a single fiber. Without optical layer protection, a fiber cut results in each traffic stream being restored independently by the client layer. In addition, the network management system is flooded with a large number of alarms for this single failure. Instead, if the optical layer were to restore this failure, fewer entities have to be rerouted (albeit larger entities), and hence the process is faster and simpler.

- Optical layer protection can be used to provide an additional degree of resilience in the network, for instance, to protect against multiple failures. An example of this is shown in Figure 9.17. Consider a SONET BLSR operating over lightpaths provided by the optical layer. Figure 9.17(a) shows normal operation of the network. Figure 9.17(b) shows what happens to a sample SONET connection in the event of a link failure. The BLSR does a ring switch and reroutes the connection around the ring. At this point, until the failed link is repaired, the network cannot handle another failure. Repairing a failed link can take several hours to days—a fairly long period during which the network is vulnerable to additional failures. Optical layer protection can be used to remove this vulnerability. In Figure 9.17(c), the optical layer reroutes the lightpath on the failed link around the failure over another optical path. At this point, as far as the BLSR is concerned, it appears as if the failed link has been restored, and the ring reverts back to normal operation. This allows the BLSR to handle additional failures while the failed link is actually being repaired.

- Finally, protection in SONET is currently based on rings (UPSR/BLSR). Ring-based schemes require that the capacity in the network reserved for protection be equal to the capacity used for working traffic. Within the optical layer, a variety of mesh-based protection schemes are being developed. These offer the promise of requiring significantly less protection capacity than ring-based schemes. Admittedly, these schemes could also be applied in the SONET layer.

However, optical layer protection does have its limitations:

- Not all failures can be handled by the optical layer. If a laser in an attached client terminal fails, the optical layer cannot do anything about it. Thus, client equipment failures need to be dealt with by the client layer.

- The optical layer may not be able to detect the appropriate conditions that would cause it to invoke protection switching. For instance, a transparent network can only monitor presence or absence of power (and in some cases, the optical signal-to-noise ratio). While it may also be able to measure power degradations, it may not know what the reasonable values for the power levels are because they vary widely depending on the type of signal being carried. Thus it can only trigger protection switching upon detecting loss of light. The bit error rate is a more precise indicator of signal quality, but a transparent network may not be able to measure bit error rate.

- The optical layer protects traffic in units of lightpaths, and it cannot protect part of the traffic within a lightpath and not protect other parts. Such functions need to be performed by the client layers.

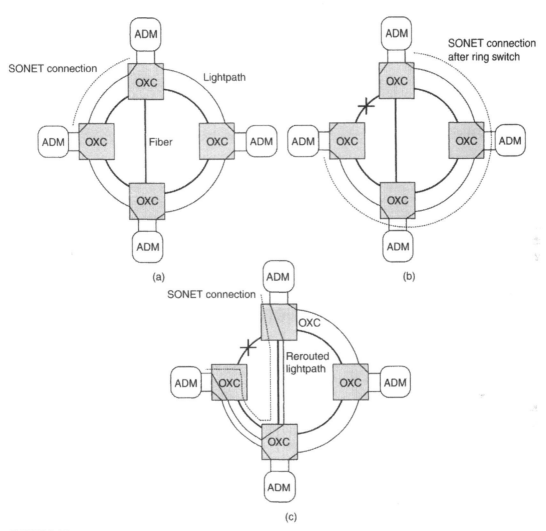

FIGURE 9.17

Optical layer protection used to enhance SONET protection. The thick lines indicate fiber
links, the thin lines indicate lightpaths provided by the optical layer between SONET ADMs,
and the dashed line indicates a SONET connection. (a) Normal operation before failure.
A SONET ring is realized using lightpaths provided by the optical layer. (b) Due to a fiber
failure, a lightpath connecting two adjacent SONET ADMs fails, causing the SONET ADMs to
invoke ring switching to rapidly restore the SONET connection. (c) The optical crossconnects
(OXCs) perform optical layer restoration and reroute the lightpath around the failure. To the
SONET ring, it appears as if the failure has been restored and the ring reverts back to normal
operation, ready to tackle another failure.

■ Protection routes in the optical layer may be longer than the primary routes, and the choice of alternate routes may be severely limited due to link budget considerations.

■ We need to pay careful attention to the interworking of protection schemes between the different layers. We will discuss some of these issues in Section 9.6.

9.4.1 Service Classes Based on Protection

Multiple classes of service can be provided by the optical layer based on the type of protection provided. The main differences in these classes lie in the level of connection availability provided and the restoration time for a connection. These different classes will likely be supported using different protection schemes. While no standards have been defined yet, we provide a likely set of services below:

Platinum. This provides the highest level of availability and the fastest restoration times, comparable to SONET/SDH protection schemes, typically around 60 ms. For example, a dedicated $1 + 1$ protection scheme could be used to provide this class of service. This class may be viewed as a premium service and is accordingly priced.

Gold. This provides high availability and fast restoration times, typically in the range of hundreds of milliseconds. For example, a shared mesh protection scheme can provide this class of service.

Silver. This class sits below gold in terms of availability and restoration time. For example, a protection scheme that provides "best-effort" restoration may fit into this category. Another example would be a scheme wherein a connection is reattempted from scratch in case of a failure.

Bronze. Here, the optical layer provides unprotected lightpaths. In the event of a failure of the working path, the connection is lost.

Lead. This class of service would have the lowest availability and the lowest priority among all the classes. For instance, we may support this class by using protection bandwidth reserved for other classes of service. If that bandwidth is needed to protect other higher-priority traffic, connections in this class are preempted.

There is a great deal of debate about what types of applications will use these service classes and which of them will proliferate. For instance, today carriers using SONET/SDH are providing primarily platinum-type services to their customers. However, we expect that the increasing dominance of data traffic will stimulate the need for lower-priced classes of service. For example, carriers interconnecting Internet routers from Internet service providers are providing in some cases platinum services and in other cases bronze (unprotected) services. In the latter case, the IP layer handles all the restoration functions. In the former situation, it is quite possible that some of that traffic could be carried over lightpaths with a lower quality of service.

9.5 OPTICAL LAYER PROTECTION SCHEMES

We next look at the different types of optical layer protection schemes. For the most part, conceptually, the schemes are similar to their SONET and SDH equivalents. However, their implementation is substantially different, for several reasons: the equipment cost for WDM links grows with the number of wavelengths to be multiplexed and terminated, link budget constraints need to be taken into account when designing the protection scheme, and there may be wavelength conversion constraints to deal with.

The optical layer consists of the optical channel (OCh) layer (or path layer), the optical multiplex section (OMS) layer (or line layer), and the optical transmission section (OTS) layer. Just as SONET protection schemes fit into either the line layer (for example, BLSR) or the path layer (for example, UPSR), optical protection schemes also belong to the OCh or OMS layers. An OCh layer scheme restores one lightpath at a time, whereas an OMS layer scheme restores the entire group of lightpaths on a link and cannot restore individual lightpaths separately. Table 9.3 provides an overview of schemes operating in the optical multiplex section layer. Table 9.4 summarizes schemes operating in the optical channel layer. These schemes have not yet been standardized, and there are many variants. We have attempted to use a nomenclature that is consistent with SDH terminology.

In SONET, there is not a significant cost associated with processing each connection separately in the path layer instead of processing all the connections together

Table 9.3 A Summary of Optical Protection Schemes Operating in the Optical Multiplex Section (OMS) Layer. Both dedicated protection rings (DPRings) and shared protection rings (SPRings) are possible

			Protection Scheme	
	1 + 1	1:1	OMS-DPRing	OMS-SPRing
Type	Dedicated	Shared	Dedicated	Shared
Topology	Point-point	Point-point	Ring	Ring

Table 9.4 A Summary of Optical Protection Schemes Operating in the Optical Channel Layer

		Protection Scheme	
	1 + 1	OCh-SPRing	OCh-Mesh
Type	Dedicated	Shared	Shared
Topology	Mesh	Ring	Mesh

in the line layer because the processing is done using application-specific integrated circuits, where the incremental cost of processing the path layer compared to the line layer is not significant. In contrast, there can be a significant difference in cost associated with OCh layer schemes relative to OMS layer schemes. An OCh layer scheme has to demultiplex all the wavelengths, whereas an OMS layer scheme operates on all the wavelengths and thus requires less equipment.

As an example, consider the two protection schemes shown in Figure 9.18. Figure 9.18(a) shows 1 + 1 OMS protection, while Figure 9.18(b) shows 1 + 1 OCh protection. The OMS scheme requires two WDM terminals and an additional splitter and switch. The OCh scheme, on the other hand, requires four WDM terminals and a splitter and switch per wavelength. Thus its equipment cost is higher than the cost of the OMS scheme. Indeed this is the case if all channels are to be protected. However, the cost of OCh protection can be reduced if not all channels need to be protected. Assuming multiplexers, splitters, and switches can be added on a wavelength-by-wavelength basis, the cost of OCh protection grows linearly with the number of channels that are to be protected. The cost of an OMS protection scheme, on the other hand, is independent of the number of channels to be

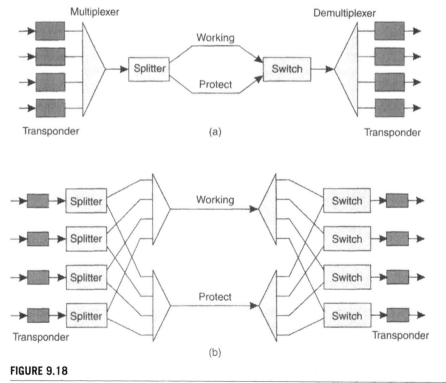

FIGURE 9.18

Comparison of (a) 1 + 1 OMS and (b) 1 + 1 OCh protection schemes.

protected. If only a small fraction of the channels is to be protected, then OCh protection is not significantly more expensive than OMS protection.

The choice of protection schemes is dictated primarily by the service classes to be supported (as discussed below) and by the type of equipment deployed. In the SONET/SDH world, protection is performed primarily by the SONET/SDH line terminals (LTEs) and add/drop multiplexers (ADMs) and not by digital crossconnects. This is the case primarily because digital crossconnects were more inefficient at performing fast protection than the LTEs and ADMs, partly because they operated on lower-speed tributaries. However, we are likely to see protection functions handled somewhat differently in the optical layer. Multiplexing equipment, such as optical line terminals and add/drop multiplexers, can provide both OCh layer and OMS layer protection in linear or ring configurations. On the other hand, optical crossconnects can provide protection in linear, ring, and mesh configurations. Unlike their digital crossconnect counterparts in the SONET/SDH world, optical crossconnects are designed to provide efficient protection. Depending on the type of crossconnect, the protection could be done either at the optical channel layer (for crossconnects that groom at the wavelength level) or at the STS-1 level (for electrical core crossconnects grooming at STS-1). Therefore one possibility is to use simple unprotected WDM point-to-point systems and rely on the optical crossconnects to perform the protection functions. Backbone networks handling large numbers of wavelengths may opt for this choice, as may operators who have already deployed a large quantity of unprotected WDM equipment in their networks. The other possibility is to rely on the WDM line terminals and add/drop multiplexers to perform this function. Metropolitan networks using small numbers of channels and not requiring the use of crossconnects may opt for this choice.

9.5.1 1 + 1 OMS Protection

This is perhaps the simplest optical layer protection scheme and is shown in Figure 9.18(a). Because of its simplicity, it has been implemented by several vendors in their OLTs. The composite WDM signal is bridged onto two diverse paths using an optical splitter. At the other end, an optical switch is used to select the better among the two signals, based primarily on detecting the presence or absence of light signals. The split incurs an additional 3 dB loss, and the switch also adds a small amount of loss (<1 dB). An alternative implementation uses optical amplifiers on each of the fibers and a passive combiner to combine both directions at the receiver. At any time, one amplifier is turned on and the other is turned off. This has the advantage of avoiding a single point of failure in the system (the selector switch in other implementations), but may be more expensive to implement.

9.5.2 1:1 OMS Protection

This scheme is similar to the SONET 1:1 scheme discussed in Section 9.2.1 and the benefits are similar: support for low-priority traffic and also the ability to

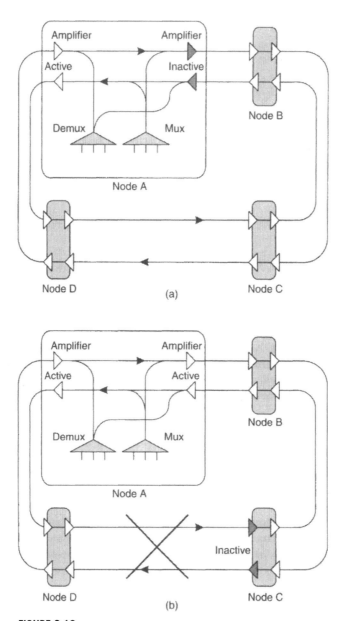

FIGURE 9.19

OMS-DPRing protection. (a) Normal operation. One pair of amplifiers is inactive (turned off) and the others are turned on, creating a bus. (b) After a failure, the currently inactive amplifiers are turned on and an amplifier pair adjacent to the failure is turned off to bring up the alternate path and restore traffic.

have N working systems share a single protection system. Compared to the $1 + 1$ scheme of Figure 9.18(a), a typical implementation uses a switch at the transmitter, instead of a splitter, resulting in a somewhat lower total loss in the path. Just as in the SONET equivalent, an APS protocol is needed to provide coordination between the two ends of the link.

9.5.3 OMS-DPRing

The OMS-DPRing (dedicated protection ring) is similar to a SONET UPSR, except that it operates at the OMS (or optical line) layer, whereas the UPSR operates in the SONET path layer. It can also be thought of as an optical unidirectional line-switched ring (ULSR).

One possible implementation of an OMS-DPRing [5][Bat98] is shown in Figure 9.19. Signals are coupled into and out of the ring via passive couplers. Each node transmits on both directions of the ring. Note that different nodes must transmit at different wavelengths; otherwise their transmissions would collide. Under normal operation, the ring functions as a bus, with one pair of amplifiers turned off on the entire ring and all the others turned on. If there is a link failure, the amplifiers next to the failed link are turned off and the ones that were originally inactive are now turned on to restore traffic. For example, in Figure 9.19(a), the amplifier pair to the right of node A is turned off under normal operation and the other amplifiers are turned on. In Figure 9.19(b), when link CD fails, the amplifier pair at C adjacent to the failed link is turned off, and the originally inactive amplifiers at node A are turned on to create a new bus and restore traffic.

9.5.4 OMS-SPRing

The OMS-SPRing (shared protection ring) is analogous to a SONET BLSR/4 with some changes. A possible implementation of a four-fiber ring is shown in Figure 9.20. Two of the fibers have WDM equipment deployed, and the remaining two fibers around the ring are used for protection purposes and do not have attached WDM equipment. In the event of a cut, the signal is either span switched or ring switched onto the protection fibers, as shown in Figure 9.21. In both cases, not having WDM equipment on the protection fibers not only saves cost but also provides a relatively lower-loss path around the ring for the protection traffic. Optical amplifiers may be needed on the protection fibers depending on the link losses.

A two-fiber version of OMS-SPRing can also be realized by dedicating half the wavelengths on each fiber for protection purposes. By making sure that protection wavelengths on one fiber correspond to the working wavelengths on the other fiber, the signals can be rerouted without requiring wavelength conversion. This scheme, however, requires the two groups of wavelengths to be demultiplexed and multiplexed at each node, and thus is not strictly operating at the OMS layer.

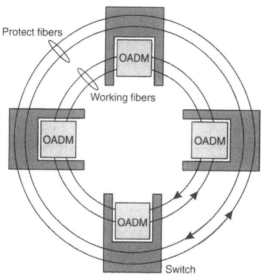

FIGURE 9.20

OMS-SPRing shown under normal operation. Only the working fibers are connected to optical add/drop multiplexers. The protection fibers are connected around the ring.

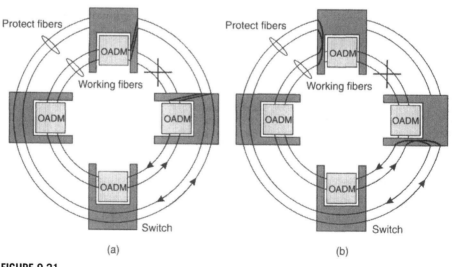

(a)   (b)

FIGURE 9.21

OMS-SPRing after a failure. (a) Span switching. (b) Ring switching.

9.5.5 l:*N* Transponder Protection

The OMS layer schemes that we discussed above handle link failures and node failures but do not handle failures of the end equipment, particularly the transponders. The transponders may be protected in a 1:*N* configuration by having a spare transponder for every *N* working transponder. One problem to overcome is that transponders today operate at fixed wavelengths, and so the spare transponder will operate at a different wavelength than the working transponder. When the signal is switched over to the spare transponder, we also need to set up a new lightpath on the new wavelength through the network. Alternatively, we could use a tunable laser in the spare transponder.

9.5.6 1+1 OCh Dedicated Protection

In 1+1 OCh protection, two lightpaths on disjoint routes are set up for each client connection. As shown in Figure 9.18(b), the client signal is split at the input and the destination selects the better of the two lightpaths. As with SONET and SDH, no signaling is required. This approach works in point-to-point, ring, and mesh configurations. In the context of a ring, the scheme is also called OCh-DPRing (OCh dedicated protection ring) or optical UPSR.

Like SONET UPSRs, this approach is bandwidth inefficient in that the protection bandwidth is not shared among multiple client connections. However, it is one of the simplest protection schemes and therefore has been implemented by several vendors in optical add/drop multiplexers and crossconnects.

Figure 9.22 shows another possible implementation of the bridge and select functions within a node. Here, the signal entering the optical layer is split and sent to two transponders, and then diversely routed across the network. At the

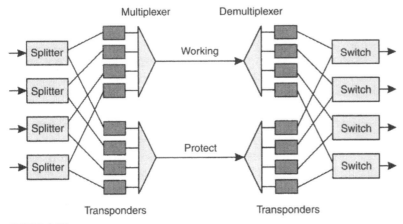

FIGURE 9.22

Another implementation of 1+1 OCh protection. The signal from the client equipment is split and sent to two transponders for transmission over diverse paths, and at the destination the better copy is selected by an optical switch at the output of the transponders.

receiving end, the signal is terminated in two transponders, and the better signal is selected afterwards to be sent to the client. In Figure 9.18, the client signal is passed through a transponder and split afterwards. At the receiving end, one of the two signals is selected by an optical switch before it is sent into a transponder and then onwards to the client. This uses half as many transponders as the previous option but does not protect against a transponder failure. Aside from this aspect, there are several other subtleties that affect the choice of one implementation versus the other, such as the criteria for switching from one path to another, and potential restoration time differences between the two approaches.

9.5.7 OCh-SPRing

The OCh-SPRing (shared protection ring) is somewhat similar to a SONET BLSR/4. However, the BLSR operates at the line (multiplex section) layer, whereas this scheme operates at the optical channel layer and not the optical multiplex section layer. Working lightpaths are set up on the shortest path along the ring. When a working lightpath fails, it is restored either using a span switch or a ring switch, just as in a SONET BLSR/4. Nonoverlapping lightpaths in the ring can share a single wavelength around the ring for protection, and this spatial reuse allows the OCh-SPRing to be more efficient than an OCh-DPRing for distributed traffic. The operation of the OCh-SPRing is essentially the same as that shown in Figures 9.5–9.7, where the fibers now correspond to wavelengths and the connections correspond to lightpaths. Just as with a BLSR, fast coordination between the ring nodes is needed in order to support node failures or low-priority traffic.

9.5.8 OCh-Mesh Protection

Ring architectures are inherently suitable for sparse physical topologies and in situations where most of the traffic is confined within the ring. Many backbone networks tend to be somewhat more densely connected than rings and are essentially meshed, with traffic being fairly distributed. A typical North American long-haul carrier's backbone network may have, say, 50 nodes, with an average node having 3–4 adjacent nodes, with some nodes having as many as 5–10 adjacent nodes. For such networks, mesh protection schemes offer more bandwidth-efficient protection than rings. The bandwidth efficiency of a mesh relative to a ring depends on several factors, including the network topology, the traffic pattern, and the type of mesh protection scheme used. In general, the more dense or meshed the topology, the greater the benefit of mesh protection. Also, if traffic in the network is primarily localized, then rings can do a good job. In contrast, if traffic in the network is distributed, then rings are inefficient—many lightpaths will need to be partitioned into multiple rings, and multiple rings need to be interconnected and protected to support these lightpaths. Efficiency improvements ranging from 20% to 60% have been reported for mesh protection schemes relative to ring protection schemes [[6]RM99a, [7]RM99b]. Here we provide a simple example to illustrate the efficiency of mesh protection relative to ring protection.

Example 9.1

Consider the network shown in Figure 9.23(a), with three lightpaths to be supported. Assume that all these lightpaths need to be protected. Each lightpath uses 1 unit of capacity on each link that it traverses.

First suppose we use $1 + 1$ OCh dedicated protection. We would then set up dedicated protection lightpaths as shown in Figure 9.23(b). In this case, a total of eight units of protection capacity is needed in the network.

Next let us consider a configuration that uses shared ring protection (OCh-SPRing). Here we have an interesting problem of how to configure the rings themselves. One solution is to configure the rings as shown in Figure 9.23(c). In this case, lightpaths X and Y each share

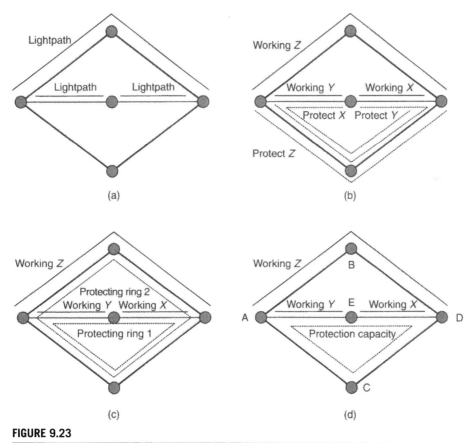

(a)

(b)

(c)

(d)

FIGURE 9.23

Example to illustrate the bandwidth efficiency of mesh protection relative to ring protection.
(a) A mesh network with three lightpaths present. (b) Protecting the lightpaths using $1 + 1$ dedicated protection. (c) Protecting the lightpaths using OCh-SPRing protection.
(d) Protecting the lightpaths using OCh-mesh protection.

the same bandwidth for protection, while lightpath Z has a separate ring for protection. This configuration requires a total of eight units of capacity for protection, which is the same as for dedicated protection above. Note, however, that the protection capacity can be reduced to six units by having lightpaths X and Y share a ring but using dedicated protection for lightpath Z. Another way to look at this is that by using the eight units of capacity, we can support additional lightpaths that can share the ring used to protect lightpath Z.

We now consider the case of shared mesh protection. Our mesh protection scheme works as follows. We will use the same routes used by the $1+1$ scheme for routing the protection lightpaths. The big difference is that the protection lightpaths are not set up ahead of time, but are only set up when there is a failure. As long as two lightpaths don't fail simultaneously, we can have them share the same protection capacity in the network. In this case, only a single lightpath fails at any given time, assuming we have to deal only with link failures. Therefore we only need to provide sufficient protection bandwidth to protect one lightpath at a time. We leave it to the reader to verify that the four units of capacity shown in Figure 9.23(d) are sufficient.

Mesh protection schemes are not new. They were used in the 1980s in networks with digital crossconnects. However, these protection schemes were centralized and operated rather slowly, taking minutes to hours to restore traffic after a failure. Also the protection was complex to manage, and there were no applicable standards. After the standardization of SONET/SDH and due to the fast 60 ms ring protection offered by SONET/SDH, these mesh-based restoration schemes were largely abandoned.

Today, we are seeing a resurrection of mesh protection schemes in the optical layer of the network for several reasons.

- The processing power available to implement mesh protection has dramatically increased over the past few decades, to the point where computationally intensive functions such as determining new routes can be performed rapidly. The communication bandwidth available for network control purposes has also gone up dramatically. To protect a network providing terabits/second of capacity, it is quite reasonable to dedicate several 2 Mb/s or 45 Mb/s lines in the network for control traffic. This was not the case earlier, where this amount of bandwidth would have been considered large, relative to the actual traffic within the network.

- Optical crossconnects and other optical layer equipment protect bandwidth at much larger granularities (lightpaths) than digital crossconnects that operate at DS1 or DS3 speeds. As a result, they have fewer entities to manage and protect. However, this situation will change as traffic grows.

- Relatively fast signaling and routing protocols have been developed for other forms of data networks, such as IP and ATM networks, and many of these protocols can be adapted for use in the optical layer.

- The 60 ms protection time requirement is not a hard number. Many carriers interested in protecting data traffic will be satisfied with protection times on the order of a few hundred milliseconds, making it easier to implement more complex protection schemes.

A variety of mesh protection schemes have been proposed, and many are currently being implemented by optical crossconnect vendors. In addition to the factors discussed above, the mesh protection schemes will have to overcome some key issues in order to facilitate widespread deployment:

- Part of the reason that SONET/SDH protection has been so successful is that the protection schemes were standardized. This is yet to happen with mesh protection schemes.

- One of the advantages of ring-based schemes is that the network is partitioned into multiple domains and each domain is protected independently. Thus one part of the network does not affect the other parts. This implies that the network can handle simultaneous multiple failures as long as they occur in different domains. Moreover, one part of the network can be serviced without impacting the protection scheme in the other parts. In order to get the full benefit of mesh protection, we will need to treat the network in its entirety as a single domain. Breaking up the network into smaller domains reduces the bandwidth efficiency unless the individual domains are reasonably large.

- Another dimension to this is the effect of software bugs or operator errors. In ring-based networks, such problems are localized, whereas in mesh networks, these problems can have a networkwide impact.

- Mesh protection schemes are considerably more complex to manage than ring protection schemes. In order to make them successful, vendors will need to provide carriers with the appropriate management tools to hide the complexity from the network operators. For instance, this could mean providing automated tools to plan and compute primary and protection routes in the network, which are otherwise fairly complex operations.

  On the plus side, however, interconnecting rings is fairly complex, and mesh protection allows for more flexible planning of capacity in the network—capacity does not have to be nailed down up front; instead it can be provisioned as needed across the network.

- The more efficient mesh protection schemes will require rapid networkwide signaling mechanisms to be implemented to propagate information related to failures and to reroute lightpaths that are affected by a failure. This in turn implies that the nodes performing the protection switching will have to be designed carefully to minimize processing latencies.

- The more efficient mesh protection schemes require that protection routing tables be maintained at the nodes. These routing tables provide information about the network topology and protection paths in the network. The tables need to be updated when lightpaths, links, or nodes are added or removed from the network. Most importantly, these tables need to be consistent across all the nodes in the network.

■ These protection routing tables are similar to the routing tables maintained in IP networks, which work well even in very large IP networks with thousands of nodes. However, we need to realize that routing tables in IP networks are not always consistent. If the tables are inconsistent, routing pathologies, such as looping, can be present in the network with fairly high probabilities. For example, at the end of 1995, the likelihood of encountering a major routing pathology in the Internet was 3.3% [8][Pax97]. These pathologies can cause packets to be forwarded incorrectly in the network, but these packets eventually find their way to their destination or are dropped by the network. In the latter event, the packets are retransmitted by a higher-layer protocol (TCP). While this approach works well in IP networks, we cannot afford to have routing pathologies in transport networks because they could prevent restoration of service after a failure. Therefore, fast and reliable topology update mechanisms need to be in place to maintain the protection routing tables.

We now look at the different variations of mesh protection. One aspect of this is whether the entire network is protected as a single domain, or whether it is broken down into multiple domains, with each domain protected independently, and the different domains then tied together. In a degenerate scenario, each domain could be a single ring, in which case we get back to the usual mode of ring-based protection.

Another important aspect that differentiates protection schemes is whether the protection routes are precomputed ahead of time (*offline*), or whether they are computed after a failure has occurred (*online*). In both cases, another dimension to consider is the degree of distributed implementation. This affects the complexity of the signaling protocols required and has a direct impact on the speed of restoration.

Let us first consider the case where the protection routes are precomputed. In this case, the protection route for a lightpath is computed at the time it is set up and stored in the network. Sufficient bandwidth is allocated on all the links so as to ensure the lightpath can be restored in the event of any possible failure. (Note that this protection bandwidth is still shared among many lightpaths and is not dedicated to a single lightpath. This is the distinction between $1 + 1$ dedicated protection and shared protection.) Depending on the sophistication of the scheme used, there may be one or many possible alternate routes for a given lightpath, based on the actual failure scenario. For example, the simplest scenario is to compute a single disjoint path through the network as the protection route. Alternatively, we may use multiple protection routes, based on which link fails in the network. Clearly the amount of information needed to be stored in the network depends on the number of protection routes per lightpath.

In a centralized implementation of this scheme, a central controller in the network is notified if a failure occurs. The central controller then sets up all the alternate routes for the lightpaths by signaling to all the affected network elements to reconfigure their switches as needed. The problem with this approach is that the central controller is a single point of failure and is likely to be a significant bottleneck, both in terms of communication and processing speed.

Several variants of a distributed implementation are possible. In one variant, the failure information is flooded to all the network nodes. Each node then looks up its routing table and reconfigures its switch, based on the exact failure that occurred. Another possibility is to signal the failure to the sources/destinations of all the affected lightpaths. Each source-destination pair then sets up the alternate routing path by signaling to the nodes along the new path.

Next let us consider computing routes on the fly. In this case, new routes are computed after the failure has been discovered. One major issue that comes up in this context is whether sufficient bandwidth is available in the network to handle all the lightpaths that need to be restored. Without essentially precomputing the routes, it is not possible to determine the amount of protection bandwidth needed a priori. In this case, it is possible that some lightpaths are restored and others aren't.

Again this scheme can be implemented in a centralized or distributed manner. The distributed implementation is more complex than for the case where routes are precomputed. Here it is possible that multiple nodes acting independently may contend for the same link or wavelength resource to restore two independent lightpaths. These contentions will have to be dealt with, making the signaling scheme more complex and the recovery possibly slower. A centralized implementation would avoid such conflicts, but would suffer even worse communication and processing bottlenecks, compared to the centralized implementation for the case where the routes are precomputed.

Based on our discussions so far, we see that mesh protection requires the following functions: route computation, topology maintenance, and signaling to set up the protection routes. These functions have been implemented in IP and ATM networks. For example, in IP networks, route computation is done using a Dijkstra shortest-path-first algorithm, and the topology is maintained using a routing protocol such as OSPF (open shortest path first). Signaling has been used to establish paths in MPLS networks and ATM networks. Several signaling protocols are available for this purpose, including the resource reservation protocol (RSVP) [9][BZB + 97], private network-network interface (PNNI) signaling protocol [10][ATM96], and Signaling System 7 (SS7) [11][ITU93]. Today, there is a significant amount of work under way to expand MPLS (called GMPLS, for generalized MPLS) [12][AR01] to provide similar capabilities in optical networks.

9.5.9 Choice of Protection Technique

We have explored a number of different optical layer protection options. It is still too early to determine which ones will be deployed widely. An operator wanting to offer the different types of protection on the lightpaths as discussed in Section 9.4.1 must use an OCh layer protection method. On the other hand, an operator who is satisfied with protecting all lightpaths together will likely prefer an OMS layer scheme. Many of the protection schemes discussed above are being implemented in commercial products.

9.6 INTERWORKING BETWEEN LAYERS

We have seen that protection functions can be done in the optical layer, SONET/SDH layers, or in the service layer (IP/ATM). How should protection in the network be coordinated between all these layers?

By default, the protection mechanisms in different layers will work independently. In fact, a single failure might trigger multiple protection mechanisms, all trying to restore service simultaneously, which would result in a large number of unnecessary alarms flooding the management center. This results in allocating protection bandwidth at each of the layers, which is inefficient.

An area of significant concern is that protection mechanisms in different layers could potentially contend with each other, preventing or delaying service restoration, although careful design can eliminate such occurrences. The following argument shows that multilayer protection schemes will eventually converge and restore traffic under the right assumptions:

Consider two network layers, a client layer operating over a server layer, each with its own protection mechanisms. If the following conditions are met, the network will always restore traffic in the event of a failure:

1. A viable protection path exists for each layer.
2. The server layer does not depend on the client layer to detect failures and invoke its protection-switching functions.
3. The client layer protection is *revertive* in the sense that it will repeatedly try switching to the other path if its current path fails.

Observe that since the server layer is independent of the client layer and does not depend on client layer indicators, in the event of a failure, the server layer will detect the failure and restore the traffic. After the failure occurs, there may be a period of time when the client layer is unable to restore service because the server layer is invoking its protection scheme. Ultimately, since the server layer converges, the client layer will see either a working path or a protection path available for it, and will therefore eventually converge.

If any of the conditions above are not met, then the protection scheme may not converge. For example, if the client layer protection is nonrevertive, it may switch over once to the protection path, discover that path is not available, and not switch back to its primary path.

While it is desirable to have some sort of coordination between protection mechanisms in different layers, this may not always be possible. For example, the protection mechanisms in different layers may actually be activated by different nodes. In some cases, it may be possible to add a priority mechanism where one layer attempts to restore service first, and only afterwards does the second layer try. One automatic way to ensure this is to have the restoration in one layer happen so quickly that the other layer doesn't even sense that a failure has occurred. For example, consider a WDM network carrying IP traffic. As we saw in Section 9.3, it can take several seconds for the IP layer to detect a failure. It is entirely feasible for the optical layer to have completed its restoration within this time scale so that the IP layer doesn't detect the failure. This may not, however, be feasible when we have SONET rings operating over a WDM network. The SONET rings detect failures very quickly and can initiate protection switching as early as $2.3\,\mu$s after a failure occurs.

Another way to implement orderly restoration would be to impose an additional *hold-off time* in the higher layer before it attempts restoration so as to provide sufficient time for the lower layer to do its restoration. However, a large hold-off time would increase the overall restoration time and is therefore not highly desirable either. In general, it would make sense to have the priorities arranged such that the layer that can provide the fastest restoration tries first.

9.7 CONCLUSION

Engineering the network for survivability plays an increasingly important role in transport networks. Protection techniques are well established in SONET and SDH and include point-to-point, dedicated protection rings, and shared protection rings. Point-to-point protection schemes work for simple systems with diverse fiber routes between node locations. Dedicated protection rings are primarily used to aggregate traffic from remote locations to one or two hub locations. Shared protection rings are used in the core parts of the network where the traffic is more distributed.

Protection in the optical layer is emerging, with several commercial products now implementing optical layer protection. Optical layer protection is needed to protect the data services that are increasingly being transported directly on the optical layer without the SONET/SDH layer being present. It can also be more efficient with respect to reducing the protection bandwidth required (by sharing the bandwidth across multiple clients) and therefore more cost-effective.

Optical channel layer protection is needed if some channels are to be protected while others are not. Optical multiplex section layer protection is more cost-effective for those cases where all the traffic needs to be protected. There is a growing trend toward the use of shared mesh protection in the optical layer, which is viewed as being more bandwidth-efficient and flexible, compared to the traditional ring-based approaches.

FURTHER READING

There is a vast literature on protection in SONET and SDH networks. SONET rings and protection schemes are described in ANSI T1.105.1 and Telcordia GR-253 and GR-1230. ITU G.841 describes the equivalent SDH architectures. We also refer the reader to the books by Sexton and Reid [13][SR97] and Wu [14][Wu92].

Providing reliable service in IP and MPLS networks is a topic of great interest today. Several protection schemes are being developed. See, for example, [15]DR00, Section 7.4], [16][CO99], and several Internet drafts available at *www.ietf.org*.

There is a lot of activity under way on optical layer protection schemes, with several being implemented in products today. These have not yet been standardized. [[17]DWY99, RM99a, RM99b, [18]Ram01, [19]MM00, [20]Bar00, [21]GR00a, [22]GR00b, [23]Dos99, [24]MBN99, [25]Wu95, [26]WO95, [27]Tel98, [28]GR96, [29]GRS97] provide good coverage of the major issues. Interworking of protection schemes between different layers is covered in [[30]Dem99, [31]MB96].

REFERENCES

[1] S. Khanna, "A polynomial time approximation scheme for the SONET ring loading problem," *Bell Labs Technical Journal*, 2(2):36–41, Spring 1997.

[2] C. Y. Lee and S. G. Chang, "Balancing loads on SONET rings with integer demand splitting," *Computer Operations Research*, 24(3):221–229, 1997.

[3] C. Alaettinoglu, V. Jacobson, and H. Yu. "Towards millisecond IGP convergence." In *North American Network Operators Group Fall Meeting*, 2000. See also IETF drafts *draft-alaettinogluisis-convergence-00.txt and draft-ietf-ospf-scalability-00.txt.*

[4] G. Hjalmtysson, J. Yates, S. Chaudhuri, and A. Greenberg, "Smart routers–simple optics: An architecture for the optical Internet," *IEEE/OSA Journal on Lightwave Technology*, 18(12):1880–1891, 2000.

[5] R. Batchellor, "Optical layer protection: Benefits and implementation" in *Proceedings of National Fiber Optic Engineers Conference*, 1998.

[6] B. Ramamurthy and B. Mukherjee, "Survivable WDM mesh networks, Part I—Protection," in *Proceedings of IEEE Infocom*, pages 744–751, 1999.

[7] B. Ramamurthy and B. Mukherjee, "Survivable WDM mesh networks, Part II—Restoration," in *Proceedings of IEEE International Conference on Communication*, pages 2023–2030, 1999.

[8] V. Paxson, "End-to-end routing behavior in the Internet," *IEEE/ACM Transactions on Networking*, 5(5):601–615, Oct. 1997.

[9] R. Bradon, L. Zhang, S. Berson, S. Herzog, and S. Jamin. *Resource Reservation Protocol—Version 1 Functional Specification*. Internet Engineering Task Force, Sept. 1997.

[10] ATM Forum. *Private Network-Network Interface Specification: Version 1.0*, 1996.

[11] ITU-T. *Recommendation Q.700: Introduction to CCITT Signaling System No. 7*, 1993.

[12] D. Awduche and Y. Rekhter, "Multiprotocol lambda switching: Combining MPLS traffic engineering control with optical crossconnects," *IEEE Communications Magazine*, 39(4):111–116, Mar. 2001.

[13] M. Sexton and A. Reid, *Broadband Networking: ATM, SDH and SONET*. Boston: Artech House, 1997.

[14] T. H. Wu, *Fiber Network Service Survivability*. Boston: Artech House, 1992.

[15] B. S. Davie and Y. Rekhter, *MPLS Technology and Applications*. San Francisco: Morgan Kaufmann, 2000.

[16] T. M. Chen and T. H. Oh, "Reliable services in MPLS," *IEEE Communications Magazine*, 37(12):58-62, Dec. 1999.

[17] P. Demeester, T.-H. Wu, and N. Yoshikai, editors. *IEEE Communications Magazine: Special Issue on Survivable Communication Networks*, volume 37, Aug. 1999.

[18] R. Ramamurthy et al., "Capacity performance of dynamic provisioning in optical networks," *IEEE/OSA Journal on Lightwave Technology*, 19(1):40-48, 2001.

[19] G. Mohan and C. S. R. Murthy, "Lightpath restoration in WDM optical networks," *IEEE Network Magazine*, 14(6):24-32, Nov.-Dec. 2000.

[20] S. Baroni et al., "Analysis and design of backbone architecture alternatives for IP optical networking," *IEEE Journal of Selected Areas in Communications*, 18(10):1980-1994, Oct. 2000.

[21] O. Gerstel and R. Ramaswami, "Optical layer survivability—A services perspective," *IEEE Communications Magazine*, 38(3):104-113, Mar. 2000.

[22] O. Gerstel and R. Ramaswami, "Optical layer survivability: An implementation perspective," *IEEE JSAC Special Issue on Optical Networks*, 18(10):1885-1899, Oct. 2000.

[23] B. T. Doshi et al., "Optical network design and restoration," *Bell Labs Technical Journal*, 4(1):58-84, Jan.-Mar. 1999.

[24] J. Manchester, P. Bonenfant, and C. Newton, "The evolution of transport network survivability," *IEEE Communications Magazine*, 37(8):44-51, Aug. 1999.

[25] T. H. Wu, "Emerging techniques for fiber network survivability," *IEEE Communications Magazine*, 33(2):58-74, Feb. 1995.

[26] L. Wuttisittikulkij and M. J. O'Mahony, "Multiwavelength self-healing ring transparent networks" in *Proceedings of IEEE Globecom*, pages 45-49, 1995.

[27] Telcordia Technologies. *Common Generic Requirements for Optical Add-Drop Multiplexers (OADMs) and Optical Terminal Multiplexers (OTMs)*, Dec. 1998. GR-2979-CORE, Issue 2.

[28] O. Gerstel and R. Ramaswami, "Multiwavelength optical network architectures and protection schemes," in *Proceedings of Tirrenia Workshop on Optical Networks*, pages 42-51, 1996.

[29] O. Gerstel, R. Ramaswami, and G. H. Sasaki, "Fault tolerant WDM rings with limited wavelength conversion," in *Proceedings of IEEE Infocom*, pages 508-516, 1997.

[30] P. Demeester et al., "Resilience in multilayer networks," *IEEE Communications Magazine*, 37(8):70-77, Aug. 1999.

[31] J. Manchester and P. Bonenfant, "Fiber optic network survivability: SONET/optical protection layer interworking," in *Proceedings of National Fiber Optic Engineers Conference*, pages 907-918, 1996.

[32] J. W. Suurballe and R. E. Tarjan, "A quick method for finding shortest pairs of disjoint paths," *Networks*, 14:325-336, 1984.

Intrusion Response Systems: A Survey

10.1 INTRODUCTION

The occurrence of outages due to failures in today's information technology infrastructure is a real problem that still begs a satisfactory solution. The backbone of the ubiquitous information technology infrastructure is formed by distributed systems—distributed middleware, such as CORBA and DCOM; distributed file systems, such as NFS and XFS; distributed coordination-based systems, such as publish-subscribe systems and network protocols; and above all, the distributed infrastructure of the World Wide Web. Distributed systems support many critical applications in the civilian and military domains. Critical civilian applications abound in private enterprise, such as banking, electronic commerce, and industrial control systems, as well as in the public enterprise, such as air traffic control, nuclear power plants, and protection of public infrastructures through Supervisory Control and Data Acquisition (SCADA) systems. The dependency dramatically magnifies the consequence of failures, even if transient. There is little wonder that distributed systems, therefore, are called upon to provide always-available and trustworthy services. The terminology that we will use in this chapter is to consider the distributed systems as composed of multiple services and the services interact with one another through standardized network protocols. Consider, for example, a distributed e-commerce system with the traditional three-tier architecture of a web server, application server, and database server. The services are typically located on multiple hosts.

The importance of distributed systems has led to a long interest in securing such systems through prevention and runtime detection of intrusions. The prevention is traditionally achieved by a system for user authentication and identification (e.g., users log in by providing some identifying information such as log-in signature and password, biometric information, or smart card); access control mechanisms (rules to indicate which user has what privileges over what resources in the system); and building a "protective shield" around the computer system (typically a firewall that inspects incoming and optionally outgoing network traffic and allows it if the traffic is determined to be benign). The prevention mechanism by itself

309

is considered inadequate, because without being too restrictive, it is impossible to block out all malicious traffic from the outside. Also, if a legitimate user's password is compromised or an insider launches an attack, then prevention may not be adequate.

Intrusion detection systems (IDSs) seek to detect the behavior of an adversary by observing its manifestations on a system. The detection is done at runtime when the attack has been launched. There are many IDSs that have been developed in research and as commercial products. They fundamentally operate by analyzing the signatures of incoming packets and either matching them against known attack patterns (misuse-based signatures) or against patterns of expected system behavior (anomaly-based signatures). There are two metrics for evaluating IDSs: rate of false alarms (legitimate traffic being flagged as malicious) and rate of missed alarms (malicious traffic not flagged by the IDS).

However, in order to meet the challenges of continuously available trustworthy services from today's distributed systems, intrusion detection needs to be followed by response actions. This has typically been considered the domain of system administrators who manually "patch" a system in response to detected attacks. The traditional mode of performing response was that first, the system administrator would get an alert from the IDS. Then, he or she would consult logs and run various system commands on the different machines comprising the entire system in an effort to determine if the attack were currently active and what damage had been caused by it. There were several sophisticated but ad hoc tools that system administrators would execute to aid in the determination process, such as a script to log into all the machines in a system to determine if .rhosts files had been tampered with and if so, set them to some overly restrictive privileges. Clearly, this process, still the dominant method today, is ad hoc and very human intensive. By the nature of the actions, this process cannot reasonably hope to respond in real time and is therefore considered offline. However, as distributed systems become larger, more complex, and ubiquitous, the number of users increases and sophisticated automated script-based attacks gain ground, automated tools for intrusion response become vitally important.[1]

The autonomous intrusion response systems (IRSs) are designed to respond at runtime to an attack in progress. The goals of an IRS may be a combination of the following: to contain the effect of a current attack if the underlying model is that it is a multistage attack, to recover the affected services, and to take longer-term actions of reconfiguration of a system to make future attacks of a similar kind less likely to succeed. There are several challenges in the design of an IRS. First, attacks through automated scripts are fast moving through the different services in a system. Second, the nature of the distributed applications enables the spread of an

---

[1]We will discuss response systems in the context of distributed systems since their application to standalone systems is simpler and does not have many of the challenges that makes this topic intellectually challenging. To distinguish between the system that the IRS protects from the IRS itself, we will call the former the *payload system*.

attack, since under normal behavior the services have interactions among them and a compromised service can infect another. Third, the owner of a distributed system does not have knowledge of or access to the internals of the different services. For example, the source code may not be available, or even if available, the expertise to understand the internals may not be available. Hence, an IRS should ideally work at the interfaces rather than in the internals. Fourth, it may not be possible to deploy detectors at each service for performance reasons (e.g., the performance overhead imposed by the packet matching at a network-based detector is excessive for a host) or deployment conditions (e.g., no host-based detector is available for the particular platform). Additionally, the detectors, if installed, may be faulty and produce false alarms or missed alarms. The IRS, therefore, has to suppress inaccurate detections and extrapolate from the available detectors to determine the appropriate services at which to take the response action. Finally, the distributed systems are often complex enough that the universe of attacks possible against such systems is not enumerable and, therefore, the IRS has to work with possibly unanticipated attacks.

The current IRSs meet only a subset of the above challenges and none that we are aware of addresses all of them. The general principles followed in the development of the IRS naturally classify them into four categories.

1. *Static decision making*. This class of IRS provides a static mapping of the alert from the detector to the response that is to be deployed. The IRS includes a basic look-up table where an administrator has anticipated all alerts possible in a system and an expert indicated responses to take for each. In some cases, the response site is the same as the site from which the alarm was flagged, as with the responses often bundled with anti-virus products (disallow access to the file that was detected to be infected) or network-based IDSs (terminate a network connection that matched a signature for anomalous behavior). The systems presented in [1–4] fall in this category.

2. *Dynamic decision making*. This class of IRS reasons about an ongoing attack based on the observed alerts and determines an appropriate response to take. The first step in the reasoning process is to determine which services in a system are likely affected, taking into account the characteristics of the detector, network topology, and so on. The actual choice of the response is then taken dependent on a host of factors, such as the amount of evidence about the attack, the severity of the response, and so on. The third step is to determine the effectiveness of the deployed response to decide if further responses are required for the current attack or to modify the measure of effectiveness of the deployed response to guide future choices. Not all IRSs in this class include all the three steps. A wide variety are discernible in this class based on the sophistication of the algorithms. The systems presented in [5–13] fall in this category.

3. *Intrusion tolerance through diverse replicas*. This class of IRS implicitly provides the response to an attack by masking the effect of the response and allowing the affected computer system to continue uninterrupted operation. The basic approach is to employ a diverse set of replicas to implement any given service. The fault model is the replicas are unlikely to share the same vulnerabilities and, therefore, not all will be compromised by any given attack. A voting process on the outputs or the state of the replicas can mask the compromised replicas, provided less than half are compromised. An advantage of this approach is the system can continue operation without a disruption. This approach is reminiscent of active replication in the fault-tolerance field. The systems presented in [14–18] fall in this category.

4. *Responses to specific kinds of attacks*. This class of IRS is customized to respond to specific kinds of attacks, most commonly, distributed denial of service (DDoS) attacks. The approach is to trace back as close to the source of an attack as possible and then limit the amount of resources available to the potentially adversarial network flows. A characteristic of this approach is cooperation is required from entities outside the computer system being protected for an accurate trace back. The systems reported in [19–21] fall in this category.

In this chapter, we will describe the primary IRSs that have been reported in the literature and label each in one of these four categories.

Next, we consider the metrics that are relevant for evaluating an IRS. Both low-level metrics and high-level metrics need to be considered for this purpose.

Low-level metrics are those that look at specific activities within an IRS, such as the latency in deploying a response, and the fraction of times a given response is successful in terminating an attack. However, these metrics need to be combined in application and domain-specific ways to evaluate the impact of the IRS on the distributed system being protected. An example of the high-level metric is the net value of transactions that could not be completed in an e-commerce system due to an attack, when an IRS is deployed. We provide a scientific basis for the high-level metrics in this chapter.

The rest of the chapter is organized as follows. Sections 10.2–10.5 present the IRSs that belong to each class introduced above. Section 10.6 presents a discussion of metrics used to evaluate an IRS and gives an example with the ADEPTS IRS applied to protect a distributed e-commerce system. Section 10.7 describes our thoughts for future evolution of the work on IRSs.

10.2 STATIC DECISION-MAKING SYSTEMS

The characteristic that defines this class of IRSs is that they respond to attacks defined exactly, prior to deployment, and using responses that are enumerated and completely configured. They are generally simple to understand and deploy and work well for a large class of systems that have determinism in the kinds of workload and where the attack modes are enumerable a priori. However, they are not very effective for dynamic systems with changing workloads, new kinds of services installed, and new vulnerabilities introduced due to hardware or software changes.

10.2.1 Generic Authorization and Access Control— Application Programming Interface

Introduction

The Generic Authorization and Access Control—Application Programming Interface (GAA-API), developed by the Information Sciences Institute [3], is a signature-based intrusion detection and response system that provides a dynamic authorization mechanism at the application layer of a computer system. The basic idea is to integrate access control policy with intrusion detection and some countermeasure according to policy, such as generating audit records. GAA-API supports access control policies and conditions defined by a BNF-syntax language. It is a generic tool that has been integrated with many applications, including Apache, SSH, SOCKS5, and FreeS/WAN (IPSec VPN), running on Linux and Sun Solaris platforms. It is designed as a generic interface based on standard C language APIs, so it can be easily ported to other platforms and applications.

Details

GAA-API extends the access control capabilities from an application, while providing the opportunity to identify application-level attacks and specify different types of real-time responses to intrusions (Figure 10.1). A key component of the API is its Extended Access Control List (EACL) language, which allows the formulation of policies for the API to evaluate, decide, and respond to possible attack scenarios. Each object in the application is associated with an EACL, where the access rights are defined along with a set of conditions necessary for the rights to be matched. The conditions can state the requirements necessary to grant or deny access (preconditions), determine what to do when an access request arrives (request-result), what must hold while the access is granted (mid-conditions), and what to do after the access ends (postconditions).

The conditions allow for the API to interact with IDSs, modify existing policy rules, and trigger a response. As an example of the interaction with an IDS, the API can report attack information such as a violation of threshold conditions and access requests with parameters that do not comply with a site's policy. The API can also request an IDS for network-based attack information, such as spoofed addresses. The API can deploy responses according to the conditions previously defined. The API might, for example, limit the consumption of resources, increase the auditing level, or request user authentication to access a certain application.

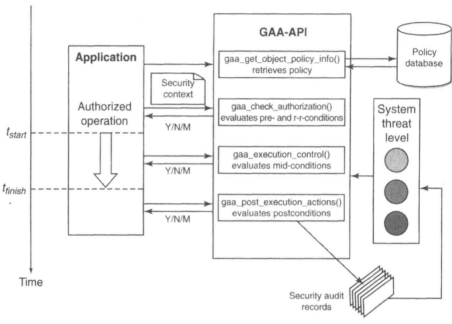

FIGURE 10.1

Application interacting through the GAA-API to enforce policies at different stages of interaction (preconditions, request-result, mid-conditions, and postconditions). The policy in effect is dependent on the threat level as communicated by the IDS. From USC, Information Sciences Institute [22].

Nevertheless, it is unclear as to which type of language or protocol is used for the framework to exchange messages with an IDS.

GAA-API defines two types of policies: systemwide policies, which can be applied to all the objects in an application, and local policies, which are selectively applied to individual objects. The final policy application to an object, for which both systemwide and local policies exist, depends on the composition mode selected. There are three alternatives: expand, which provides access to an object if either system or local policy allows it; narrow, where mandatory access control rules defined by systemwide policies overrule any discretionary rule defined at the local policy level; and stop, where local policies are ignored if a corresponding systemwide policy exists.

The policies defined and implemented allow for the GAA-API framework to also interact with system administrators. An administrator can receive messages and validate the impact and effectiveness of the response actions taken by the framework. An example would be a rule defined for an Apache web server that states updating the list of malicious Internet provider (IP) addresses after a potential attack is detected and sending an email with the IP address of the potential attacker, the URL attempted, and the reported time of the attack. The administrator would later validate the effectiveness of the response.

The authors at USC [22] report that GAA-API functions introduce a 30% overhead for an Apache web server function call when email notification to administrators is disabled. If the email notification is enabled, the overhead rises to 80%.

Significance

The authors at USC [22] present an extended approach to the regular access control model found in popular Unix-based applications. The access control policies interact with other important security mechanisms such as IDS and firewalls, allowing for a richer set of potential responses in the presence of attacks. More recently, the authors further developed the concepts presented in GAA-API with the introduction of dynamic detection and response mechanisms during the trust negotiation phase between two parties, usually client and server, and the support they can provide for stronger access control. A potential drawback to this model could be the complexity introduced by such policies, with many variables and the interaction among them, making it hard to administer in a large environment.

10.2.2 Snort Inline

Introduction

Snort Inline is a mode of operation for Snort, the popular open-source IDS. Originally developed as an independent, modified version of Snort, it was integrated in version 2.3.0 RC1 of the Snort project to provide intrusion prevention capabilities. It requires the Netfilters/IPtables software developed by the same project. Snort Inline provides detection at the application layer to the IPtables firewall so it can dynamically respond to real-time attacks that take advantage of vulnerabilities at the application level.

Details

Snort Inline is the intrusion prevention component of Snort, a popular network intrusion detection and prevention system capable of real-time IP network traffic analysis. Snort was originally developed by Martin Roesch and is currently owned and developed by Sourcefire, a company founded by Roesch. Snort Inline started as a separate project that used Snort for its packet logging and traffic analysis capabilities, but has since been included in the Snort distribution, providing the intrusion response capabilities that the popular IDS had hitherto lacked.

The Netfilter/IPtables software allows for the implementation of the response mechanism while Snort Inline provides the policies based on which IPtables make the decision to allow or deny packets. After an incoming packet to a network is provided by IPtables, Snort performs the rule matching against the packet. There are three new rule types included in Snort for Snort Inline to define the actions that IPtables might take after receiving an incoming packet. All three rule types drop the packet if it matches a predefined rule. The second type of rule also logs the packet and the third type sends a control message back. The rules are applied before any alert or log rule is applied. The current version of Snort also allows a system to replace sections of a packet payload when using Snort Inline. The only limitation is that the payload selected must be replaced by a string of the same length. For example, an adversary that is looking to propagate malicious code through the PUT command could have it replaced by the TRACE command, thus halting further propagation of the code.

In order for Snort Inline to interface with IPtables, two C libraries are needed: libipq and libnet. Libipq [23] is a library for IPtables packet queuing that allows Snort Inline to exchange messages with IPtables. Libnet is the popular networking interface to construct, handle, and inject packets into a network.

Significance

The inclusion of Snort Inline to the popular Snort project is a good example of the evolution of IDSs as more proactive—dynamic capabilities are necessary to assist systems against today's attacks. However, the rule matching is against a statically created rule base and thus needs a prior estimate of the kinds of attacks that will be seen and the action is taken at the site of detection.

10.2.3 McAfee Internet Security Suite

Introduction

The McAfee Internet Security Suite (ISS) is a commercial product developed for the Windows operating system platform that integrates many security technologies to protect desktop computers from malicious code, spam, and unwanted or unauthorized access. The suite also includes monitoring and logging capabilities as well as backup, file and print sharing, privacy, spam filtering, and file wiping utilities. The interaction between several of these technologies allows for prevention, detection, and response of various types of attacks, chief among them being attacks related to malicious code. However, for this system, it is impossible to find detailed technical material while there is an overabundance of documents listing the features of the solution.

Details

The two main components of ISS are an anti-virus subsystem and a firewall subsystem. The anti-virus subsystem allows for the detection of viruses, worms, and other types of malicious code by using a signature-based approach along with a heuristic engine for unknown attacks. The firewall subsystem can be configured to scan multiple points of data entry, such as email, storage devices, instant messaging, and web browser. An intrusion detection module allows the firewall to interact with the anti-virus, providing a limited set of automatic responses to ongoing attacks. Another component of the ISS that is relevant to intrusion response is a system monitor. The system monitor detects and blocks changes on important components of the operating system, such as configuration files, browser settings, startup configuration, and active protocols and applications.

Significance

The evolution from an anti-virus product to an all-in-one security solution is a natural transformation that vendors such as McAfee and Symantec have experimented with in the last few years. The increase in complexity, speed, and variety for malicious code, along with the requirement to respond to attacks in real time, have led these vendors to integrate multiple security mechanisms. The response mechanisms implemented are still static and limited but one could expect more dynamic responses in future versions of these suites.

10.2.4 Other Systems

McAfee IntruShield Intrusion Prevention System

This forms part of the Network Intrusion Prevention product offering from McAfee. There is no technically rigorous publication describing the product. Our discussion is based on the documents put on the specific McAfee web page [24]. This system can be described as a network intrusion prevention system (IPS). It provides real-time prevention of encrypted attacks, while its ASIC-based architecture provides deep packet inspection and shell-code detection leading to zero-day protection. It employs purpose-built appliances (i.e., specialized hardware). The hardware is of different types depending on deployment—at the core of the network or the perimeter of the corporate network. It claims to prevent a wide variety of attacks, such as botnets, voiceover IP (VoIP) vulnerability-based attacks, and encrypted attacks.

   In terms of response, it provides hints for creating some offline response in the manner of forensics. It delivers unique forensic features to analyze key characteristics of known and zero-day threats and intrusions. IntruShield's forensic capabilities provide highly actionable and accurate information and reporting related to intrusion identification, relevancy, direction, impact, and analysis. There is a host-based intrusion prevention system also from McAfee [25].

10.3 DYNAMIC DECISION-MAKING SYSTEMS

10.3.1 Broad Research Issues

Dynamic decision-making-based IRS involves the process of reasoning about an ongoing attack based on observed alerts and determining an appropriate response to take. There have been various designs and architectures proposed for this kind of dynamic decision-making-based IRS system. However, the core issue underlying all these systems is how the decision making should be achieved. Many factors can contribute to and complicate the decision-making process. For instance, a response can come with a certain cost such as the computation resource required for executing the response and the negative impact on the system after the execution of this response. Also, a response can fail with some probability. So, at the highest level of abstraction for each applicable response option, an IRS has to consider both the outcome from deploying the specific response and not deploying it, and makes a decision between these two choices based on some metric. From this point, we can see three potential research issues regarding dynamic decision-making-based IRSs. One is modeling the effect of an attack on a system, and this is directly related to the outcome from a decision on not using any response. The second issue is modeling the effect of the responses, and this is related to the outcome from a decision on using responses. Finally, there's the issue of how to decide the *set of responses* for deployment for a given attack, considering that responses are deployed on different hosts or services in a distributed environment and that they are not all independent.

There has been some work done on modeling the effect from responses and incidents. For example, Balepin et al. [5] propose the "gain matrix," which formulates the effect of using response A_k in a system with M potential states $S_1, S_2, \ldots, S_M$ as:

$$(q_1 a_{k1} + q_2 a_{k2} + \cdots + q_m a_{km})$$

where q_i is the probability of the system being in state S_i and a_{ki} is the benefit from using response A_k in state S_i. The benefit is derived from the response cost (say, in terms of negative impact on functional services), the likelihood of success of the response, and the potential damage from the system remaining in that system state. Following this formulation, the "optimal" response A_i from a set of response alternatives $\{A_1, A_2, \ldots, A_N\}$ is determined by:

$$i = \arg \max_{1 \leq k \leq N} (q_1 a_{k1} + q_2 a_{k2} + \cdots + q_m a_{km})$$

The gain matrix brings out two challenging facts in the design and implementation of a dynamic decision-making-based IRS. One is the number of system states to be considered. There are likely to be a vast number of states for a real production system and this would preclude any approach that relies on statically enumerating the states and creating the responses in each state. This underpins the desirability of dynamic intrusion response approaches. An example is the work by Toth and Kruegel [10], in which they use a dependency tree structure to dynamically calculate the impact on a system from a response.

The second challenge is about selecting the optimal set of responses in real time. A *response plan* is composed of multiple response operations that will be carried out in a certain sequence and at specific times. For example, {tightening the firewall rules for the entry point to the network at time x, rebooting the web server at time y, and resetting the firewall rules at time z} is a response plan composed of three response operations. Now, consider that the IRS has a choice of N response operations, say one each at a service site. There can be at least 2^{N-1} possible response plans even without considering the timings in the sequence of response operations. This imposes a challenge on the response decision process, which is to pick the best choice from all potential plans. A naive dynamic approach of scanning through the gain matrix and evaluating the expected gain for the large number of response plans will not work well, in general, since an IRS usually has to respond to incidents in a timely manner. Existing work, such as ADEPTS [26, 27], relies on heuristics for limiting the size of the set of response plans by considering only the response operations that are applicable near the sites where an incident was detected. ADEPTS also evaluates the responses with respect to a local optimality criterion (e.g., effect on the specific service, rather than on the system as a whole). While this is certainly an improvement over static decision-making-based IRS systems, much work needs to be done to determine how good a given heuristic is for a specific payload system. Now we provide the details of some representative dynamic IRSs.

10.3.2 **ADEPTS**

Design Approach

ADEPTS [26, 27] makes use of the characteristics of a distributed application in guiding its response choices. It considers the interaction effects among the multiple services both to accurately identify patterns of the intrusions relevant to the response process (e.g., cascading failures due to service interactions) and to identify the effectiveness of the deployed response mechanism. In designing an IRS, a possible approach is to consider different attacks and provide a customized sequence of response actions for each step in an attack. A second approach, subtly yet significantly different, is to consider the constituent services in the system and the different levels of degradation of each individual service due to a successful attack. For easier understanding, one may visualize a malicious adversary who is trying to impact the constituent services (the subgoals) with the overall goal of either degrading some system functionality (e.g., no new orders may be placed to the e-store) or violating some system guarantee (e.g., credit card records of the e-store customers will be made public). In ADEPTS, the authors take the latter approach. This is motivated by the fact that the set of services and their service levels are finite and reasonably well understood, while the possible universe of attack sequences is potentially unbounded. They focus on the manifestations of the different attacks as they pertain to the services rather than the attack sequence itself. This leads them to use a representation called an intrusion graph (I-Graph), where the nodes represent subgoals for the intrusion and the edges represent preconditions/postconditions between the goals. Thus, an edge may be OR/AND/Quorum indicating any, all, or a subset, respectively, of the goals of the nodes at the head of the edge that need to be achieved before the goal at the tail can be achieved.

In ADEPTS, the response choice is determined by a combination of three factors: static information about the response, such as how disruptive the response is to normal users; dynamic information, which is essentially the history of how effective the response has been for a specific class of intrusion; and out-of-band parameters of the response, such as expert system knowledge of an effective response for a specific intrusion or policy-determined response when a specific manifestation occurs. Importantly and distinct from other work, ADEPTS points out the need for the IRS to provide its service in the face of unanticipated attacks. Thus, it does not assume that the I-Graph is complete nor that there is a detector to flag whenever an I-Graph node is achieved. However, it assumes that the intrusion will ultimately have a manifested goal that is detectable. ADEPTS also considers the imperfections of the detection system that inputs alerts to it. The detectors would have both type I and type II errors, that is, false alarms and missed alarms. If false alarms are not handled, this can cause the IRS to take unnecessary responses, potentially degrading the system functionality below that of an unsecured system. If missed alarms (or delayed alarms) are not compensated for, the system functionality may be severely degraded despite the IRS. ADEPTS can coexist with off-the-shelf detectors and estimates the likelihood that an alarm from the detection system is false or there is a missing alarm. The algorithm is based on following the pattern of nodes being achieved in the I-Graph with the intuition that a lower-level subgoal is achieved with the intention of achieving a higher-level subgoal.

The design of ADEPTS is realized in an implementation that provides intrusion response service to a distributed e-commerce system. The e-commerce system mimics an online bookstore system and two auxiliary systems for the warehouse and the bank. Real attack scenarios are injected into the system with each scenario being realized through a sequence of steps. The sequence may be nonlinear and have control flow, such as trying out a different step if one fails. ADEPTS' responses are deployed for different runs of the attack scenarios with different speeds of propagation, which bring out the latency of the response action and the adaptive nature of ADEPTS. The survivability of the system is shown to improve over a baseline system, with a larger number of runs leading to greater improvement.

Contributions and Further Work

ADEPTS presents a worthy framework for reasoning about and responding to multistage attacks in systems that have the nondeterminism and imperfections of real-world distributed systems. It provides fundamental algorithms for diagnosis of the affected service, taking a proactive response and evaluating the effect of a response by observing further alerts in the system.

However, the responses in ADEPTS only achieve a local optima and are deployed in sites close to where the detector flagged the alarm. It is unclear how close ADEPTS can get to the theoretically best achievable response. Also, ADEPTS needs to consider variants of previously observed attack scenarios and completely unanticipated attack scenarios.

10.3.3 **ALPHATECH Light Autonomic Defense System**

Design Approach

This is a host-based autonomic defense system (ADS) using a partially observable Markov decision process (PO-MDP) that is developed by a company called ALPHATECH, which has since been acquired by BAE systems [28–30]. The system ALPHATECH Light Autonomic Defense System (a LADS) is a prototype ADS constructed around a PO-MDP stochastic controller. The main thrust of the work has been the development, analysis, and experimental evaluation of the controller. At the high level, Armstrong et al. [28, 29] and Kriedl and Frazier [30] have two goals for their ADS: it must select the correct response in the face of an attack and it must not take actions to attacks that are not there, notwithstanding noisy signals from the IDS.

The overall framework is that the system has a stochastic feedback controller based on PO-MDP that takes its input from a commercially available anomaly sensor (CylantSecure, from Software Systems International, Cyland Division, http://www.cylant.com/), calculates the probability that the system may be in an attack state, and invokes actuators to respond to a perceived attack. The system is partially observable because the sensors (the intrusion detectors) can give imperfect alerts; the system is also partially controllable since the effect of an action by the ADS will not deterministically bring the system back to a functional state.

The authors set up PO-MDP formulas to determine for each $x \in X$, $b_k(x) = P_r(x_k = x/I_k)$, where I_k denotes the set of the first k observations received and all controls selected through the $(k - 1)$st decision stage. Let $B_k = \{b_k(x) : x \in X\}$ be the set of all individual state estimates after the kth observation. The objective is to choose a response policy μ that outputs the selected control $\mu_k = \mu(B_k)$ (as a function of B_k). The choice of the optimal response is given by:

$$\mu^*(B_k) = \arg\min_{u \in U} \left| \sum_{x \in X} a^*(u, x) b_k(x) \right|$$

where $\alpha^*(u, x)$, for each $u \in U$ and $x \in X$, is proportional to the optimal *cost-to-go*, given current state $x_k = x$ and current decision $u_k = u$. That is, $\alpha^*(u, x)$ is the expected cost obtained through an optimal selection of controls at future decision stages, given current state $x_k = x$ and current decision $u_k = u$. However, determining the optimal response policy that minimizes the infinite horizon cost function is intractable and heuristics must be applied to find near-optimal policies. The heuristics Armstrong et al. [28, 29] and Kriedl and Frazier [30] apply is to consider the single-step combination of current state and control.

For the evaluation, the authors build a Markov state model for the worm attack on a host. The prototype ADS receives observations from two intrusion detector sensors. One intrusion detector sensor monitors activities on the IP port and the other sensor monitors processes operating on the host computer. These two sensors are calibrated against activity that is determined to be representative of how the computer system will typically be used. For the experiments, the training data were a combination of stochastic http and ftp accesses plus random issuances of commands that are commonly used by operators of Linux. The first experiment demonstrates that an ADS built on a feedback controller is less likely to respond inappropriately to authorized system activity than a static controller (i.e., is less susceptible to noises from the detection system) and is thus able to effectively use a more sensitive anomaly detector than a static controller. The second experiment demonstrates the ability to respond to attacks not seen before—αLADS was trained with a worm attack on the ftp server and able to thwart similar worm attacks to the named and rpcd servers. The surprising result is αLADS is able to thwart every single instance of the not-seen-before attacks. To interpret the results, a crucial piece of information is the degree of similarity between the different worms, which is not available in the published papers.

Contributions and Further Work

The work is significant in its use of a formal modeling technology (i.e., PO-MDP) in intrusion response. The design is rigorous and while the modeling technique has the challenge of determining the correct transition matrix from suitable training data, this challenge is not unique to the αLADS system. It is expected that the work will mature and use more sophisticated techniques for creation of the matrices that are available in related literature.

What has gotten short shrift in this work is the development of the actual responses that would be effective in a distributed environment. In fact, their experiments only use the ability to kill a process or shut down a computer (apart from just observation or human notification). The system has to be made hierarchical and distributed so that it can respond to attacks in different parts of a distributed infrastructure.

10.3.4 Cooperating Security Managers and Adaptive, Agent-Based Intrusion Response Systems

Design Approach

Both systems come from the same research group with cooperating security managers (CSMs) preceding adaptive, agent-based intrusion response system (AAIRSs) in chronology. CSM is designed to be used as an intrusion detection tool in a large network environment. CSM follows an approach in which individual intrusion detection monitors can operate in a cooperative manner, without relying on a centralized director to perform the network intrusion detection. To stress the role of the individual components in managing intrusions, not just monitoring them, the term used is *security managers*. CSM employs no centralized director; instead, each of the individual managers assumes this role for its own users when that manager suspects suspicious activity. Each CSM reports all significant activity to the CSM for the host from which the connection originated. This enables

CSM to track a user as he or she travels from one host to another in a distributed environment.

If an intruder is suspected or detected, it is up to the intruder-handling (IH) component to determine which action to take. This is where the intrusion response capability is embedded in CSM. The responsibility of the IH module is to take appropriate actions when intrusive activity is detected. Performing a specific action in response to an abuse will depend on the perceived severity of the detected abuse. Simple notification of the system manager on the detecting system is still the first step. The second step is to also notify all other CSMs in the trail for this user. This information is obtained from the user-tracking module. Beyond this, several other activities may be deemed appropriate. Two actions would be to kill the current session of the suspected intruder and to lock the account that was used to gain access so the intruder cannot simply return. However, they have to be done with care only when the evidence is strong and the disruption due to lack of response is severe.

A later work coming from the same group is the AAIRS [20, 21]. In AAIRS, multiple IDSs monitor a computer system and generate intrusion alarms. The interface agents receive the alerts and use an iteratively built model of false alerts and missed alerts from the detectors to generate an attack-confidence metric. The agents pass this metric along with the intrusion report to the master analysis agent. The master analysis agent classifies whether the incident is a continuation of an existing incident or is a new attack using several different parameters, such as the target application and target port. The decision algorithm for determining if an alarm corresponds to a new attack or an existing attack is adopted by other systems, such as ADEPTS.

If the master analysis agent determines this is a new attack, it creates a new analysis agent for handling this attack. The analysis agent analyzes an incident and generates an abstract course of action to resolve the incident, using the response taxonomy agent from Hiltunen et al. [18] to classify the attack and determine a response goal. The analysis agent passes the selected course of action to the tactics agent, which decomposes the abstract course of action into very specific actions and then invokes the appropriate components of the response toolkit.

The proposed methodology provides response adaptation through three components: the interface, analysis, and tactics agents. The interface agent adapts by modifying the confidence metric associated with each IDS. As the analysis components receive additional incident reports, these reports may lead to reclassification of the type of attacker and/or type of attack. This reclassification may lead to the formulation of a new plan or a change in how the response goal is accomplished. The analysis component may change the plan steps being used to accomplish the goal if alternative steps are available and can be substituted into the plan. Alternatively, the tactics components may have multiple techniques for implementing the plan step and adapt by choosing alternate steps. These components maintain success metrics on their plans and actions, respectively, and weight the successful ones so that they are more likely to be taken in subsequent instances of an attack.

The work provides a good framework on which the IRS can be built. However, it does not provide any of the system-level techniques and algorithms that will be required for the AAIRS to work in practice. It leaves many unanswered questions, most important of which are: How is the algorithm to determine a sequence of response actions to an incident, how does the system measure the success of previous responses, or how are multiple concurrent attacks handled?

Contributions and Further Work

CSM highlights the trade-offs to be made in any autonomous response system. Its module for tracking a user and the architecture for distributed detection are valuable in an IRS for a distributed system. However, the work is lacking in system-level details and actual design decisions made for a specific application context. The evaluation does not shed any light on the IH component of the system.

AAIRS presents a compelling architecture with different modules that make up an IRS. The modules are at two basic levels of abstraction: application system neutral and application system specific. These levels are important to the extensibility of an IRS to new applications. AAIRS also raises important concerns for any IRS: the imperfections of any IDS both for false alarms and missed alarms have to be accounted for in the IRS and there should be feedback about the success or failure of a deployed response. However, the work is lacking in specific algorithms for any of the steps of an IRS. There are no system-level details provided and this is especially critical for IRS since many trade-offs in algorithms are brought out by actual implementations and deployments. The system description indicates competent system administrators may still need to be involved in the loop (e.g., in manually determining if an alert from an IDS was a false one).

10.3.5 EMERALD

Design Approach

Event Monitoring Enabling Responses to Anomalous Live Disturbances (EMERALD) developed an architecture that inherits well-developed analytical techniques for detecting intrusions and cast them in a framework that is highly reusable, interoperable, and scalable in large network infrastructures [8, 31]. Its primary goal is not to perform automated intrusion response. However, its modular structure and tools can enable effective response mechanisms.

The primary entity within EMERALD is the monitor, with multiple monitors deployed within each administrative domain. The monitors may interact with the environment passively (reading activity logs or network packets) or actively (via probing that supplements normal event gathering). The monitors may interact with one another. An EMERALD monitor has a well-defined interface for sending and receiving event data and analytical results from third-party security services. An EMERALD monitor is capable of performing both signature analysis and statistical profile-based anomaly detection on a target event stream. The work on these components represents state-of-the-art development in the intrusion detection literature within each domain. In addition, each monitor includes an instance of the EMERALD resolver, a countermeasure decision engine capable of fusing the alerts from its associated analysis engines and invoking response handlers to counter malicious activity.

A feature that makes EMERALD well suited to intrusion response in a distributed environment is its capability for alert aggregation. This is achieved through a tiered arrangement of monitors and exchange of CIDF-based [32] alert information. Thus, resolvers are able to request and receive intrusion reports from other resolvers at lower layers of the analysis hierarchy, enabling the monitoring and response to global malicious activity. Each resolver is capable of invoking real-time countermeasures in response to malicious or anomalous activity reports produced by the analysis engines. The countermeasures are defined in a field specific to the resource object corresponding to the resource in which the monitor is deployed. Included with each valid response method are evaluation metrics for determining the circumstances under which the method should be dispatched. These criteria are the confidence of the analysis engine that the attack is real and the severity of the attack. The resolver combines the metrics to formulate its monitor's response policy.

Contributions and Further Work

An important lesson from the design of EMERALD is the separation of generic and target-specific parts of the system. Target-specific refers to the service (FTP, SSH) and the hardware resource (router) that EMERALD is deployed on. This design approach simplifies reusability of components and extensibility and enhances integration with other data sources, analysis engines, and response capabilities. While we see the great potential in EMERALD to build automatic responses in the resolver, we did not find any detailed description of its capabilities or its application. The infrastructure provides the common EMERALD API, event-queue management, error-reporting services, secondary storage management (primarily for the statistical component), and internal configuration control. The statistical and P-BEST (Production-Based Expert System Tool) components are integrated as libraries and provide powerful intrusion detection capabilities. The EMERALD API can likely be used to build a powerful intrusion response engine. However, this has not been reported in the project.

10.3.6 Other Dynamic Intrusion Response Systems

There are some other systems that employ dynamic decision making for intrusion response. In the interest of space, we will limit the discussion of these systems to their key contributions.

1. In Toth and Kruegel [10], the authors propose a network model that allows an IRS to evaluate the effect of a response on the network services. There

exist dependencies between entities in the system either as a direct dependency (user A depends on DNS service) or an indirect dependency that needs to be satisfied for the direct dependencies (if DNS service is on a different subnet, then firewall rules must allow access to that subnet). A dependent entity may become unavailable either because no path exists in the network topology or firewall rules disallow access. Indirect dependencies are determined automatically by analyzing the network topology (which is encoded in routing tables) as well as firewall rules. Dependencies are represented using an AND-OR tree and the degree of dependency is represented by a number between 0 and 1. Capability of an entity is the portion of the entity's functionality that is available under the current response strategy (number between 0 and 1). The capability is computed from the dependency tree. A penalty is assigned for the unavailability of each entity. The net penalty cost of an entity is capability × penalty. At each step, the system takes the response that minimizes the penalty. This is a greedy algorithm and does not necessarily lead to a global optima.

2. Security agility [33] is a software flexibility technique that extends the functionality of software components to accommodate the dynamic security properties of their environment. Thus, when access control is tightened in the environment, the software does not fail. The security agility toolkit provides the means to integrate more sophisticated response capabilities (than simply killing an offending process) into processes to realize more flexible intrusion-tolerant systems. At its heart, the response actions are changes to access control rules with activation criteria specified. The chief contribution of this work is policy reconfiguration techniques at runtime. A secondary contribution is that the reconfiguration capability enables reconfiguration as part of a response.

In general, dynamic decision-making-based IRSs are a promising technology that is still in its nascent phase. There is scarce deployment of them in real-world production systems, at least what is reported in open literature. Part of the reason is the many open issues that need to be solved before generalizable design principles can be presented. For example, the heterogeneity among real-world systems has been an obstacle for modeling the effect on a system from incidents and responses. In a sense, an IRS has to figure out what the services are in the system, what their functionalities are, what the interactions are among them, and what the effects are of a response on the system. Each of these is a topic of active research in distinct fields, such as system management. Besides, there are many properties in the response decision-making process that need to be quantitatively modeled and analyzed, such as the optimality of a response. There is surprisingly little in the way of comparative evaluation of the different techniques with respect to each other and with respect to an idealized scenario. We believe this is an exciting field of development in IRS technology and we hope to see many worthwhile research efforts in it in the years to come.

10.4 INTRUSION TOLERANCE THROUGH DIVERSE REPLICAS

The use of diverse replicas in IRS borrows ideas from the field of natural fault tolerance and from observations of biological systems. By introducing artificial diversity, a common phenomenon in biological systems, an attack specific to a vulnerability in a system cannot affect another system that lacks that vulnerability. Coupled with redundancy, the effect of an attack can be masked, allowing the system to provide continued service in the presence of disruptions. The basic approach is to employ a diverse set of replicas for a given service, such that they provide the same high-level functionality with respect to other services, but their internal designs and implementations differ. The fault-masking techniques used are similar to methods in natural fault tolerance, such as voting and agreement protocols. The use of diverse replicas is attractive because provable theoretical improvements to the survivability or security of the system can be obtained, compared to other techniques that are more suitably classified as heuristics. Evaluation techniques from the mature field of natural fault tolerance are more readily adapted to this class of IRSs.

A common assumption is to assume, at most, a fraction of the servers in a network may fail. This assumption is strengthened through the use of active and periodic recovery. Another common assumption is that failures in the system are independent, which motivates the use of diversity. Extending this argument to vulnerabilities, the assumption states that vulnerabilities do not occur across different operating systems and applications.

10.4.1 Broad Research Issues

Two main issues that arise are (1) how to introduce diversity into a system and (2) how to achieve redundancy that improves survivability and security of a system. To handle the first issue, most system architects have chosen to manually introduce diversity, such as installing different operating systems and applications. Taking it a step further, different versions of an application are also used. Introducing diversity automatically is a topic of much ongoing research, such as through the OASIS and SRS programs within DARPA [14, 16, 34, 35]. We survey two of these papers here. The second issue is system specific and, in general, advances in the fields of cryptography and dependability have given us a better idea of how redundancy impacts the survivability of the system. The following are sample systems in this domain.

10.4.2 Building Survivable Services Using Redundancy and Adaptation

Hiltunen et al.'s paper [18] advocates the use of redundancy and adaptation to build survivable services and presents a general approach to do so. The authors introduce various forms of redundancy: redundancy in space and time and the use of redundant methods. Redundant methods enforce a security attribute and the attribute remains valid if at least one of the methods remains uncompromised. An example is to perform multiple encryption operations using different cipher systems. They motivate the use of redundancy to avoid single points of vulnerability and to introduce artificial diversity and unpredictability into a system. They provide a useful characterization of the effectiveness of redundancy as the independence of the redundant elements, and the main goal of the design is to maximize this independence.

As an example, they apply redundancy to a secure communication service called *SecComm*. SecComm provides customizable secure communication by allowing user-specified security attributes and algorithms for implementing these attributes. The traditional approach of selecting a better encryption algorithm or increasing the key size to increase security is not survivable, since they in essence still contain single points of vulnerability. Therefore, Hiltunen et al., propose using two or more techniques to guarantee an attribute rather than a single method. For maximal independence, a different key established using different key distribution methods is used for each method. Fragmentation is also proposed when there are multiple connections. At a basic level, they implement redundancy by sequentially applying multiple methods to the same data. They suggest numerous general ideas to vary the application of the methods, with the main goal being to maximize the independence as mentioned above. The increase in survivability is relatively hard to quantify, therefore, their experimental results only measure the cost of redundancy against performance.

Hiltunen et al. have done a good job motivating the use of redundancy and diversity with respect to the security of computer systems. They provided many examples on how to use diverse replicas for various purposes, and the next two sections illustrate specific architectures that use diverse replicas.

10.4.3 Scalable Intrusion-Tolerant Architecture

Design Approach

Scalable Intrusion-Tolerant Architecture (SITAR) is an intrusion-tolerant system that relies heavily on redundancy [14]. The main components of the SITAR architecture are proxy servers that validate incoming and outgoing traffic and detect failures within the application servers and among themselves. The mitigation of adverse effects due to intrusions is through the use of redundant and diverse internal components. The diversity is achieved manually by choosing different server codes (e.g., Apache, Internet Information Server for web servers) and different operating systems (e.g., Linux, Solaris, MS). Through this, the authors of [14] assume that only one server can be compromised by a single attack, allowing them to build a simple model for their system.

A specific subsystem that employs redundancy is their ballot monitor subsystem. The monitors receive responses from acceptance monitors, perform validation of responses, and apply a voting algorithm to detect the presence of an attack and respond to the attack by choosing the majority response as the final response.

Contributions and Further Work

SITAR is a good example of using diverse replicas to improve the survivability of a system. The architecture used clearly illustrates the practical benefits of diversity and replication, and how they can be used to detect and respond to attacks. However, the work does not lay down generalizable design principles for diverse replicas.

10.4.4 Survival by Defense Enabling

Design Approach

Pal et al. [16] propose an approach to survivability and intrusion tolerance called *survival by defense*. The main idea is to introduce defense mechanisms that enhance the common protection mechanisms with a dynamic strategy for reacting to a partially successful attack. Due to their assumption that they lack control over the environment (e.g., OS, network), they focus on ensuring correct functioning of the critical applications. Therefore, defense enabling is performed around the application, with the assumption that it can be modified.

The type of attack considered is the corruption that results from a malicious attack exploiting flaws in an application's environment (they conclude it is most likely). Since the knowledge and actions within the environment are limited, an assumption they make is that administrator privileges will eventually be obtained by an attacker. In this context, defense enabling is divided into two complementary goals: (1) attacker's privilege escalation is slowed down and (2) defense responds and adapts to the privileged attacker's abuse of resources. Therefore, an application is defense enabled if mechanisms are in place to cause most attackers to take significantly longer to corrupt it (these mechanisms tend to be in the middleware).

To prevent the quick spread of privilege, the main idea is to divide a system into distinct security domains consisting of user-defined elements (e.g., host, LAN, router), such that each domain has its own set of privileges. Pal et al. suggest the use of a heterogeneous environment (various types of hardware, OS) to prevent domain administrator privileges from one domain to be converted into domain administrator privileges in another domain. Also, applications are distributed across the security domains (i.e., application redundancy) to reduce the effect of privilege escalation within a domain. Not limited to replicating applications, Pal et al. suggest other forms of replication such as communication redundancy.

A strong assumption made is that attacks proceed sequentially (staged attacks) instead of concurrently, that is, an attack on an application in multiple domains is slower than an attack on one single domain. Their design approach is to design applications intelligently distributed across security domains, so that privilege in a set of domains is needed to compromise the application. However, there is no discussion on how the staging is to be enforced.

Contributions and Further Work

With respect to the use of diverse replicas, the significance of this work is their higher-level approach to the use of redundancy. This is illustrated by partitioning a network into various domains, such that an attack on a domain only has a limited affect on another domain.

10.4.5 Implementing Trustworthy Services Using Replicated State Machines

Schneider and Zhou's article [17] is a comprehensive survey on techniques to implement distributed trust. In essence, the problem of distributing trust is solved by using replicas, and the issues faced are the same as the general theme of this section. By distributing trust, it is possible for the fault tolerance of the distributed system to exceed the fault tolerance of any single server. The first emphasis of the authors is the use of proactive recovery to transform a system that tolerates t failures in its lifetime to a system that tolerates t failures within a time window. This is useful because it strengthens the assumption that not more than t failures will exist at any one time, though additional complexity to the system design is introduced. Next, they discuss service key refresh and scalability, which is achieved through the use of secret sharing protocols. This allows periodic changes to the shared secret keys to be transparent to the clients. With regards to server key refresh, Schneider and Zhou discuss three solutions, namely the use of trusted hardware, offline keys, or read-only service public keys.

The independence assumption of failures is discussed and methods to reduce correlated failures are mentioned. They are:

1. Developing multiple server implementations, which is generally an expensive endeavor.
2. Employing preexisting diverse components, such as using different operating systems.
3. Introducing artificial diversity during compile or runtime, which will not eliminate flaws inherent in the algorithms implemented.

The next important requirement in distributed trust is replica coordination. This is mainly required for consensus, which is impossible to implement deterministically in the asynchronous model. The solutions provided are:

1. Abandon consensus and use quorum systems or embrace all the sharings of a secret (rather than having to agree on one sharing).
2. Employ randomization to solve Byzantine agreement.
3. Sacrifice liveness (temporarily) for weaker assumptions of the asynchronous model.

Finally, Schneider and Zhou discuss the problems and solutions that arise when confidential data are involved. The main problems of confidential data are that they cannot be changed by proactive recovery, and at any time they are unencrypted, their confidentiality may be lost. By using either reencryption or blinding, it is possible for clients to retrieve encrypted data in the case where services implement access control.

Schneider and Zhou's article is a well-written introduction to the issues and solutions of distributing trust, which are the same issues one would face when using diverse replicas in a system. The next section presents a specific approach to this problem.

10.4.6 Distributing Trust on the Internet

Design Approach

Cachin [15] presents an architecture for secure state machine replication in an asynchronous and adversarial network. This is achieved through recent advances in threshold cryptography and protocols for atomic broadcast. Depending on the level of diversity in the replicated servers, guarantees of liveness and safety can be made under certain assumptions (e.g., there are n static servers and at most t may fail). The designer of the distributed system can easily define meaningful attributes, such as the location and type of an operating system, which represent the different measures of diversity within the system. From these attributes, one can produce a description of how the servers may be compromised simultaneously (which is formalized as a general adversary structure in [15]) and design a secret sharing scheme that ensures that the guarantees of the distributed system are kept.

The use of diversity enables the authors of [15] to avoid making the standard independence assumption of faults, allowing the system to tolerate malicious acts and better approximate reality. The consensus protocol described within Cachin [15] is part of the Secure Intrusion-Tolerant Replication Architecture (Sintra) toolkit.

Contributions and Further Work

Cachin [15] presents specific techniques for distributing trust in an untrusted environment. This work is significant in that a clear approach is presented that allows a system designer or administrator to easily incorporate this architecture into a network with no existing use of diverse replicas and obtain an improvement in the survivability of the system.

Extensions to the scheme are discussed, such as using proactive recovery, dynamic grouping of servers, hybrid failure structures that distinguish between natural and malicious failures, and optimistic protocols that adapt their speeds depending on the presence of adversaries (due to the significant overhead of the atomic broadcast protocols).

10.5 RESPONSES TO SPECIFIC KINDS OF ATTACKS

This class of IRS is customized to respond to specific kinds of attacks, most commonly, DDoS attacks. There are scarce efforts at responses to other kinds of specialized attacks. One example is responding to internal attacks, where approaches proposed include changing the access control rules or dropping some connections when a high threat level is perceived [36]. However, such techniques so far have been human intensive and little exists in the literature in terms of rigorous validation of an automated system against different internal attacks. Hence, we focus on the DDoS attack response technology here.

DDoS attacks present a growing problem for network administrators around the world. On the Internet, a DDoS attack is one in which a multitude of compromised systems attack a single target, thereby causing denial of service (DoS) for users of the targeted system. The flood of incoming messages to the target system essentially forces it to shut down, thereby denying service to the system to legitimate users. An adversary begins a DDoS attack by exploiting a vulnerability in one computer system and making it the DDoS "master." It is from the master system that the intruder identifies and communicates with other systems that can be compromised. The intruder loads cracking tools available on the Internet onto multiple—sometimes thousands of—compromised systems. With a single command, the intruder instructs the controlled machines to launch one of many flood attacks against a specified target. The inundation of packets to the target causes a denial of service.

Increasingly powerful DDoS toolkits are readily available to potential attackers and essential systems are ill prepared to defend themselves. Both their ease of use and effectiveness make them the perfect tool for malicious individuals attempting to disrupt networks and web services. Accordingly, corporations and academia are working overtime to solve this complex problem and several systems exist that work to address DDoS. Unfortunately, none of the solutions fully handles the ever-evolving DDoS toolkits being used today and fails to present an all encompassing solution to the problem. Despite this failing of existing DDoS handling systems, systems such as Cooperative Intrusion Traceback and Response Architecture (CITRA) and the cooperative architecture hold much promise for the future.

10.5.1 Primitives for Responding to DDoS

DDoS attacks typically require four components: an attacker, master hosts, zombie hosts, and a victim host. Using exploits in a remote system, an attacker installs the attack program that can be remote controlled by the master host. When the attack begins, it usually falls into one of two classes: *bandwidth depletion* and *resource depletion*. Attackers can perform these attacks directly or through reflection. Reflection makes it more difficult to track down the source of the problem and offers a greater challenge to DDoS handling systems by bouncing packets off other hosts. The first line of defense against DDoS attacks is intrusion prevention. Rate-limiting filters are commonly used for preventing DDoS attacks [37, 38]. The reason why intrusion prevention and intrusion detection are unlikely to solve all kinds of DDoS attacks is that it is often difficult to tell the two kinds of traffic apart. Although some DDoS traffic can be easily distinguished from legitimate traffic, this is not true in the general case. More sophisticated DDoS toolkits generate traffic that "blends in" with legitimate traffic and, therefore, cannot be blocked. Hence, autonomous intrusion response is called for. Responses when a DDoS attack is detected usually involve some type of trace back or packet marking procedure to locate the source of the attack and block it.

Fundamentally, response mechanisms for DDoS attacks have to be distributed in nature as pointed out in Koutepas et al. [21]. This is due to several factors: (1) attackers most of the time spoof the packet source IP's address, (2) the possibility of the attack initiating from a wide range of networks worldwide, and (3) the inability of a domain to enforce incoming traffic shaping. Detected malicious flows can be blocked locally but the assistance of the upstream network is still needed in order to free the resources occupied on the incoming link.

10.5.2 **Citra**

Design Approach

CITRA is one of these systems currently in development working to handle bandwidth depletion attacks [19, 39]. Originally, CITRA (and the Intruder Detection and Isolation Protocol (IDIP) on which CITRA is based) did not have DDoS response as their goal. They were developed to provide an infrastructure enabling IDSs, firewalls, routers, and other components to cooperatively trace and block network intrusions as close to their sources as possible. Later CITRA was adapted for responding to DDoS attacks. CITRA is used by creating a cooperative network of nodes, each installed with the CITRA software. A node registers itself and coordinates efforts with the rest of the nodes through the discovery coordinator (DC). When an attack is detected, the CITRA nodes trace back toward the source through the use of network audit data. Along the path of the trace back, temporary action lasting only two minutes is taken to decrease the network flooding. During this two-minute window, the DC formulates a more reasoned plan of how to handle the attack.

At each CITRA component along the path of attack, responses are taken in accordance with the CITRA policy mechanisms. Traffic rate limiting is used rather than packet filtering, because of the difficulty of telling a legitimate packet from one that is part of the adversarial stream of packets. This response strategy is approximate since some DoS traffic may get through while some legitimate traffic may get blocked out. But with well-chosen parameters, enough bandwidth should be available for legitimate traffic even though it may be at a reduced speed. So the authors of CITRA [19, 39] integrated a rate limiter function using a token bucket rate limiting service available with netfilter. Experiments using RealPlayer were carried out on a test bed composed of several subnets, each with their own CITRA-enabled router. Results showed that when the system was active it allowed uninterrupted viewing but at reduced quality. It took ten seconds to slow the attack even on their small-scale test bed, bringing up a possible issue of scalability. On more powerful hardware, however, the delay was reduced to two seconds and the quality was not reduced.

Contributions and Further Work

The architecture presented is appealing and points in the direction of further development for DDoS mitigation. It does not require universal deployment to be meaningful, which is a big positive factor for any DDoS response mechanism.

Possible problems with the system involve slower-than-optimal trace back and scalability limitations. The system currently needs more effective means of dealing with attacks than simply limiting the bandwidth due to more sophisticated, multi-pronged attacks. Also, monitoring all packets coming in from all other networks is not scalable without smart algorithms. There is considerable ongoing work in the area of making routers fast by developing high-speed algorithms for packet look-ups and classification (see work by George Varghese et al. from the University of California at Davis and Nick McKeown et al. at Stanford University).

10.5.3 Cooperative Counter-DDoS Entity

Design Approach

Similar to CITRA, the cooperative architecture [21] attempts to locate the source of an attack but through the use of cooperative domains that internally check if they are sending a DDoS attack, and if so, alert the other networks that may be affected. To deal with the scalability of this system and increased network conges-tion from the message, the system uses multicast transmission of alerts. Multicast allows a source host to send a message to multiple hosts through an optimal span-ning tree by only sending the message once and replicating it only when the path along the spanning tree splits. Within each domain, there are entities that deter-mine the probability of an attack internally by looking at the alerts coming in from other entities and domains and the results of local IDSs. If one entity fails, another entity has the ability to take over. Once the number of alerts exceeds a threshold, the entities take action through use of a reaction table. This reaction table pro-vides the action that should be taken given the current state. This system lacks any experimental evidence to support its claims and offers a different approach than CITRA. By not using a traditional trace-back mechanism, the system can react faster and more efficiently. However, it heavily relies on the multicast backbone, and should an attacker target the backbone, the system may be rendered ineffective.

Contributions and Further Work

The work lays out an impressive architecture for quickly reacting to DDoS attacks. It moves away from the reliance on trace back that underlies the vast majority of approaches in this domain. However, problems facing the systems in existence today are how to detect legitimate packets sent to a network and packets intended to perform a DDoS attack without disrupting the legitimate users. This is no easy task when one considers that a network may simply be undergoing an increase in legitimate traffic or a DDoS attack may even use legitimate requests. Another prob-lem deals with determining the source of an attack. How does one find the source of the attack if it is constantly switching sources or it passes through a network with a less-than-helpful network administrator? Lastly, what is the universe of responses that should be included with any DDoS mitigation system—are the current ones of bandwidth throttling or packet filtering sufficient?

DDoS handling systems today have several weaknesses that can be exploited. They still need a better way of determining the source of an attack and better ways of responding to a detected attack. Blocking the remote host at the source would be optimal but trace-back procedures are too slow and resource intensive. Also, they rely on the cooperation of other networks and a limited set of responses. The aforementioned actions either fail to stop the attack and only slow it down or stop the attack but in the process block legitimate users. Better response, detection, and trace-back technology will have to be developed if these systems are to be deployable in real-world systems.

10.6 BENCHMARKING INTRUSION RESPONSE SYSTEMS

It is important to benchmark any IRS using quantifiable metrics. This is a nascent field within IRS design and development and one that needs significant work to get to maturity. Hence, this section is based around a suggested course of action for future development and an example from an existing IRS, ADEPTS. The metrics should capture the two essential goals of IRSs: to provide gracefully degraded functionality in the presence of attacks and to make a system more robust to future attacks. These two notions are addressed respectively by the metrics *survivability* and *vulnerability*.

One commonly accepted definition of *survivability* is the capacity of a system to provide essential services in the face of intrusions [40, 41]. The challenge with this definition is how to define essential services: Is this by the different categories of users for the different services, or by business criticality, or by some other measure? Also, the question arises if there exists a minimum essential service level that can be guaranteed. In Jha et al. [42], the authors inject errors into a network specification and visualize effects in the form of scenario graphs. Model checking is used to verify if states that violate certain temporal properties can be reached. Hiltunen et al. [18] present Cactus, which is a framework for constructing highly customizable and dynamically adaptable middleware services for networked systems. The fine-grained customization allows customized trade-offs between QoS attributes, including performance, reliability, and survivability, while the dynamic adaptation allows services to change behavior at runtime as a reaction to incoming intrusions.

To start, consider a simple combinatorial model for survivability. Let us define G as the overall goal of the system (e.g., sell products or services on the Internet), which is accomplished through several subgoals G_i (e.g., the different transactions that are possible on the system), $i = 1, ..., N$. Each subgoal G_i is given a weight W_i indicating its importance in the achievement of the system goal G, $(\sum_i W_i = 1)$.

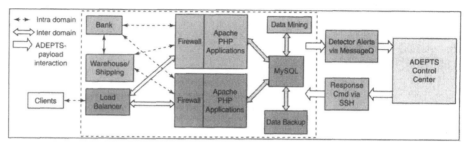

FIGURE 10.2

Layout of e-commerce test bed for the experiments on ADEPTS.

This can be estimated by the number of users who reach the subgoal as a fraction of the total number of users, a fraction of the usage of the subgoal, or a quantity defined by the system owner. Each subgoal G_i is decomposed into a conjunction of sets of services $\vec{S}_{ij}$, $j = 1, \ldots, N_i$, such that each set of services must be functional for goal G_i to be reached. Each such set can be further decomposed to be a disjunction of basic services $\vec{S}_{ijk}$, $k = 1, \ldots, N_{ij}$, such that any service of this set being functional causes the set to be functional. Let p_x denote the probability that a service X is affected by a disruption and cannot be used, and P_Y denote the probability that a goal y cannot be reached. Then, $P_{G_i} = \text{Max}(\text{Min}(p_{S_{ijk}})$ over all $k = 1, \ldots, N_{ij})$, over all $j = 1, \ldots, N, P_G = \sum_i W_i P_{G_i}$. The survivability is given by $1 - P_G$.

To apply this formulation, we will have to decompose a goal into the services and estimate the probability of a service being nonfunctional. The former can be deduced from a Service Net (network indicating interactions between services during normal operation) through a training phase when the transaction corresponding to a particular subgoal G_i is executed and the service interactions observed. We may use techniques from software reliability engineering of path testing [43] to determine the conjunction and disjunction of services.

To illustrate the concept, let us consider an example of its application as shown by Foo et al. in ADEPTS [26]. Figure 10.2 depicts the test bed that is used for experiments on ADEPTS. The payload system mimics an e-commerce web store, which has two Apache web servers running web store applications based on Cube-Cart [44–49] and are written in the PHP scripting language. In the backend, there is a MySQL database that stores all the store's information, which includes products' inventory, products' description, customer accounts, and order history. There are two other organizations with which the web store interacts: a bank and a warehouse. The bank is a home-grown application that verifies credit card requests from the web store. The warehouse is also a home-grown application that takes shipping requests from the web store, checks inventory, applies charges on the customers' credit card accounts, and ships the products. The clients submit transactions to the web store through a browser. Some important transactions are given in Table 10.1.

Table 10.1 List of Important Transactions in E-Commerce System. The weight is unitless and gives the relative importance of each transaction to the system owner

Name	Description	Services Involved	Weight
Browse web store	Customer uses web browser to access web store and browse the products available	Apache, MySQL	10
Add merchandise to shopping cart	Customer adds products to shopping cart	Apache, MySQL	10
Place order	Customer can input credit card information, submit orders, and web store will authenticate credit card with bank	Apache, MySQL, bank	10
Charge credit card	Warehouse charges credit card through bank when order is shipped	Warehouse, bank	5
Administrative work	Admins/webmasters can modify various source codes	Variable	10

There are certain security goals for the system, the complement of which are specified in Table 10.2, along with the weights. Thus, adding the word "prevent" before each gives the goal. The attached weights to the transactions and security goals are used for survivability computation as discussed below.

The authors define survivability based on the high-level transactions and security goals. Thus, the metric shows the effect of ADEPTS on the high-level functioning of the e-commerce system:

$$\text{Survivability} = 1000 - \Sigma \text{ unavailable transactions} - \Sigma \text{ failed security goals}$$

When a transaction becomes unavailable or the security goal is violated, the survivability drops by its corresponding weight, which was given in Table 10.1 and Table 10.2. Transactions become unavailable due to ADEPTS responses, such as rebooting a host or due to attacks. Security goals may be violated due to the successful execution of an attack step or an erroneous response action. If a security goal is violated multiple times during an attack, then each violation causes a decrease in the survivability.

The survivability metric considers the state of the system at the present time and does not consider the resilience of the system to future disruptions. This is an important measure and is captured by the *vulnerability* metric. The basic idea of this metric is to fit a temporal distribution for the probability that a given goal in a multistage attack is reached. This curve is analogous to unreliability curves

Table 10.2 List of Security Goals for E-Commerce Test Bed		
Illegal read of file (20)	Corruption of MySQL database (70)	Unauthorized credit card charges (80)
Illegal write to file (30)	Confidentiality leak of customer information stored in MySQL database (100)	Cracked administrator password (90)
Illegal process being run (50)	Unauthorized orders created or shipped (80)	

seen in traditional fault-tolerant systems. To get the vulnerability at a point in time T, we aggregate the individual unreliability curves using some structure as an attack graph and map the nodes to the services that are affected. Then an analysis similar to the survivability analysis above is performed. Note that the different curves are not independent. Given the Service Net with times for interaction between services, the edges in the attack graph will also have time for the delay between a lower-level goal and a higher-level goal being achieved. We believe the dependence introduces substantial complexity in the analysis and requires further investigation.

10.7 THOUGHTS ON EVOLUTION OF IRS TECHNOLOGY

We anticipate that for IRSs to be widely deployed, they will have to evolve in several directions over the coming years, including:

- *Ability to withstand unpredictable attack scenarios*. It is inconceivable that all attack scenarios would be "programmed" in the IRS. The IRS should, therefore, be able to extrapolate strategies available in its knowledge base and take responses to hitherto unseen attacks. This will be an important requirement since polymorphic worms, viruses, and other forms of attacks are rampant in today's security landscape. In this matter, there is a delicate balancing game between learning from the past and being agile to respond to future attacks. It is possible to build up large knowledge bases and do exact matches with them to choose appropriate responses from the history. However, this may affect the ability of the system to respond quickly. Also, in taking lessons from the past, the IRS should take into account the fact that the impact of the attack may be different even though the attack steps may be the same. Thus, a more drastic or quicker response may be called for.

- *Dynamic responses with changing network configurations*. The IRS will have to deal with topology and configuration changes in the distributed system. It may take inputs from change notification software systems, such as

Tripwire, and modify its response strategies accordingly. In any medium- to large-size distributed system, there are multiple administrators responsible for maintaining the system. The tools are often not standardized or uniform across different administrators. Thus, modifying the tools to send notification to the IRS seems daunting. A more feasible approach appears to be software to observe the resultant changes and notify the IRS. A change in the configuration may render some responses unnecessary (such as a critical service being made accessible from only inside the corporate network) or some responses more critical (such as a service being made web accessible).

- *Interaction with other components of the security framework.* The response strategy decided on by the IRS is predicated on confidence placed on other components of the security framework, such as IDS, change notification software, firewalls, and so on. The confidence placed on these components should not be predefined constant values. The confidence should change as new software is installed, rules updated, or configurations change. This also indicates why a probabilistic framework for the IRS seems the promising avenue, rather than deterministic response decisions. On another point, the IRS may depend on various basic functionalities in the system, such as firewalls or an access control system, to deploy the computed responses.

- *Separation of policy and mechanism.* It is important for the IRS to provide mechanisms for determining the appropriate response based on security policy settings. As far as practicable, the two aspects should be clearly delineated. This will enable a system administrator to set the policy, which can be at various levels of abstraction, such as a paranoid versus *laissez faire* policy at the systemwide level, to policy levels for individual services. In the absence of this, an IRS will not have buy-in for production systems.

- *User interface design.* Visualizing the different effects of an attack and its responses in a distributed environment is inherently challenging. The speed of the processes (attacks as well as responses) makes this a particularly daunting task. However, for critical functions, all the stake holders (system administrators to chief information officers of an organization) will likely have a human-digestible form of the information available to them. This should include online tools that let them visualize the network while an attack or its responses are being deployed, as well as offline tools that will aid in forensics action.

10.8 CONCLUSION

In this chapter, we present the motivation for designing IRSs for distributed systems. We lay out the design challenges in designing and implementing IRSs. Then, we present existing work in the field, classified into four classes. The first category of

IRSs, called *static decision making*, provides a static mapping of the alert from the detector to the response that is to be deployed. The second class, called *dynamic decision making*, reasons about an ongoing attack based on the observed alerts and determines an appropriate response to take. The third class, called *intrusion tolerance through diverse replicas*, provides masking of security failures through the use of diverse replicas concurrently for performing security critical functions. The fourth class includes IRSs meant to target specific kinds of attacks, with our focus being on DDoS attacks. Then, we present a discussion on the nascent field of benchmarking of IRSs. Finally, we present five key areas in which IRSs need to evolve for a widespread adoption. In summary, we find that the design and development of IRSs have been gaining in research attention and we expect that they will become mainstream in the computer security landscape in the near future.

REFERENCES

[1] W. Metcalf, V. Julien, D. Remien and N. Rogness, "Snort Inline," http://sourceforge.net/projects/snort-inline/.

[2] Symantec Corp., "Norton Antivirus," at http://www.symantec.com/home_homeoffice/products/overview.jsp?pcid=is&pvid=nav2007.

[3] T. Ryutov, C. Neuman, K. Dongho, and Z. Li, "Integrated Access Control and Intrusion Detection for Web Servers," *Proceedings of the 23rd International Conference on Distributed Computing Systems* (ICDCS), Providence, RI, 2003, pp. 394–401.

[4] McAfee Inc., "Internet Security Suite," at http://us.mcafee.com/root/package.asp?pkgid=272.

[5] I. Balepin, S. Maltsev, J. Rowe, and K. Levitt, "Using Specification-Based Intrusion Detection for Automated Response," *Proceedings of the 6th International Symposium on Recent Advances in Intrusion Detection (RAID)*, Pittsburgh, PA, 2003, pp. 136–154.

[6] S. M. Lewandowski, D. J. Van Hook, G. C. O'Leary, J. W. Haines, and L. M. Rossey, "SARA: Survivable Autonomic Response Architecture," *Proceedings of the DARPA Information Survivability Conference & Exposition II (DISCEX)*, Anaheim, CA, 2001, vol. 1, pp. 77–88.

[7] G. B. White, E. A. Fisch, and U. W. Pooch, "Cooperating Security Managers: A Peer-Based Intrusion Detection System," *Network, IEEE*, 10:20–23, 1996.

[8] P. G. Neumann and P. A. Porras, "Experience with EMERALD to Date," *Proceedings of the Workshop on Intrusion Detection and Network Monitoring*, Santa Clara, CA, 1999, pp. 73–80.

[9] D. Ragsdale, C. Carver, J. Humphries, and U. Pooch, "Adaptation Techniques for Intrusion Detection and Intrusion Response Systems," *Proceedings of the IEEE International Conference on Systems, Man, and Cybernetics*, Nashville, TN, 2000, pp. 2344–2349.

[10] T. Toth and C. Kruegel, "Evaluating the Impact of Automated Intrusion Response Mechanisms," *Proceedings of the 18th Annual Computer Security Applications Conference (ACSAC)*, Las Vegas, NV, 2002, pp. 301–310.

[11] M. Atighetchi, P. Pal, F. Webber, R. Schantz, C. Jones, and J. Loyall, "Adaptive Cyber Defense for Survival and Intrusion Tolerance," *Internet Computing, IEEE*, 8:25–33, 2004.

[12] M. Tylutki, "Optimal Intrusion Recovery and Response through Resource and Attack Modeling," Ph.D. Thesis, University of California at Davis, 2003.

[13] W. Lee, W. Fan, M. Miller, S. J. Stolfo, and E. Zadok, "Toward Cost-Sensitive Modeling for Intrusion Detection and Response," *Journal of Computer Security*, 10:5-22, 2002.

[14] D. Wang, B. B. Madan, and K. S. Trivedi, "Security Analysis of SITAR Intrusion Tolerance System," *Proceedings of the ACM Workshop on Survivable and Self-Regenerative Systems*, Fairfax, VA, 2003, pp. 23-32.

[15] C. Cachin, "Distributing Trust on the Internet," *Proceedings of the International Conference on Dependable Systems and Networks (DSN)*, Göteborg, Sweden, 2001, pp. 183-192.

[16] P. Pal, F. Webber, and R. Schantz, "Survival by Defense-Enabling," in Jaynarayan H. Lala (Ed.), *Foundations of Intrusion Tolerant Systems (Organically Assured and Survivable Information Systems)*. Los Alamitos, CA: IEEE Computer Society, 2003, pp. 261-269.

[17] F. B. Schneider and L. Zhou, "Implementing Trustworthy Services Using Replicated State Machines," *Security & Privacy Magazine, IEEE*, 3:34-43, 2005.

[18] M. A. Hiltunen, R. D. Schlichting, and C. A. Ugarte, "Building Survivable Services Using Redundancy and Adaptation," *IEEE Transactions on Computers*, 52:181-194, 2003.

[19] D. Sterne, K. Djahandari, B. Wilson, B. Babson, D. Schnackenberg, H. Holliday, and T. Reid, "Autonomic Response to Distributed Denial of Service Attacks," *Proceedings of the 4th International Symposium on Rapid Advances in Intrusion Detection (RAID)*, Davis, CA, 2001, pp. 134-149.

[20] C. Douligeris and A. Mitrokotsa, "DDoS Attacks and Defense Mechanisms: Classification and State-of-the-Art," *Computer Networks*, 44:643-666, 2004.

[21] G. Koutepas, F. Stamatelopoulos, and B. Maglaris, "Distributed Management Architecture for Cooperative Detection and Reaction to DDoS Attacks," *Journal of Network and Systems Management*, 12:73-94, 2004.

[22] University of Southern California, Information Sciences Institute, "Generic Authorization and Access-control API (GAA-API)," at http://gost.isi.edu/info/gaaapi/.

[23] Netfilter Core Team, "Libipq—Iptables Userspace Packet Queuing Library," at http://www.cs.princeton.edu/~nakao/libipq.htm.

[24] McAfee Inc., "Network Intrusion Prevention," at http://www.mcafee.com/us/smb/products/network_intrusion_prevention/index.html.

[25] McAfee Inc., "McAfee Host Intrusion Prevention," at http://www.mcafee.com/us/local_content/datasheets/partners/ds_hips.pdf.

[26] B. Foo, Y. S. Wu, Y. C. Mao, S. Bagchi, and E. Spafford, "ADEPTS: Adaptive Intrusion Response Using Attack Graphs in an E-commerce Environment," *Proceedings of the International Conference on Dependable Systems and Networks (DSN)*, Yokohama, Japan, 2005, pp. 508-517.

[27] Y. Wu, B. Foo, Y. Mao, S. Bagchi, and E. H. Spafford, "Automated Adaptive Intrusion Containment in Systems of Interacting Services," *Elsevier Computer Networks Journal,* Special Issue on "From Intrusion Detection to Self-Protection," 51(5):1334-1360, April 2007.

[28] D. Armstrong, S. Carter, G. Frazier, and T. Frazier, "Autonomic Defense: Thwarting Automated Attacks via Real-Time Feedback control," *Wiley Complexity*, 9:41-48, 2003.

[29] D. Armstrong, G. Frazier, S. Carter, T. Frazier, and I. Alphatech, "A Controller-Based Autonomic Defense System," *Proceedings of the DARPA Information Survivability Conference and Exposition*, Washington, DC, 2003, vol. 2, pp. 21-23.

[30] O. P. Kreidl and T. M. Frazier, "Feedback Control Applied to Survivability: A Host-Based Autonomic Defense System," *IEEE Transactions on Reliability*, 53:148-166, 2004.

[31] P. A. Porras and P. G. Neumann, "EMERALD: Event Monitoring Enabling Responses to Anomalous Live Disturbances,"*Proceedings of the National Information Systems Security Conference,* Baltimore, MD, 1997, pp. 353-365.

[32] P. Porras, D. Schnackenberg, S. Staniford-Chen, M. Stillman, and F. Wu, "The Common Intrusion Detection Framework," CIDF working group document, at http://www.gidos.org.

[33] M. Petkac and L. Badger, "Security Agility in Response to Intrusion Detection," *Proceedings of the 16th Annual Computer Security Applications Conference (ACSAC)*, New Orleans, LA, 2000, pp. 11-20.

[34] P. P. Pal, F. Webber, R. E. Schantz, and J. P. Loyall, "Intrusion Tolerant Systems,"*Proceedings of the IEEE Information Survivability Workshop (ISW-2000)*, Boston, MA, 2000, pp. 24-26.

[35] V. Stavridou, B. Dutertre, R. A. Riemenschneider, and H. Saidi, "Intrusion Tolerant Software Architectures,"*Proceedings of the 2001 DARPA Information Survivability Conference & Exposition*, 2001, pp. 230-241.

[36] S. M. Khattab, C. Sangpachatanaruk, D. Mosse, R. Melhem, and T. Znati, "Roaming Honeypots for Mitigating Service-Level Denial-of-Service Attacks,"*Proceedings of the 24th International Conference on Distributed Computing Systems (ICDCS)*, 2004, pp. 328-337.

[37] W. J. Blackert, D. M. Gregg, A. K. Castner, E. M. Kyle, R. L. Hom, and R. M. Jokerst, "Analyzing Interaction between Distributed Denial of Service Attacks and Mitigation Technologies," *Proceedings of the DARPA Information Survivability Conference and Exposition (DISCEX)*, 2003, vol. 1, pp. 26-36.

[38] D. K. Y. Yau, J. C. S. Lui, L. Feng, and Y. Yeung, "Defending against Distributed Denial-of-Service Attacks with Max-Min Fair Server-Centric Router Throttles," *IEEE/ACM Transactions on Networking*, 13:29-42, 2005.

[39] D. Schnackenberg, K. Djahandari, and D. Sterne, "Infrastructure for Intrusion Detection and Response,"*Proceedings of DARPA Information Survivability Conference and Exposition (DISCEX)*, 2000, vol. 2, pp. 3-11.

[40] Carnegie Mellon University, Software Engineering Institute, "Survivable Network Technology," at http://www.sei.cmu.edu/organization/programs/nss/surv-net-tech.html.

[41] R. J. Ellison, R. C. Linger, T. Longstaff, and N. R. Mead, "Survivable Network System Analysis: A Case Study," *IEEE Software*, 16(4): 70-77, Jul./Aug. 1999.

[42] S. Jha, J. Wing, R. Linger, and T. Longstaff, "Survivability Analysis of Network Specifications," *Proceedings of International Conference on Dependable Systems and Networks (DSN)*, New York, NY, 2000, pp. 613-622.

[43] J. R. Horgan, S. London, and M. R. Lyu, "Achieving Software Quality with Testing Coverage Measures," *Computer*, 27:60-69, 1994.

[44] Devellion Limited, "CubeCart: PHP and MySQL Shopping Cart," at http://www.cubecart.com/.

[45] V. Srinivasan, G. Varghese, and S. Suri, "Packet Classification Using Tuple Space Search," *Proceedings of ACM SIGCOMM*, Sept. 1999, pp. 135-146.

[46] M. Waldvogel, G. Varghese, J. Turner, and B. Plattner, "Scalable High Speed IP Routing Lookups," *Proceedings of ACM SIGCOMM*, Sept. 1997, pp. 25-36.

[47] P. Gupta and N. McKeown, "Algorithms for Packet Classification," *IEEE Network*, 15(2): 24-32, 2001.

[48] P. Gupta and N. McKeown, "Packet Classification Using Hierarchical Intelligent Cuttings," *Hot Interconnects VII*, Aug. 1999.

[49] P. Gupta, S. Lin, and N. McKeown, "Routing Lookups in Hardware at Memory Access Speeds," *Proceedings of IEEE INFOCOM*, 8:1240-1247, Mar. 1999.

Index

Printed and bound by CPI Group (UK) Ltd, Croydon, CR0 4YY

14/10/2024

01773692-0001